CW00407917

An Illustrated History of

LNWR ENGINES

By the same author

Steam from Kenya to the Cape
Steam in Turkey
LNWR Miscellany (Volume 1)
LNWR Miscellany (Volume 2)
The Locomotive Names of British Railways
A Pictorial Record of British Railways Standard Steam Locomotives

An Illustrated History of

LNWR ENGINES

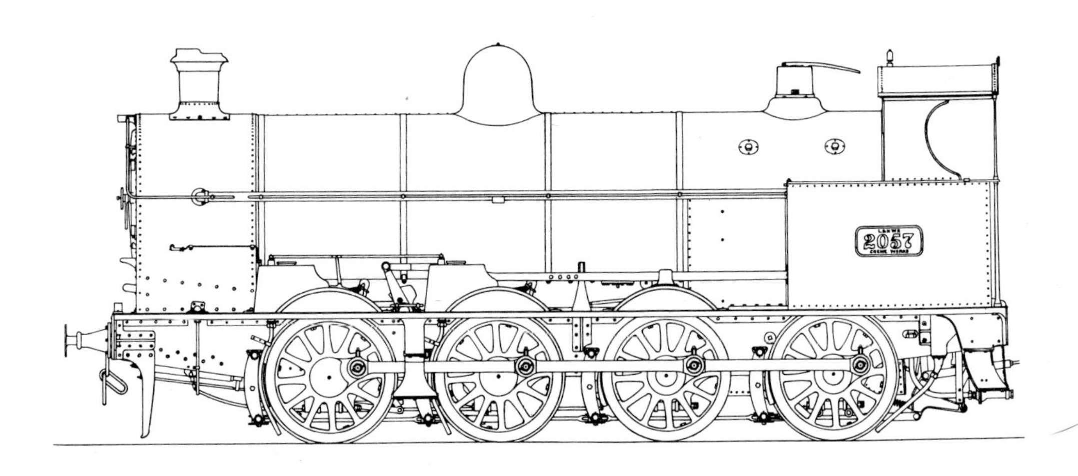

Edward Talbot

Oxford Publishing Co.

ISBN 0-86093-209-5

Typeset and printed in Great Britain by:
Netherwood Dalton & Co. Ltd., Huddersfield, Yorks.

Published by:
Oxford Publishing Co.
Link House
West Street
POOLE, Dorset

Acknowledgements

The information in this book has been gathered from many sources, from books and magazines, from the study of many photographs and drawings, and not least from correspondence and conversations with many railwaymen, fellow enthusiasts and friends. When the manuscript was completed, it was checked by G. H. Platt, who kindly provided photographs from his own collection, drawings by F. C. Hambleton, which had been left to him, and drawings which he had made himself. The text was then read by C. P. Davis, who added particularly useful details to the section on Webb compounds and provided information for the appendix on tenders from his article for the LNWR Society. Finally, the text was read by J. P. Richards, who made several valuable suggestions, contributed further information, especially on the Whale and Bowen Cooke periods, and generously provided some of his own drawings and photographs, as well as others taken by his father, R. P. Richards.
Many other individuals have kindly helped in a variety of ways by providing photographs, drawings or information and have often gone to great pains to do so. Particularly valuable contributions have been made by Roger Bell, Michael Bentley, W. T. Butler, W. A. Camwell, F. W. Chubb, David Clarke, G. J. Clarke, Fred Davies, E. Dutton, F. E. A. Eades, John Edgington, Bill Finch, Brian J. Gills, Eric Hannan, L. Hanson, Jack Hassall, Ted Higgs, G. E. Hughes, Malcolm Lewis, Bernard Matthews, Ken Morgan, G. N. Nowell-Gossling, D. J. Patrick, Brian Reed, John Easter Roberts, F. W. Shuttleworth, H. B. Spencer, Clive Taylor, Harry Townley, Laurie Ward, V. R. Webster and G. Dudley Whitworth. Alan Gettings made his superb drawings of name and numberplates available, Richard D. Foster and Keith Lawton re-drew some of the drawings, and Peter J. C. Skelton, Les Tindall and Peter Ward printed some of the photographs.
The majority of the photographs are from the author's own collection, which has been assembled from many sources over many years. Credit for them rightly belongs with the photographers who took them in the first place but sadly they are now almost entirely anonymous, though doubtless W. H. Whitworth was responsible for many. The remaining photographs and drawings have come from many sources as detailed below:
M. Bentley collection: *Plate, 81, 97, 238, 258, 271, 276, 368, 371.*
BR/OPC Joint Venture: *Figure 15, 17, 18, 19, 21, 22, 25, 27, 30, 32, 33, 34, 36, 39, 40, 41, 42, 44, 51, 55, 57, 58, 60, 61, 62, 65, 66, 67, 70, 71, 72, 73, 75, 76, 80, 87, 88, 90, 91, 93, 94, 97, 99, 101, 103, 105, 110, 111, 112, 113, 114, 115, 117, 119, 121, 123, 124, 125, 127, 130, 131, 132, 133, 136, 137, 138, 139, 141; Plate 164, 172, 191, 233, 265, 277, 278, 279, 357, 358, 458.*
W. T. Butler collection: *Figure 84.*
R. S. Carpenter collection: *Plate 407.*
F. W. Chubb: *Figure 64.*
G. J. Clark: *Figure 115, 122.*
E. Dutton collection: *Figure 77; Plate 69, 77, 88, 98, 105, 112, 119, 132, 143, 187, 203, 215, 218, 219, 239, 244, 269, 284, 291, 292, 296, 308, 315, 328, 334, 336, 339, 349, 353, 356, 362, 372, 378, 390, 397, 408, 421, 434, 443, 452, 457, 459, 461, 464, 475, 484, 488, 489, 490, 500, 509.*
A. G. Ellis collection: *Plate 114, 115, 131, 134, 194, 222, 236, 237, 248, 249, 251, 273, 302, 310, 312, 323, 324, 332, 333, 345, 346, 348, 352, 355, 370, 379, 380, 381, 382, 413, 425, 439, 441, 455, 460, 463, 482, 499, 503.*
W. Finch collection: *Figure 95; Plate 213.*
V. Forster collection: *Plate 89, 90.*
Alan Gettings: *Figure 144–52.*
Brian J. Gills collection: *Figure 74.*
Glasgow Museum: *Plate 477.*
F. C. Hambleton, reproduced courtesy of G. H. Platt: *Figure 2, 3, 7, 9, 12, 13, 14, 23, 26, 38, 43, 47, 48, 49, 50, 53, 54, 81, 83, 85, 86, 89, 92.*
L. Hanson: *Plate 156.*
T. Hinkley, courtesy of W. A. Camwell: *Plate 72, 216, 221.*
Historical Model Railway Society collection: *Plate 392.*
H. G. W. Household: *Plate 418.*
G. E. Hughes collection: *Plate 43.*
W. H. C. Kelland, courtesy Bournemouth Railway Club: *Plate 92, 406.*
T. A. Lindsay: *Figure 78, 79, 133.*
LNWR Society collection: *Plate 189, 193, 195, 209, 260, 280, 289, 331, 394, 396, 401, 402, 409, 420, 422, 430, 442, 465, 501.*
J. N. Maskelyne, courtesy of Argus Books Limited: *Figure 52, 59, 126, 136.*
Bernard Matthews collection: *Plate 130, 177, 245, 252, 344.*
Mitchell Library, Glasgow: *Figure 1.*
Ken Morgan: *Figure 37, 68, 140.*
E. R. Morten: *Plate 440.*
National Railway Museum, Crown Copyright, courtesy of the Keeper: *Figure 8; Plate 83, 87, 109, 113, 151, 158, 170, 171, 211, 229, 263, 266, 267, 275, 286, 321, 322, 343, 400, 423, 432, 448, 470, 483, 485, 502, 507, 516, 518.*
Ken Nunn collection, courtesy of the Locomotive Club of Great Britain: *Plate 9, 99, 103, 120, 231, 253, 376.*
D. J. Patrick collection: *Plate 57, 75, 137, 160, 240, 264, 274, 316, 435.*
G. H. Platt: *Figure 28, 118, 120, 128.*
G. H. Platt collection: *Figure 4, 5, 6, 35, 45, 56, 69; Plate 46, 86, 110, 116, 127, 159, 167, 173, 230, 287.*
Brian Reed collection, courtesy LNWR Society: *Figure 20; Plate 208, 226, 334, 510.*
J. P. Richards: *Figure 24, 29, 31, 63, 96, 98, 100, 104, 106, 108, 109, 142.*
J. P. Richards collection: *Plate 190, 250.*
R.P. Richards, courtesy J. P. Richards: *Plate 82, 140, 154, 338, 511.*
G. M. Sholto: *Plate 437.*
H. B. Spencer collection: *Plate 375.*
A. E. L. Thorne, courtesy V. R. Webster: *Plate 318.*
Harry Townley, courtesy M. Bentley: *Plate 126.*
G. Dudley Whitworth collection: *Plate 297.*
W. H. Whitworth, courtesy W. A. Camwell: *Plate 133, 146, 147, 148, 149, 150, 152, 153, 155, 449.*
Once again, the LNWR Society (membership enquiries: 7 Walnut Grove, Winchester, Hants, SO22 5HR) has played a valuable role in facilitating contact with like-minded enthusiasts. Its friendly informal meetings are rarely attended without learning something new.
To all who have helped in any way I offer my sincere thanks.

Edward Talbot
Stafford
January 1984

Contents

Preface

My earliest recollection of an LNWR engine is of a 'Prince of Wales' at Stafford in 1946. To me then it seemed a strange machine. With its straight running plate, plain boiler, unusual nameplate and simple tender, it had a very stark and austere appearance by comparison with the Stanier and Fowler engines that worked the majority of trains. It was also somewhat dirty and neglected, as were most of its more modern counterparts for that matter. Yet it had a certain style, an indefinable quality that caught the imagination and roused the curiosity as to its origins. It had an air of dignity, like an aristocrat that had fallen on hard times but knew how to behave though forced into the company of lesser mortals. Soon I found that despite its strange appearance it worked quite effectively. On the local passenger trains to Shrewsbury and Nuneaton it started away from stations with a very purposeful manner and it bowled along well between stops too. Later I came across pictures of 'Princes' in lined North Western black and realised that they had once been superbly painted in a style that complemented their lines magnificently. In 1946 they were survivors from the golden age of railways.

Very soon, of course, I became aware of other engines from the same school, of various Webb 0-6-0s and sundry tank engines, and above all of the 'Super Ds'. These too had the air of having known better days and the same purposeful manner, and they were fascinating machines with their distinctive exhaust beat, accompanied quite often by wheezings from leaks of steam at the front end. Nevertheless, they appeared to perform their work competently, and this was confirmed by my father who drove them regularly. Though he sometimes spoke of them with amusement—'Up in the roof for the brake, down in the cellar for the water', referring to the positions of the brake handle and injector water cock—it was always with approval and affection. As a young fireman at Monument Lane, he had worked on the various Webb tank engines that handled the Birmingham suburban services and he spoke of them too with the same approval. On one turn which he particularly remembered, they started out from New Street, usually with a 'Klondyke' ('Watford Tank') bunker first, and stopped at all stations to Tutbury via Lichfield and Burton. At Tutbury they ran round the train and then went all stations via Walsall and Darlaston to Wolverhampton (High Level). There they ran round again and then went all stations to Four Oaks via New Street. From Four Oaks they ran back light to Monument Lane Shed. They took water at Lichfield twice, both going out and on return, atWolverhampton and either at Monument Lane during the ticket stop or at New Street. In a day's work they had run round twice, taken water four times and covered 98 miles.

So began my interest in the engines of the LNWR. It has ultimately led to the production of this book in which I have tried to put on record all the information I have been able to gather about them. I hope that it will not only give pleasure to all who read it and help some to make good models but also serve as a modest tribute to the engines themselves and not least to those who designed, built, worked and maintained them.

Introduction

In its pre-eminent position as the largest of the pre-Grouping railway companies, serving most of the main cities and industrial centres in the country, the London & North Western Railway had engines of a quite distinctive character and style, that immediately set them apart from the engines of lesser railways. This was not because of any conscious or deliberate effort on the part of Crewe Works to be different for its own sake. It was simply because engines were built by the company to suit its own needs and features of design adopted by one engineer were retained by his successor unless there was some practical reason for change. So although Crewe followed technical developments elsewhere quite closely and often led the way itself, as in the application of superheating, it generally ignored the trends and fashions of the day, confident in its own ability to know what was best for the leading railway in the land. If as a consequence its engines differed from those of other companies, that was a matter of no concern whatsoever.

Most obviously, at a time when elaborate liveries of green, red and blue were commonplace on other railways, North Western engines were black although the sheen on their paintwork was generally so deep and glossy that it came to be described, quite aptly, as 'blackberry black'. Moreover, the whole style of the engine was unmistakably different, following a line of development from the earliest days of Crewe right up to the Grouping. So just a glimpse of a chimney, cab or footstep was enough to identify an engine as North Western. The word 'Grecian' has been applied by Jack Nelson to LNWR signals and could equally well be applied to the engines also.

Even on closer examination, many detail fittings not only looked different but actually worked differently on North Western engines. Again, this was because over the years Crewe had developed its own designs for every fitting, including injectors and brakes, which on other railways were obtained from outside suppliers. So long as these worked well and could be produced more cheaply than they could be bought, there was every reason for not changing them.

Many of the engines even sounded different, over and above the usual differences between one class and another, and between the whistles of the different companies. Webb's three-cylinder compounds made only two very heavy exhaust beats per revolution, and the 'Georges', 'Princes' and 'Super D's had an uneven exhaust, with the second beat louder than the first, and the third and fourth quieter than them both.

Outward appearances, however, were never of any great concern to North Western locomotive engineers. Their prime aim was always strictly functional, to produce engines which would work the company's traffic with the greatest possible economy. To this end they invariably pursued a policy of building small highly standardised engines, which thanks to the efficiency of Crewe Works, were very low in first cost. Because many of the company's trains were heavy, these small engines had to be worked hard to keep time, and this in turn meant harder work for the enginemen, especially the firemen. Hard driving came to be accepted by the men as quite normal, however, since their morale and company loyalty were high, and it became yet another tradition in which the North Western differed from other companies. Though it increased both coal consumption and maintenance, the additional cost was minimal, since coal was cheap and repairs were effected at the sheds by a cheap competent labour force, using cheap spares from Crewe and with the advantages of standardisation. Indeed, the whole operation of the company was only made possible by the sheer hard work, organisation, dedication and discipline of its servants at all levels, which was a product of the social order of the times and would be quite impossible today. So the trains were worked to time, earning the company a good reputation for punctuality. Locomotive Department costs were kept lower than those of comparable companies, and economy overall was achieved, to the benefit of the shareholders and ultimately the nation.

All these things contributed to the uniqueness of North Western engines and to their unique fascination for enthusiasts. Their character was effectively captured by H. F. F. Livesey, in comparing them with the trains of South London, with which he was familiar: 'Almost they were not real trains at all, or, at least, not in the sense that the LNWR expresses were. Euston was the gateway to the North, whose fells I loved, and through the Doric arch you came to magic. In the gloom of Euston you heard the hiss of fiercer steam, the rasp of angrier exhaust. Here the engines had about them something of the brisk naval air of destroyers stripped for action and ready to rush through rain and storm to their goal. And rush they did, screaming their way through stations with whistle-note pitched high, until at last we reached Carlisle. In those days the LNWR was indeed the "Premier Line".'

This book relates the history of LNWR engines through photographs, drawings and exhaustive captions. Complete coverage of the whole period from 1846 to 1922 is, unfortunately, impossible. The company built many hundreds of engines before photography was perfected or widely practised. No photographs exist of Trevithick engines in original condition or of many of the early Southern Division types, and there are only about twenty in all of LNWR engines before the time of Webb, most of them in Ramsbottom condition.

This early period has therefore been described as thoroughly as possible in the circumstances but inevitably has been relatively neglected. From then on, however, coverage is much more complete. Fortunately, the LNWR seems to have been one of the most popular railways with enthusiast photographers and many examples of their work have survived, as well as the superb official pictures taken by the company's own photographer. Incidentally, the use of official pictures is sometimes criticised by enthusiasts ('too many grey pictures') but although they are not always representative of engines in traffic, such pictures were intended as a record of the company's engines and are therefore ideal for a book of this type. After the photographs had been taken, of course, the engines would have been returned to the paintshop to be finished in glossy black, with or without lining as appropriate. In any case, every effort has been made to include a balanced selection of photographs showing each class in service at all the main stages in its life.

Generally, pictures taken in LMS livery have been avoided but some are included exceptionally, either because they show features of which no earlier photograph has been found or because they illustrate LNWR designs which were completed after the Grouping, such as Beames 0-8-4 tank engine. Features of purely LMS origin are mentioned in the captions of such photographs but no attempt has been made to complete the story of LNWR engines in LMS days. That is the concern of a companion volume, *An Illustrated History of LMS Locomotives*.

So far as possible, the changes in each class are illustrated from their original condition either to withdrawal or to the end of the LNWR period, whichever was earlier. Related classes are grouped into chapters, so that, for example, the development of the eight-coupled goods engines or of the 'Jumbos' can be followed in successive pages, and the chapters are arranged in roughly chronological order. Some classes present difficulties in that they might logically appear in more than one chapter. The 'Renowns', for instance, could be included either with the

'Jubilee' and 'Alfred the Great' four-cylinder compounds, on the grounds of being direct rebuilds from them, or with the Whale engines as one of his designs, and the first compound tank engine could appear with the 'Metropolitan' tanks, from one of which it was converted, or with the other compound tanks. In such cases, ease of reference has been the deciding factor. The reader is unlikely to expect to find the 'Renowns' with the four-cylinder compounds and so they are included with the Whale engines, and the compound 'Metropolitan' tank has been put with the other compound tanks, since the fact that it was converted to compound is its over-riding feature of interest. Similarly, all the eight-coupled goods engines are grouped in the same chapter, even the Whale and Bowen Cooke engines, so as to show their successive development, although all the other designs by those two engineers are contained in separate chapters.

As a rule, the names of the various classes used in this book are those by which they seem to be best known today. In many cases, the official names or descriptions, which often differed from those used generally by railwaymen and by enthusiasts, are also given, but the nicknames used by enginemen alone, which are often interesting and sometimes very amusing, have been avoided.

Ideally, a book such as this should contain a list of all LNWR engines, cross-referenced to the relevant chapters, so that the details of any particular engine could be readily identified. Owing to the nature of the LNWR numbering system, however, such a list would occupy most of the book itself and so is obviously out of the question. Basically, a new engine was accounted for in the company's books either on revenue account or on capital account. If on the former, it received the number of an engine recently withdrawn or transferred to the duplicate list, and so replaced it in capital stock. When all vacant numbers had been filled, a new engine was given the lowest blank number available and was charged to capital account. At the end of every six-monthly accountancy period, there would be no vacant numbers in the capital list and the highest number in it would be the same as the total number of engines in the company's capital stock. This system clearly suited the accountancy needs of the company, since it went unchanged throughout its existence, but it meant that engines of the same class were not numbered consecutively but had numbers scattered at random through the list and so cannot be summarised. The only major exceptions were the Webb 0-8-0s and four-cylinder compound 4-4-0s, which were numbered 1801-1900 and 1901-1980 respectively. These 200 numbers had been reserved for the duplicate list, into which engines were renumbered on becoming 'capital-expired', and so fell vacant when it was decided to number duplicate-list engines in the 3000 series after April 1897. The text, therefore, refers to different groups of engines by the batches in which they were built (for example, 'the 1915 batch'), so that the running numbers can be ascertained by reference to a complete list of LNWR engines. Fortunately, such a list has recently been published for the first time in *The British Locomotive Catalogue, Volumes 2A and 2B* by Bertram and David Baxter, published by the Moorland Publishing Company.

Chapter 1 Northern Division Engines

Trevithick 6ft 2-2-2

Plate 1: When the LNWR was formed on 16th July 1846, Francis Trevithick was Locomotive Superintendent of the Grand Junction Railway works at Crewe and continued in that position on the Northern Division of the new company. While he was in charge, only two main classes of the same basic design were produced, 2-2-2s for passenger work and 2-4-0s for goods. For many years these engines were known as the 'Old Crewe' type or 'Allan Type', but strictly neither of these terms is correct, since the type neither originated at Crewe nor is attributable to Alexander Allan. The complicated history of these engines is thoroughly discussed in an excellent study by D. H. Stuart and Brian Reed, *Loco Profile No. 15 The Crewe Type.* The type was originally developed to overcome the problem of crank-axle fractures commonly experienced with inside-cylinder engines. Double frames were used for strength and rigidity and the cylinders were placed outside so that the driving axle could be straight. Over the years the design was improved in many ways. At first 'crooked frames' were used; that is, the inside frames were not straight throughout their length but were narrowed over the driving-axle journal. Gab motion was originally used but was later replaced by Stephenson motion, first through rocking levers ('indirect action') and then with direct drive. Small fireboxes were later succeeded by large, and the wheelbase was altered a number of times. So although in a sense this was an early instance of standardisation, there were many differences in the 400 odd 'Crewe Types' built. Full information on the early engines is scanty. Contemporary drawings have not survived, if they ever existed, and the earliest photographs show the engines in Ramsbottom days. This drawing shows a Trevithick 6ft. 2-2-2 of the 1845 small firebox type, with 5ft 6in. plus 7ft 6in. wheelbase.

Plate 2: The earliest known photograph of a 6ft. 2-2-2, No. 500 *Menai* sometime between July 1865, when the 'Problem' on the right was built, and the end of 1872, when *Menai* lost its nameplates. Traditionally, the location is said to be Stafford, but this seems very unlikely. The engine is in green livery with black lining and has acquired an ornamental chimney top, standardised at Crewe during Ramsbottom's superintendence. It also has its original dome and safety valves, horizontal smokebox door, two lamp sockets on the wooden bufferbeam, and a hook-type coupling. The original four-wheel tender has been replaced by a six-wheel Ramsbottom tender. *Menai* was originally built in 1847 as No. 169 *Huskisson*.

Plate 3: A small-firebox 6ft 2-2-2, built before 1853, photographed around 1875 in the early Webb period. It has the original boiler fittings except for the Webb chimney, and the wheelbase is 6ft. plus 7ft. There is a lamp socket at the top of the smokebox, and a hook-type coupling is fitted.

Plate 4 (above): No. 1876, originally the last of the small-firebox 6ft. singles No. 291 *Prince of Wales*, after being reboilered in 1869 with two safety valves and no dome, as on the original 7ft. singles. The photograph was probably taken in 1879 before the engine was transferred to service stock as *Engineer Crewe*. Though unfortunately 'chopped' by the camera, the tender is the original four-wheel Trevithick type.

Plate 5 (right): No. 1873, which was originally No. 19 *Princess*, one of the early 1845 2-2-2s with 5ft. 6in. plus 7ft. 6in. wheelbase. It is seen in the mid-1870s, being withdrawn in August 1876.

Plate 6 (right): Trevithick 6ft. single No. 365 *Vesta*, built in 1855, running about 1880 after rebuilding in 1870 and after acquiring a Ramsbottom boiler and mountings, Webb chimney, black livery and numberplates, and a screw coupling; it has a Ramsbottom six-wheel 1,500 gallon tender. On the cabside is the winch used to wind up the chain brake. This winch is usually seen on the left-hand side, so perhaps the engine has worked a train tender first. The nameplate is of interest, having only a single row of subsidiary inscription.

Plate 7 (left): No. 1848 *Sefton*, originally No. 285, one of the last batch of large-firebox 6ft. singles built in 1857. It is seen at Prestbury between 1884 and 1887, and is basically in the same condition as *Vesta*. An additional sandpipe has been rigged on the front of the tender to assist braking.

Plate 8 (right): *Engineer Bangor* at Llanfairfechan about 1890, with original boiler but with Webb chimney, cab and vacuum brakes. This style of cab was used with the original boiler. The engine was originally No. 49 *Columbine*, which used to be regarded as the first engine built at Crewe Works, though that distinction belongs correctly to No. 32 *Tamerlane*. Quite a number of 6ft. singles passed into service stock.

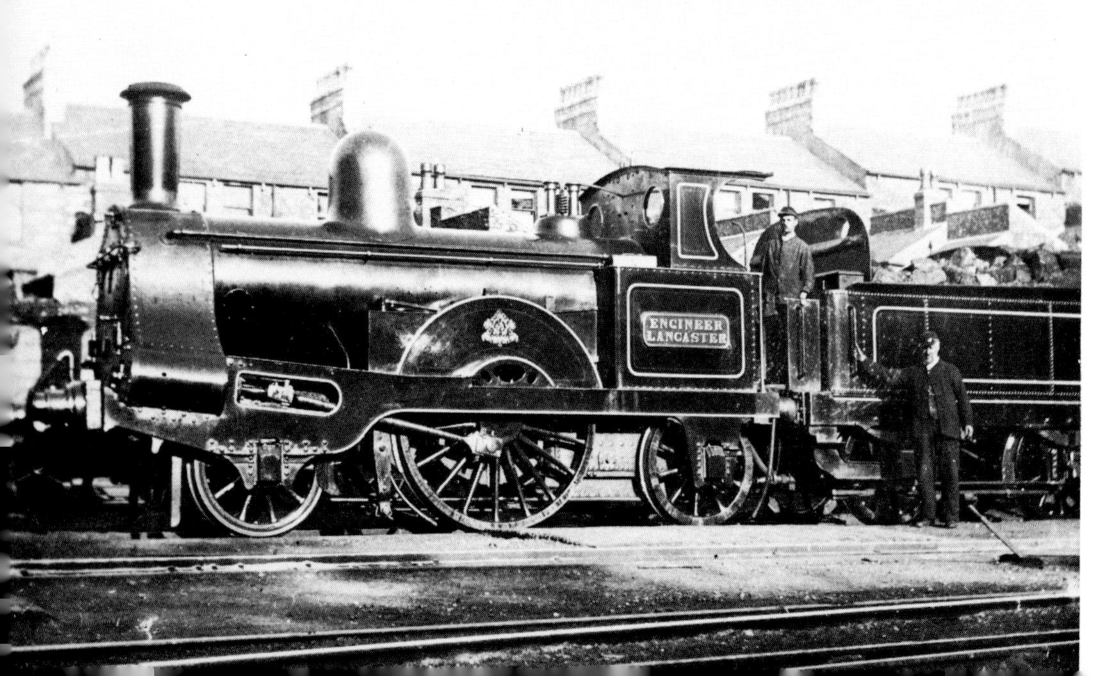

Plate 9 (left): *Engineer Lancaster* at Lancaster on 12th August 1902, with Webb boiler, chimney, dome and cab, and Ramsbottom safety valves and horizontal smokebox door. The Ramsbottom tender has a spectacle plate for running tender first, and rolled up on the front of it is a tarpaulin, to be attached to the rear edge of the cab roof in wet weather. The engine was originally No. 110 *Canning*, built in 1857.

Plate 10 (above): *Engineer Manchester*, originally No. 323 *Greyhound*, as running in the 1890s with a McConnell four-wheel tender from a Southern Division engine.

Plate 11 (left): *Engineer South Wales*, originally No. 135 *Bat* built in 1852, as running between 1911 and 1920, with Webb boiler ('Samson' type) and fittings, including safety valves and circular smokebox door. No centre lamp socket is fitted on the bufferbeam.

Trevithick 7ft 2-2-2

Figure 1: From the 6ft. 'Crewe Type' was developed the 7ft. single, introduced with No. 144 *Raven* in 1853. This general arrangement drawing is of the last batch of 7ft. singles built in 1857 but is essentially the same. It has the then new castellated chimney, wheelbase the same as the large firebox 6ft. singles and the same boiler but pitched 6in. higher. The grate slopes backwards (to allow a larger front damper and easier air access, so as to reduce smoke emission) and has a rocking-bar section at the front operated by levers from the footplate and a pull-and-chain operated front damper.

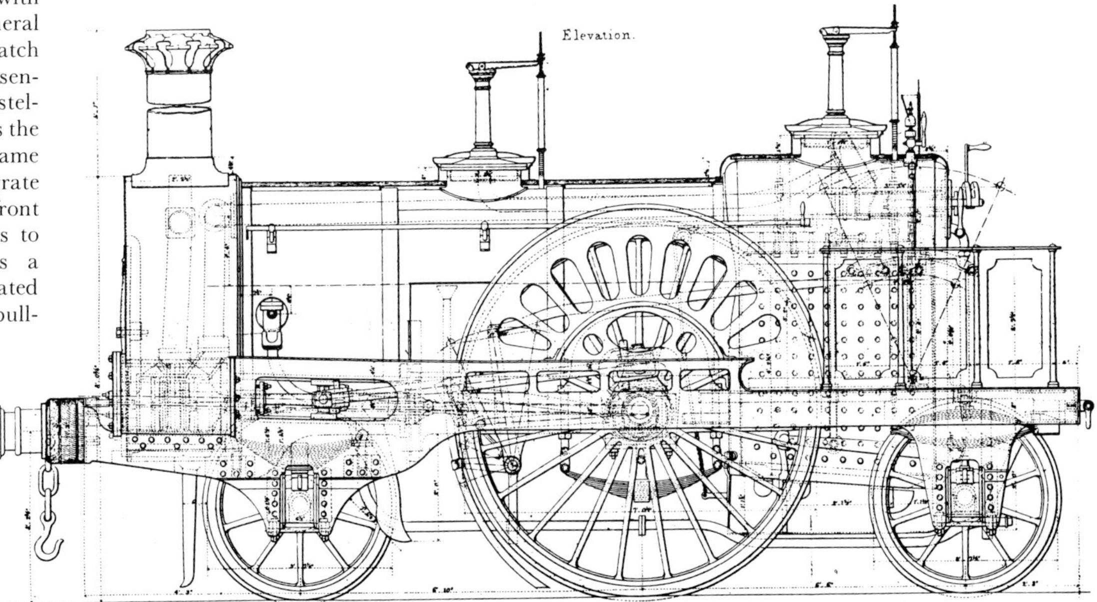

Plate 12: 7ft. single No. 1840 *Pegasus*, originally No. 31, after rebuilding in 1865 with a 'DX' boiler, and the fitting of a Webb chimney in the 1870s. It became No. 1840 in May 1876 and was scrapped in January 1880. This is the only known photograph of a Trevithick 7ft. single other than the one of *Velocipede*.

Trevithick 2-4-0 Goods

Figure 2: The goods engine counterpart of the 'Crewe Type' 2-2-2 engine was the 5ft. 'Crewe Goods' 2-4-0, exemplified here by No. 292 *Hardwicke*, in original condition.

Figure 3: The essential feature of the 'Crewe Type' engine was the combination of outside cylinders and double frames to overcome the problem of crank-axle breakages with inside cylinders. This drawing shows the arrangement of the straight frames of a 'Crewe Goods' 2-4-0.

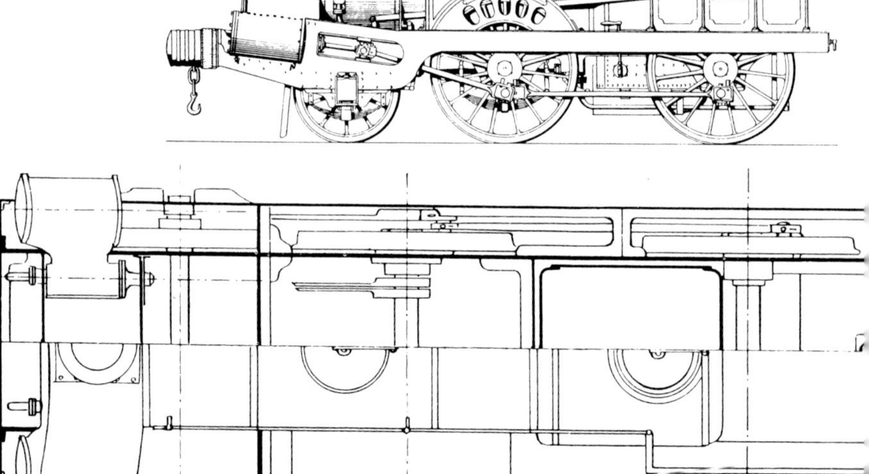

Plate 13 (below): The earliest known photograph of a Trevithick 5ft 2-4-0 No. 512, which was built originally as No. 18 *Cerberus* in January 1857 with large firebox and direct action, was sold to the Lancaster & Carlisle Railway soon afterwards and on its return to the LNWR in August 1859 was numbered 512 but was not again named. It is seen here in original condition, with its original four-wheel tender. The chimney appears to be the ornamental type, standardised by Ramsbottom.

Plate 14 (right): Another early photograph of a Trevithick 5ft 2-4-0, this time No. 155 *Ousel*, which was built in 1854 with large firebox, straight frames and direct action. It was later rebuilt in 1867. It is seen here about 1870 in green livery with black lining, and with Ramsbottom chimney. The tender is of the first six-wheel type, built as replacements for four wheelers and thought to be of Trevithick design, having the same footsteps as the fourwheelers, round ends to the bufferbeams and square buffers at the front. A few six-wheelers were built before Trevithick left but this is possibly an early design by Ramsbottom. The steps and buffer beam were redesigned to suit the 'DX' 0-6-0s but no other changes were made until round buffers were introduced. The engine nameplate is also of interest, being the early type with only a single row of subsidiary inscription.

Plate 15 (above): Trevithick 2-4-0 No. 72, formerly *Phlegethon*, built in 1853 in the same class as *Ousel*. It is seen here as rebuilt in the 1860s but with Webb chimney; the date is sometime between 1872, when the nameplates were removed, and 1880, when the engine was renumbered in the duplicate list. Basically, it is in the same condition as *Ousel*, but has a Webb chimney and is in plain black with painted numbers. It has also been given a rear sandpipe, on the right-hand side only.

Plate 16 (below): Quite a number of the 2-4-0s ended up at Buxton for working on the Cromford & High Peak section, where this one, No. 3074, is seen in the 1890s. It is as rebuilt in 1872, and has a Webb chimney and black livery with painted numbers. The engines for the High Peak line all had spectacle plates on the tenders for running tender first, and plain link couplings front and rear. A route-indicator bracket is carried on the chimney, which has perhaps come from a tank engine used on London suburban services.

Plate 17: No. 3046 at Buxton in the 1890s. It has a shorter chimney than No. 3074, 4ft. 3in. instead of 5ft., but otherwise is in similar condition.

Trevithick 2-4-0 Tank

Plate 18: In 1857 two of the last class of Trevithick 5ft. 2-4-0 goods engines, with large firebox, straight frames and direct action, were turned out as side tanks, and by 1871 over 100 of the small-firebox 2-4-0s had been similarly converted. This view shows No. 37 *Hawk* on 7th October 1867 inRamsbottom livery with castellated chimney, and with the original curved nameplate from the tender engine on the tank side. It was previously a straight-frame, small-firebox, indirect-action tender engine.

Plate 19: Trevithick 2-4-0 tank No. 953, which was originally built as No. 283 *Croxteth*, a small-firebox, straight-frame, direct-action tender engine, in April 1852. It was converted to a tank engine by Mr Webb and is seen here about 1880, with Trevithick boiler, Webb chimney and black livery, screw couplings front and rear but no cab. The leading sandboxes are in front of the tanks and the rear ones in the coal bunker, supplying pipes running down beside the guard-irons.

Plate 20: No. 3097 on the High Peak section. It was originally built as No. 295 *Penmaenmawr* in 1852, renumbered 3097 in November 1887 and sold in January 1903. The cab is typical of Webb in the 1880s; the angle from which the picture is taken clearly shows the whistle between the safety-valve balance and the spectacle plate. Another view of this engine at the same period shows the front coupling to be of the plain three-link type, signifying that the engine was intended purely for goods work. The coupling has probably been removed as in other pictures taken on the High Peak line, with the hook being hidden by the buffer.

Plate 21: No. 3022 at Buxton Shed in the 1890s. It was originally 2-4-0 No. 307 *Fury*, was converted to a tank engine in January 1867, renumbered 3022 in April 1887 and scrapped in June 1904. It has screw couplings and black coupling rods with polished connecting rods. Some observers say the tanks of these engines were made from those of scrapped tenders but a minute dated November 1859 instructed that tenders released by these conversions should be broken up. In any case, the tanks of four-wheel tenders would be too short.

Trevithick 2-4-0 Saddle Tank

Plate 22 (right): In 1873-7 Mr Webb converted some of the large-firebox 2-4-0 tender engines to saddle tanks. This is No. 161, originally built in March 1856 and named *Cuckoo*. It became a saddle tank in September 1876 and is seen here about 1880 with Webb chimney, dome and black livery, Ramsbottom safety valves, screw couplings and no cab.

Plate 23 (right): No. 1924, originally built as No. 310 *Isis* in 1853, at Manchester (London Road) in 1884-9.

Cornwall

Figures 4 & 5 (right): In the mid-1840s advocates of the broad gauge asserted that the development of standard-gauge engines had reached its limit. The speed and power of the Great Western's broad-gauge engines, such as Daniel Gooch's recently completed *Great Western*, was well beyond the capacity of the 'Crewe Type' singles, and in an attempt to match them, Crewe built three experimental engines of widely different designs in 1847, *Cornwall*, *Courier* and *Velocipede*. No 173 *Cornwall* was designed by Trevithick with the boiler slung beneath the driving axle, the aim being to achieve a low centre of gravity, thought to be essential for stable running at speed, with large driving wheels; the 8ft. 6in. driving wheels of *Cornwall* were 6in larger than those of *Great Western* and were clearly intended to beat it for speed. These drawings show *Cornwall* as originally built.

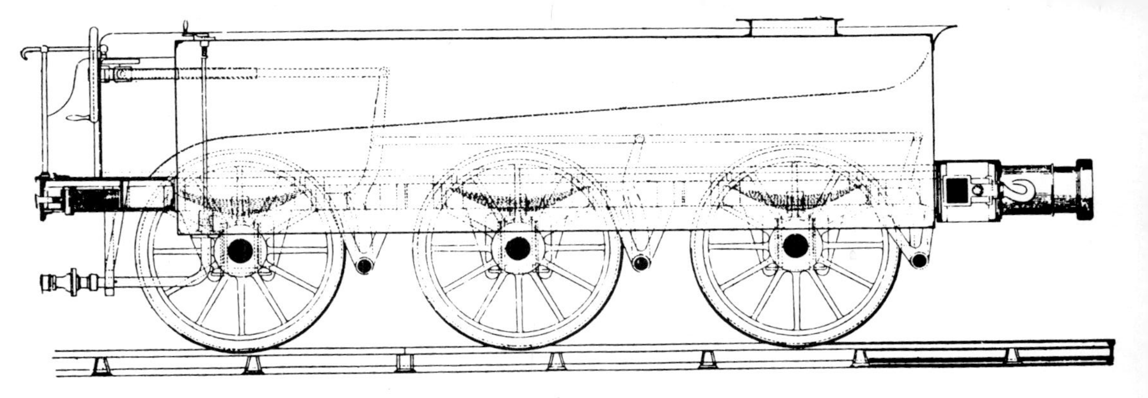

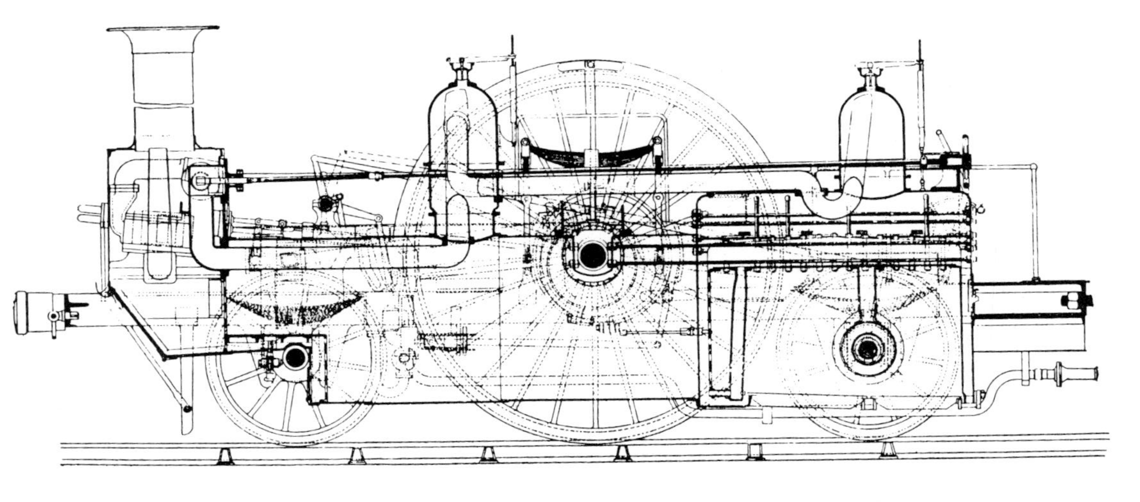

Figure 6 (below right): Drawing of the original boiler fitted to *Cornwall*, showing the way the driving axle passed through a notch in the top of the boiler.

Figure 7 (below): Another drawing of *Cornwall* as first built.

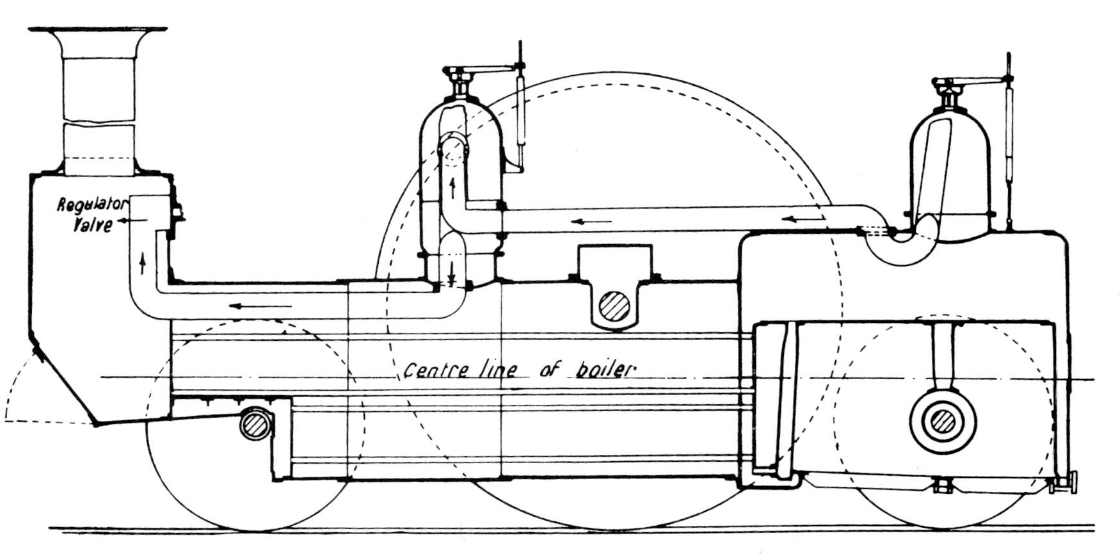

Figure 8 (above): *Cornwall* proved to be most unsatisfactory and in September 1848 Trevithick was directed to 'put an additional pair of wheels under the *Cornwall* engine' presumably in the interests of smooth riding and to alleviate harmful effects on the track; it was then put to work on cattle and goods trains. This drawing shows *Cornwall* as a 4-2-2 and probably in the form in which it was exhibited at the Crystal Palace in 1851.

Figure 9 (right): All attempts to make *Cornwall* into a reliable machine failed and in 1858 it was extensively rebuilt by John Ramsbottom along the lines of a 'Crewe Type' but with a standard 'DX' boiler, with backward sloping grate, and the original 8ft. 6in. driving wheels. The design was prepared by F. W. Webb, who was then in charge of the Crewe drawing office. This drawing shows *Cornwall* in rebuilt condition, with the usual Ramsbottom features of the day, castellated chimney, safety valves and green livery with painted numbers.

Plate 24: No. 173 *Cornwall* as it was between 1873 and 1877, when it acquired a new boiler. It has a Webb chimney and cab, and full lining on the boiler bands, as was first applied with the black livery up to 1876. The tender is an early six-wheeler but with round buffers in place of square.

Plate 25: In 1886 *Cornwall* was renumbered 3020 on the duplicate list and is seen here as running at that time. It is in much the same condition as in the previous picture except for the new boiler with Webb safety valves acquired in 1877, a screw coupling and a more modern tender. The chimney cap is finished bright and the large Ramsbottom displacement lubricators are prominent on either side of the smokebox by the tail rods of the valve spindles.

Plate 26: A view of the left-hand side of *Cornwall* taken about the same time, 1886-7, but after being fitted for working vacuum-braked trains.

Plate 27 (above): In 1887 *Cornwall* was given a new boiler and in 1895 a circular smokebox door, and is seen here so fitted about 1900. Webb displacement lubricators have replaced the Ramsbottom type, and an 1,800 gallon tender with coal rails and oil axleboxes has replaced the 1,500 gallon tender which had grease axleboxes. The axleboxes on the engine have similarly been replaced.

Plate 28 (right): *Cornwall* was withdrawn in 1907 but was restored to the duplicate list again in May 1911 and allocated to working the chief mechanical engineer's saloon. By then it had lost its communication-cord whistle and, of course, its tender, which it did not need when it was attached to the saloon; it also acquired Cooke axleboxes for the carrying wheels. During World War I, it was tried for motor train working on the Northwich branch from Sandbach but without success, because the driver had no means of knowing when the engine was slipping. This view shows the engine at Crewe on 20th July 1920 after double-heading *Patriot* from Euston with the 1.15 p.m. 'Corridor'. Its dome is now polished brass (before Webb changed to steel, domes were made of brass generally, because it was easier to shape, but were painted to save the labour of polishing them) and it ran like this from about 1918 to 1927. It also has long-tapered buffers and rear sanding. The tender is not the previous one, which was damaged in an accident, but has come from a Webb engine. On the front of the tender beside the fireman is the stanchion to support the cable running along the base of the tank for communication when hauling the saloons; the plate explaining the bell code is still in the cab. Except for the polished dome, *Cornwall* is now preserved in this condition, though with a different tender and without its Bowen Cooke axlebox covers. The tender it was preserved with originally (No. 1509) was put back into traffic during World War II and replaced with one which was life-expired (No. 1691).

Plate 29: *Cornwall* at Euston on 25th September 1938, while on display in connection with the London & Birmingham Centenary.

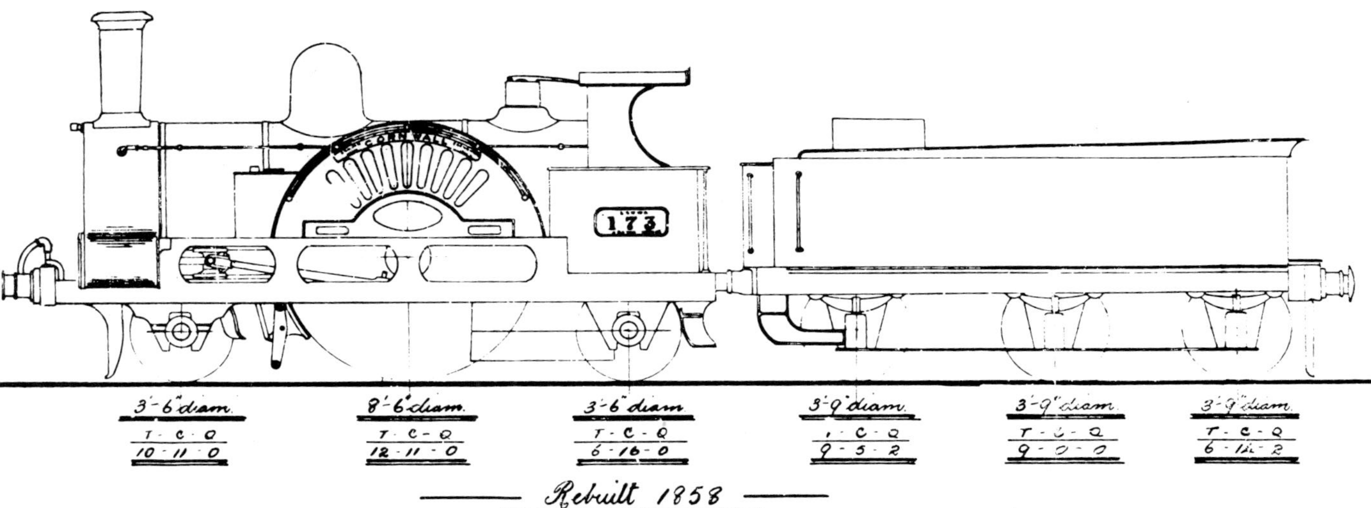

Figure 10 (right): Official Crewe weight diagram of *Cornwall*. Despite the engine number and the date, the details refer to the engine's condition after the 1887 rebuilding. The diagram is signed by George Whale.

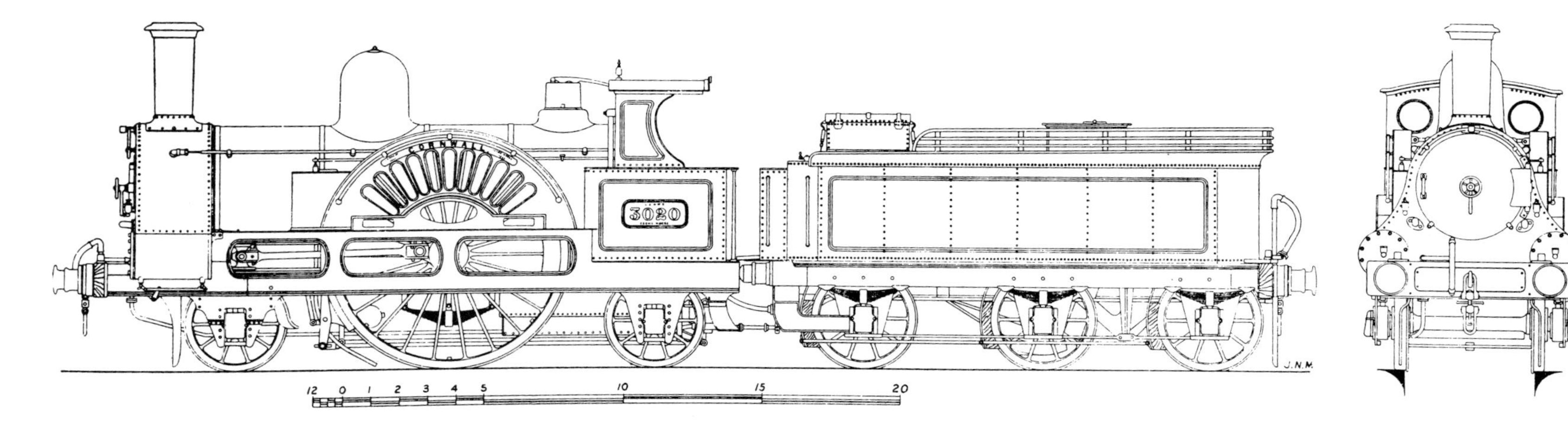

Figure 11 (below): Drawing of *Cornwall*, as running about 1900.

Courier

Figure 12 (right): The second experimental engine to appear from Crewe in 1847 was No. 176 *Courier*. It was built to the patent design of T. R. Crampton, the essential feature of which was to place a single pair of large driving wheels so that the axle passed to the rear of the firebox. While this achieved the desired combination of a low-pitched boiler (and so a low centre of gravity) and large driving wheels, the adhesive weight on the driving wheels was low and so the power of the engine was limited. *Courier* was found to have a harmful effect on the track, like *Cornwall*, did little real work and was withdrawn in 1854. This drawing shows *Courier* as built in 1847.

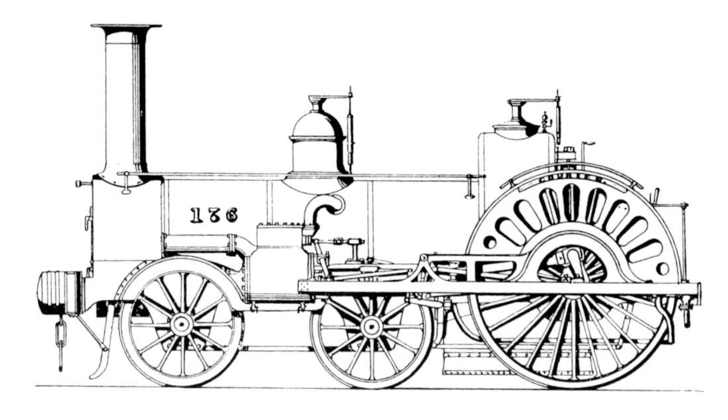

Velocipede

Plate 30: The third experimental engine was a 7ft. single version of the standard Trevithick 6ft. type and was No. 187 *Velocipede*. It seems to have been reasonably successful, as it lasted until about 1860 before being rebuilt. This drawing shows it in original condition, with huge slotted eccentrics for the outside valve gear. These were later replaced by the standard-size inside type, as they wore excessively and tended to run hot. The close similarity to the 6ft. singles is apparent. Incidentally, the nameplate is probably more accurate than it might seem, as plates such as this, showing the name only without the subsidiary inscriptions which later became standard, were used for a time in the early days.

Plate 31 (left): In 1869 *Velocipede* was rebuilt again, this time as a standard 7ft. single of the 'Raven' class; in 1877 it was renumbered 1932 on the duplicate list and in 1881 it was scrapped. This view, probably taken at the time of withdrawal, shows it with a Webb chimney and dome, Ramsbottom safety valves and no cab. The sandbox is reminiscent of the small ones fitted originally on the 'Problems', to which there is something of a family likeness generally.

Sharp 2-2-2 Saddle Tank

Figure 13 (right): Drawing of 'Sharpie' No. 402, which was erected at Longsight as a 2-2-2 tender engine in 1857, and converted to a saddle tank in 1868. These tank engines worked local passenger trains in the North Eastern Division.

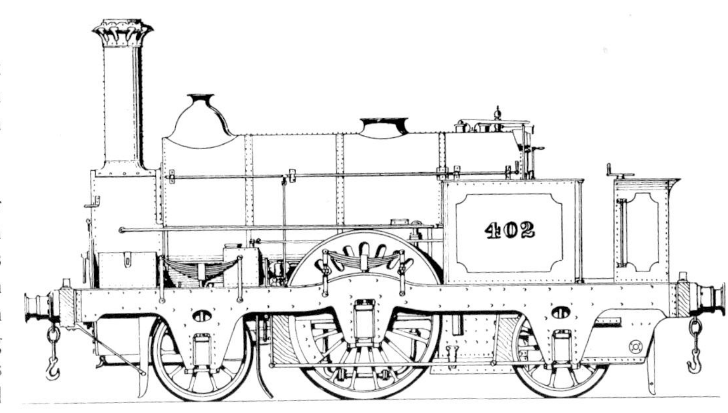

Plate 32 (below): 2-2-2 saddle tank No. 446. Originally built as 2-2-2 tender engine *Brook* for the Huddersfield & Manchester Railway by Sharp Bros. in 1847, it was rebuilt as a saddle tank in 1862 and was re-boilered in 1870. It has a Ramsbottom chimney, lamp sockets and hook coupling, and is in green livery with painted numbers. The driving and trailing wheels have wooden brake blocks, and there is no sanding gear. A bucket, possibly containing sand, is hanging on the fire-iron hook on the back of the bunker. This photograph was taken at Crewe Works by E. Pouteau in 1873. The general offices, then being built, have been painted out on this print to give a clear background.

Fairbairn 0-4-2 Tank

Figure 14 (right): A North Eastern Division Fairbairn 0-4-2, originally No. 75 built in 1853, as running about 1880 with Ramsbottom 'DX' boiler, Webb chimney and cast-iron H-section wheels.

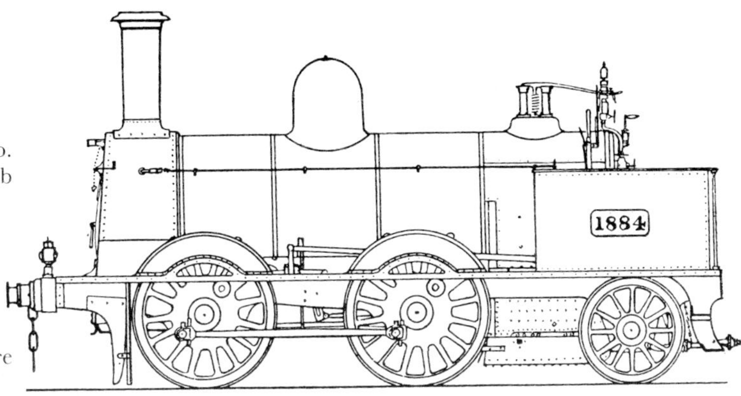

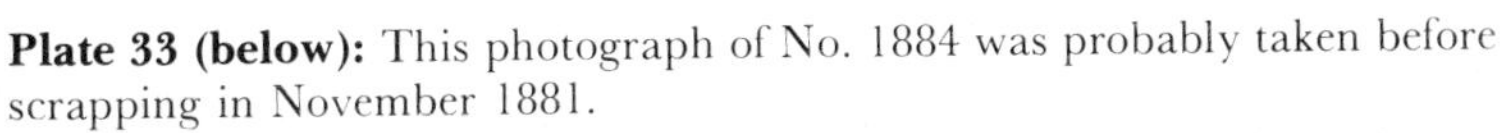

Plate 33 (below): This photograph of No. 1884 was probably taken before scrapping in November 1881.

Chapter 2
Southern Division Engines

Long-boiler 4-2-0

Plate 34: Early Southern Division engines comprised a wide variety of types. As well as Bury engines surviving from the London & Birmingham, there were Sharp singles, long-boiler passenger and goods engines, and an assortment of singles and four-coupled engines from various builders, to which J. E. McConnell, the Locomotive Superintendent, added his own designs. Sadly, except for McConnell's 'Bloomers', very few photographs of these engines exist. This is one of the long-boiler 4-2-0s built in 1847 by Jones, Potts & Co. The first batch of six had haystack fireboxes but the next ten had round-topped fireboxes, as seen here. All the latter were scrapped or sold in the 1860s.

Long-boiler 4-2-2

Figure 15: Drawing of a long-boiler 4-2-2 designed by Robert Stephenson & Co. for the Southern Division about 1848.

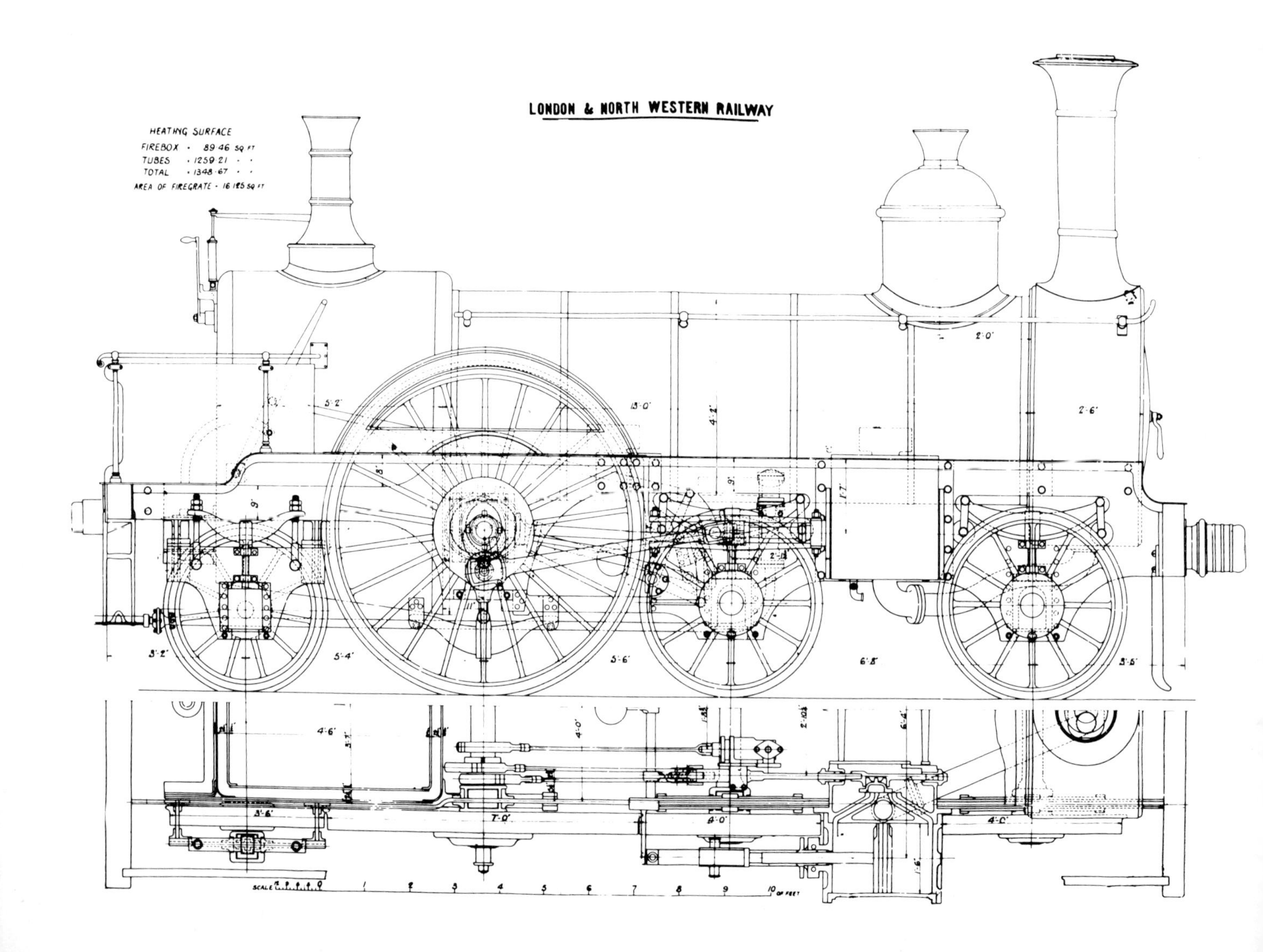

London

Figure 16: At about the same time that Crewe was building its experimental engines, among them the Crampton *Courier*, the Southern Division also tried two examples of the Crampton principle, *London* and *Liverpool*. No. 200 *London* was built by Tulk & Ley in 1847 to the 4-2-0, perhaps more accurately (2-2)-2-0 wheel arrangement. It had quite a large boiler of oval section, with the firebox extending beneath the driving axle, and with 8ft. driving wheels was a considerable advance in hauling power over the Bury engines. Whereas the long-boiler type suffered from hunting at speed, the Crampton engines were stable, thanks to their low centre of gravity and long rigid wheelbase. For the same reasons, however, they transmitted heavy sideways thrusts to the track, which caused considerable wear, and they were extremely rough riding. This drawing shows *London* as built; it was the first named engine on the Southern Division.

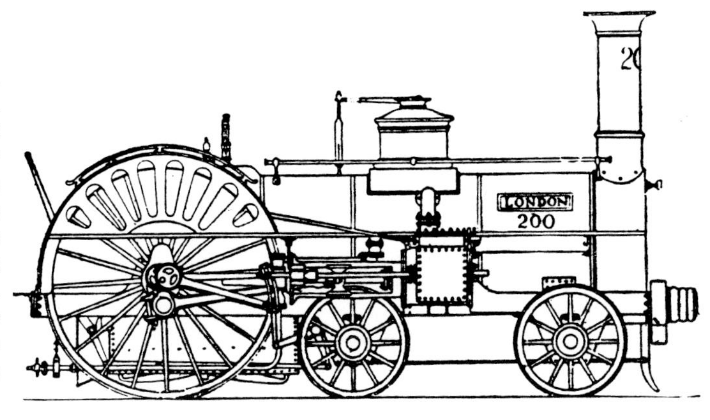

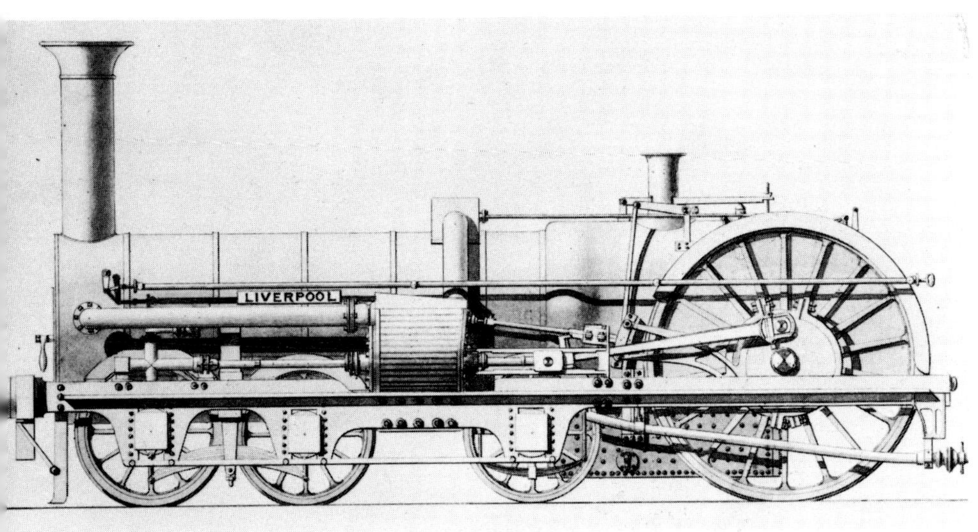

Liverpool

Plates 35 & 36 (below): Two views of *Liverpool*, which was built by Bury, Curtis & Kennedy of Liverpool in 1848 and was exhibited at the Great Exhibition of 1851. It was the largest Crampton ever built. All axles were rigid in the frame, the wheel arrangement being denoted as 6-2-0 or (4-2)-2-0. Though quite powerful, the engine damaged the track unduly and was withdrawn in 1858. No doubt the large unbalanced driving wheels, with their solid eccentrics, produced considerable hammer blow.

Heating Surface
1½ Inch Scale

Plate 38 (right): 'Large Bloomer' No. 992, which was built in 1862 and named *Stork* in 1872. It has a Ramsbottom chimney and appears to be in green livery. When McConnell retired in 1862, Ramsbottom became Locomotive Superintendent of the whole railway and his green livery became standard throughout.

'Large Bloomer'

Plate 37 (above left): The most famous engines on the Southern Division were the 'Bloomers'. They were inside-cylinder inside-frame single-wheelers and were designed by McConnell. The first to appear were the so-called 'Large Bloomers', introduced in 1851. This is No. 249, which was built by Sharp Bros. in 1851 and is seen here at Wolverton in shop grey, possibly in 1861 when the photographs of the 'Extra Large Bloomer' No. 373 and the standard goods No. 371 seem to have been taken. It would normally have been painted in the Southern Division's green livery but after this picture was taken may have received the red livery introduced about this time. In either case it would have been a fine sight, with plenty of polished brass — dome, safety valves, splasher beading, numberplates and numbers on the chimney.

Figure 17 (left) & Figure 18 (below): Works drawings of the first 'Large Bloomer', No. 247, and of its tender, built by Sharp Bros. in 1851.

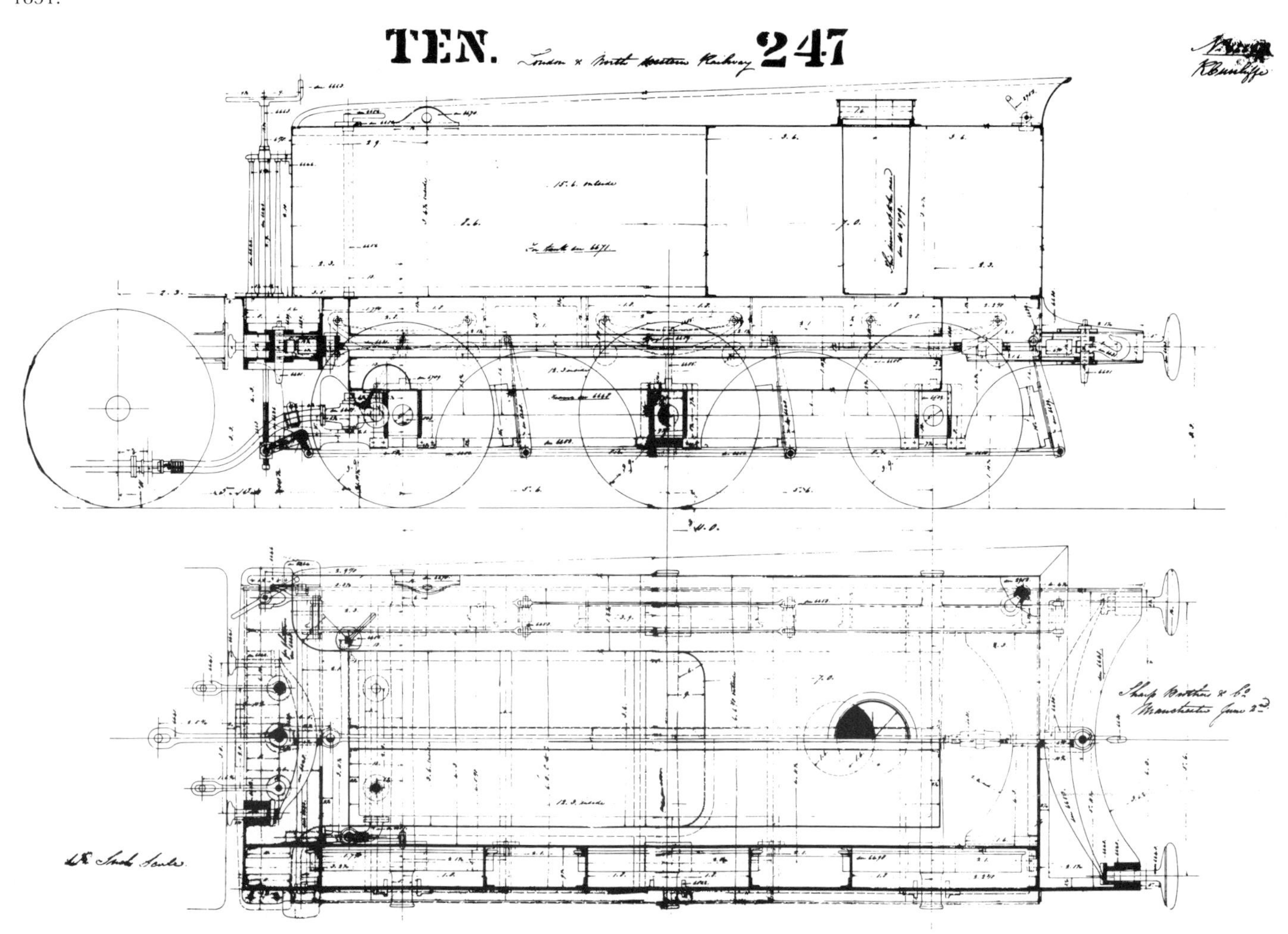

Plate 39: Another of the 1862 batch of 'Large Bloomers', No. 896, which was named *Daedalus* in 1872. It has a Ramsbottom chimney and appears to be in green livery. Compared to No. 992, however, its driving splasher is quite open.

Plate 40: No. 1008 *Rowland Hill* at Camden with the famous roundhouse in the background about 1875. It is largely in original condition with the original boiler fittings, but has a Webb chimney and black livery of the first style, with boiler bands lined red, cream and grey, and lining round the steps and tender frames as in the Southern Division red livery. From 1876 boiler bands had two parallel red lines only, and there was no lining below footplate level.

Plate 41 (right): 'Large Bloomer' No. 998 *Una* in the late 1870s. It has a Ramsbottom boiler, Webb chimney, black livery like *Rowland Hill*, and sandboxes under the running plate of typical Webb style.

Plate 42 (below): No. 1002 *Theseus*, in the late 1870s in much the same condition as *Una* but with the addition of a cab.

McConnell's 'Patent' 2-2-2

Figure 19: After the 'Large Bloomers', McConnell produced his 'Patent' 2-2-2s, as the directors wanted a larger engine which could work London-Birmingham trains in two hours. The 'Patents', which appeared in 1852, were not only larger than the 'Large Bloomers' but differed from them in many features of design. They had outside bearings and the boiler was pitched very low, with a recess to accommodate the cranks and upward inclined cylinders. The 'patent' feature concerned the design of the firebox with a combustion chamber to burn coal instead of coke. This drawing shows 'Patent' No. 300, built by Fairbairn in 1852.

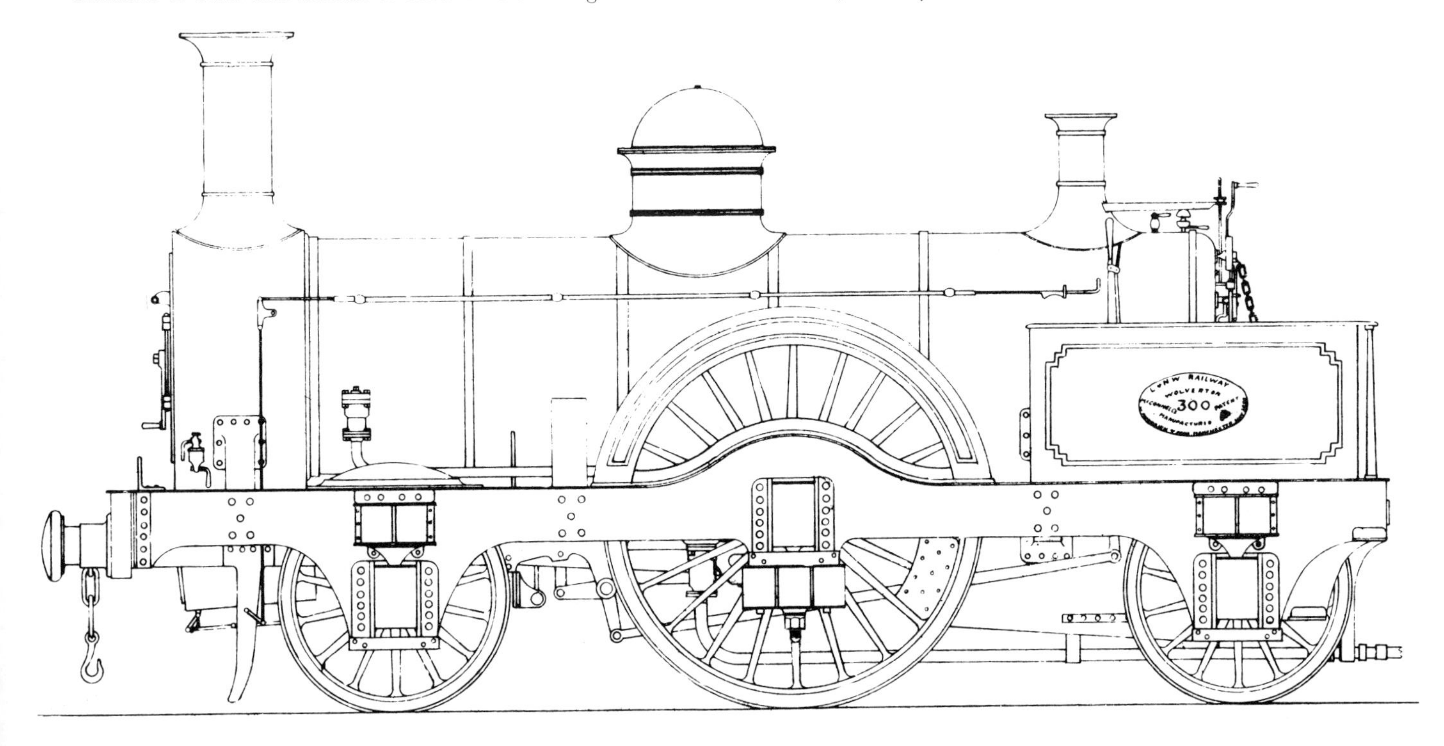

'Small Bloomer'

Plate 43: In 1854 the 'Small Bloomers' were introduced. They were basically similar to the 'Large Bloomers' but had smaller boilers and smaller driving wheels, 6ft. 6in. instead of 7ft. This fine photograph shows No. 103, built at Wolverton in May 1857, in original condition, and is probably the earliest surviving picture of a 'Bloomer'. The engine seems quite new and is probably in the Southern Division livery of 'medium chrome green' — 'the colour of GN locomotives in Patrick Stirling's time'. The lining on the cab side-sheet and tender panels seems most unusual and is thought to be in red and yellow, the red not being visible owing to early films being insensitive to it. Quite probably, however, this was the standard Southern Division livery until 1861. There is plenty of polished brasswork and the numberplate between the double beading on the driving splasher also serves as a maker's plate, as on other Wolverton engines. The tender is the usual McConnell style but again the springing is unusual.

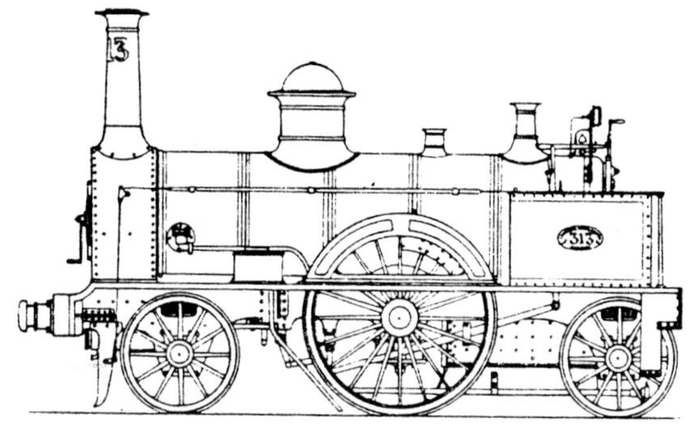

Figure 20: Drawing of 'Small Bloomer' No. 313.

Plate 44: The last of the 'Small Bloomers', No. 381, which was built at Wolverton in 1861. It is in the red livery of the Southern Division, with brass cabside numberplates and brass numbers on the front of the chimney.

Plate 45 (left): Most of the 'Bloomers' were renumbered twice. 'Small Bloomer' No. 3 was built at Wolverton in 1859 and renumbered 603 in 1862 when 600 was added to Southern Division numbers so as to number all LNWR engines in one sequence. It was named *Langdale* in 1872 when Mr. Webb decided that the 'Bloomers' should be named. As seen here about 1865, it has acquired the green livery with black lining and painted numbers, but otherwise appears to be in original condition, even with its original chimney.

Plate 46 (above): 'Small Bloomer' No. 602 at the old Trent Valley shed at Rugby about 1870. It is basically still in original condition, even with its Southern Division numberplate on the driving splasher, but appears to have paid a visit to Crewe Works, having acquired a Ramsbottom chimney and safety valves, and green livery.

Plate 47 (left): 'Small Bloomer' No. 630, built as No. 320 by R. & W. Hawthorn in 1854, and named *Ribble* in 1872. It is in full Ramsbottom condition probably in the late 1860s, with his chimney top (unfortunately just 'clipped' by the camera), dome, safety valves, smokebox door and green livery lined in black — in fact, with all the usual Crewe features of the day, though the diminutive spectacle plate is typical of all 'Bloomers' before cabs were fitted. The brass beading on the driving splasher has been painted over. Though 'Small Bloomers' were painted black in the 1870s and received Webb chimneys, none were ever fitted with cabs.

'Extra Large Bloomer'

Plate 48: In 1861 McConnell produced three enlarged 'Bloomers' at Wolverton Works, which are commonly referred to as 'Extra Large Bloomers'. They had 7ft. 6in. driving wheels and boilers with various McConnell patent features. This is No. 373, probably in shop grey on completion. On the right is No. 249, which is also painted grey and was probably photographed on the same occasion.

Figure 21: Drawing of No. 373 as displayed at the 1862 International Exhibition. It was later named *Caithness*.

Fairbairn 0-6-0

Plate 49: A Southern Division long-boiler type 0-6-0 goods engine, originally built in 1853 as No. 270 by W. Fairbairn & Sons. It has lost its original boiler with raised firebox and now has a Webb boiler with Webb chimney and dome and Ramsbottom safety valves. It was renumbered 1824 in June 1877 and scrapped in 1880. It has a 'top' lamp socket on the smokebox door instead of on top of the smokebox, and early type round-section coupling rods. The tender has an early style of framing and axleboxes.

Figure 22: Drawing of long-boiler 0-6-0 No. 281, built by Fairbairn in 1853, showing the firebox flush with the top of the boiler. Earlier examples had raised fireboxes. Various types of long-boiler 0-6-0s were acquired by the Southern Division for goods work in the 1840s and 1850s.

Plate 50: Another re-boilered Fairbairn long-boiler 0-6-0, No. 1905, a number which it carried for about ten months in 1877-8. It originally had a flush-top firebox with midfeather and two firehole doors, but is seen here with a Webb boiler, rectangular-section coupling rods and the later type of McConnell tender.

Plate 51 (left): A long-boiler 0-6-0, converted by Webb to a saddle tank. It is in much the same condition as No. 1905 as regards boiler fittings, rods and cab but has cast-iron H-section wheels, open coupling-rod splashers and a top lamp socket in the normal position.

McConnell 0-4-2

Plates 54 (right) & 55 (below): Two views of McConnell's 0-4-2 No. 778, built at Wolverton in 1862. It never carried a Southern Division number and is seen here in the late 1860s with Ramsbottom chimney and green livery lined in black. It was scrapped in 1874 as No. 1961.

McConnell Goods 0-6-0

Plate 52 (left): Whereas McConnell's predecessor at Wolverton, Edward Bury, had pursued a small-engine policy with diminutive 2-2-0 passenger and 0-4-0 goods engines, McConnell himself built large engines by the standards of the day. His 'Bloomers' were considerably bigger than their Crewe contemporaries and the Southern Division had various six-coupled goods engines to compare with Trevithick's 2-4-0s. McConnell's standard 0-6-0 was introduced in 1854 and was of similar size to Ramsbottom's 'DX' which it preceded by four years. This is No. 371, a Wolverton goods of the 1861 batch, and its family likeness to the 'Bloomers' is immediately apparent. The lower line of the maker's plate reads 'Manufactured at the Engine Works, Wolverton'; above is the number and above that 'London & North Western Railway'.

Plate 53 (below left): The last engines to be built at Wolverton were ten 0-6-0s of Class 'G', which were ordered before Ramsbottom took over in 1862 and responsibility for locomotive affairs was centralised at Crewe. They were built in 1863 and were like McConnell's standard goods, introduced with No. 332 in 1854, with 5ft. 6in. driving wheels but probably 17in. cylinders instead of 16in. This photograph shows No. 1073 after rebuilding with a Ramsbottom boiler and Webb cab and chimney, about 1880.

McConnell 0-4-2 Well Tank

Plate 56: One of McConnell's 0-4-2 well tanks, built in 1862. It was originally LNWR No. 983, was renumbered 1857 in the duplicate list in 1874 and was scrapped in 1877. It has a Webb chimney but is in green livery lined in black in the Webb style, with rounded corners. There is a top lamp socket, not fitted on the smokebox in front of the chimney but on the smokebox door about a foot lower down. Possibly, McConnell's circular smokebox door left insufficient room at the top for the lamp socket to be in the usual position.

Chapter 3
Six-Coupled Goods Engines and Related Tank Classes

'DX'

Plate 57: The 'DX' 0-6-0s were designed by John Ramsbottom and no less than 943 were built in 1858-72 including 86 for the Lancashire & Yorkshire Railway. This was a remarkable instance of standardisation at a time when most railways had many different classes, each one consisting of only a few engines. As originally built, the 'DXs' naturally incorporated all the usual Ramsbottom features: his own designs of chimney top, safety valves and screw reverse, horizontal smokebox door, coupling rods with split ends and wedge adjustment, slotted splashers, wooden bufferbeams and brake blocks, no brakes on the engine and green livery lined in black. This photograph shows No. 568 *Stewart* outside the Old Works on completion in August 1861. 'DXs' carried nameplates for only a short time. In 1862 it was decided that goods engines would no longer be named and in 1863 the plates were removed. They were replaced by numberplates in the same style and showing the date of building, as on the original unnamed engines. No. 568 is fitted with a 2,000 gallon tender, a type which seems to have been soon made obsolete by the widespread adoption of water-troughs. On the rear is a white diamond, as used on LNWR wagons for many years.

Figure 23: The first 'DX', No. 355 *Hardman*, as built.

Plate 58: 'DX' No. 613 was the 1000th engine to be built at Crewe Works and is seen here bearing number 1000 on completion in December 1866. It became a company tradition that every 1,000th engine should carry that number for publicity purposes before assuming its allocated number in the capital list. Presumably, it was not thought worthwhile to make a special splasher numberplate for No. 1000. The tender is the standard 1,500 gallon type with square front buffers.

Plate 59 (above): 'DX' class 0-6-0 No. 1651, as built in January 1868. The 'DXs' originally had only two lamp sockets, at either side of the bufferbeam, the socket at the top of the smokebox being added about 1872-3. The lamps seen here are of a little-known type; LNWR lamps traditionally had glasses front and rear but these have glasses on three and possibly all four sides. On the side of the firebox is the steam valve for the Giffard injector.

Plate 60 (right): 'DX' No. 578, in original condition as built in 1861. With numberplates on the driving splashers, the number was displayed five times on each engine, being painted on the cab sidesheets and on the front bufferbeam.

Plate 61 (left): From March 1872, after Webb had succeeded Ramsbottom, splasher numberplates were taken off and from January 1873 cast-iron numberplates (brass from January 1877) replaced painted numbers on the cab side-sheets, the engines then being painted black instead of green. This picture shows No. 453 as running after these changes in the late 1870s. It has acquired a Webb chimney, plain black livery and numberplates, and also has a lamp socket on the top of the smokebox.

Plate 62: 'DX' No. 823 in identical condition to No. 453.

Plate 63: At first Mr Webb continued to build 'DXs' but fitted them with cabs, closed splashers and his own style of chimney, the first so built being No. 2044. Earlier examples were then modified to conform. This view shows No. 568; it has lost its Giffard injectors, replaced by Webb's type on the back of the firebox, and also has his chimney and cab but retains slotted splashers. The last of the class built for the LNWR appeared at the end of 1872 but construction continued up to March 1873 for the Lancashire & Yorkshire and East Lancashire Railways.

Plate 64: No. 114, as running in the 1870s and early 1880s. It was built in August 1872 and had cab, Webb chimney and closed splashers from the outset. In June 1883 it was rebuilt as a 'Special DX'. Couplings such as this had gone out of use by 1881-2.

Plate 65: No. 411, built in November 1860, was renumbered 1834 in the duplicate list in December 1886, and was renumbered No. 3302 in April 1897. Except for the Webb safety valves, it is in the same condition as No. 114.

Plate 66: A 'DX' in final condition. It has all the Webb features, 4ft. chimney, cab, closed splashers and safety valves, but there are still no brakes on the engine. So far as photographic evidence is concerned, No. 3330 is unique among unrebuilt 'DXs' in having an 1,800 gallon tender, but many of the survivors in the late 1890s would probably have acquired early 1,800 gallon tenders also, in place of the 1,500 gallon type, which had no coal rails. The photograph was taken at Shrewsbury between November 1898, when No. 1867 (originally No. 594) was renumbered 3330, and March 1902 when the engine was withdrawn. On 1st July 1898 there were 205 original 'DXs' in service; all were scrapped by 1904.

Plate 67: In April 1881 Mr Webb rebuilt 'DX' No. 460 with a new 150 lb. p.s.i. boiler of the same kind as fitted to the '17in. Coal Engines' and 'Precursor' 2-4-0s, except that the latter were 140lb. As seen in this photograph taken on completion, it has his usual features of the time — cab, chimney and safety valves — as well as new coupling rods with solid ends. Contrary to many accounts, the first rebuilds were not fitted for working vacuum-braked trains (the simple vacuum brake was adopted by the LNWR in 1883 and was replaced by the automatic vacuum brake in 1887). Nor did they have circular smokebox doors, which were introduced only in 1884 and first appeared on the 'SDXs' in 1889. Both these features, however, soon became typical of 'Special' or 'Vacuum DXs' as they were called, and neither was ever fitted to an unrebuilt 'DX', 'Non-Vacuum DX' or 'Black DX' (as they were known, because none were ever lined). Indeed, the term 'Special' was perhaps only used after the engines were vacuum-fitted, to denote those specially fitted with vacuum brakes to work passenger trains. The same explanation may also apply to the 'Special Tanks', although in that case it may have arisen because they were built for the special job of working the Abergavenny to Merthyr line. No definite information on the origin of the term seems to be available.

Plate 68 (left): 'Special DX' No. 1538, as running in the late 1880s in lined black livery. It was converted in July 1881 and has new coupling rods; it seems only the earlier conversions had new rods as most retained their Ramsbottom rods until about 1905. After the first conversions, the boiler was pitched higher and a shorter chimney, 3ft. 9in., was fitted, as seen here. The engine is vacuum-fitted but still retains its horizontal smokebox door. There are steam brakes on the engine and wooden brake blocks on both engine and tender.

Plate 69: Official view of 'Special DX' No. 2022, taken on 18th February 1891. It has all the usual 'Special DX' features including a circular smokebox door but as a June 1885 rebuild, it retains its original rods.

Figure 24: Drawing of a 'Special DX'.

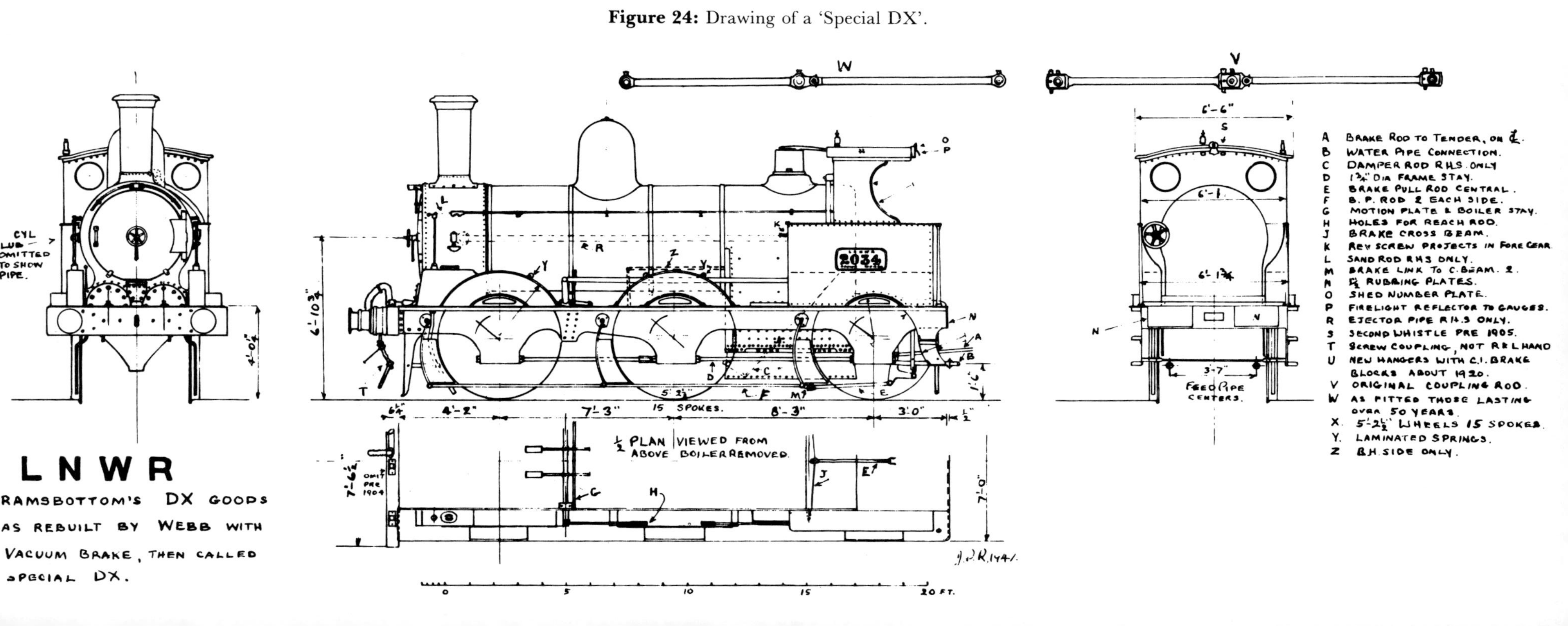

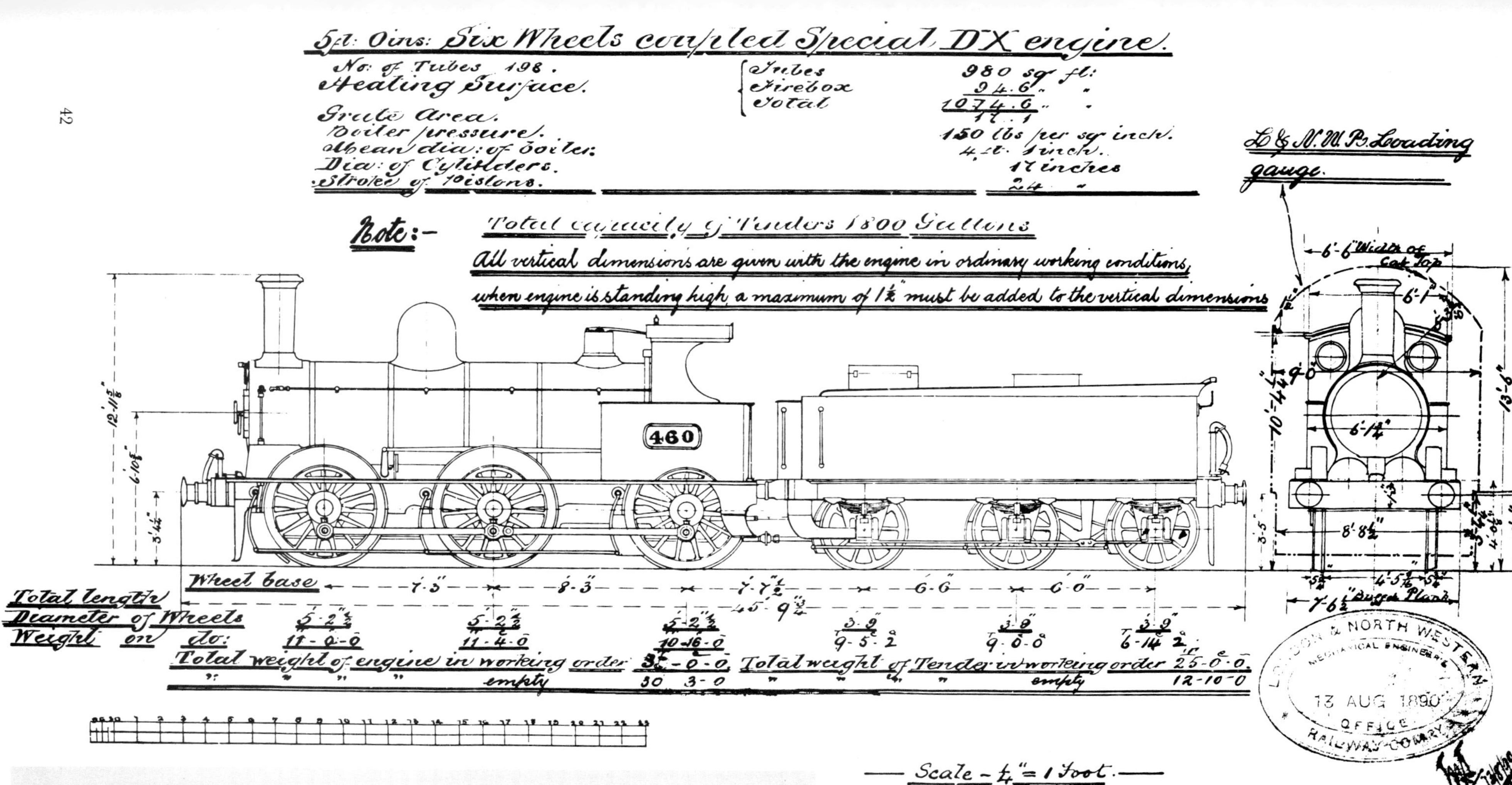

Figure 25: Official weight diagram of a 'Special DX'.

Plate 70 (left): 'Special DX' No. 2034, as running in the late 1890s. The mushroom-shaped fitting in front of the cylinders is an anti-vacuum or snifting-valve. These valves were fitted to many engines in the 1890s. In photographs they are often seen to be leaking and presumably needed frequent 'lapping in'. They were removed as unnecessary about 1903 when Mr Webb had left.

Plate 71: 'Special DX' No. 1795, as running about 1900 with coal rails on the tender and still with Ramsbottom coupling rods. All 'SDXs' had 1,800 gallon tenders and acquired coal rails in due course.

Plate 72: 'SDX' No. 3121 at Rugby about 1910.

Plate 73: 'SDX' No. 3461 at Chester about 1920. It still has wooden brake blocks but has acquired long-tapered buffers. Having been reboilered in December 1880, only months before the final conversion, this engine was the last to be converted to 'Special' in June 1898, when no doubt it obtained Webb coupling rods.

Plate 74: 'SDX' No. 3331 at Carnforth about 1915. It was originally the third 'DX' to be built, No. 358 *Falstaff*, in October 1858.

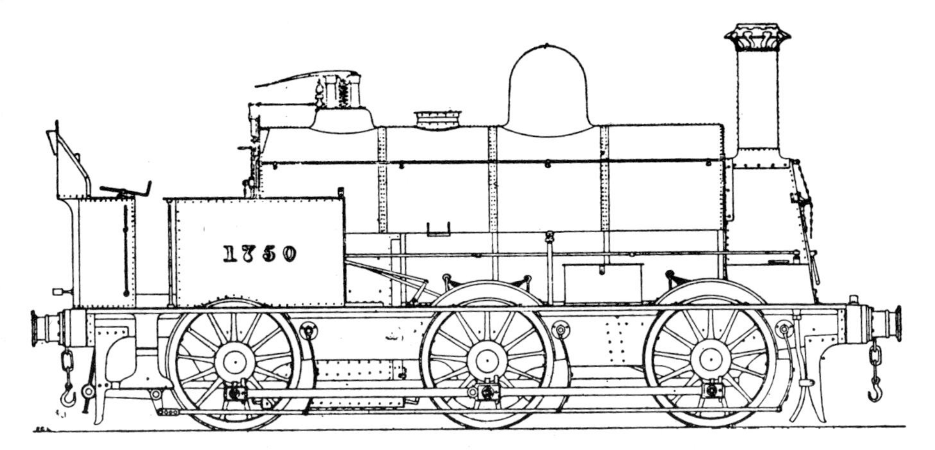

'Special Tank'

Figure 26: Ramsbottom's last design was the 'Special Tank', which was in effect a saddle tank version of the 'DX' for shunting, with the same cylinders and wheelbase but slightly smaller wheels and boiler. Only the first twenty were built before Mr Webb took over, all of them in 1870; they had all the usual Ramsbottom features but unfortunately no photograph exists of one in original condition. This drawing is believed to show the first of the class, No. 1750, as originally built.

Plate 75: 'Special Tank' No. 2047, built in November 1871, at Camden in the 1870s. This was one of the first of the class to be built under Mr Webb's superintendence. On the first twenty, the frames were made of iron and so were deeper to give the required strength, with the lower edge straight between the leading wheels. Webb introduced steel frames, shaped as in this picture; they seem weaker but were in fact both lighter and stronger. Other Webb features are the numberplates, safety valves, chimney and black livery. No. 2045, the first of the batch, was almost certainly the first new engine to be painted black, but what type of chimney was originally fitted is not known. The batch possibly had Ramsbottom chimneys, as Webb had only just been appointed; but the short chimney seen here (to allow them to work over the Great Eastern via Victoria Park and Stratford into Thames Wharf, where there were some low bridges) was carried by Nos. 2045-54 in the 1870s, though standard ones were fitted later. Ramsbottom features on No. 2047 are the splashers, coupling rods and conventional wheels; after the first fifty, plain splashers were fitted, and after the first seventy, H-section cast-iron wheels.

Plate 76: A Ramsbottom 'Special Tank' as running between 1913, when it was fitted with a cab, and 1919, when it became No. 3638 in the duplicate list. The majority received cabs in the period 1912-16 but some had them in the 1890s and others never received them at all. Ramsbottom features are the wheels, coupling rods, splashers and horizontal smokebox door; otherwise No. 501 is in typical Webb condition. By the 1920s it was commonplace to find Ramsbottom engines with Webb wheels, and Webb engines with Ramsbottom wheels.

Plate 77: Official photograph of No. 2141, taken in June 1890 when 'Special Tanks' began to be painted in the lined black livery for shunting passenger stock in station areas. This engine is a typical example of the Webb version of the 'Special Tanks'. On the 0-4-0 saddle tanks, the '4ft. Shunters', the whistle was in the same position, beside the safety valves. So far as is known from photographs, the class was unusual in having no lining on the back of the bunker.

Plate 78 (left): Another of the first fifty Ramsbottom engines, No. 3148 at Stockport about 1920 (originally No. 185, built in January 1872). It has acquired cast-iron wheels and Webb coupling rods, but retains its original splashers.

Plate 79 (right): No. 672, a Webb 'Special Tank' built in April 1878, as running before 1895 when it was renumbered in the duplicate list. It is in typical Webb condition of the time. When shunting in goods yards, which was what the class was designed for, the crew of a 'Special Tank' was constantly busy, the driver working the screw reverser back and forth and the fireman winding the handbrake on and off. The screw reverser at least overcame the inherent dangers of the lever reverse, which could kick viciously at times, but with wooden brake-blocks in wet weather, the handbrake was of dubious effectiveness and must have been a cause of anxiety to the men at times. With no cab, working on these engines in winter must have been a trial to the fittest of men.

Plate 80 (left): No. 3217 at Crewe about 1915. A typical Webb 'Special Tank', it has been fitted with a cab (by 1913) and with vacuum brake. The driver's drinking bottle is standing on the handrail in front of the cab, while the driver himself appears to be working the screw reverser.

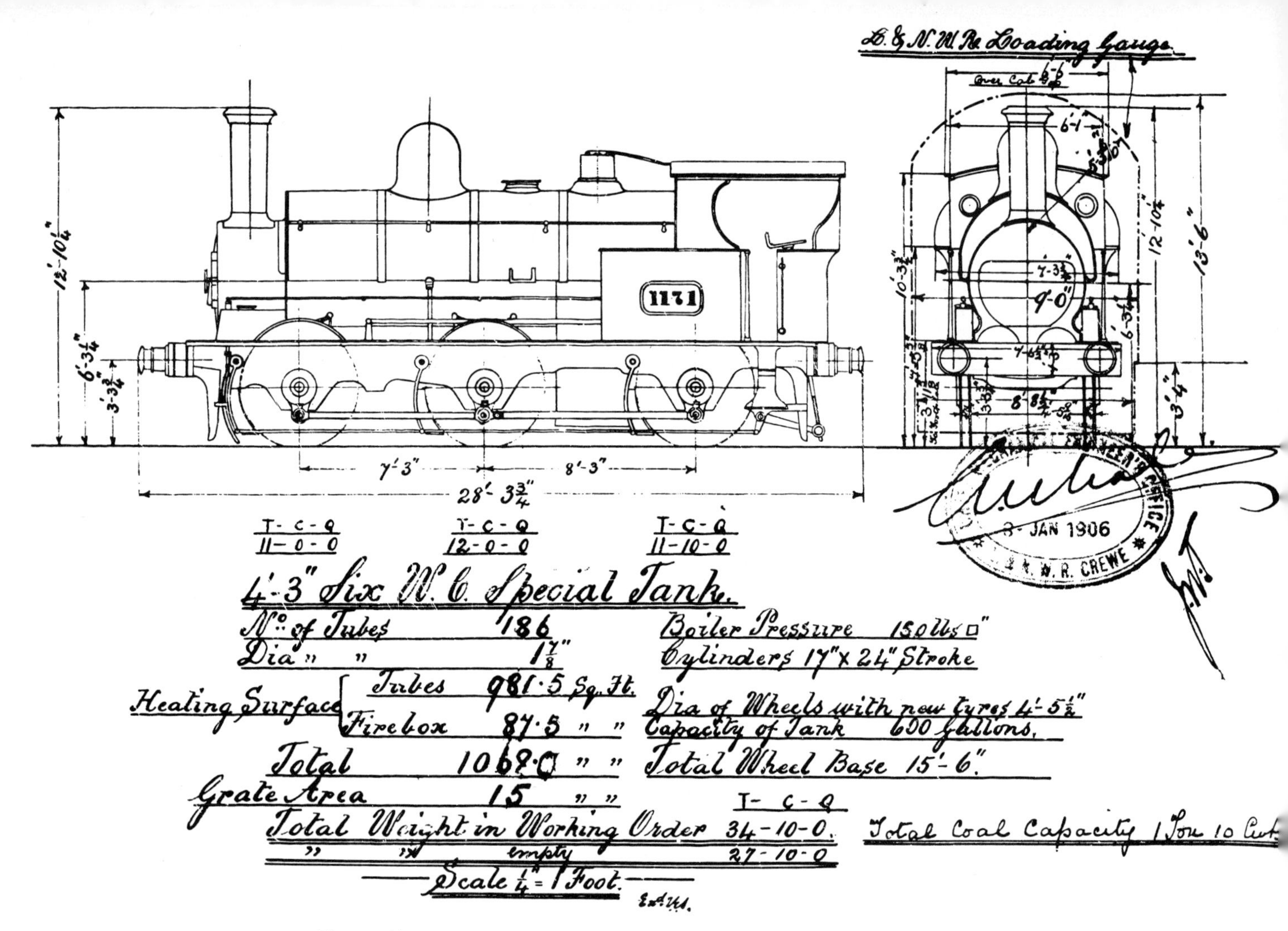

Figure 27: Official weight diagram of a 'Special Tank', dated 1906.

Figure 28: Drawing of a 'Special Tank' fitted with vacuum brake and cab.

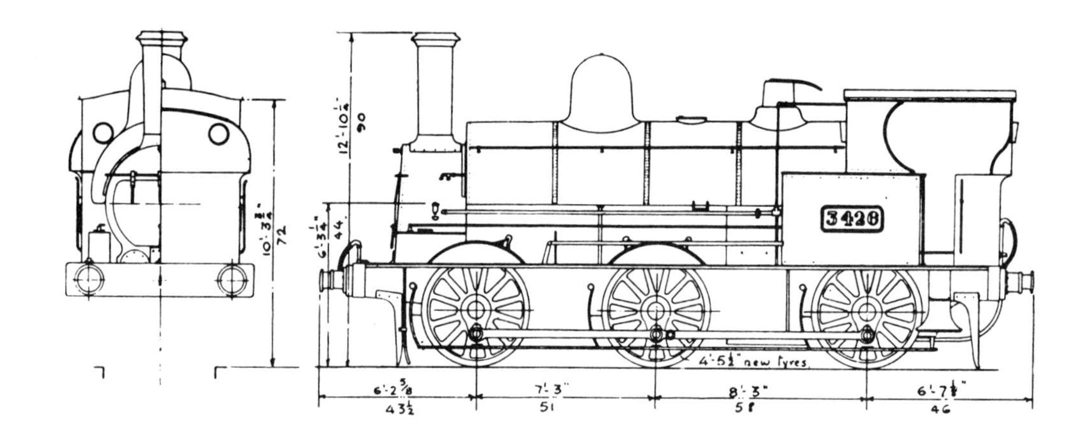

Plate 81: 'Special Tank' No. 3408, as running in the early 1920s with a circular smokebox door. It is possibly the only photograph showing a 'Special Tank' so fitted in LNWR condition, though in LMS days of course it became a common feature.

Plate 82: Two 'Special Tanks', Nos. 528 and 50, were turned out in January 1876 with square saddle tanks and condensing apparatus for working Wapping Tunnel traffic in Liverpool . They had rudimentary cabs, nothing more than roofs supported by four pillars, with no spectacle plates front or rear. No. 50 became No. 3021 on the duplicate list in May 1893 and is seen here soon afterwards in Crewe Works.

Plate 83: In 1895 they were assigned to work into Liverpool Riverside, particularly on boat specials, were fitted with better cabs and vacuum brakes, named *Euston* and *Liverpool*, and painted in the full lined black livery, complete with the coat of arms, which was applied only to passenger engines. *Euston* is seen here in an official photograph taken on 17 December 1897.

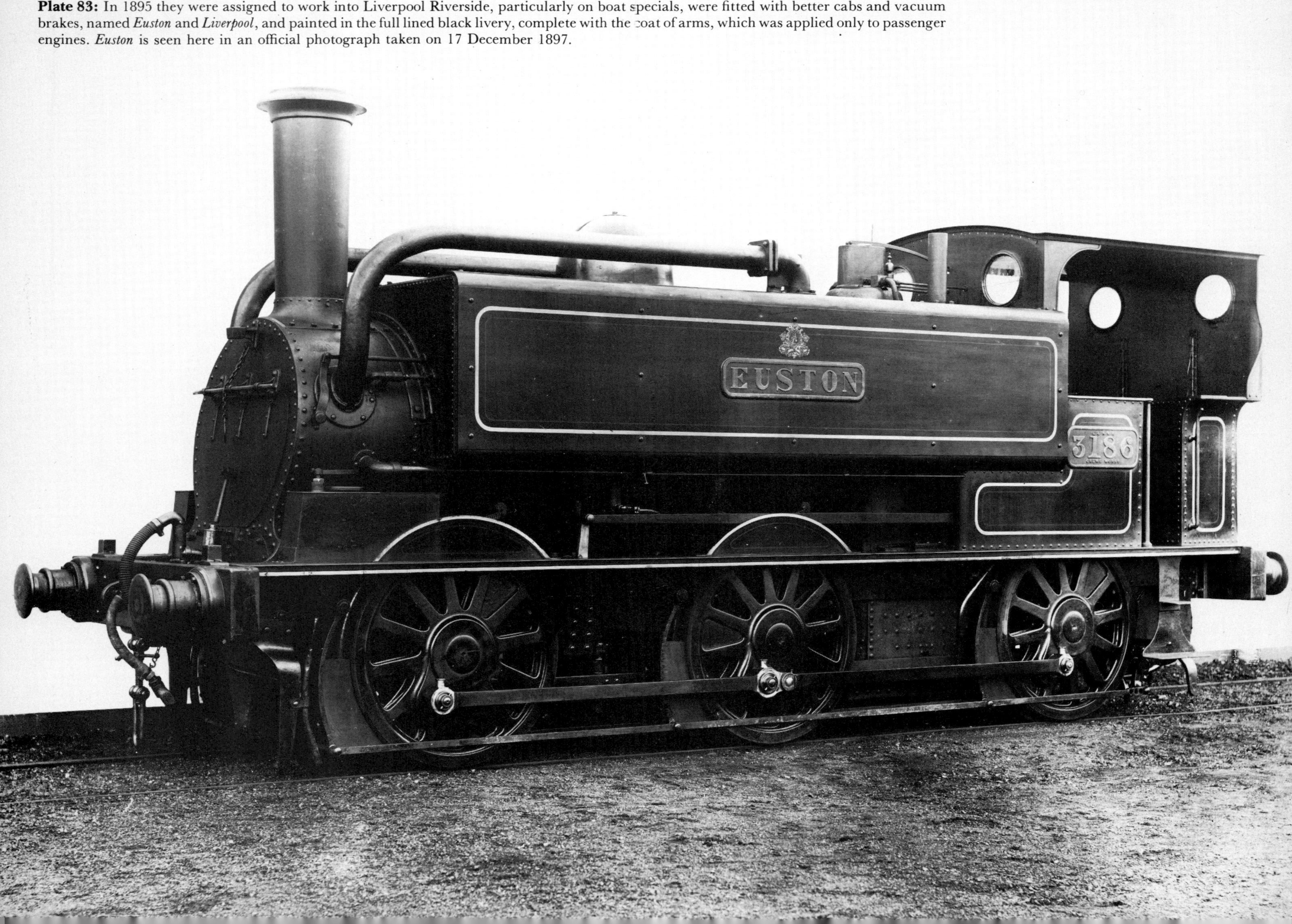

Plate 84: The lining on the cab sides of *Euston* and *Liverpool* differed, as this photograph well shows.

Plate 85: *Euston* and *Liverpool* lost their condensing apparatus during World War I and were transferred away from Liverpool. *Euston* is seen here at Camden in early LMS days. It has long-tapered buffers, vacuum brake, carriage-heating apparatus (the second pipe on the bufferbeam), plain black livery and a circular smokebox door.

‘17in. Coal Engine’

Plate 86: In February 1873 Mr Webb introduced the famous ‘17in. Coal Engines’, the first new engines for which he was entirely responsible. The design was based on that of the ‘Special Tanks’ and at first used the same boiler uprated to 140 lb. p.s.i.; later the whole class had boilers with larger fireboxes. This beautiful picture is the earliest known photograph of the class and shows No. 433 at Heaton Chapel with a local passenger train to Manchester (London Road) about 1880. This engine was one of the first batch, being built in April 1873. It has Ramsbottom safety valves but Webb chimney, cab, coupling rods and cast-iron wheels. The horizontal smokebox door, wooden bufferbeam and brake blocks, absence of brakes on the engine and the style of the 1,500 gallon tender with grease axleboxes all date from the earliest Crewe designs, well before Ramsbottom.

Plate 87: An official view of an unidentified ‘17in. Coal Engine’ as built, with hook-type coupling at the front end and Webb safety valves.

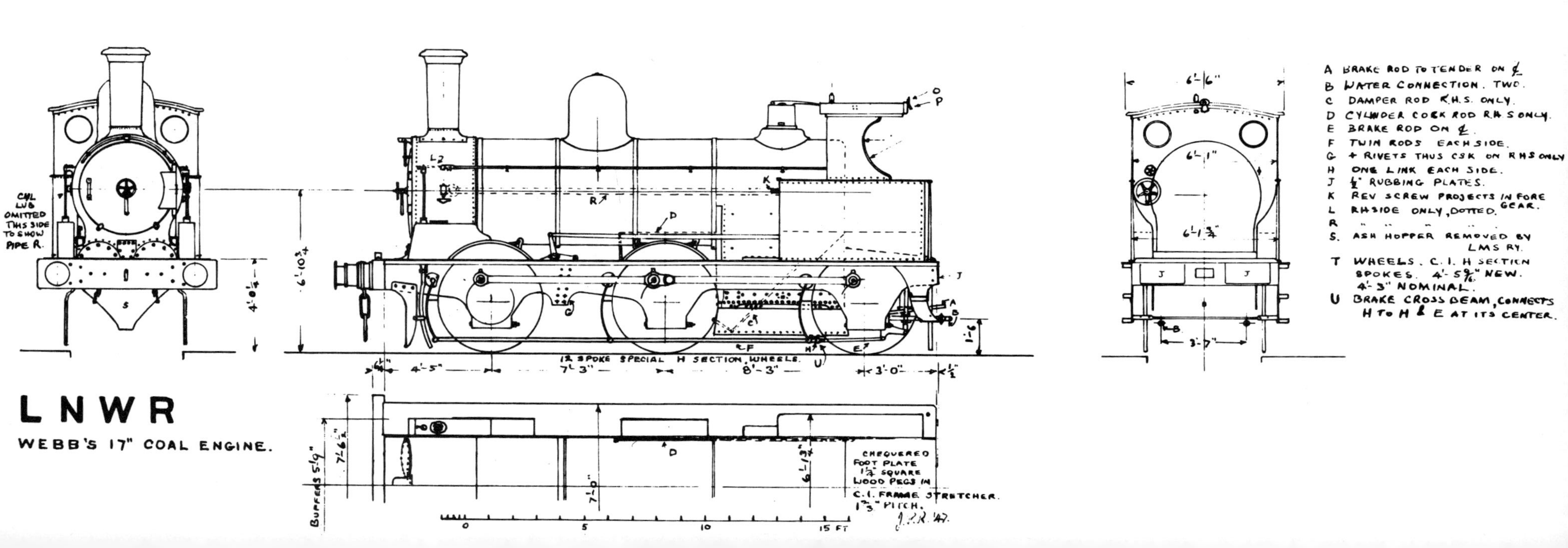

Plate 88: Official view of No. 360, built in November 1880, taken in June 1890, probably to show the engine finished in lined livery. It is usually said that the first goods engines to be lined out were the 0-8-0s of 1892-3, after which lining was applied to goods engines generally; but it seems quite likely, from this picture and *Plates 77* and *98*, that lining of goods engines began in mid-1890. Before then, the '17in Coal Engines' were invariably plain black. They were never fitted for working vacuum-braked trains and so probably did little work on passenger trains after the adoption of the simple vacuum brake, though the chain brake did not finally disappear until 1892. The tender is a pre-1882 1,800 gallon type, with grease axleboxes and open handrails at the front. The hooks at the rear, designed to hold fire-irons, can be clearly seen.

Figure 29: Drawing of a '17in. Coal Engine'.

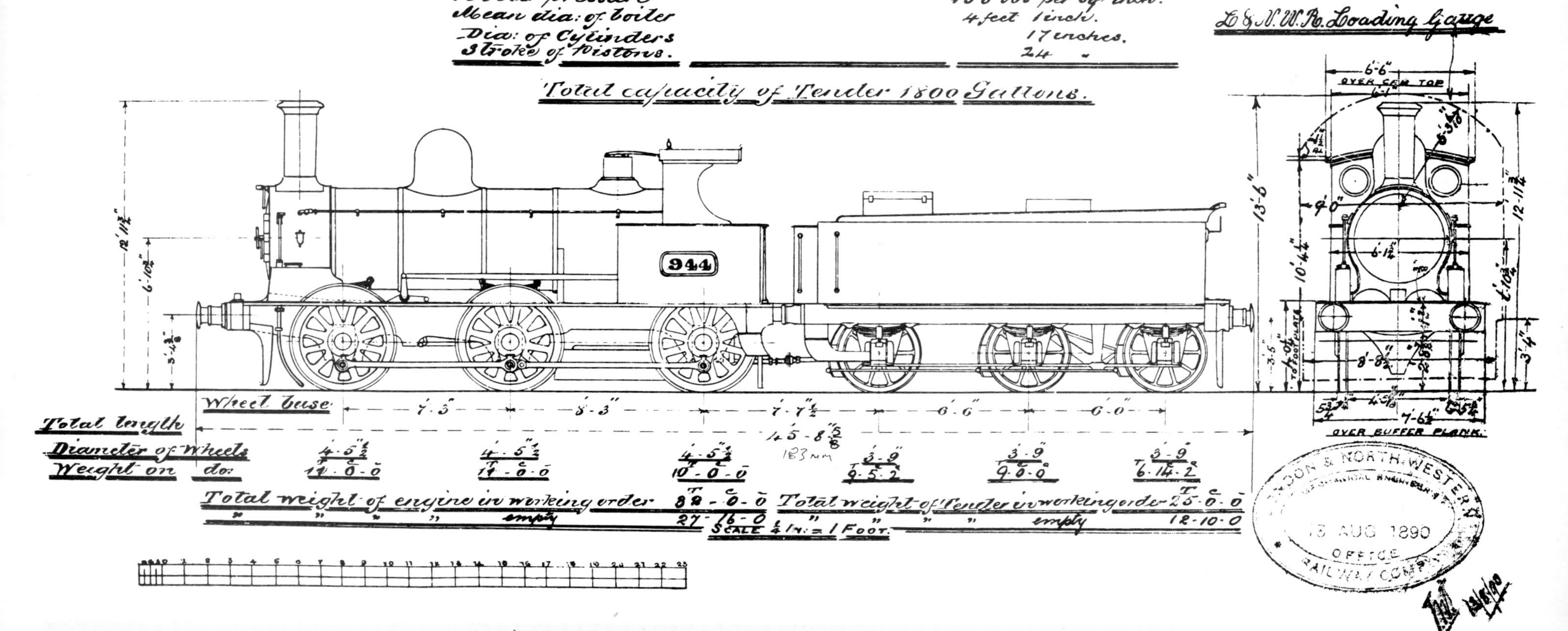

Figure 30: Official weight diagram of a '17in. Coal Engine', dated 1890.

Plate 89: The final batches of '17in. Coal Engines' were built in the early 1890s. They had steam brakes with wooden blocks on the engine and circular smokebox doors from new, and probably the 1892 batch at least came out in lined livery also. An example, No. 85, is seen here in the late 1890s; its tender is an early 1,800 gallon type with open handrails but oil axleboxes and coal rails. Fire-iron hooks are still fitted to the rear. No. 85 was converted to a saddle tank in 1905.

Plate 90: Another view of No. 85, showing cab fittings and stanchion handrails well polished. The footsteps are the type built up from plate; cast steps with replaceable treads were introduced later and are noticeably wider. The way the lining on the footplate edging curved round and down at the outer end of the drag box can be clearly seen; it was the same later when cast drag boxes were used as on the 'Precursors'. The floor seems to be made simply of wooden boards, the oak peg type presumably being a later innovation. By the driver's feet is his drinking bottle. Shed 7 was Netherfield & Colwick.

Plate 91: No. 3099 at Willesden on 21st August 1920, still in lined livery. It has H-section cast-iron wheels on the tender, as did quite a number of both this class and the various Webb eight-coupled coal engines. Webb buffers on the engine have been replaced by the Bowen Cooke type.

Plate 92 (right): No. 713 at Blisworth in 1921, though it would have appeared much the same ever since the fitting of a circular smokebox door and engine brakes, and the application of lined livery in the 1890s.

Plate 93 (above): During World War I, some 'Coal Engines' were sent overseas with the Railway Operating Division, for which they were fitted with larger tenders mostly of the 2,500 gallon type. No. 137, originally No. 2224 built in January 1876, is seen here at Willesden on 21st June 1922, still with its big tender, which is in fact a 2,000 gallon model. The engine has Cooke buffers but the tender still has the Webb type.

Plate 94: No. 3456 at Camden on 2nd May 1925, still in LNWR lined livery and with H-section cast-iron wheels on the tender. Apart from the metal brake-blocks, duplicate list number and centre lamp socket on the bufferbeam fitted in 1903, it is in much the same condition as Mr Webb would have known thirty years before. Fluted coupling rods were never fitted to this class.

'Coal Tank'

Plate 95: In September 1881, some eight years after the first '17in. Coal Engine' appeared, a tank-engine version was introduced. This view of No. 1076 shows the class as originally built and as running in the 1880s. It has a horizontal smokebox door, wooden bufferbeams and brake blocks and all the usual Webb fittings of the day. The livery is plain black, as the 'Coal Tanks' were originally intended only for goods trains and shunting.

Plate 96: 'Coal Tank' No. 205, one of the first batch built in 1881, is pictured at Heaton Chapel with a local passenger train to Manchester (London Road) in the early 1880s. The plain black paintwork is well polished and the handrails are finished bright, but the overall appearance is very austere; only the touch of red on the bufferbeams and numberplates offers any relief from plain black. The only form of braking on the engine is the handbrake but the train is fitted with the chain brake, the cable for which can be seen passing between the engine and the first carriage on the far side. From their introduction, the 'Coal Tanks' were found to be very suitable for local passenger work; in modern times they would have been described as 'mixed traffic' engines.

Plate 97 (left): No. 252 outside the engine shed at Whaley Bridge about 1892. This shed originally belonged to the Stockport, Disley & Whaley Bridge Railway.

Plate 98 (below): Official view of No. 848, taken in June 1890 probably to show the lined passenger livery on the class. Apart from that, and the exceptionally tall water-filler manhole, the engine is virtually in original condition.

Plate 99 (right): No. 771 at Lancaster, on 12th August 1902, in full lined livery and fitted with vacuum brake. Because their brake power was restricted by poor leverage for some reason, the 'Coal Tanks' were often used on passenger work rather than unfitted goods trains, and when shunting often ran coupled to a large fitted van for extra brake power. The '4ft 6in. 2-4-2 Tanks' were preferred for goods work as they had powerful steam brakes. Bowen Cooke improved the vacuum brake on the 'Coal Tanks' but many never received the modifications and, thanks to running lower mileages, survived longer, the preserved No. 1054 among them.

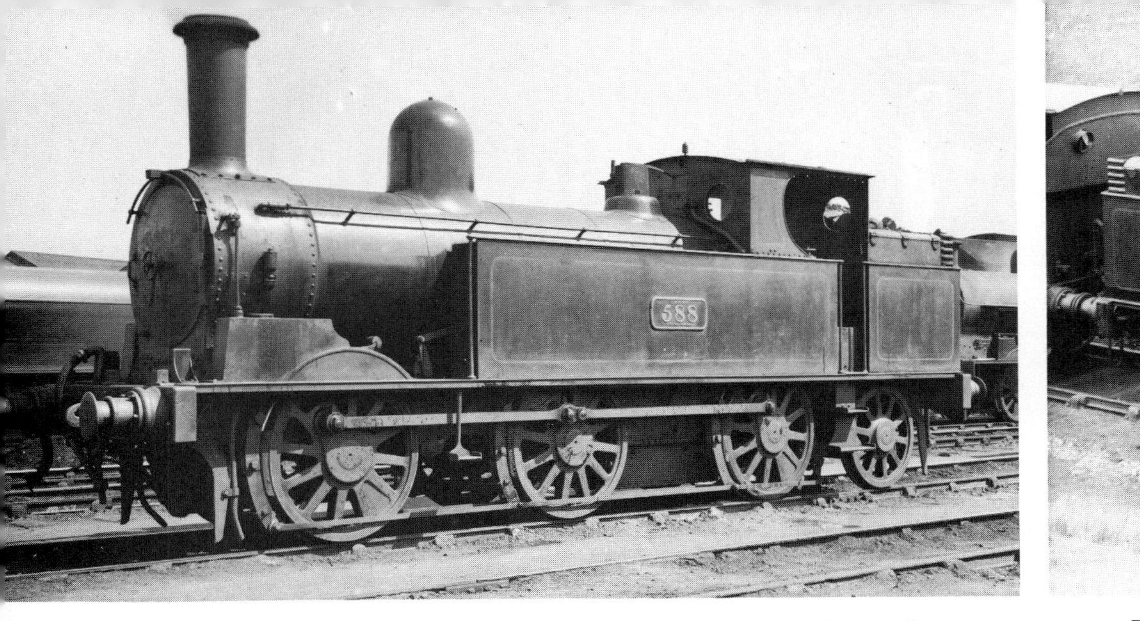

Plate 100: No. 588 at Willesden about 1920. It has destination-board brackets on the front bufferbeam for working London area suburban traffic and metal brake blocks. When coal rails were fitted to the bunkers in the early 1900s, the toolboxes were moved up to the rear spectacle plates, and doors giving access to them were provided from inside the cab in the same way as on the 2-4-2 tanks and '18in. Tanks'.

Plate 101: No. 549 as running about 1920, with metal brake blocks. The access door to the right-hand toolbox can be clearly seen, as can the gap between the frames at the front, not covered by footplating. On the far side of the bufferbeam, beyond the vacuum-brake pipe, is a bracket associated with motor-train working while on the near side, lower down, is the train-heating pipe.

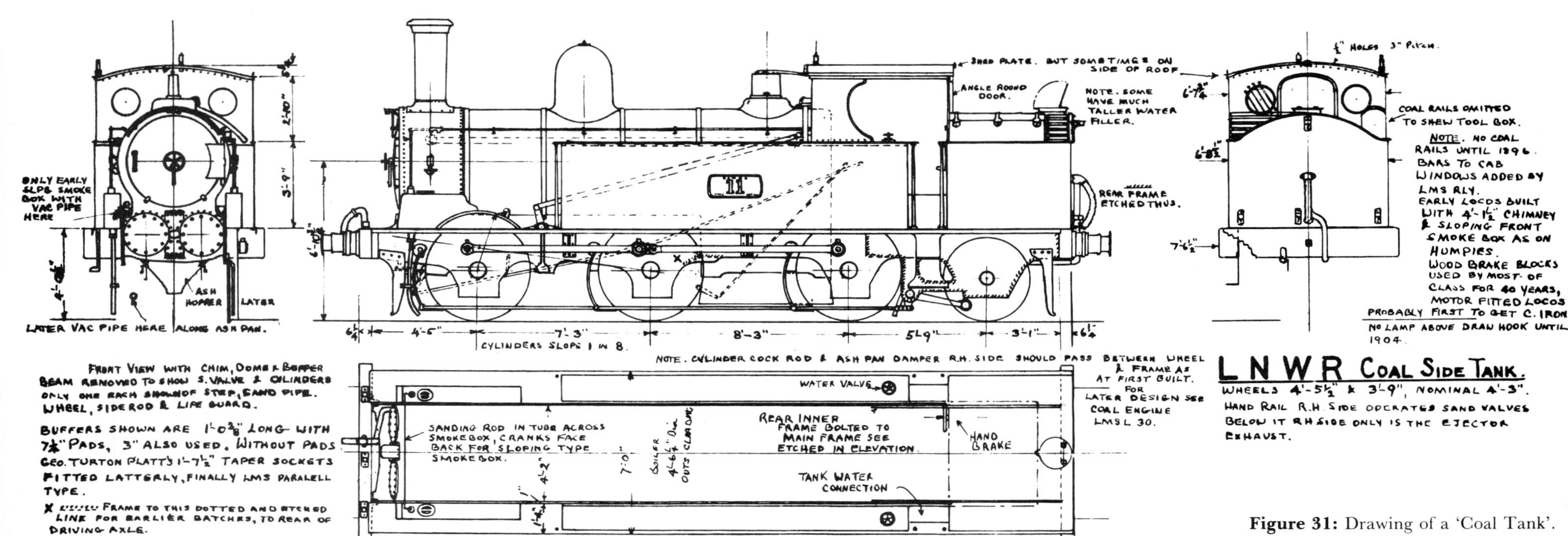

Figure 31: Drawing of a 'Coal Tank'.

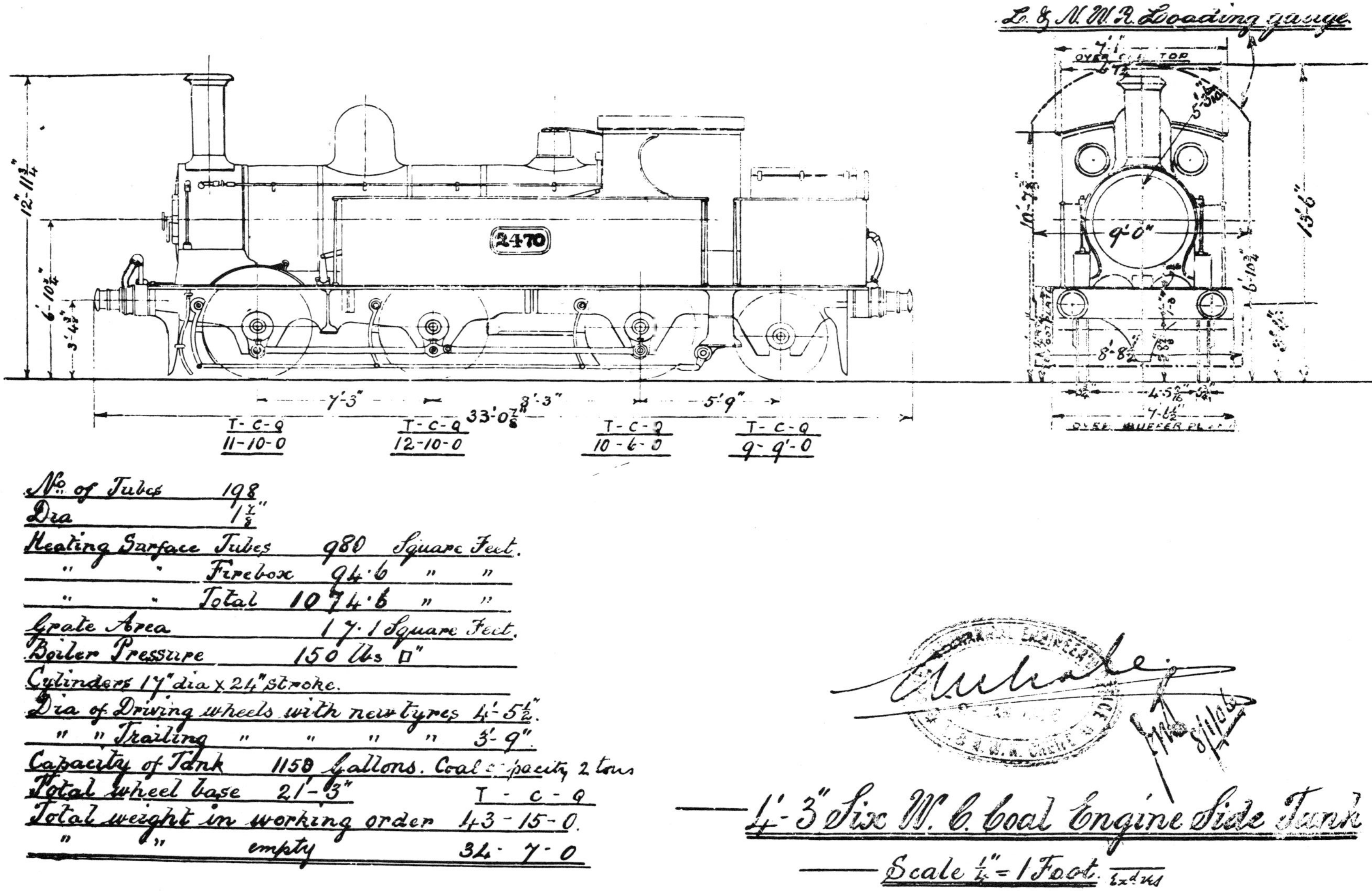
L. & N.W.R. Loading gauge
13'-6"
10'-7 3/8"
9'-0"
6'-10 3/4"
8'-8 1/2"
4'-5 3/16"
7'-1 1/2"
12'-11 3/4"
6'-10 3/4"
3'-4 3/4"
7'-3"
8'-3"
5'-9"
33'-0 7/8"
2470
T-C-Q
11-10-0
T-C-Q
12-10-0
T-C-Q
10-6-0
T-C-Q
9-9-0
No. of Tubes 198
Dia 1 7/8"
Heating Surface Tubes 980 Square Feet.
" " Firebox 94·6 " "
" " Total 1074·6 " "
Grate Area 17·1 Square Feet.
Boiler Pressure 150 lbs □"
Cylinders 17" dia x 24" stroke.
Dia of Driving wheels with new tyres 4'-5 1/2".
" " Trailing " " " " 3'-9".
Capacity of Tank 1150 Gallons. Coal capacity 2 tons
Total wheel base 21'-3" T - C - Q
Total weight in working order 43-15-0.
" " empty 34-7-0
4'-3" Six W. C. Coal Engine Side Tank
Scale 1/4" = 1 Foot.

Figure 32: Official weight diagram of a 'Coal Tank'.

Plate 102 (right): No. 2461 in immaculate condition about 1920. It has metal brake-blocks, destination-board brackets and Cooke buffers.

Plate 103 (right): A rear view of No. 605 in early LMS days at Liverpool (Lime Street), showing destination-board brackets on the bunker, Cooke buffers and the vacuum reservoir under the bunker, but still with LNWR lamp sockets and shed-plate holder on the rear of the cab roof.

Plate 104 (left): No. 3736 at Willesden on 22nd August 1925. It has metal brake blocks and long-tapered buffers. The train-heating pipe is out of use — they were usually taken off in the summer. LMS lamp irons have not yet replaced the LNWR socket type.

'Coal Saddle Tank'

Plate 105 : In 1904-5, forty-five '17in. Coal Engines' were converted into tank engines for shunting. Because of the box-like tanks with which they were fitted, they were known as the 'square saddle tanks'. Although they looked very different, they were really only a larger variation of the 'Special Tanks' of 1870, from which the '17in. Coal Engines' were developed. No. 808 is seen in this official view taken on 23rd June 1905. Apart from the steel bufferbeams and short-tapered Whale buffers, the engine has been little modified in the conversion. It has the usual steam brakes with wooden brake blocks.

Figure 33: Official drawing of a 'Saddle Tank Coal Engine'.

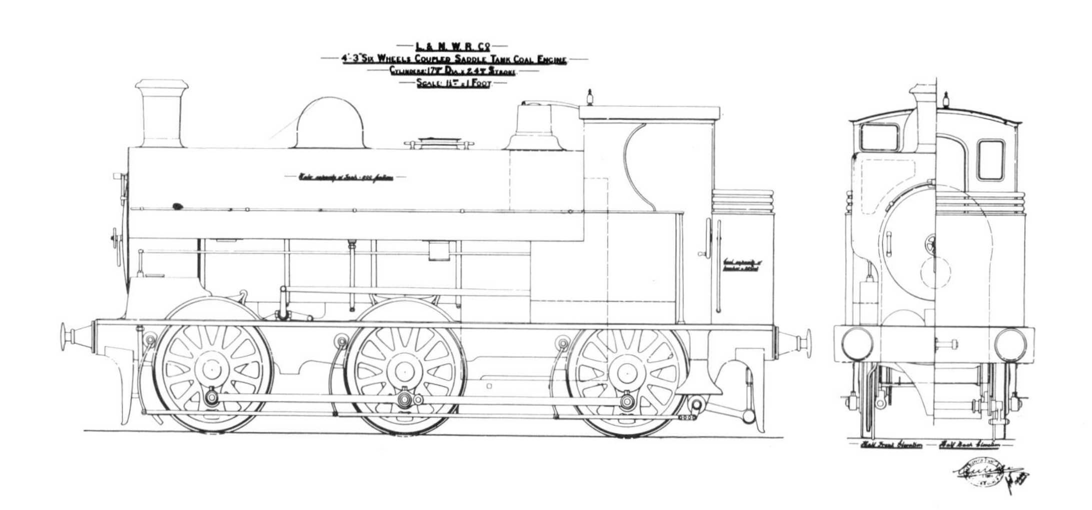

Plate 106 (right): No. 1096, fitted with vacuum brake and screw couplings. Running beneath the tank are the controls for the blower and the right-hand sandbox, and the ejector exhaust-pipe.

Plate 107 (left): A broadside view of No. 2079, which is in much the same condition as No. 1096 apart from having an ordinary three-link coupling.

Plate 108 (right): A rather murky view of No. 3694 at Willesden, on 2nd June 1923. It has metal brake blocks and Cooke buffers, though it is still in lined livery. The lip appears to have come off the chimney and is lying round the base!

'Cauliflower' or '18in. Express Goods'

Plate 109: The famous '18in. Goods' or 'Cauliflowers' were introduced in June 1880. They were intended for express goods work and had 18in. cylinders, the same boilers as the 'Precedents' and 5ft. (actually 5ft. 2½in.) driving wheels; they were the first LNWR engines to have Joy valve gear. This official view shows the first of the class, No. 2365, on completion. Unusual features are the chimney, which is probably unique for an LNWR engine in not having the usual pressed steel base, the flush finish of the smokebox with no rivets visible, the grate, which has a 'water bottom' as did some of the three-cylinder compounds later, and by comparison with later members of the class, the low pitch of the boiler. There is a hook-type front coupling, wooden bufferbeam, horizontal smokebox door, no brakes on the engine and cast-iron H-section driving wheels. After trials with No. 2365, nine more of the class were built in 1882; owing to the absence of photographs, full information on the detail fittings is not known but they certainly had cast-iron driving wheels and probably horizontal smokebox doors also. A further batch of ten was built in early 1887, with conventional driving wheels of cast steel and circular smokebox doors, which became standard on subsequent batches. No. 2365 was exhibited at an Institute of Mechanical Engineers meeting at Barrow, which may account for the finish of the smokebox with curved leading edge. Probably the smokebox is lagged in the same way as the boiler, and the base of the chimney is attached to the smokebox proper and is covered by a skirt fitting on to the cleading, for appearance sake only.

Plate 111 (right): Another of the same batch, this time No. 34, but slightly later about 1890 when fitted with vacuum brake and screw couplings. It seems to have new cast-steel wheels. The 'Cauliflowers', also occasionally known as the 'Crested Goods', were so called because of the LNWR coat of arms on the centre splasher, and were the only 0-6-0 class to be so adorned.

Plate 110 (above): One of the second batch, No. 1026, is seen here as built with wooden brake blocks and black rectangular-section coupling rods. It also seems to have wrought-iron wheel centres from a withdrawn 'DX'. The engine is well polished and the chimney cap, handrails and sandbox control rod are finished bright. On the second batch, and possibly the rest of the first batch after No. 2365, the boiler centre line was raised from 6ft. 10⅛in. to 7ft. 4¼in. to allow access to the valve gear, and there was no water bottom.

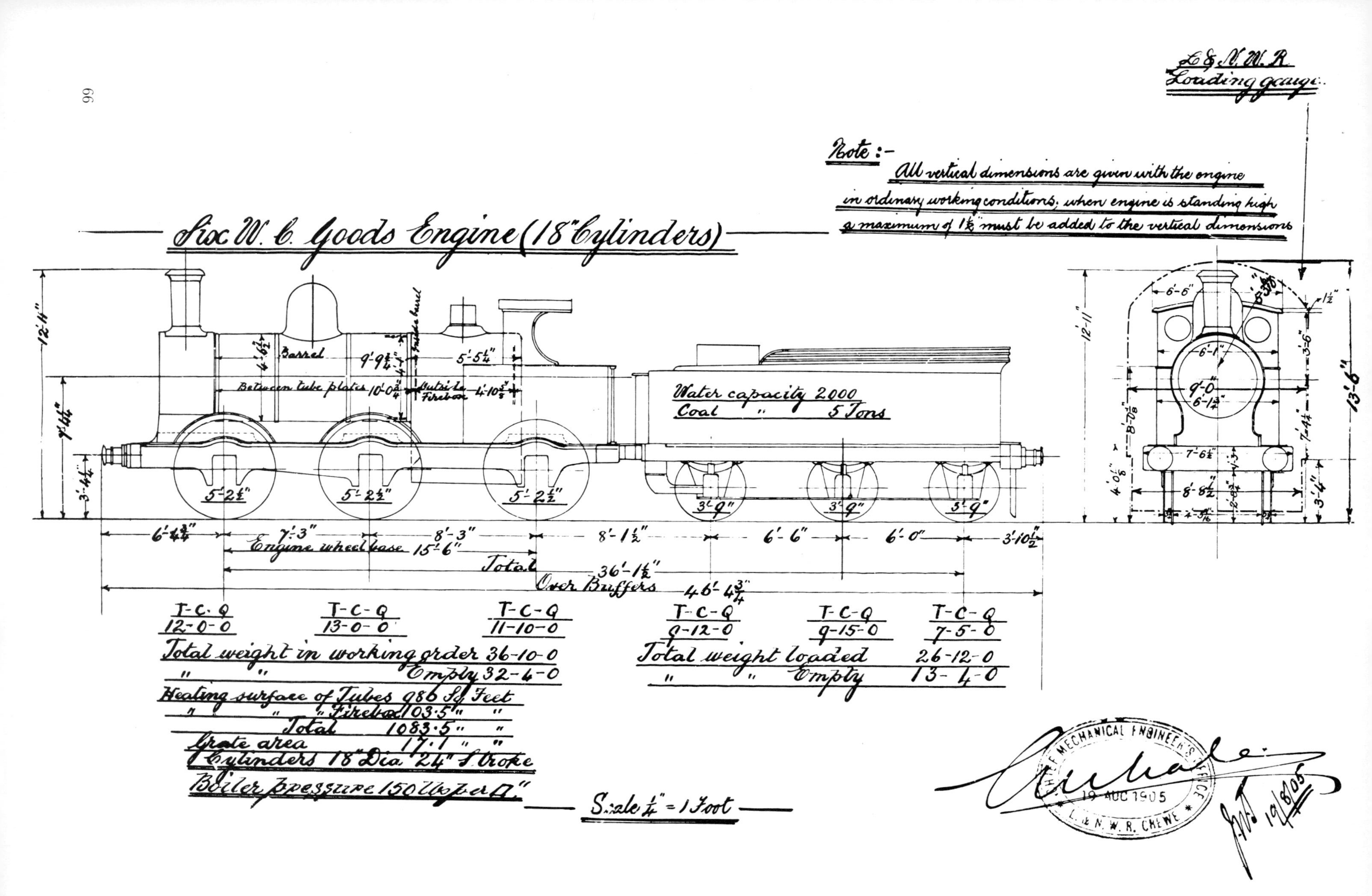

Figure 34: Weight diagram of a 'Cauliflower', dated 1905.

Plate 112: Official view of No. 1269, taken on 9th October 1892, in identical condition to No. 34. This engine was the last of the fourth batch of ten, which were built new with 17in. cylinders. It is thought to have been the last to have frames with the lower edge straight between the leading axles. On all subsequent engines, the frames were deepened and shaped accordingly, at the point where the cross members supporting the slide bars were riveted to them.

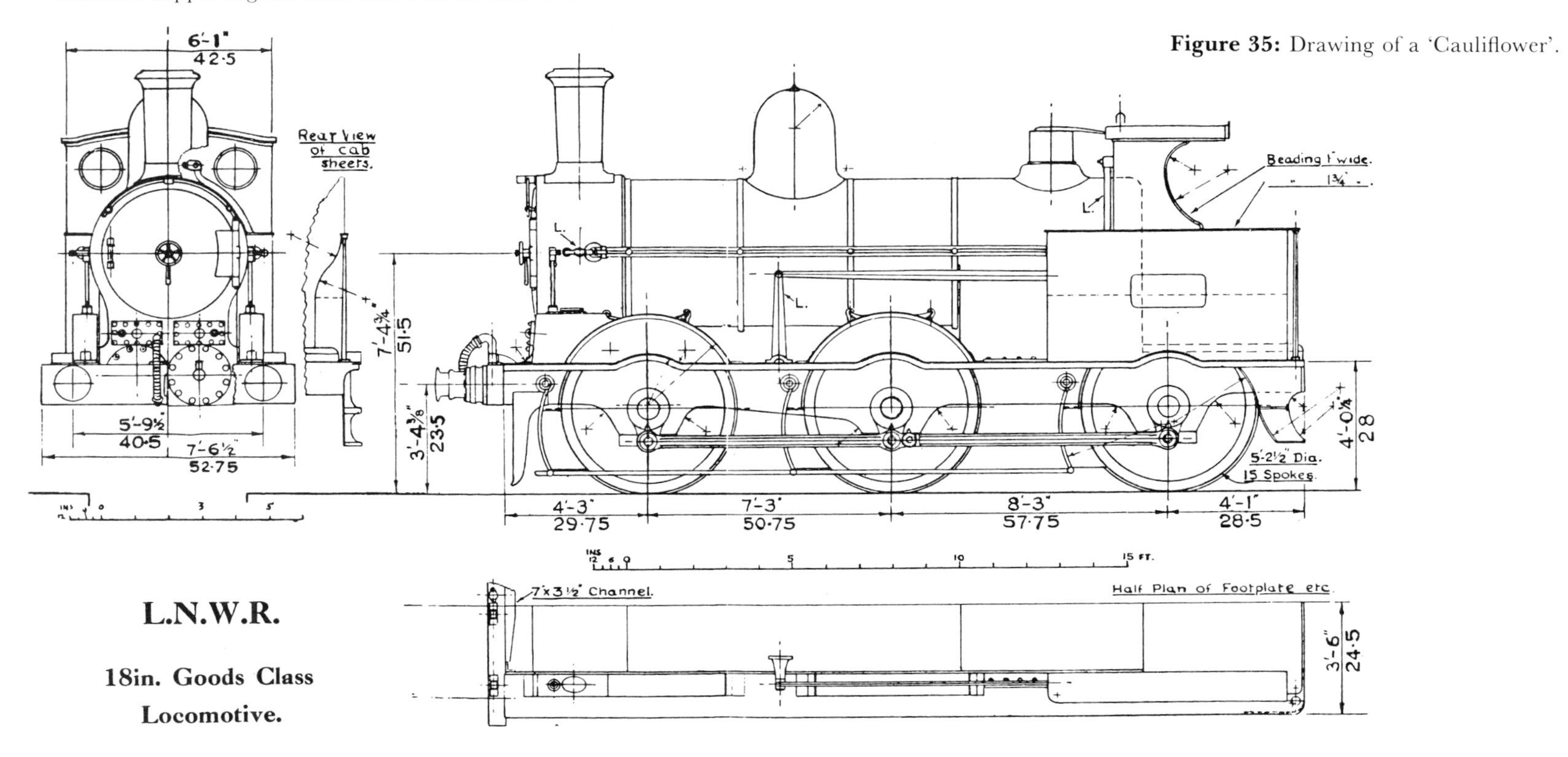

Figure 35: Drawing of a 'Cauliflower'.

Plate 113 (above): An official view of No. 9 in Crewe Works on 29th September 1899. Fluted coupling rods were first fitted to the class on the late 1898 batch. The engine has clearly been working passenger trains, being equipped with supports for the communication cord, and the tender also has coal rails.

Plate 114 (right): No. 9 a few years later, in much the same condition except for the removal of the communication-cord supports and the associated second whistle.

Plate 115 (left): No. 2466, one of the first batch, still with its H-section wheels, at Manchester (London Road) about 1910. The engines with these wheels were known as 'duckfoots' or 'duckfooted Cauliflowers'.

Plate 116 (left): The last thirty 'Cauliflowers' were originally intended to be built as '18in. Tanks'. They had piston valves, which were later replaced by flat valves, and the frames had the deepened portion by the firebox to take the support brackets for the side tanks. Both these features can be seen in this photograph of No. 801 at East Croydon on a train from Willesden.

Plate 117 (below): No. 1244 at Willesden in the early 1920s, by which time it had acquired long-tapered buffers but was otherwise unchanged from the late 1890s.

Plate 118 (right): An early LMS view of No. 560, built in April 1901 and photographed about 1926 in a somewhat 'mixed up' condition! The Belpaire firebox with Ross pop safety valves was an LMS innovation, though designed by H. P. M. Beames, and was fitted in 1925. But the LNWR lamp sockets have not been replaced by LMS irons. At the other extreme, the driving wheels are the cast-iron type and must have been originally fitted to one of the first ten of the class, while metal brake blocks and Cooke buffers have been fitted. To complete the ensemble, the tender is the 2,500 gallon type as fitted to '17in. Coal Engines' for service with the ROD.

'Watford' or '18in. Tank'

Plate 119: Eighteen years after the 'Cauliflowers' had appeared, a tank-engine version was produced for suburban and local passenger work. Officially, they were the '18in. Six-coupled Side Tanks', which was commonly shortened to '18in Tanks', but they are also sometimes referred to as 'Watford Tanks', though they were to be found all over the LNWR system. This official view shows the first of the class, No. 1597, after completion on 12th September 1898. It has the refinements of the day: fluted coupling rods, steel bufferbeams, metal brake blocks and carriage warming apparatus. But coal rails, introduced for passenger tender engines in late 1895, were not fitted until the 1900s, so the water-filling manhole is clearly visible in the usual position at the rear of the bunker. When first built, seventy of the eighty in the class had piston valves, although many later had them replaced by flat valves. The projection from the front of the valve chest is a snifting or anti-vacuum valve, to admit air to the steam chests when running with the regulator closed. The '18in. Tanks' were immediately successful and showed that Webb could produce exactly what was required very quickly, in just the same way that Whale did later. They pulled well and ran fast, and though many completed high mileages, thirty lasted for more than forty years.

Plate 120 (left): No. 309 at Willesden Junction in the early 1900s. There are three destination boards in the bracket on the front of the engine.

Plate 121 (right): No. 16 at Birmingham (New Street) about 1910, after the fitting of coal rails. The bunker is piled so high with coal that it would be impossible to take water without moving some of it.

Plate 122 (below): No. 972 at Birmingham (New Street). The circular covers for the piston-valves can be clearly seen.

Plate 123 (left): A head-on view of No. 2037, showing the shape of the piston valve covers. The snifting valves have been removed and blanked off.

Plate 124 (right): Yet another view at Birmingham (New Street), this time of No. 55 about 1910, still fitted with piston valves. One of the headlamps has been turned to one side, and a shovel and pricker are lying on top of the tank.

Plate 125 (below): No. 2019 about 1915.

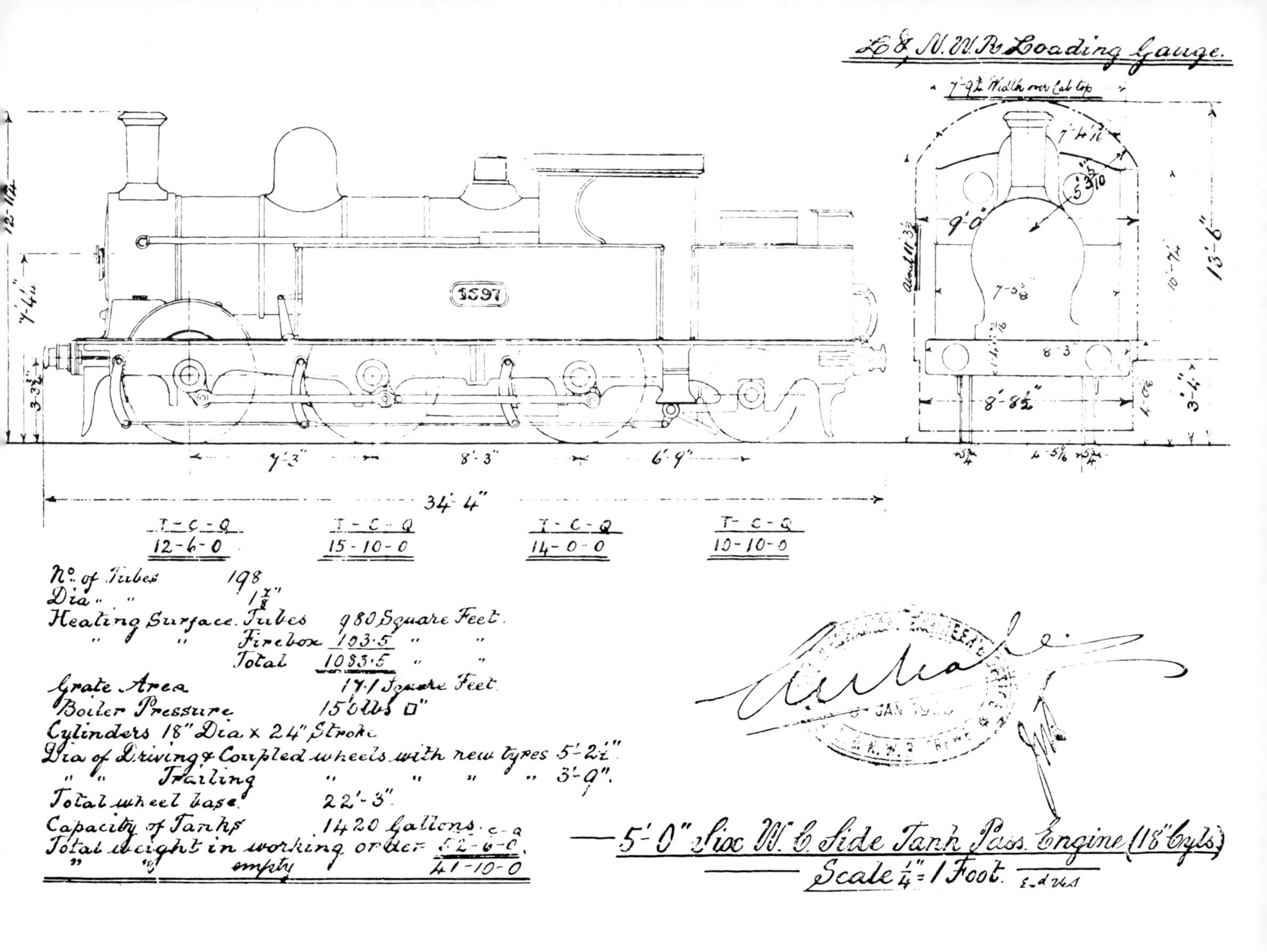

Figure 36: Official weight diagram of an '18in. Tank', dated 1906.

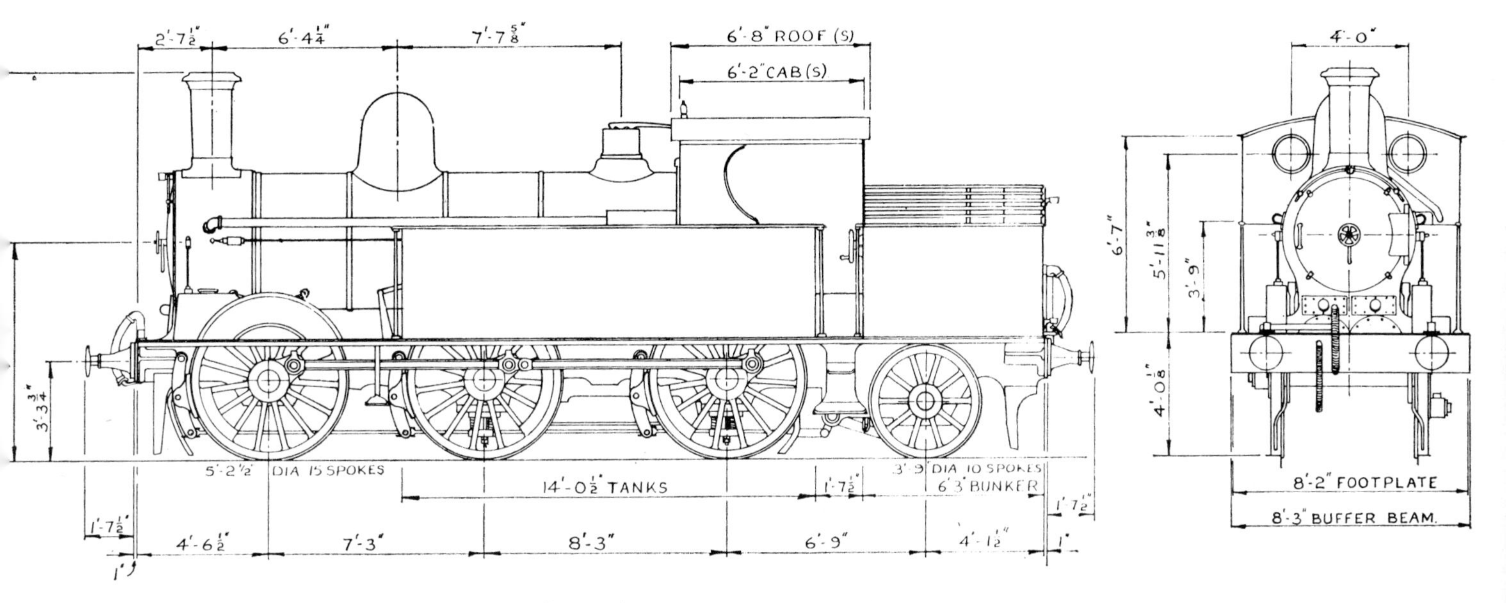

Figure 37: Drawing of an '18in. Tank'.

Chapter 4
Four-Coupled Shunters

'4ft. Shunter'
Plate 126: In December 1863 Ramsbottom introduced a class of 0-4-0 saddle tanks, generally known as the '4ft. Shunters'. They were the first engines to have cast-iron H-section driving wheels, and coupling rods with solid ends but otherwise had the usual Ramsbottom features, ornamental chimney top, safety valves, wooden bufferbeams and brake blocks, no cab, hook couplings and green livery lined in black. This official view of No. 1437, built in August 1865, was taken in the usual position at the time, outside the erecting shop at the Old Works. The engine has been specially prepared for photography, with the black lining represented in white, possibly over-elaborately. The right-hand cab side-sheet was later raised to increase coal capacity.

Plate 127 (below): This view is one of the earliest known of a '4ft. Shunter'. It is one of five built in March 1872, after Webb had taken over, for the Lancashire & Yorkshire Railway, and has Ramsbottom chimney and safety valves, LYR lamps and no sign of ownership.

Figure 38: The first '4ft. Shunter', No. 835, as built.

Plate 128 (below): Ramsbottom 0-4-0 saddle tank No. 1957, originally No. 1364, shunts at Manchester (London Road) in the late 1880s. There was no access to the footplate on this side and the side-sheet was higher, since it served as the coal bunker. The single footstep at the rear and the vertical handrail on the side-sheet are for use by the shunter, not by the crew. There is a stylish sandbox on the running plate at the front (later photographs show only one central sandbox) and the centre one has the same sort of lid, while other features are the Webb chimney and plain black livery. The pipe from the bottom of the rear of the tank passes under the boiler to the other side to equalise the water-levels.

Plate 129 (below): No. 3068, possibly at Rugby between 1890 and 1905, with one central sandbox and screw couplings. Vacuum brakes are fitted, but only for working attached vehicles.

Plate 130: A rear view of No. 3068 at Rugby about 1900, showing the large opening in the rear of the cab to permit the use of fire-irons. The shed plate, 8 (Rugby), is visible, and the driver is taking a swig from his bottle, probably containing cold tea!

Figure 39: Weight diagram of a '4ft. Shunter', dated 1906.

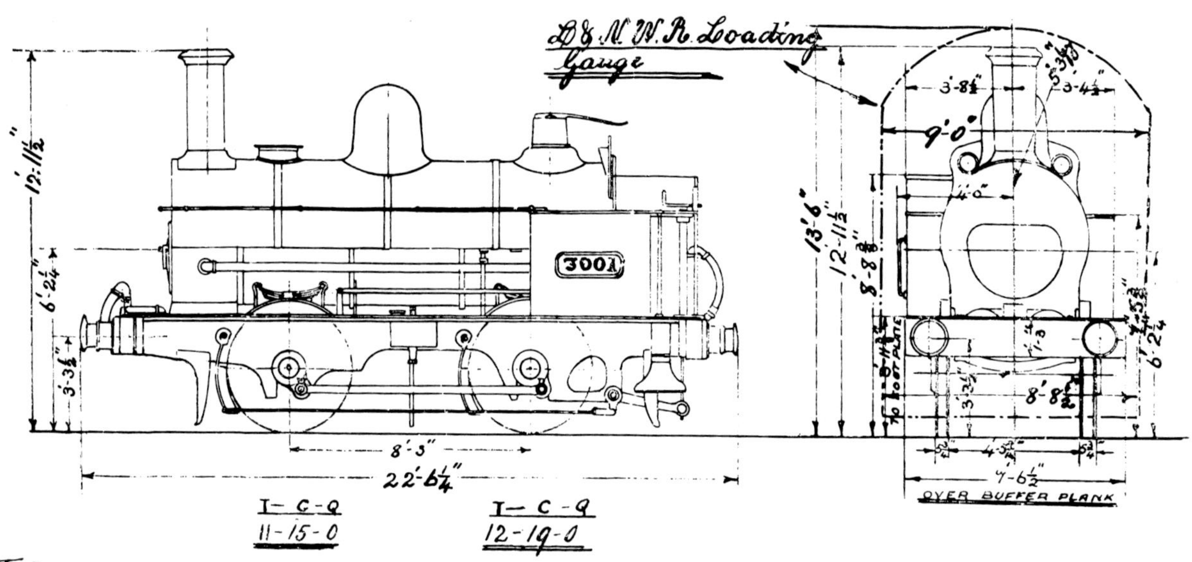

No. of Tubes 120
Dia " " 1¾"
Heating Surface, Tubes - 374.3 Square Feet
" " Firebox 40.7 " "
" " Total 415.0 " "
Grate Area 11·0 Square Feet
Boiler Pressure 120 lbs □"
Cylinders 14" Dia × 20" Stroke
Dia of Driving Wheels with new tyres 4'-3"
" " Leading " " " " 4'-3"
Total wheel base 8'-3"
Capacity of Tank 420 Gallons

	T - C - Q
Total weight in working order	24-14-0
" " empty	20-11-0

8 - JAN 1906

4'-0" Four W.C. Saddle Tank Engine.

Scale ¼" = 1 Foot

Plate 131 (right): No. 3060 about 1910 with dumb buffers, three-link couplings and a toolbox on the front of the running plate.

Plate 132 (above): In November 1892, Mr Webb built ten more 4ft. saddle tanks, the last three being turned out as 0-4-2 crane tanks. This is the official view of the second of the batch, No. 2526, taken on completion; it was very soon renumbered, first to 2126 and then to 3240. Apart from Webb safety valves, there is little difference from the original batch except for the lined black livery. The pipe leading downwards from a valve at the base of the safety valves conveys steam to the vacuum-brake ejector, the exhaust steam pipe from which runs parallel to the bottom of the tank to the smokebox.

Plate 133 (right): No. 3039, one of the 1872 batch, as running about 1922-3 with a larger spectacle plate and roof, shorter chimney, metal brake blocks and dumb buffers at the front end only.

Plate 134 (left): Two shunters at Liverpool for work in the docks, probably about 1920. On the right is 0-4-0 saddle tank No. 3243 with short chimney, dumb buffers front and rear, large spectacle plate with roof, on top of which is a bell, and moveable spark arrester plate over the chimney. The bunker is well stacked with coal and a somewhat mangled fire-iron is lodged behind the handrail. On the left is 0-4-2 'Bissel Tank' No. 3464, originally No. 317, the first of the class. It is similarly equipped for the docks with bell and spark arrester, but has ordinary buffers on the front. There is a toolbox on the tank behind the chimney.

Plate 135 (above): '4ft. Shunter' No. 3084 at Crewe about 1910, specially modified for working the Crewe Works 'cab'. It has a cut-down chimney, dome and cab roof for restricted clearances in the works, metal brake blocks but no front coupling or vacuum-brake gear.

Plate 136 (right): The last of the 1872 batch, originally No. 1210, in departmental service as LMS No. 3009 about 1930, with a short chimney, LMS lamp irons, metal brake blocks and coupling rods of the kind fitted to the '2ft. 6in. Shunters'.

'4ft. Crane Shunter'
Plate 137: The last three of the 1892 batch of '4ft. Shunters' were turned out as 0-4-2 crane tanks, and except for the modifications required by the cranes, they were identical to the 0-4-0 saddle tanks. This is the official view of No. 3247 taken on completion. Originally, the crane was designed to lift four tons and was secured, when not in use, by chains anchored to the tank seams just ahead of the safety valves. Later a longer jib was fitted, on some engines at least, to lift three tons only, and the chains were then secured to brackets on the tank ahead of the line of the dome. Both sizes of jib continued in use side by side into LMS days.

Plate 138: Two 'Crane Shunters' back to back, probably in the works during the early 1900s. On the left is No. 3248 in lined livery, and on the right No. 3249, the first of the 1894 batch of five. Both engines have three-ton cranes with jibs secured ahead of the domes.

Plate 139 (left): '4ft. Crane Shunter' No. 3246 at Crewe, probably about 1915, with the original arrangement of a four-ton crane but with a large spectacle plate and cab roof added.

Plate 142 (above right): No. 3248 in LMS livery and with LMS lamp irons; otherwise it is in late LNWR condition with metal brake blocks.

Plate 140 (above): Rear view of No. 3248 at Crewe Works in plain black; it is perhaps awaiting entry to the paintshop for final painting. Beyond it is a 'cab'.

Plate 141 (left): 'Crane Shunter' No. 3249 at work about 1920 with cab roof, enlarged spectacle plate and metal brake blocks.

Figure 40 (right): Weight diagram of a 'Crane Shunter', dated 1906.

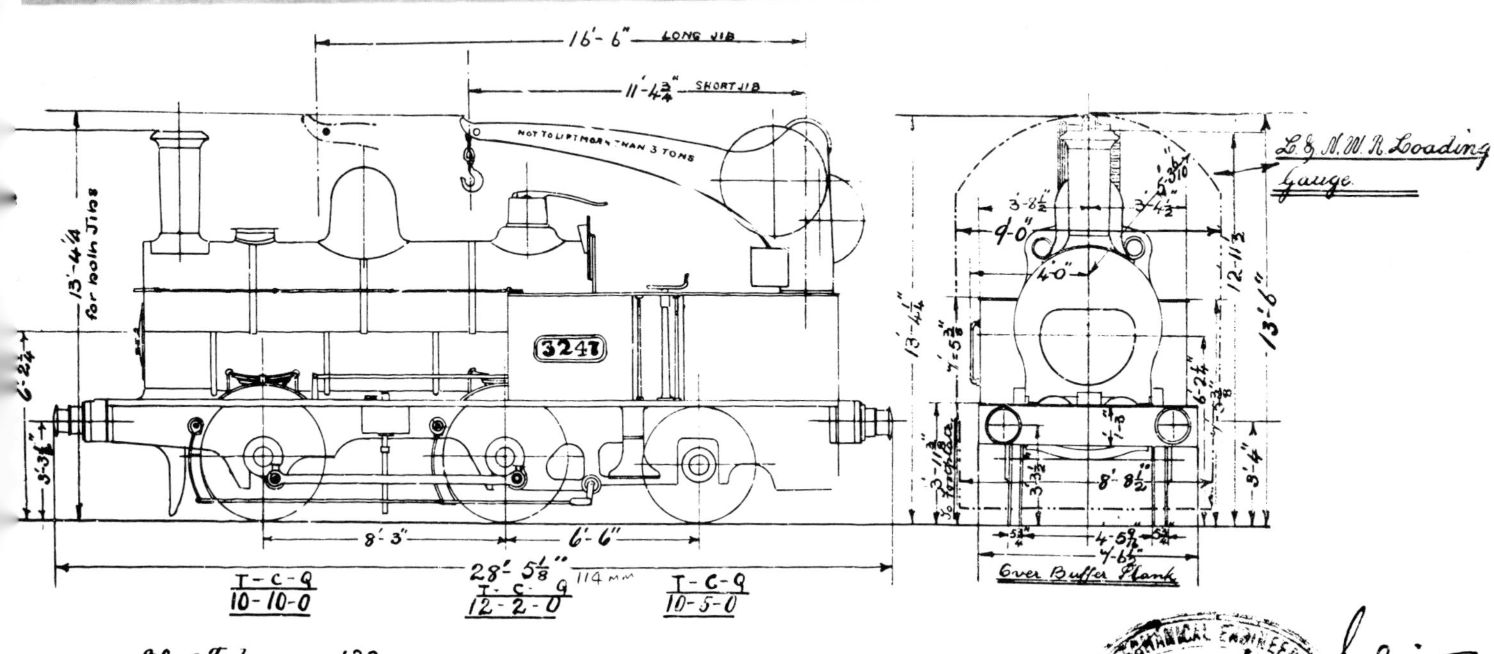

No. of Tubes 120
Dia " 1¾"
Heating Surface Tubes 374.3 Square Feet
" " Firebox 40.7 " "
" Total 415.0 " "
Grate Area 11.0 Square Feet
Boiler Pressure 120 lbs per sq. inch
Cylinders 14" Dia × 20" Stroke
Dia of Leading & Driving wheels with new tyres 4'-3"
" " Trailing wheels with new tyres 3'-9"
Total wheel base 14'-9"
Capacity of Tank 420 Gallons
Total weight in working order T-C-Q 32-17-0.
" " empty 28-7-0.
Coal Capacity — — — 1 Ton.

4'-0" Four W. C. Crane Engine
Scale ¼" = 1 Foot.

'Dock Tank'

Plate 143: In 1896 Mr Webb introduced a class of 0-4-2 square saddle tanks for work in docks, and twenty were built by early 1902. To enable them to negotiate sharp curves, they had a coupled wheelbase of only 7ft. 6in. and a Bissell truck at the rear with solid wheels. The style of the square tank was followed in 1905 when some '17in. Coal Engines' were converted to shunting tanks. This is the official view of the first 0-4-2 'Dock Tank' No. 317, taken on 3rd December 1896. It has the usual Webb features of the day. Wooden bufferbeams were presumably preferred for a shunting engine, as steel had already appeared on both passenger and goods engines, but it has fluted coupling rods, being one of the first engines

Plate 144 (above): The 'Dock Tanks' were perhaps better known as 'Bissell Tanks', from their trailing trucks. No. 3527, of the 1901 batch, poses here probably in early LMS days. Its full lined LNWR livery can still be seen clearly although there is no coat of arms on the tank. Probably only the first of the class was so adorned, specially for the official photograph. There is a large toolbox on the running plate, metal brake blocks are fitted, and there are dumb buffers at the rear.

Plate 145 (above right): No. 3528, in plain black livery but otherwise in much the same state as No. 3527. The brackets for the fire-irons can be seen inside the rear spectacle plate.

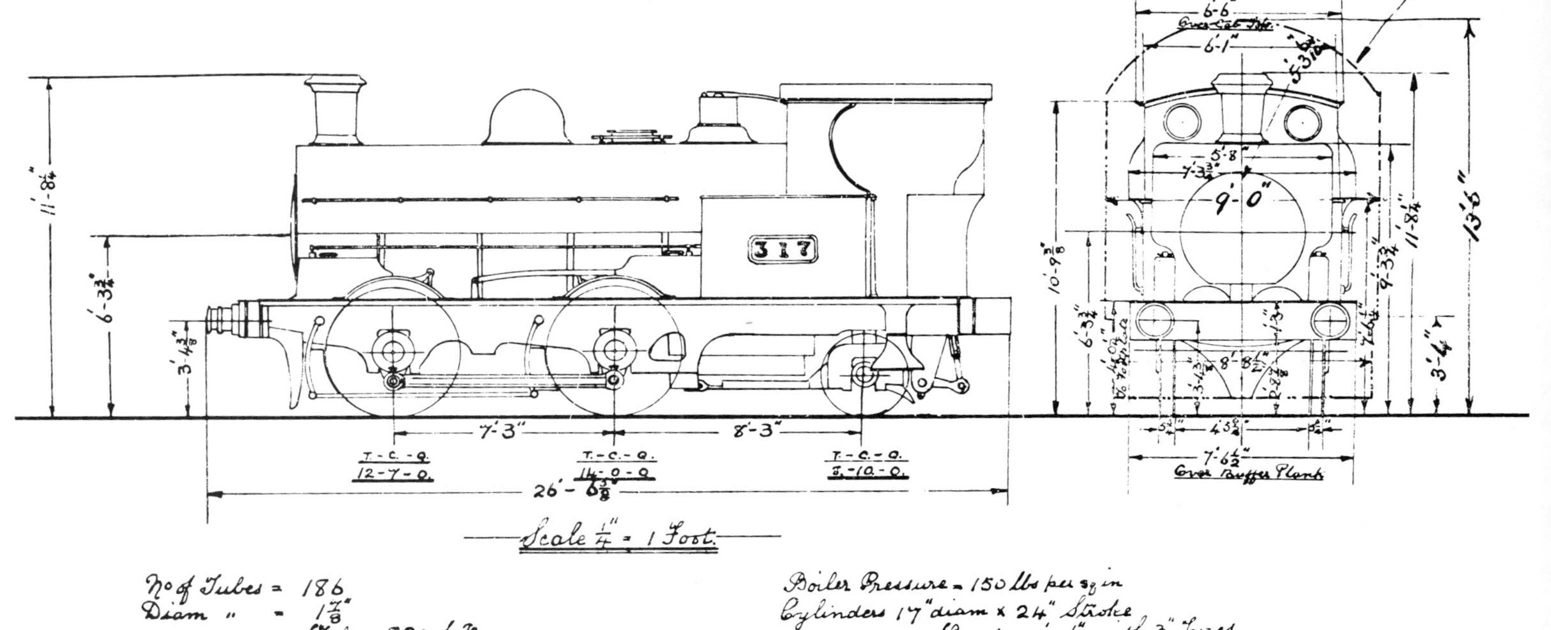

Figure 41 (left): Weight diagram of a 'Dock Tank', dated 1914.

'2ft. 6in. Shunter'

Plate 146: In 1880 Mr Webb produced five of the most unusual engines ever to be built, even at Crewe Works, and another five were built in 1882. Known as the '2ft. 6in. Shunters', they were mostly used in the works itself and after 1886 were numbered 3010-9. The driver and fireman worked at opposite ends, either being able to attach couplings, and both the brake and the reversing gear were operable from either end. The boiler was oil-fired, the firebox being semicircular top and bottom with a water-tube grate, and having a small combustion chamber extending into the barrel. To save heat, the smokebox was completely surrounded by water and the chimney passed through the dome. Full details of all these engines are not known but there seem to have been three sub-classes, though whether this was so originally or came about through rebuilding or modification is uncertain. The most common sub-class was as shown in this view of No. 3016. It has an extra pair of buffers for shunting chauldron wagons, no sanding gear and no protection from the elements for the crew.

Plate 147 (right): No. 3012 at Shrewsbury. It has a central sandbox but otherwise is similar to No. 3016. The squarish opening at the fireman's end gave access to the firebox, while the circular opening at the driver's end allowed work to be done on the smokebox.

Figure 42 (below): Weight diagram of a '2ft. 6in. Shunter', dated 1906.

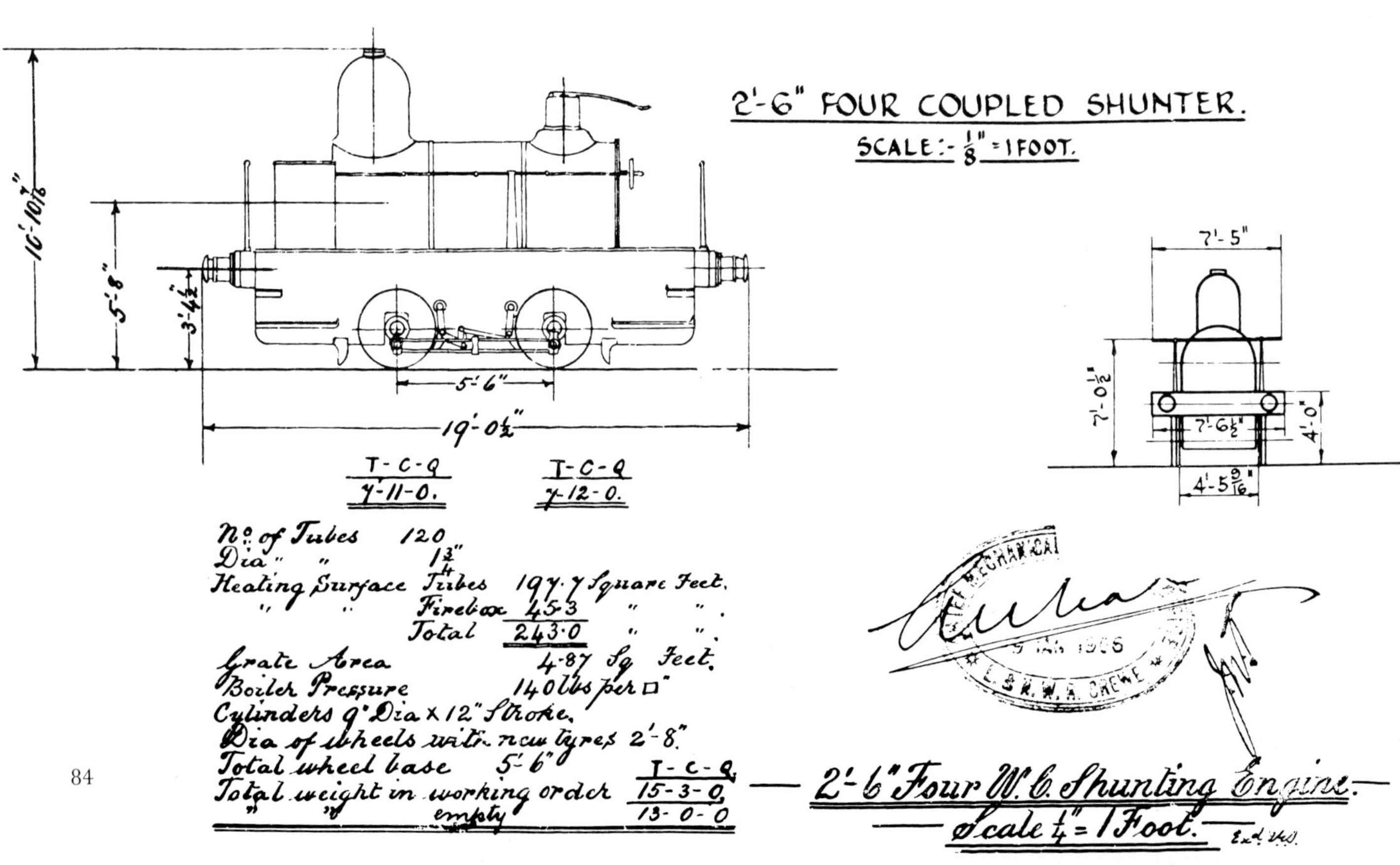

Plate 148 (right): The driver's end of No. 3018. It obviously had the extra pair of buffers at one time because of its deep bufferbeam, though they have since been removed. The board on the side of the footplate at the fireman's end seems to imply coal-firing.

Plate 149 (left): Nos. 3016, 3010, 3018 and 3017, probably photographed in Crewe Works around the time of withdrawal in 1926-7. No. 3010 seems to have a deep bufferbeam for four buffers at the near end, and an ordinary one for two at the other!

Plate 150 (right): A closer view of No. 3018 taken at the same time as the previous picture.

Plate 151 (left): No. 3017 was fitted with a canopy and bell for working in Liverpool Docks, and so became a sub-variety of the '2ft. 6in. Shunters'. It is seen at Crewe Works in late 1896; perhaps the photograph was taken because the canopy had just been fitted. It has a bracket for a shed plate on the roof at the driver's end.

Plate 152 (left): Two of the '2ft. 6in. Shunters', Nos. 3014 and 3015, had boilers with safety valves positioned centrally, no domes and no buffers, and so constituted the third sub-variety of the class. Whether they were originally built like this is uncertain; the alteration is thought perhaps to have been made by the LMS (the numbers are no guide, as the class was not renumbered by the LMS). As seen here in Crewe Works, they both have boards on the footplate at the fireman's end, which implies that they were coal-fired, at this time anyway.

Plate 153 (below): A close-up view of No. 3014. The fireman appears to be provided with the luxury of a seat!

18in. gauge Crewe Works Shunters

Plate 154: In 1862, when responsibility for all LNWR locomotive matters was concentrated at Crewe, John Ramsbottom reorganised Crewe Works and laid down an 18in. gauge railway for internal transport between the various shops. To work on the system, he built an 0-4-0 tank engine named *Tiny* and eventually four more, *Pet*, *Nipper*, *Topsy* and *Midge*. This view shows *Tiny* inside the tender shop in the 1890s. It is black with the usual lining around the casing.

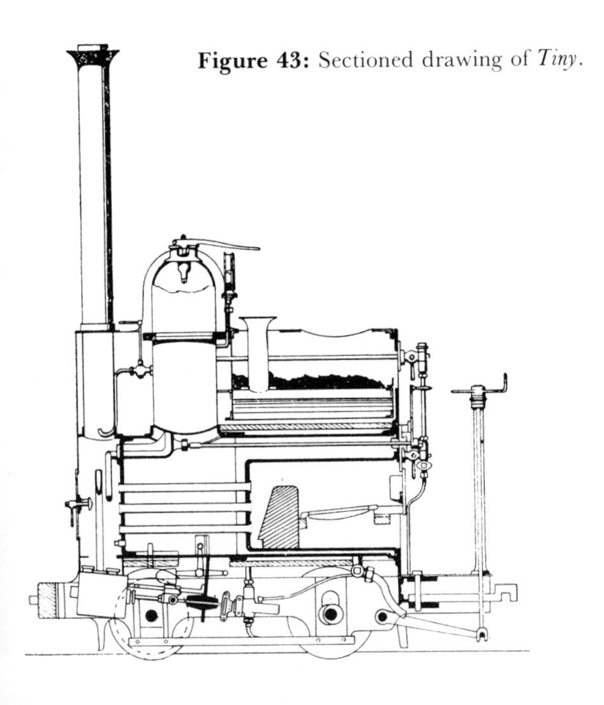

Figure 43: Sectioned drawing of *Tiny*.

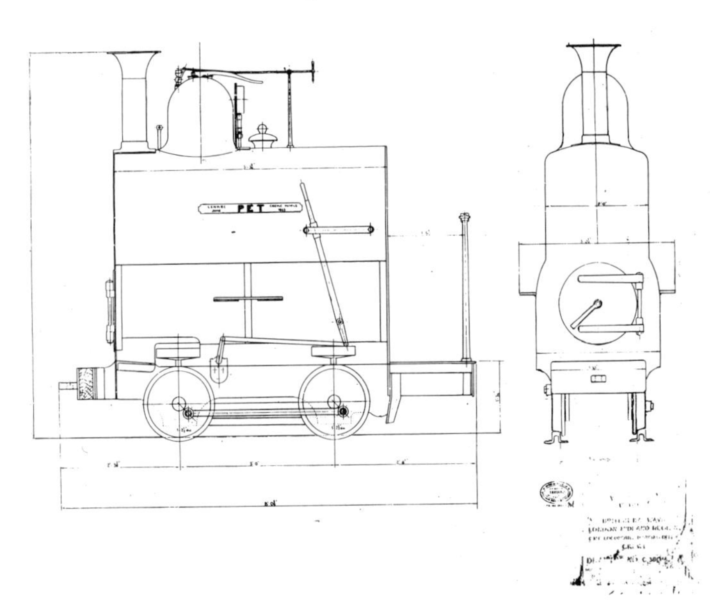

Figure 44: Official drawing of *Pet*.

Plate 155 (left): *Topsy* loaded on to a wagon in the 1920s, probably to be moved to the erecting shop for repair. Coal was carried in a hopper in the casing to the rear of the dome.

Plate 156 (below): All five of these engines were withdrawn in October 1929. Here *Pet* is seen inside the paintshop at Crewe Works on 18th April 1937. Happily, it is now preserved in the Narrow Gauge Railway Museum at the Talyllyn Railway's Wharf station in Towyn.

being built by the firm of William Rylance rather than at Crewe, and in being named *Billy*, after the proprietor of the firm, and *Dickie*, after his son. Both had cylindrical boilers containing a hexagonal flue with small cross tubes. From the flue, three chimneys, each with its own blast nozzle, passed up through the dome which also housed the safety valves. Like the '2ft. 6in. Shunters', which came later, they could be driven from either end and probably had a crew of one man only. *Billy* was originally built with a Brotherhood three-cylinder rotary engine, positioned between the frames and driving on to one axle through gearing, the other axle being driven by coupling rods in the usual way. This somewhat tattered drawing shows *Billy* as built.

Figure 46: An engraving of *Billy* as built.

Plate 157 (left): Just how long *Billy* ran in its original form is not known but it seems to have been rebuilt quite soon like *Dickie*, with outside cylinders of 5½in. by 6 in. The date on the nameplate reads 'July 1875'.

Plate 158 (right): An official view of *Dickie*. The nameplate differs from that of Billy in having no full stop, and the date reads 'May 1876'.

Chapter 5
The 'Problem' or 'Lady of the Lake' or '7ft. 6in. Single' 2-2-2

Plate 159: The 'Problem' class 2-2-2s were designed by John Ramsbottom and introduced in 1859, the first of the class being No. 184 *Problem*. This name came from a withdrawn Trevithick 2-4-0 goods engine and originally had a mathematical connotation, another of the class being named *Theorem*. Officially, the engines were known as the '7ft. 6in. Singles'. They incorporated all the usual Ramsbottom features: his design of chimney top, safety valves and screw reverser, green livery lined in black, hook-type coupling, horizontal smokebox door, no cab, no brakes on the engines and no top lamp socket; they were the first engines to have the ash chute under the smokebox. This is the earliest known photograph of a 'Problem' and shows the second in the class, No. 229 *Watt*, at Preston in the early 1860s with the East Lancashire Railway platforms in the background. It is in original condition, with small sandbox and nameplate showing the name only, without any subsidiary inscriptions. The blower is operated by the handle pointing downwards at the footplate end of the boiler handrail; the blower steam supply is carried by the pipe curving down behind the handrail from the top of the firebox. The tender is the 2,000 gallon type, introduced before the adoption of water troughs and fitted to some 'Problems' and 'DXs'. The engine number has been wiped clean but the engine as a whole is quite dirty. Little can be seen of the lining on the cabside and streaks of dirt have run down from the slots in the driving splasher.

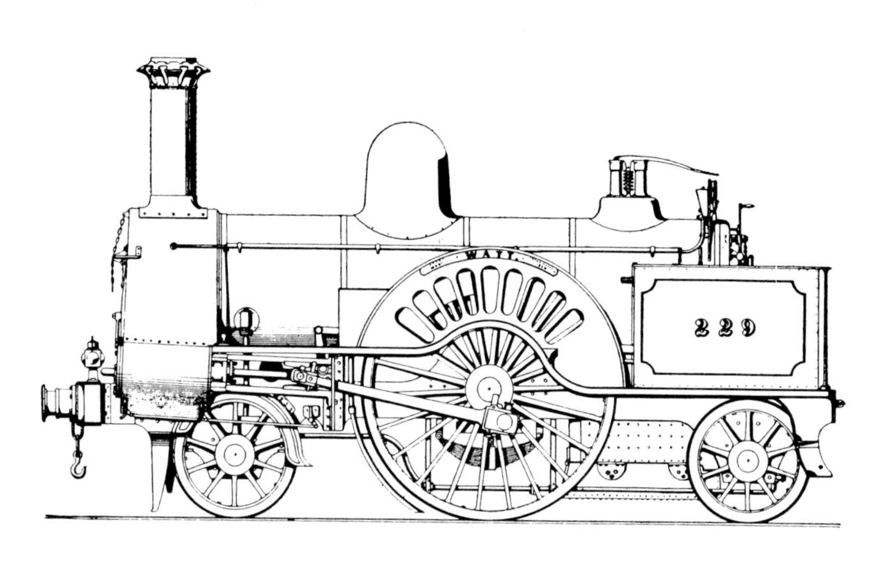

Figure 47: A drawing of *Watt* as built; the sandbox is shown too large in error.

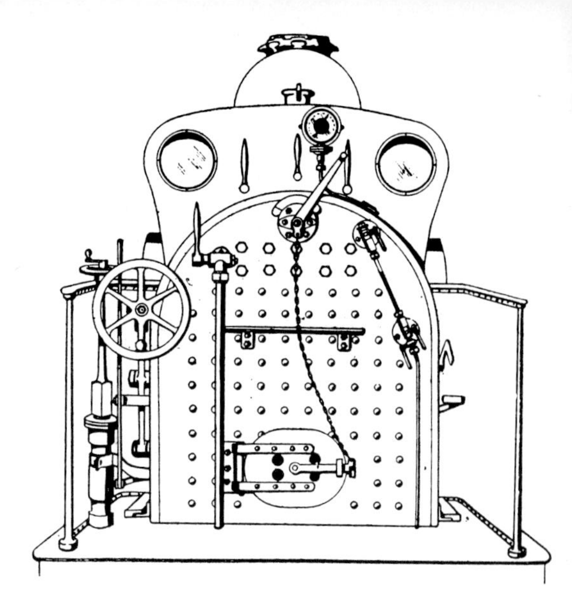

Figure 48: Footplate view of No. 165 *Star*. This was the first engine to be fitted with a Giffard injector, seen here on the left-hand side; the wheel on the top controlled the water supply, while the steam was controlled by a hand-wheel on the side of the firebox. Subsequently, this injector was adopted for all Ramsbottom's engines.

Plate 160: This is one of the earliest official photographs and shows 'Problem' No. 565 outside the Old Works at Crewe, probably on completion in May 1861. The livery is green with black lining, shown here in white for photographic purposes. According to the *S.L.S. Journal*, Nos. 561-5 ran unnamed for about two years, bearing splasher numberplates in the same style as nameplates, as used on the 'DXs', but no photograph exists of one in this condition. No. 565 was eventually named *Napoleon*. The sandbox is larger than that on *Watt*, which implies that the small type was used on the first fifteen engines only. Again, a 2,000 gallon tender is fitted.

Plate 161: The most famous engine of the class was No. 531 *Lady of the Lake*, since it was awarded a bronze medal at the International Exhibition in 1862. As a result, its name came to be used colloquially as the class name. This view shows the engine in green livery with the medal on the cab side-sheet, and was taken by the clock tower of the Old Works at Crewe, probably in 1862. It is the only photograph showing double black lining, which seems to be applied to the tender only; possibly, this was a feature of the early Crewe livery that was abandoned by Ramsbottom for the sake of simplicity, but was specially revived on this engine for the exhibition. There is a screw coupling on the rear and a hook-type on the front.

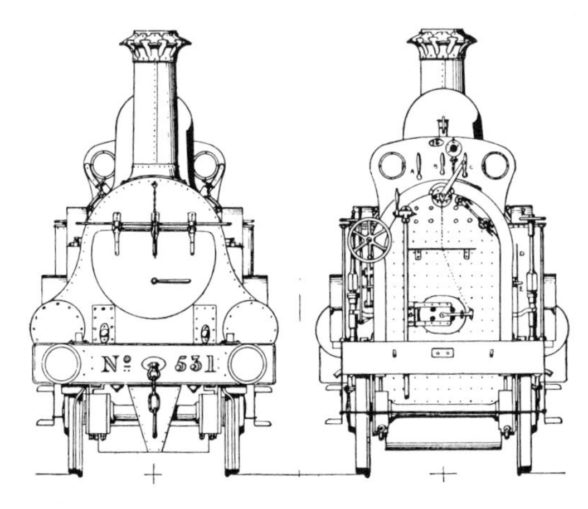

Figure 49 (right): Drawings of the front end and footplate of *Lady of the Lake*.

Figure 50 (below): Drawing of *Lady of the Lake* as displayed at the 1862 International Exhibition but showing single black lining.

Plate 162: When the Shah of Persia visited Crewe Works on 27th June 1873, No. 806 *Waverley* was temporarily renamed *Shah of Persia* in Persian script and decorated with a crown on the boiler, presumably for working the Shah's special train. As seen here, it has a Webb chimney, cab and lamp socket at the top of the smokebox, a feature introduced about this time; the Giffard injector seems to have gone too, presumably replaced by the Webb type, but otherwise it is in original condition, with Ramsbottom safety valves, slotted splashers and the larger sandbox on the front of the driving splasher. This is the earliest photograph showing the lined black livery and No. 806 may well have been the first passenger engine to be so finished. The lining is more complicated than that which later became standard, being applied to the lower edge of the tender frame, spring pads and possibly the buffers, like the white lining in some ex-works photographs of Ramsbottom engines.

Plate 163 (right): No. 618 *Princess Alexandra*, in much the same condition as No. 806 but with a large sandbox on the driving splasher and a toolbox on the front of the tender, which has square buffers. Another photograph exists of this engine in black livery but before the fitting of a cab.

Plate 164 (below): No. 531 *Lady of the Lake* as rebuilt by Mr Webb in 1876, with Webb chimney, cab, large sandbox and Webb safety valves but still with slotted splashers, hook-type front coupling and no brakes on the engine. The handrail at the rear of the cab side-sheet has been inadvertently painted out in the dark room along with the background!

Plate 165: In 1879-83 the 'Problems' were given new boilers having a pressure of 140lb. p.s.i., but they still retained horizontal smokebox doors. No. 127 *Peel* is seen here at Prestbury, as running in the early 1880s after this rebuilding, with Webb chimney, cab, closed safety valves and large sandbox on the driving splasher. The large pipe running from the cab alongside the boiler to the smokebox is the ejector exhaust-pipe for the vacuum brake, but the engine itself still has no brakes. There is a displacement lubricator on the side of the smokebox and the front coupling is the screw type which has long been fitted at the rear. An extra sandpipe has been rigged at the front of the tender, probably to improve adhesion for braking purposes, but the train is fitted with the chain brake. At this stage, all the class retained their Ramsbottom 1,500 gallon tenders.

Plate 166: No. 618 *Princess Alexandra*, as running in the late 1880s after the 1879-83 re-boilering. It now has brake blocks acting on the leading side of the driving wheels. The pipe round the firebox in front of the cab connects the driver's brake valve to the train pipe, while the engine itself has steam brakes with metal brake blocks acting on the driving wheels.

Plate 167: No. 1436 *Egeria* at Bletchley with a train for Oxford in the late 1880s or early 1890s, after the first reboilering of 1879-83 and before the final rebuilding in 1895-9. This view shows front end detail very well: horizontal smokebox door, lubricators on cylinder and slide-valve ends, wooden bufferbeam, ash chute and vacuum-brake pipe. The carriages are the Bletchley No. 2 set (the leading 30ft. 6in. vehicle still has separate upper footsteps) and are presumably now fitted with the automatic vacuum brake; the engine still has a small ejector for maintaining running vacuum.

Plate 168: No. 1430 *Pandora*, as running before the final rebuilding of 1895-9 and fitted with a crosshead vacuum pump.

Plate 169 (left): No. 44 *Harlequin* in 1884, with an experimental generator mounted on the tender to provide electric lighting on both engine and train. Three different sets were tried. First, tender No. 230 had a dynamo driven by a Brotherhood 3-cylinder engine; then tender No. 140 had one driven by a rotary engine supplied by Parker & Elwalls of Coalbrookdale; finally, tender No. 230 had an improved Brotherhood engine.

Plate 170 (below): Official view of No. 531 *Lady of the Lake*, taken on 29th August 1893 before the final rebuilding of the late 1890s.

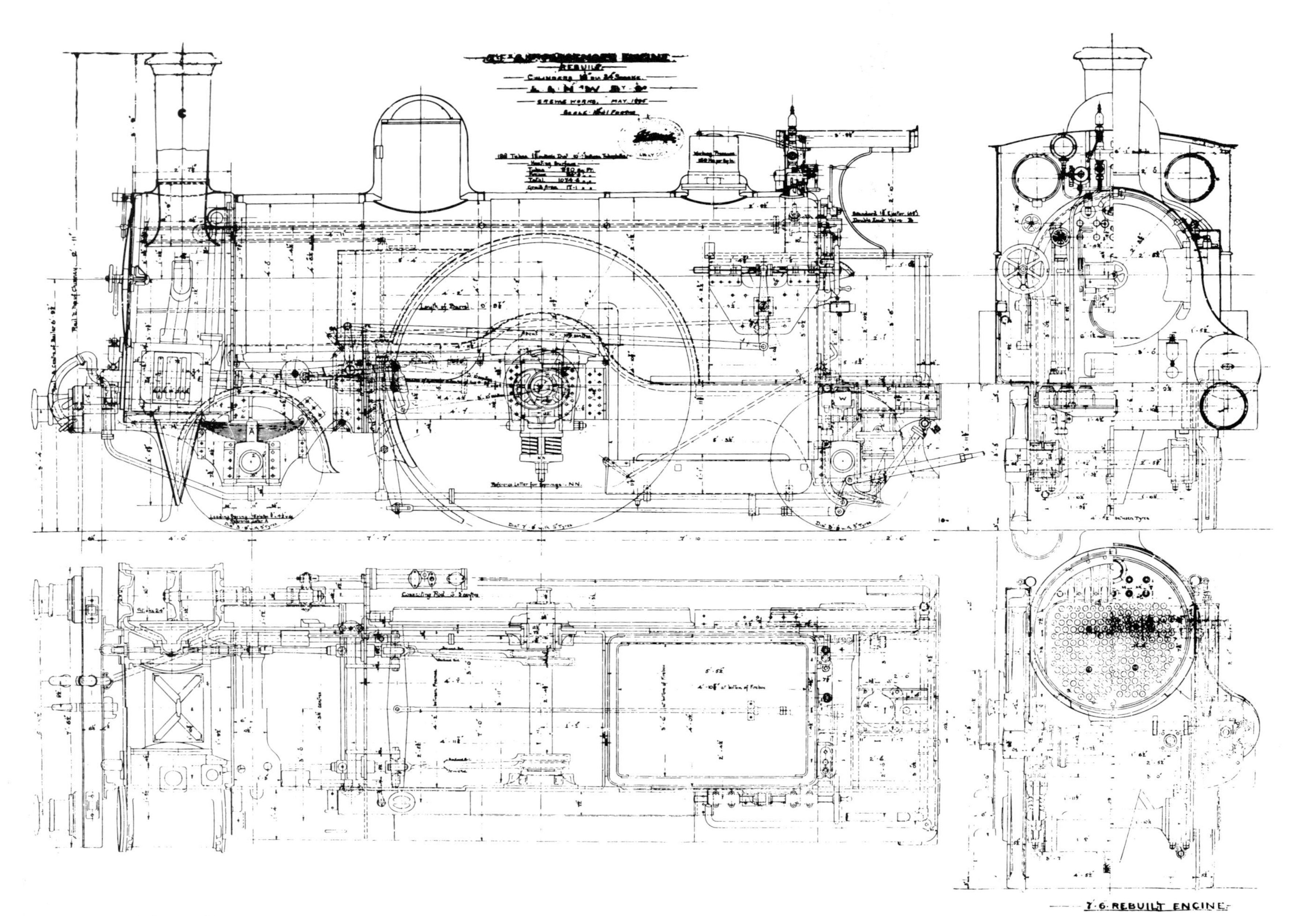

Figure 51: General arrangement drawing of a 'Problem' as finally rebuilt.

Plate 171 (opposite): In the late 1890s, Mr Webb rebuilt the 'Problems' with new frames and 150 lb. p.s.i. boilers. This is the official view of No. 134 *Owl*, but renamed *Princess Royal* for some special occasion, taken on completion of the final rebuilding on 23rd March 1896. Engines in the final rebuilt state are easily recognisable by the circular smokebox doors, shorter chimneys (due to the higher pitch of the boiler) and almost invariably,

Figure 52: Drawing of No. 1 *Saracen* in final form, to a scale of 4mm.

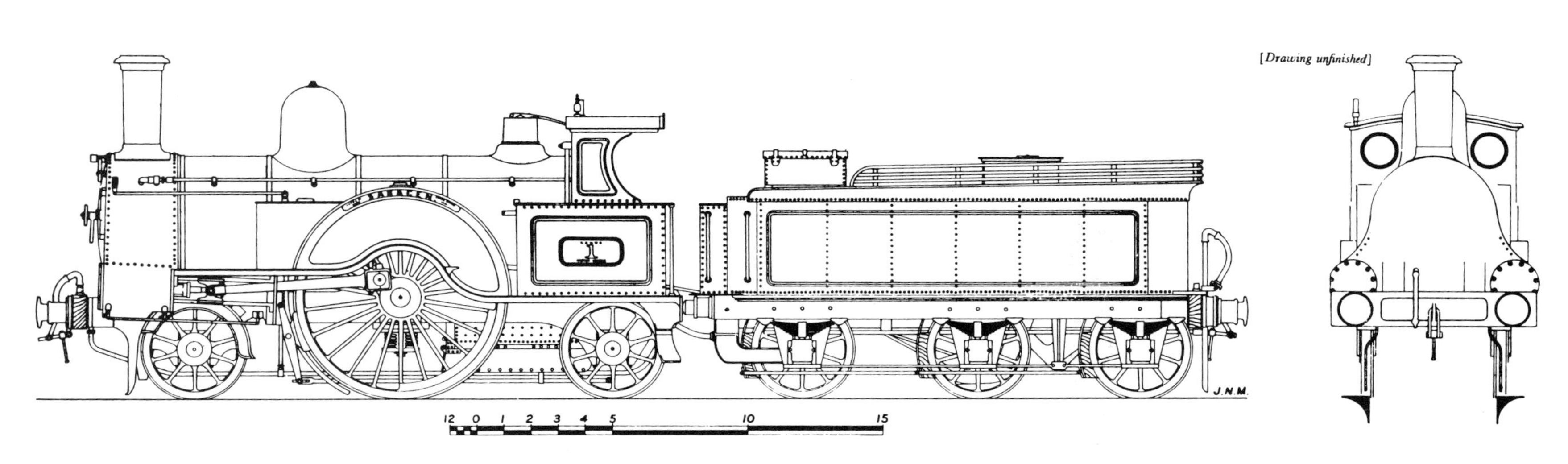

Plate 172: No. 184 *Problem*, the first of the class, in final rebuilt condition about 1900. In addition to a crosshead vacuum-pump, it is fitted with a lubricator on the side of the smokebox, being the only member of the class to have piston valves, which were fitted in 1897.

Plate 173: Head-on view of No. 184 *Problem* at Euston in the late 1890s, showing the circular covers for the piston valves.

Plate 174 (above): No. 1429 *Alfred Paget* as running about 1900 after the final rebuilding. Despite Mr Webb's thorough rebuilding, all the 'Problems' were scrapped by George Whale in 1903-7, not so much because they were worn out as because they were too small for the greatly increased train loads of the early 1900s.

Plate 175 (right): No. 111 *Russell* at Llandudno about 1900.

Plate 176 (right): Rear view of No. 33 *Erebus*, taken at Crewe in the early 1900s, showing the stylish design of footsteps on engine and tender.

Chapter 6
Ramsbottom and Webb 2-4-0s

'Samson'

Plate 177: The 'Samson' class 2-4-0s were introduced by John Ramsbottom in 1863. They were officially known as '6ft. curved link passenger engines' and were the first LNWR passenger engines to have coupled driving wheels. This view shows No. 633 *Samson* outside the Old Works at Crewe on completion. It has the usual Ramsbottom features: the standard chimney, safety valves and horizontal smokebox door, slotted splashers, 'box type' sandboxes and the green livery lined in black (the white lining is for photographic purposes only); there are no brakes on the engine and no cab. The coupling rods are of the early Ramsbottom type, with forked ends having wedge adjustment and cottered fastenings.

Figure 53: Drawing of *Samson* as built.

Plate 178 (left): No. 633 *Samson* in the mid-1870s, still much as built but with Webb chimney and lined black livery. The hook-type leading coupling can be clearly seen; the rear one would be the early screw type. The tender now has round buffers on the front.

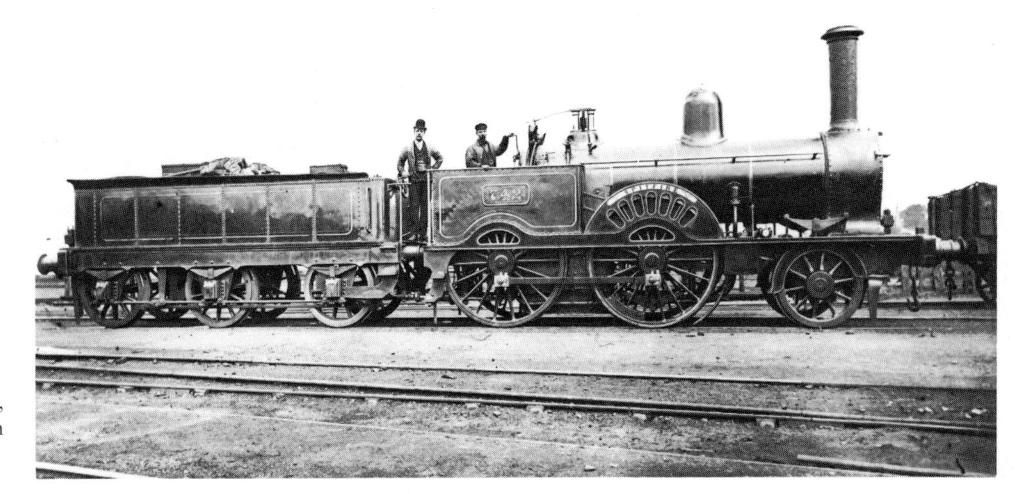

Plate 179 (right): No. 742 *Spitfire*, another Ramsbottom 'Samson' but with Webb chimney and lined black livery.

Plate 180 (below): Yet another Ramsbottom 'Samson', No. 737 *Roberts*, with Webb chimney and cab but retaining slotted splashers and open Ramsbottom safety valves. The square buffers on the front of the tender, as on the original *Samson*, can be clearly seen.

Plate 181: In 1873-9 Mr Webb constructed more 'Samsons', basically to Ramsbottom's design but with cabs, his own style of chimney and sandboxes, coupling rods with solid ends, and lined black livery. At first, slotted splashers were retained but were later replaced by the closed type; and from late 1874 the open Ramsbottom safety valves began to be replaced by Webb's enclosed type. The 1879 batch had 140 lb. p.s.i. boilers when built; the rest of the class probably had this boiler pressure also but they certainly received 1879 type boilers when their old ones were due for replacement. This view shows Webb 'Samson' No. 90 *Luck of Edenhall* in virtually 'as built' condition, with Webb chimney, cab, sandboxes, coupling rods and lined black livery. The boiler bands are fully lined in red, cream and grey as in the previous three pictures; from 1876 two red lines only were applied. There is also lining along the tender frames.

Plate 182 (below): Another Webb 'Samson', No. 2154 *Loadstone*, with all the usual Webb features about 1880, including closed splashers, but still with open Ramsbottom safety valves, no brakes on the engine and no vacuum brake. The leading coupling is now the screw type.

Plate 183 (below): No. 2156 *Sphinx*, a Webb 'Samson' built in 1874, as running in the early 1890s, still with open safety valves but with closed splashers, steam brakes on the engine and fitted for working vacuum-braked trains.

Plate 184 (above right): As Mr Webb introduced various modifications, so they were applied to the original Ramsbottom engines as well as to his own. This view shows No. 609 *The Earl of Chester*, built by Ramsbottom in 1866, as running in the early 1890s. It has acquired all the usual Webb features, including closed driving splashers, closed safety valves and steam brakes on the engine, and is fitted for working vacuum-braked trains, but it still retains Ramsbottom coupling rods.

Plate 185 (right): No. 852 *Kestrel*, one of the last Webb 'Samsons' to be built, in 1879. Except for steam brakes and vacuum fittings, it is in original condition and remained so until withdrawal in 1894, the 1879 batch being among the few Webb engines to remain largely unaltered throughout their lives.

Plate 186 (below): No. 445 *Ixion*, a Webb 'Samson' built in 1873, at Shrewsbury as running in final condition before withdrawal in 1892. The angle shows good detail of the 1,500 gallon tender with grease axleboxes; a plate has been added inside the tender handrail. Main-line passenger engines began to get oil-box tenders from about 1889.

Plate 187: When No. 757 *Banshee*, one of the original Ramsbottom 'Samsons' built in 1863, was withdrawn in 1892, it was used by Mr Webb for experiments with friction drive and is seen here at Crewe Works in May 1896. The idea was to combine the free-running qualities of the single-driver with the extra adhesion of coupled driving wheels. The drive was transmitted from the leading to the trailing driving wheels, not by the usual coupling rods, but by means of a friction wheel, which could be raised or lowered as required by the driver. When starting from rest or working hard up steep gradients, the friction wheel would be raised, giving in effect a four-coupled engine, but at speed the wheel would be lowered, so disengaging the rear driving wheels and converting the engine into a single-driver. The 1,500 gallon tender seen here has oil axleboxes.

Plate 188: Between 1889 and 1896 eighty 'Samsons' were scrapped and replaced by new 'Whitworth' class 2-4-0s, which took their names and numbers. Ten 'Samsons' survived and were eventually transferred to the Engineer's Department. This view shows *Engineer Watford* in the late 1890s, fitted with a short chimney; it was originally built in 1879 as Webb 'Samson' No. 773 *Centaur*. The 1,500 gallon tender has grease axleboxes and has acquired a spectacle plate. So far as is known, 1,500 gallon tenders never received coal rails.

Plate 189: *Engineer*, originally No. 885 *Vampire*, stands at Manchester (London Road) about 1910. It retains its tall chimney but has acquired an 1,800 gallon tender with coal rails and a somewhat rudimentary tender cab.

Plate 190: No. 2157 *Unicorn* became spare engine in 1905 and is seen here at Manchester (London Road) with an inspection saloon. It has a short chimney and a centre lamp socket on the bufferbeam. This view also shows quite clearly the unusual design of coupling used by the LNWR. One side of the first link was hammered flat so that it could be passed through a slot behind the hook and then worked round into the desired position. Early screw couplings, however, were of the usual design used on other railways; there was no slot, the first link being secured by a pin through a hole behind the coupling.

'Newton'

Plate 191: The 'Newton' class 2-4-0s were designed by John Ramsbottom and introduced in 1866. Officially known as '6ft. 6in. curved link passenger engines', they were developed from the 'DX' 0-6-0s and were intended for express passenger working on the Lancaster & Carlisle line, where the 'Problems' were having difficulties in adverse weather conditions. Naturally, they had all the standard Ramsbottom features: his own style of chimney and safety valves, slotted splashers, horizontal smokebox door, 'box type' sandboxes, green livery with black lining, no cab and no brakes on the engine. Like the '4ft. Shunters', they had coupling rods with solid ends and circular bushes. This view shows No. 1480 *Newton* on completion by the clock tower of the Old Works at Crewe. The white lining is for photographic purposes only and would be replaced by black before the engine entered traffic. There is a screw coupling on the tender but there would be a hook-type coupling on the engine.

Plate 192: No. 1745 *John Bright*, in original Ramsbottom condition about 1870, before the fitting of a lamp socket at the top of the smokebox, which took place about 1872-3.

Figure 54: Drawing of *Newton* as built.

Plate 193: When Mr Webb took over, he continued to build 'Newtons' to Ramsbottom's basic design but with cabs (the first engines to be so fitted) and with his own style of chimney. There was also, possibly, a change in the boiler, with fewer tubes and perhaps a pressure of 140 lb. p.s.i., as on the 'Newtons' built for the Lancashire & Yorkshire Railway. The first Webb 'Newton' was No. 1211, which was appropriately named *John Ramsbottom*. It is seen here as first built in April 1872. Before it entered traffic, it would have been repainted in Ramsbottom green with black lining in place of photographic grey with white lining. Or, quite possibly, it was an experimental paint scheme and a trial of red, cream and grey, as used later. There is now no way of knowing. Certainly, the style of lining differs from that used by Ramsbottom and has the same contours as used later by Webb on black engines, with rounded corners instead of reversed; but the number is painted on the cabside, as cast numberplates were not introduced until February 1873 on the '17in. Coal Engines'.

Plate 194 (right): Another Webb 'Newton', this time No. 1218 *Phaeton*, photographed soon after completion in April 1872 and painted in green livery with black lining in the Webb style.

Plate 195: No. 1684 *Speke*, a Ramsbottom 'Newton' in original condition except for the fitting of a Webb chimney and lamp socket at the top of the smokebox, at Crewe shed about 1873. The bufferbeam is painted red with a black rectangle, as used by Webb on black engines; it no longer carries the engine number normally displayed in that position on engines in Ramsbottom green.

Plate 196 (left): No. 1516 *Byron*, a Ramsbottom 'Newton' in original condition except for Webb chimney, lined black livery and cast numberplates. The Ramsbottom screw reverser can be clearly seen above the cab side-sheets.

Plate 197 (below): Another Ramsbottom 'Newton', No. 2006 *Princess*, as running about 1875 with Webb chimney, cast numberplates and lined black livery.

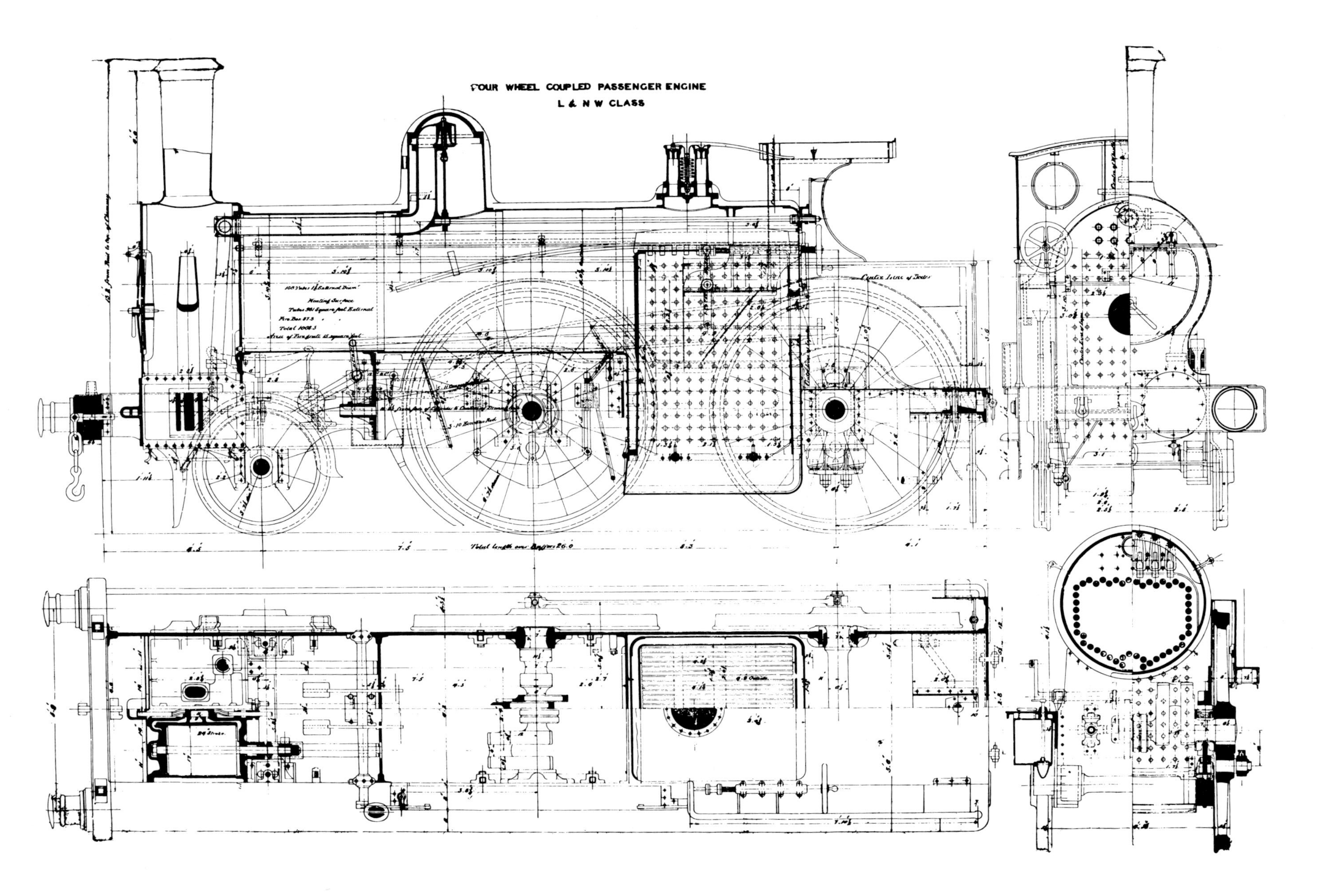

Figure 55: General arrangement drawing of a Webb 'Newton' built at Crewe for the Lancashire & Yorkshire Railway in 1873.

Plate 198: No. 1525 *Abercrombie*, as running in the late 1870s with Webb chimney, cab and black livery. It still retains its open safety valves and slotted splashers and there are still no brakes on the engine.

Plate 199 (below): In 1878-82, Mr Webb rebuilt the 'Newtons' with 140lb. boilers having larger fireboxes. No. 1745 *John Bright* is seen here as rebuilt, and has closed splashers with side valances, closed safety valves and a screw coupling on the front of the engine in place of the hook type. It has steam brakes on the engine and is fitted for working vacuum-braked trains, the pipe connecting the driver's brake-valve with the train pipe being clearly visible round the front of the cab; but there is no front vacuum hose, which dates the picture to the late 1880s or 1890. The original 1,500 gallon tender has been replaced with an 1,800 gallon one which still has grease axleboxes but has been fitted with panel plates instead of the old pillar and handrail.

Plate 200 (below): Another rebuilt 'Newton', No. 2005 *Lynx*, which was the last to be withdrawn, in 1894, and is seen here in its final form. It is much the same as *John Bright* but has a front vacuum hose and oil axleboxes on the tender. The ejector exhaust-pipe can be seen running along the boiler side to the smokebox, where a lubricator is fitted. All the 'Newtons' were withdrawn in 1887-94, their names and numbers passing to the 'Improved Precedents' which replaced them.

'Precursor'
Plate 201: In 1874 Mr Webb introduced two new classes of 2-4-0 passenger engines, the 'Precursors' and the 'Precedents'. They were identical mechanically but the 'Precursors' had boilers identical to the '17in. Coal Engines' while the 'Precedent boilers had larger fireboxes. They also differed in the size of the driving wheels. The 'Precursors' had 5ft. 6in. driving wheels, which were thought to be better suited to hill climbing on the Crewe- Carlisle line, whereas the 'Precedents' had 6ft. 6in. driving wheels. This view shows No. 2145 *Precursor* in photographic grey as first built. In addition to the expected Webb features, such as the chimney, cab and curved sandbox, it has open Ramsbottom safety valves, horizontal smokebox door, hook-type front coupling and no brakes on the engine.

Plate 202: 'Precursor' class 2-4-0 No. 1144 *Druid*, as running about 1885. Compared with *Precursor* as built, it has steam brakes on the engine, Webb closed safety valves, a screw coupling at the front end and a lubricator on the side of the smokebox. It is fitted for working vacuum-braked trains; the ejector exhaust-pipe is positioned alongside the boiler below the handrail but there is no hose at the front end. Instead of Ramsbottom's double-beat regulator, which needed no oil and was always easy to operate, these engines had Webb's regulator, which basically consisted of one pipe working inside another. It was located in the smokebox, not the dome, and needed oil, which was supplied by the lubricator behind the chimney. This type of regulator valve was commonly referred to by the men as the 'bible valve', because when dismantled and seen end-on, it was reminiscent of the pages of a book being turned over.

Plate 203 (above): Official Crewe photograph of No. 2147 *Champion*, taken on 18th February 1891, still fitted with a horizontal smokebox door

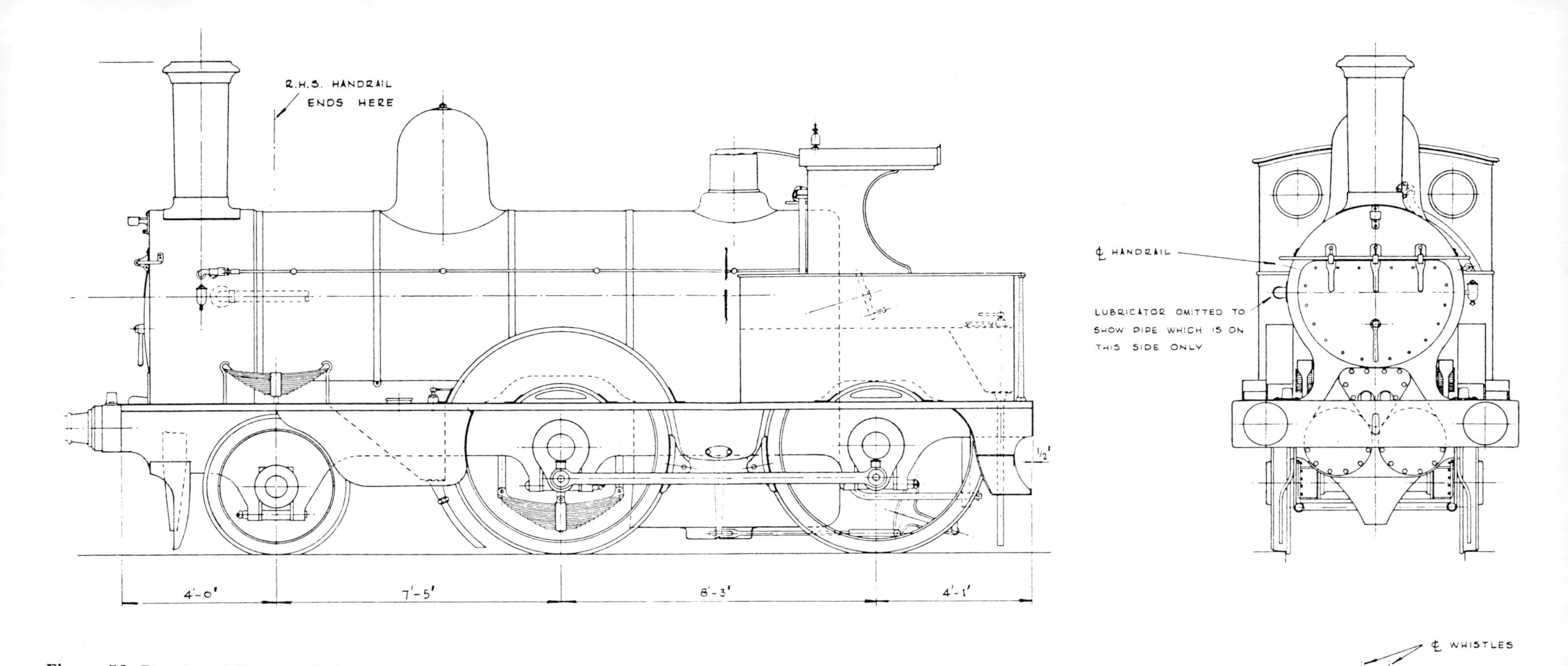

Figure 56: Drawing of 'Precursor' class 2-4-0.

LNWR WEBB PRECURSOR CLASS

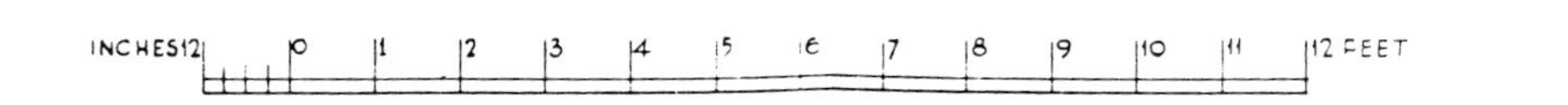

Plate 204 (above): No. 1148 *Boadicea*, as running in the early 1890s with circular smokebox door. The boiler handrail operates the blower valve when twisted in the cab by means of a handwheel.

Plate 205 (left): No. 481 *Etna*, one of the 1879 batch of 'Precursors',as running in the late 1880s and up to withdrawal in December 1892, with a circular smokebox door but with a T-shaped lubricator behind the chimney. The blower valve is now on the right-hand side and no doubt the pipe carrying oil pipes has been fitted on the left.

Plate 206 (below): No. 1147 *John Rennie*, in final condition as running in the early 1890s before withdrawal, fitted with circular smokebox door and with the later type of lubricator behind the chimney. The large pipe beneath the boiler handrail conveys pipes from the sight-feed lubricator in the cab to the front end. All the 'Precursors' were withdrawn in 1892-5 and replaced by their tank engine counterparts, the '5ft. 6in. 2-4-2 Tanks' or '910' class, which were introduced in 1890.

'Precedent'

Plate 207: The 'Precedents' were the 6ft 6in. counterparts of the 'Precursors' and were introduced in December 1874. They had 140lb. boilers and ⅞in. frames. This view shows No. 2187 *Penrith Beacon*, probably soon after completion in April 1875 and in photographic grey paint. The practice of displaying the company's coat of arms on the driving splasher was begun in June 1878, when it was applied to certain 'Precedents' after overhaul. Among them were *Amazon*, *Balmoral*, *Meteor* and *Penrith Beacon*. The first new engines to receive it were the batch of 'Precedents' which began in August 1878 with No. 1173 *The Auditor*, the 1877 batch being the last without. 'Precursors' got the coat of arms as they went through works in 1880. There is also full lining on the boiler bands and along the tender frames.

Plate 208: When first built, the 'Precedents' had no brakes on the engine and hook-type front couplings, like the 'Precursors', but they possibly had Webb's closed safety valves from the outset. This view shows *Precedent* around 1880, with brakes and front screw coupling. The winch on the cab is for the chain brake.

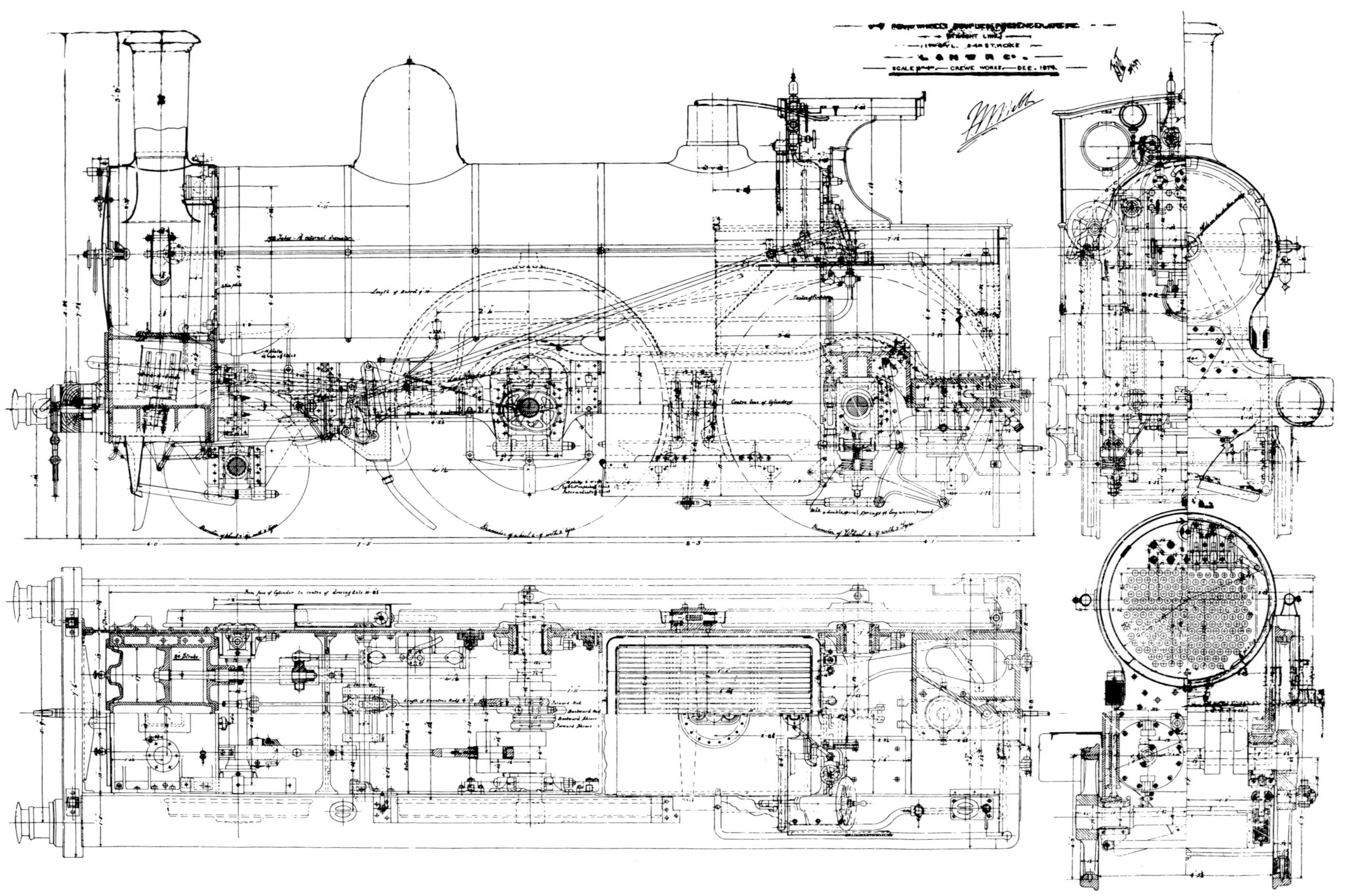

Figure 57: General arrangement drawing of *Precedent*.

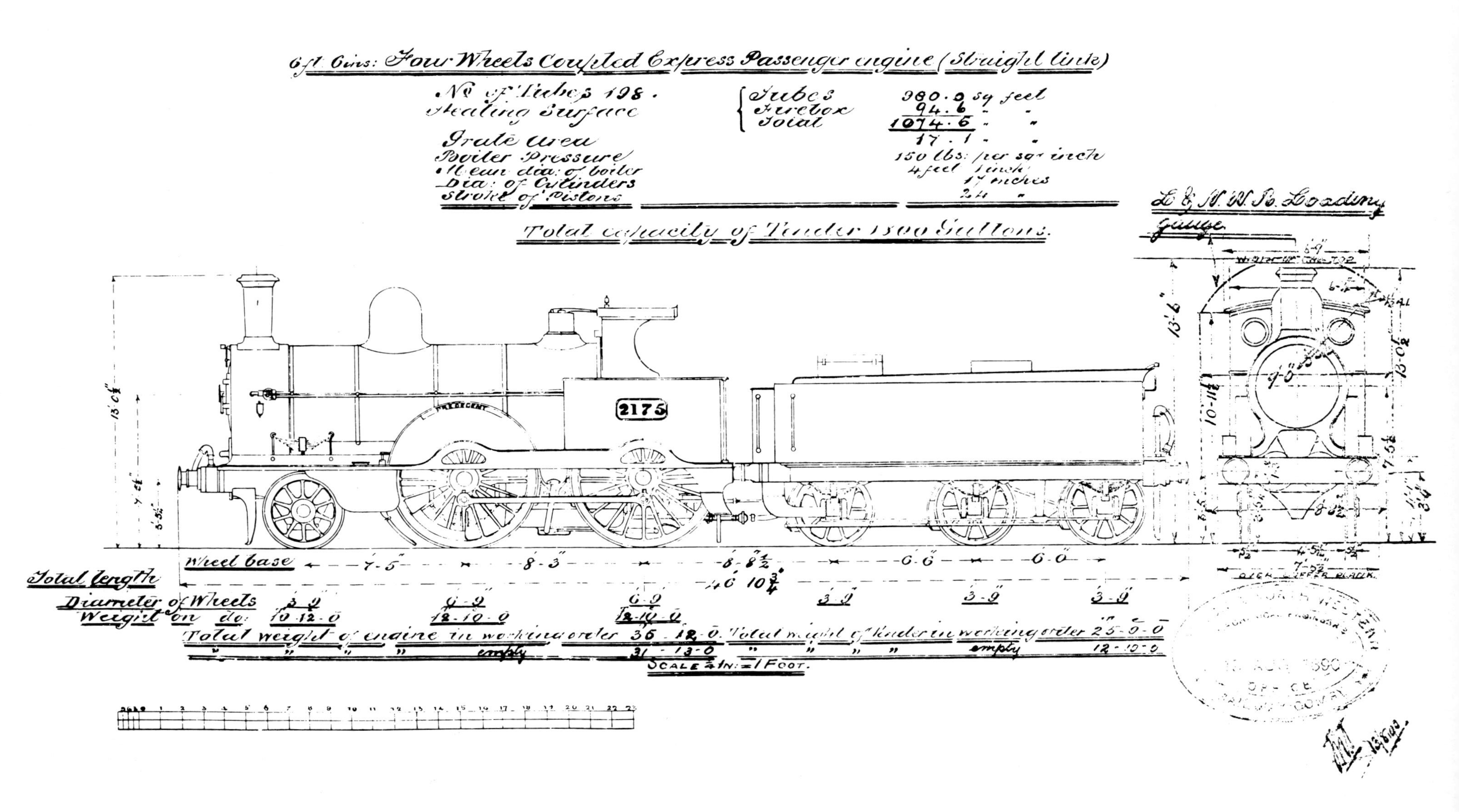

Figure 58: Weight diagram of *Precedent*.

Plate 209: The most famous of the 'Precedents', No. 955 *Charles Dickens*, at Manchester (London Road) about 1885. It is fitted with steam brakes on the engine, a screw coupling at the front as well as the rear and a T-shaped lubricator behind the chimney, but it is not yet vacuum-fitted. The driver is leaning on the winch for the Clarke & Webb chain brake and the stanchion associated with it can be seen on the front of the tender. The 1880 batch of 'Precedents', beginning with No. 619 *Mabel*, were the first LNWR engines to be fitted with steam brakes. *Charles Dickens* was specially rostered to accumulate a large mileage by working a return trip from Manchester to London six days a week.

Plate 210: 'Precedent' class 2-4-0 No. 2186 *Lowther* at Bletchley in the early 1890s, in a view which shows the front-end details well. It is fitted for working vacuum-braked trains and has a tender with oil axleboxes. The nickname 'Jumbos' first came to be applied to the 'Precedents'. None of the class is thought to have ever been fitted with a circular smokebox door or a tender with coal rails; at least, no photograph is known showing such features, but any not replaced by 1896 should have acquired coal rails. In 1893-1901 they were withdrawn and were replaced by new 'Improved Precedents' with 1in. frames and 150lb. boilers, which took the same names and numbers.

'Improved Precedent' or 'Large Jumbo'

Plate 211: Mr Webb next introduced the 'Improved Precedent' or '6ft. 6in. straight link' class. The design was basically the same as that of the original 'Precedents' but the frames were stronger, of 1 in. plate instead of ⅞ in., and the boilers were of 150 lb. pressure instead of 140 lb. They were built continuously in batches from 1887 to 1901 and were officially rebuilds, first of the 'Newton' class (up to 1894) and then of the original 'Precedents' themselves, some parts of the latter perhaps being utilised in the new engines. As these classes were withdrawn, so the names and numbers of withdrawn engines passed to newly built 'Improved Precedents'. In 1889, the 'Whitworth' or '6ft. straight link' class was introduced and in the same sort of way replaced the 'Samsons'. Except for their smaller driving wheels they were identical to the 'Improved Precedents'. The latter then became known as 'Big Jumbos' and the 'Whitworths' as 'Small Jumbos'. In fact, the official description used nominal wheel sizes; with new 3in. tyres the actual diameters were 6ft. 9in. and 6ft. 3in. respectively. Earlier tyres were 2¼in. thick, so the 'Newtons' and original 'Precedents' had 6ft. 7½in. driving wheels. This official view shows 'Improved Precedent' No. 1482 *Herschel*, which replaced a Ramsbottom 'Newton' on completion in October 1889. The most obvious external difference from an original 'Precedent' is the circular smokebox door. Otherwise, in all its basic details, it is similar. The rectangular-section coupling rods would be black in service, here photographic grey. There is a lubricator on the side of the smokebox and the boiler handrail, beneath which is the pipe conveying small oil pipes from the sight-feed lubricator in the cab, operates the blower valve in the smokebox when twisted in the cab. But there is still no front vacuum pipe.

Plate 212: 'Big Jumbo' No. 1673 *Lucknow*, which replaced the 'Newton' of the same name and number in May 1891. Behind the chimney is the later type of lubricator for the regulator in the smokebox. This type replaced the T-shaped fitting shown on *Herschel*. The lubricator on the side of the smokebox has gone, replaced by a supply from the sight-feed lubricator in the cab, and there is now a front vacuum pipe.

Plate 213: Shortly before building the four-cylinder compound *Iron Duke* with a double chimney in 1897, Mr Webb fitted a similar arrangement to a 'Big Jumbo', No. 1532 *Hampden*, presumably to see how the idea worked in practice. It was known that some tubes in a boiler conveyed more of the exhaust gases from the firebox than others. By dividing the smokebox into two halves horizontally across the front tube plate and arranging for each half to exhaust through its own separate chimney, he hoped that the draught on each half would be more equal. Here, *Hampden* is seen at Crewe as first modified, its double chimney having a stovepipe top.

Plate 214: Eventually, *Hampden* was fitted with a double chimney having a top of normal Webb outline, as fitted to *Iron Duke*, and seems to have run with it for some months if not years. How well the device achieved its purpose is not known, but it was not adopted for any other LNWR engine.

Plate 215 (above): The famous *Hardwicke*, photographed at Crewe Works on 29th September 1899. It has tender coal rails, introduced in 1895, and fluted coupling rods, introduced in 1896-7 and kept polished instead of being black. The blower valve is now on the right-hand side and the tops of the boiler, dome and safety valves have been painted for photographic purposes to subdue the shine. This was apparently done on a print from the original negative which was then re-photographed, rather than on the engine itself.

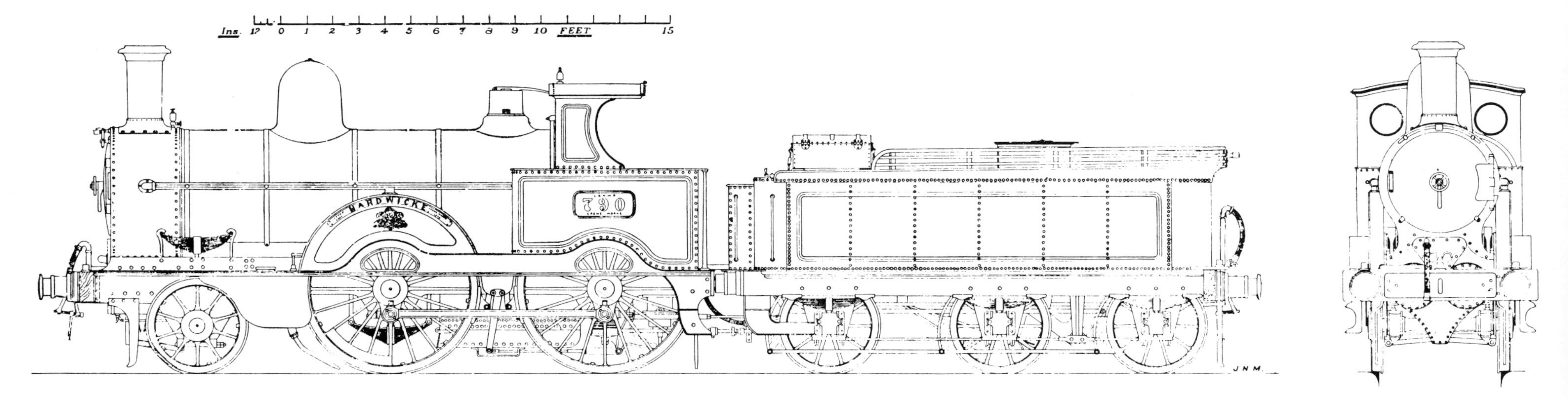

Figure 59: Drawing to 4mm scale of No. 790 *Hardwicke* as running about 1900.

Plate 216: 'Big Jumbo' No. 1531 *Cromwell* at Rugby Shed about 1910. The communication-cord supports have now gone, along with the second whistle, but the carriage-warming relief valve, in the front corner of the cab roof, and the final type of regulator lubricator with handwheel and horizontal T-handle, introduced by Mr Whale, can be clearly seen.

Plate 217: No. 1666 *Ariadne* at Nottingham (London Road, Low Level) on a local train to Northampton about 1920. It has lost its Webb buffers and has acquired Cooke ones in their place.

Plate 218: Eight 'Precedents' were never officially replaced, in that new engines of the '6ft. 6in. straight link' class with new Crewe motion numbers were never built to replace them. It is certain, nevertheless, that they were fitted with new 150lb. boilers during normal overhaul at Crewe and most with new 1in. frames as well. One of these eight was No. 955 *Charles Dickens*, seen here at Crewe Works on 11th August 1902, after completing two million miles. Outwardly, at any rate, it is identical to any other 'Big Jumbo'.

'Whitworth', 'Waterloo' or 'Small Jumbo'

Plate 219: In the same way that the 'Big Jumbos' replaced the 'Newtons' and 'Precedents', so in 1889-96 the 'Small Jumbos' replaced the 'Samsons'. Officially designated the '6ft. straight link' class, they came to be known equally well as the 'Whitworth' or 'Waterloo' class. This arose because although No. 748 *Waterloo* was the first of the class, in the sense of having the lowest Crewe motion number, No. 1045 *Whitworth* was the first into traffic, in September 1889. This is the official photograph of *Waterloo*, taken in October 1889. It has the usual fittings of the day: circular smokebox door, rectangular-section coupling rods, black in service, no tender coal rails and T-shaped lubricator behind the chimney. This view shows clearly how the handrail was fitted above the wide pipe running along the boiler and containing oil pipes from the cab to the front end. The blower valve is now on the right-hand side of the boiler and since it is on the left-hand side in the photograph of *Herschel*, taken in the same month, *Waterloo* was almost certainly the first 'Jumbo' on which it was so re-located.

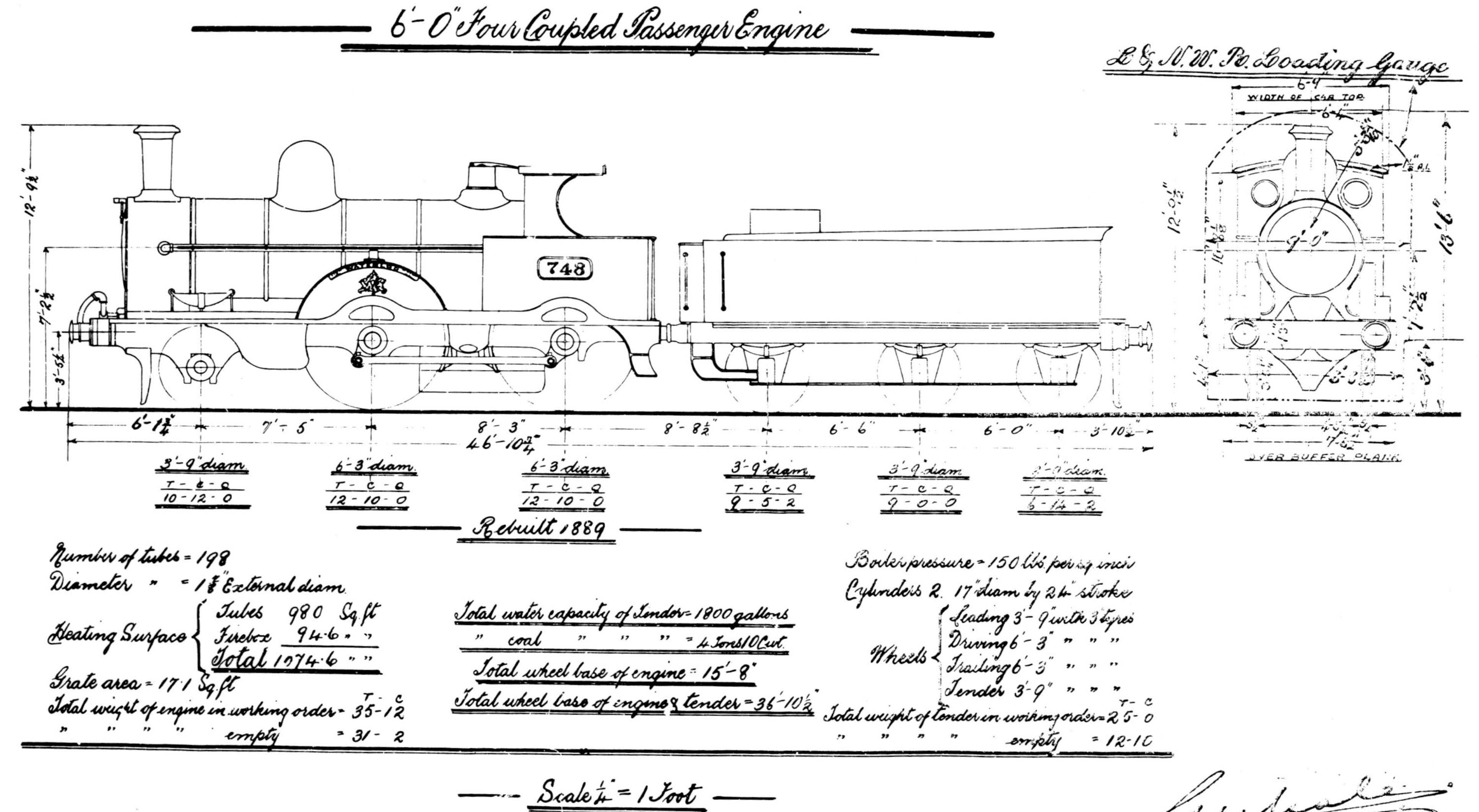

Figure 60: Weight diagram of *Waterloo*

Plate 220: Another early view of a 'Whitworth' or 'Waterloo', this time in service, No. 419 *Zillah*. The date must be very soon after completion in 1890, as there is no front vacuum-pipe and the stanchion for the chain brake is still fitted on the tender (visible between the two enginemen). These engines could be distinguished from the 'Improved Precedents' not only by their smaller driving wheels but also by the frames which were less deep above the running plate.

Plate 221: A very fine close up view of 'Whitworth' No. 901 *Hero* at Rugby in 1910.

Plate 222 (left): No. 1045 *Whitworth*, with fluted coupling rods, tender coal rails, later type of lubricator behind the chimney and centre lamp socket on the bufferbeam, a feature introduced in 1903.

Plate 223 (right): Like the 'Samsons', some of the 'Small Jumbos' were transferred to the Engineering Department. No. 2156 *Sphinx* became *Engineer Manchester* in 1914 and as such is seen here, fitted with a tender cab. The second whistle, used in connection with the communication cord, has been removed from the cab roof but the carriage-warming reducing valve, on the right-hand front corner of the roof, is retained. A windshield is fitted to the sand-pipe.

Plate 224 (left): No. 2158 *Sister Dora* at Camden on 25th June 1922. It has clearly been putting in some hard work on the main line, as the smokebox door is badly burned. Cooke buffers have replaced the original Webb ones.

Plate 225: Cab view of No. 2157 *Unicorn* at Chester on 8th July 1921. It is allocated to shed 15W, Whitchurch. In front of the reverser, on top of the left-hand splasher, is the driver's seat, a home-made model. Beneath it is the filler lid for the rear sandbox. Parallel to the splasher, out of sight near the floor, is the rod controlling the cylinder drain cocks. Beyond the reverser, in the left-hand corner, is the sight-feed lubricator, supplying oil through pipes carried in a large pipe on the left of the boiler to the valves and cylinders at the front end. The bracket on the cab side-sheet, with some papers behind it, is for a lamp, to enable the driver to see the lubricator at night. Immediately behind the reverser is the lever controlling the sanders; this is duplicated on the fireman's side. The reverser could be held in a set position by means of the chain, another home-made device, hanging by it. The chain is suspended from the horizontal handwheel used to blow steam back through the injector to clear dirt or foreign matter blocking the water feed. To set the injector, situated below the footplate, the vertical lever above the regulator was pulled to supply steam, and the water-valve on the tender opened. The lever low down on the same column as the horizontal wheel was then adjusted until the injector began to 'sing'. Water was then delivered to the boiler by the large pipe to the right, the clack valve being situated behind the vertical handwheel, which could be used to close the valve if it stuck open. The Webb injector was thus an excellent design, having features enabling the crew to overcome common problems in service. The other injector, on the fireman's side, is basically the same except that the slaking pipe, controlled by a plunger, comes off the delivery pipe, and the steam control on the manifold is horizontal. The wheel in the centre of the manifold controls steam for carriage heating, delivered to the train by the lagged pipe on the right. The wheel to the right of the manifold controls steam to the vacuum ejector, or 'torpedo', on the right — a cloth wound round the equilibrium valve on the top gave a little more brake power for steep banks or emergencies. All these handwheels were operated by the wheel spanner hanging below the two gauges showing boiler pressure and carriage heating pressure, on the right-hand cab side-sheet. The two prongs on the lower end fitted over the spokes of these wheels, while the other end fitted between the spokes of the smokebox-door wheel. Below the spanner, just beyond the torpedo, is the horizontal handle which worked the blower by twisting the boiler handrail. On the left of the cab is the brake gauge. Just below it, to the right, is the valve controlling the vacuum brakes on the train. In the centre of the valve is a spindle, which is linked to its left by a horizontal rod to the engine steam brakes, so that when the brake handle below the valve was moved to the right, both brakes were applied simultaneously. To re-create the vacuum and release the brakes, the handle was moved to the left. Once the train was moving at about 15m.p.h., the handle was moved slightly to the right into the 'running position', shutting off steam to the ejector and leaving the vacuum pump to maintain vacuum. If the driver wanted to release the train brakes but keep the engine brakes on, he held the spindle in the centre of the valve out by means of some sort of wedge or perhaps a knotted cloth; when he released the spindle, the brakes came off the engine also. This was a very useful facility, especially in conjunction with the fine control provided by the Ramsbottom regulator on Whale and Bowen Cooke engines, enabling them to re-start heavy trains on banks in impressive fashion. The regulator in this case, of course, is the Webb type; to the left of it is the lubricator cup supplying it with oil. To the right is the single water gauge, fitted with plungers to test the level. The level could easily be seen because the diagonal stripes on the enamelled plate behind the tube appeared to be reversed when seen through water. The firehole door is operated by the ratchet handle on the left and swings into the firebox, forming a baffle plate. Above it is the coffee plate, on which is the holder for the oil lamp to light the water gauge at night. Though a Webb engine, this may be regarded as a typical LNWR cab, since Whale and Cooke engines were closely similar.

Summary of the Ramsbottom and Webb 2-4-0s

The history of the various Ramsbottom and Webb 2-4-0 classes often confuses students of LNWR locomotives. Even knowledgeable modern writers sometimes make errors in identifying classes and seem to hope that they are on safe ground, so long as they describe any 2-4-0 as a 'Precedent'. Unfortunately, the subject cannot be simplified quite so much as that but basically it is straightforward enough so long as two underlying complications are understood.

Firstly, certain classes are superficially very similar if not identical to one another. This applies particularly to some earlier classes which were altered in appearance when fitted with Webb boilers and so look the same as engines built by Webb himself. The only reliable means, then, of identifying the class of a particular engine is to refer to a full locomotive list.

Secondly, the Crewe accounting concept of renewal is often misunderstood. When an engine was renewed, it was not partially or even thoroughly rebuilt but scrapped and replaced by a new engine. Even though the new engine sometimes took the name and number of the engine it replaced, its status as a new engine was officially recognised by the allocation of a new Crewe motion number. This is particularly relevant in the case of the 'Precedents', which were renewed by being scrapped and replaced by engines which looked identical to them but had 150lb. instead of 140lb boilers, stronger frames and new cylinders, and so were really much superior, more modern machines.

The history of the 2-4-0s may be summarised in four main stages:

1) The 'Samsons' and 'Newtons' were built by Ramsbottom and were basically small- and large-wheeled variants of the same design. Webb built more of both classes with his own boilers, cabs and other fittings, and also modified Ramsbottom's engines to conform. The simplest way of determining whether one of these engines in Webb condition was originally a Ramsbottom or a Webb engine is by reference to a full locomotive list.

2) Webb next built two new classes, the 'Precursors' and the 'Precedents'. The 'Precursors' had small driving wheels, which identify them immediately, and were eventually scrapped. The 'Precedents' had large driving wheels and were Webb's front-line non-compound express engines. In 1882 the nickname 'Jumbo' was applied by the men to the last ten then being built (this was in reaction to the public outcry caused by the separation of two famous elephants at London Zoo, Jumbo and Alice, when Jumbo was sold to the American showman, P. T. Barnum); the name soon came to be applied to the class as a whole and later to their replacements.

3) Webb then built the 'Improved Precedents', which were outwardly identical to the original 'Precedents' but had 150lb. boilers instead of 140lb., stronger frames of 1in. plate instead of ⅞in. and new cylinders. 'Improved Precedents' were built first to replace the 'Newtons', which were scrapped, and then to replace the original 'Precedents' themselves, which were also scrapped. Eight of the latter were never renewed in this way, but except for No. 2191 *Snowdon*, which is known to have retained its original ⅞in. frames, they all received the new components at major overhauls, in most cases before the 1893-1901 official renewal of the class took place. The 'Improved Precedents' were nicknamed 'Big Jumbos', perhaps because they were more powerful than the 'Precedents' but also to distinguish them from the smaller-wheeled 'Whitworths', which were known as 'Small Jumbos'.

The 'Improved Precedents' can be distinguished easily from the 'Newtons' in Webb condition, because the latter are clearly smaller and older engines, but to distinguish them from the 'Precedents' is more problematical. The 'Improved Precedents' always had circular smokebox doors and the 'Precedents' originally all had the horizontal type, but some 'Precedents' acquired circular doors before renewal, in which case there is no means of distinguishing between the two classes in a photograph taken about 1890, unless the photograph can be dated precisely and a locomotive list referred to. Later, when such features as fluted coupling rods, which were never fitted to 'Precedents', and tender coal rails enable a photograph to be dated more accurately, reference to a list generally eliminates any doubt.

4) In the same way as the 'Newtons' were replaced by the 'Improved Precedents' so Webb next replaced their small-wheeled counterparts, the 'Samsons', with a small-wheeled version of the 'Improved Precedents', called the 'Whitworths'. They can be distinguished from the 'Improved Precedents' by their smaller driving wheels, which gave them the nickname 'Small Jumbos', and by their frames, which are less deep above the running plate. In fact, except for the modifications needed to lower the whole design by 3in. to suit the smaller driving wheels, they are identical. Nowadays, these alterations would be too costly and only one design would be built, but clearly relative costs were different then and Mr Webb thought the advantages of having both designs in service were worthwhile.

The following table summarises the history of the 2-4-0s:

Common Name	*Official Name*	*Enthusiast Name*	*Nickname*	*Number built*	*Date*	*Notes*
'Samson'	'6ft. Curved Link'	Ramsbottom 'Samson'		50	1863-9	Eighty scrapped 1889-96; ten transferred to Engineer's Department. Replaced by ninety 'Whitworths' with
		Webb 'Samson' or 'Prospero'		40	1873-9	same names and numbers.
'Newton'	'6ft. 6in. Curved	Ramsbottom 'Newton'		76	1866-71	Scrapped 1887-94. Replaced by 96 'Improved
	Link'	Webb 'Newton'		20	1872-3	Precedents' with the same names and numbers.
'Precursor'	'5ft. 6in. Straight Link'			40	1874-9	Scrapped 1892-5. Replaced by '5ft. 6in. 2-4-2 Tanks'.
'Precedent'	'6ft. 6in. Straight Link'		'Jumbo'	70	1874-82	Replaced by 'Improved Precedents'.
'Improved Precedent'	'6ft. 6in. Straight Link'		'Big Jumbo'	166	1887-1901	Replaced 'Newtons' and 'Precedents', taking their names and numbers.
'Whitworth' or 'Waterloo'	'6ft. Straight Link'		'Small Jumbo'	90	1889-96	Replaced 'Samsons', taking their names and numbers.

Chapter 7
Four-Coupled Passenger Tank Engines

'Metropolitan Tank'
Plate 226: In 1871 sixteen 4-4-0 tank engines were ordered from Beyer Peacock to that company's standard 'Metropolitan Tank' design. It was the only occasion in LNWR history that engines of a non-LNWR design were ordered from an outside manufacturer, except for the early days of the Southern Division. They were fitted with condensing apparatus and were intended to work suburban services in the London area, on the North London line from Willesden and on the 'Outer Circle' from Broad Street via Willesden and Earl's Court to Mansion House. This view shows No. 2057 of the first batch in original condition. It has a Beyer Peacock chimney, which is fitted with a bracket to hold a route indicator, and there are brackets on the front bufferbeam for destination boards. Screw couplings are fitted front and rear. The vertical pipe from the tank side above the numberplate is a breather pipe for the tank.

Plate 227: 'Metropolitan Tank' No. 1964, photographed while numbered in the 1800 series duplicate list between March 1886 and July 1890. Externally at least it is still in much the same condition as when originally built, except that it is vacuum-fitted and has a Webb chimney. The dome is polished brass and the coupling rods are black, though the connecting rods are polished.

Plate 228: No. 1964 was renumbered 3090 in July 1890 and scrapped in November 1892. It is in the same condition as in the previous pictures but this view shows front-end detail more clearly, particularly the linkage across the smokebox controlling the valves for condensing operation, and the lever attached to it and linked to the cab by a pull rod.

Plate 229: The 'Metropolitan Tanks' were displaced from the Mansion House trains by the condensing fitted '4ft. 6in. 2-4-2 Tanks', the so-called 'Mansion House Tanks'. One had already been converted to a three-cylinder compound 4-2-2-0 tank and now five were scrapped in 1892-3. The remaining ten, however, were quite extensively rebuilt by Mr Webb as non-condensing 4-4-2 tanks, receiving new steel boilers with typical Webb fittings, new cylinder castings, new bogies in place of the original Bissell trucks and quite sizeable bunkers. Many of the rebuilds, if not all, worked on suburban trains in the Manchester area. This is the official photograph of No. 3092, taken on 23rd February 1891 after conversion to a 4-4-2 tank. It has a circular smokebox door and destination-board brackets on the front bufferbeam (and presumably on the back of the bunker). The tank filler can be seen in the centre of the rear of the bunker.

Figure 61: Weight diagram of a converted 'Metropolitan Tank'.

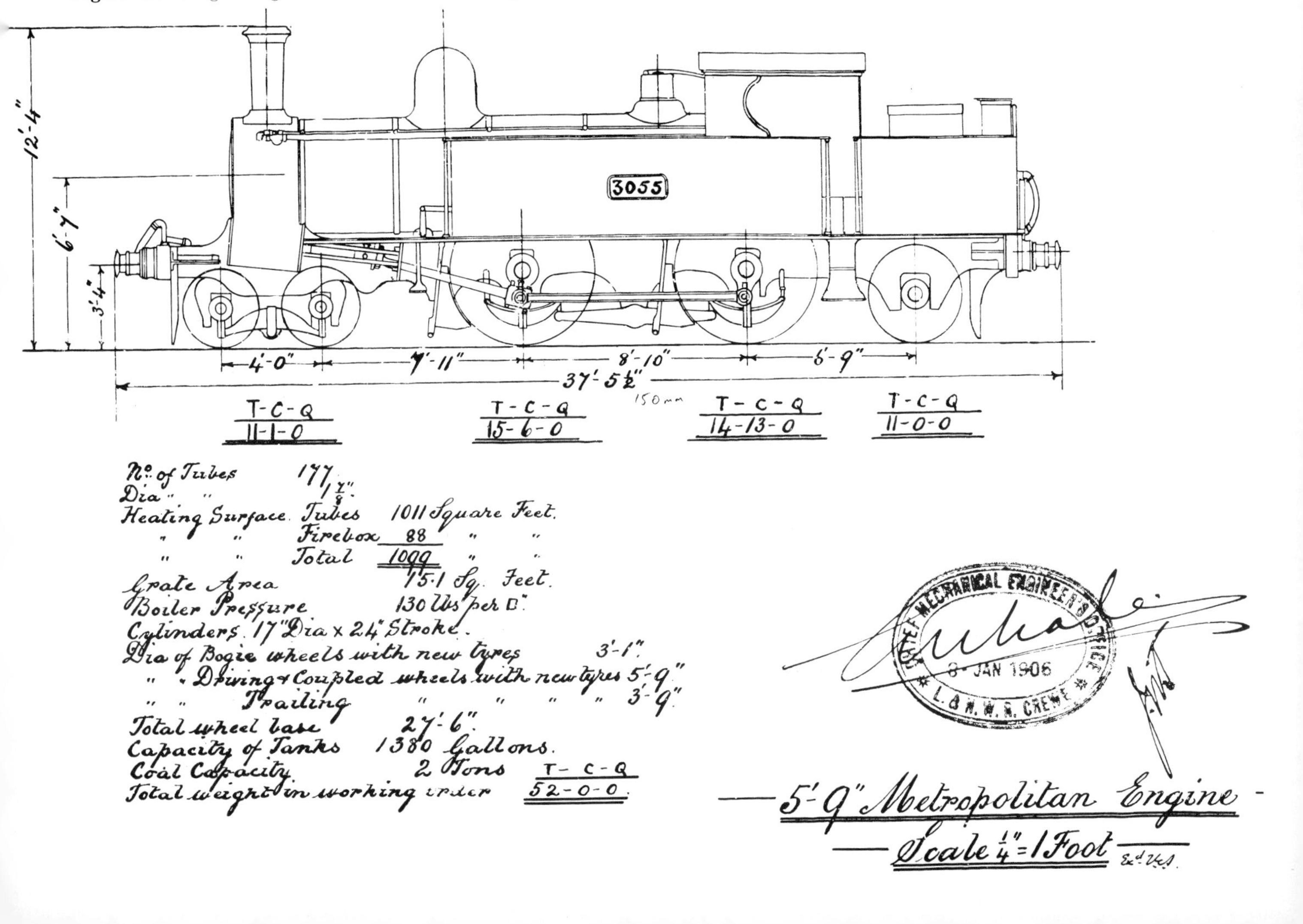

Plate 230 (left): No. 3036 in the 1890s, soon after rebuilding. It still has black rectangular-section coupling rods.

Plate 231 (left): No. 3072 at Stockport, on 16th August 1902. It now has fluted coupling rods, and the chimney cap and cylinder ends have been scoured bright with bath brick and oil.

Plate 232 (below): No. 3044 at Stockport in 1898 with a goods train. It is fitted with fluted rods and a crosshead vacuum pump. All the 4-4-2 tanks were withdrawn in 1907-11.

'4ft. 6in. 2-4-0 Tank'

Plate 233: In 1876 Mr Webb introduced the '4ft. 6in. 2-4-0 Tank' engines and fifty of the class were built in 1876-80. They were intended for local passenger work and operated in the Manchester and Birmingham areas, and on the Broad Street — Mansion House service. The first to be built was given Crewe motion number 2000, out of correct sequence, and is seen here so numbered (its true running number was 2233) and with the following legend painted alongside near the numberplate: 'The two thousandth engine built at Crewe Works, May 24, 1876'. That was the date of both Queen Victoria's birthday and Empire Day, so possibly the Crewe numbers were juggled to enable the first of the new class to be both the 2,000th engine and to be completed on that day. As seen here, in original condition, these engines had condensing apparatus, cabs as fitted to tender engines (half cabs), wooden brake blocks and bufferbeams, rectangular-section coupling rods, horizontal smokebox doors, 3ft. 6in. chimneys and Webb closed safety valves. They were also the first engines to be fitted with Webb's radial axle. The lever at the side of the smokebox controlled the valve which directed exhaust steam through the large pipe to the condenser in the tank, and was operated by means of the boiler handrail. There are both front and rear sand-pipes.

Plate 234: No. 2251 in original condition. A toolbox on top of the tank was a common sight with this class; there was no room for it anywhere else!

Plate 235 (left): An early view of No. 2234, probably taken in the mid-1880s, with route-indicator boards front and rear and destination boards on the front bufferbeam. The chimney also has brackets for route-indicator boards. A rear spectacle plate and overall roof have been added to make a more complete cab, and the engine is now fitted for working vacuum-braked trains.

Plate 236 (right): In 1879, to give greater coal and water capacity, the '4ft. 6in. 2-4-2 Tanks' were introduced and found to be more widely useful. Consequently, in the late 1890s, forty of the 2-4-0 tanks were scrapped and the parts used with new 1in. plate frames to make 2-4-2 tanks, while ten continued as 2-4-0 tanks for use on the Cromford & High Peak section. One of the latter was No. 2238, seen here at Buxton about 1915. It has lost its condensing apparatus and has a full cab, circular smokebox door and coal rails on the bunker. It still retains wooden brake blocks and rectangular-section coupling rods.

Plate 237 (left): In 1908 five of th engines built new as 2-4-2 tanks wer converted to 2-4-0 tanks for workin motor trains. One of them was No. 1001 seen here at Llandudno about 1915. Th sandbox filler lid is just visible inside th front of the tank side-sheet.

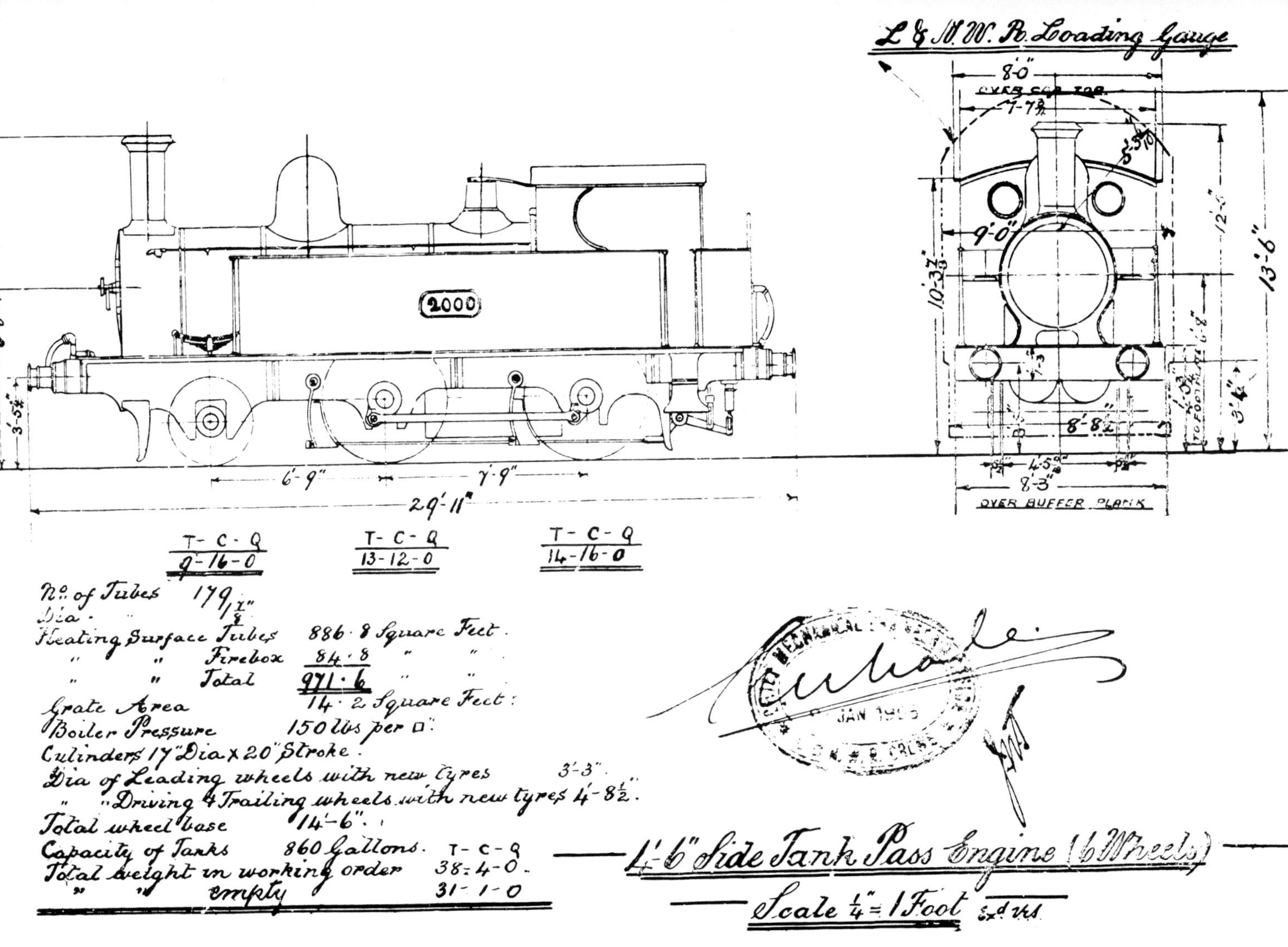

Figure 62: Weight diagram of a '4ft 6in. 2-4-0 Tank'.

'4ft. 6in. 2-4-2 Tank'

Plate 238: The '4ft. 6in. 2-4-2 Tanks' were designed by Mr Webb to give greater coal and water capacity than the 2-4-0 tanks and had a radial axle at either end. With new steel tyres, the actual driving-wheel diameter was 4ft. 8½in. Eventually, there were 220 of them, 180 built new in 1879-90 and forty built as replacements of 2-4-0 tanks in 1895-8. No. 798, seen here at Manchester (London Road) with driver Marcus Weaste of Buxton Shed on the left, was built in March 1882. It has condensing apparatus, horizontal smokebox door, wooden bufferbeams and brake blocks, rectangular-section coupling rods and no coal rails. The rear cab windows are opened upwards and inwards, and made fast by a clip under the cab roof.

Plate 239: The official photograph of 'Mansion House' 2-4-2 tank No. 2524, as built in January 1890. It was soon renumbered 729, being charged to revenue account instead of capital account as originally intended. By comparison with No. 798, it has a circular smokebox door, ventilators in the cab roof and a tall exhaust or breather pipe over the water filler at the back of the bunker. There was no condenser as such. The handrail operated a valve directing exhaust steam into the top of the side tanks above the water level; the pipes under the cab roof conveyed it to the bunker tank (which was U-shaped, round the coal space) and any still not condensed exhausted through the breather pipe. Destination-board brackets would be fitted later at front and rear, and the chimney cap may well have been burnished in service. Coal rails on the bunker and metal brake blocks began to be fitted after the turn of the century. The name 'Mansion House' tanks was applied to the batch of 2-4-2 tanks which were fitted with condensing apparatus specially for working on the Mansion House services.

Plate 240: No. 2498 at Birmingham (New Street) about 1900. A centre lamp socket would have been fitted to the left of the vacuum pipe in 1903, and coal rails sometime in the 1900s. A bucket has been hung from the shed plate bracket on the rear of the cab roof!

Plate 241: One of the conversions from a 2-4-0 tank, No. 1176, as running in the 1900s. It has coal rails but retains wooden brake blocks; the condensing apparatus has been removed. The sandbox and its filler lid are visible behind the front of the tank side-sheet and on top is a small box, possibly a toolbox but perhaps containing the driver's food. Route indicator brackets are fitted to the chimney and destination-board brackets are fitted just to the rear of the bufferbeam. The space between the frames in front of the valve chests was not covered with footplating but was left open in most Webb engines. The pipe to the left of the vacuum pipe is for carriage heating.

Plate 242: No. 786 at Willesden on 21st August 1920. It has condensing gear, destination-board brackets, carriage-heating apparatus, metal brake blocks and coal rails right up to the cab, with toolboxes inside them and covered with coal. In addition, it is fitted with rodding for motor-train working (the T-shaped bracket above the bufferbeam and girder in front of the guard iron), and conventional lamp irons have replaced the LNWR socket type.

Plate 243: No. 1446 at Willesden about 1920. It is in much the same condition as No. 786 except that it has no condensing gear. The doors in the rear of the cab giving access to the toolboxes can be clearly seen, as can the reservoir under the bunker, an indication that the engine itself has vacuum brakes. The motor-fitted engines, and a few others, had their brakes changed from steam to vacuum from about 1913 onwards and had the reservoir added to speed up the release of the brake. Lamp irons were fitted to take the tail lamp when running with the engine pushing, so that only two lamps need be carried, one head and one tail, both fitting over the irons. Coupling rods are still rectangular-section, though fluted rods were introduced on other classes in 1896-7.

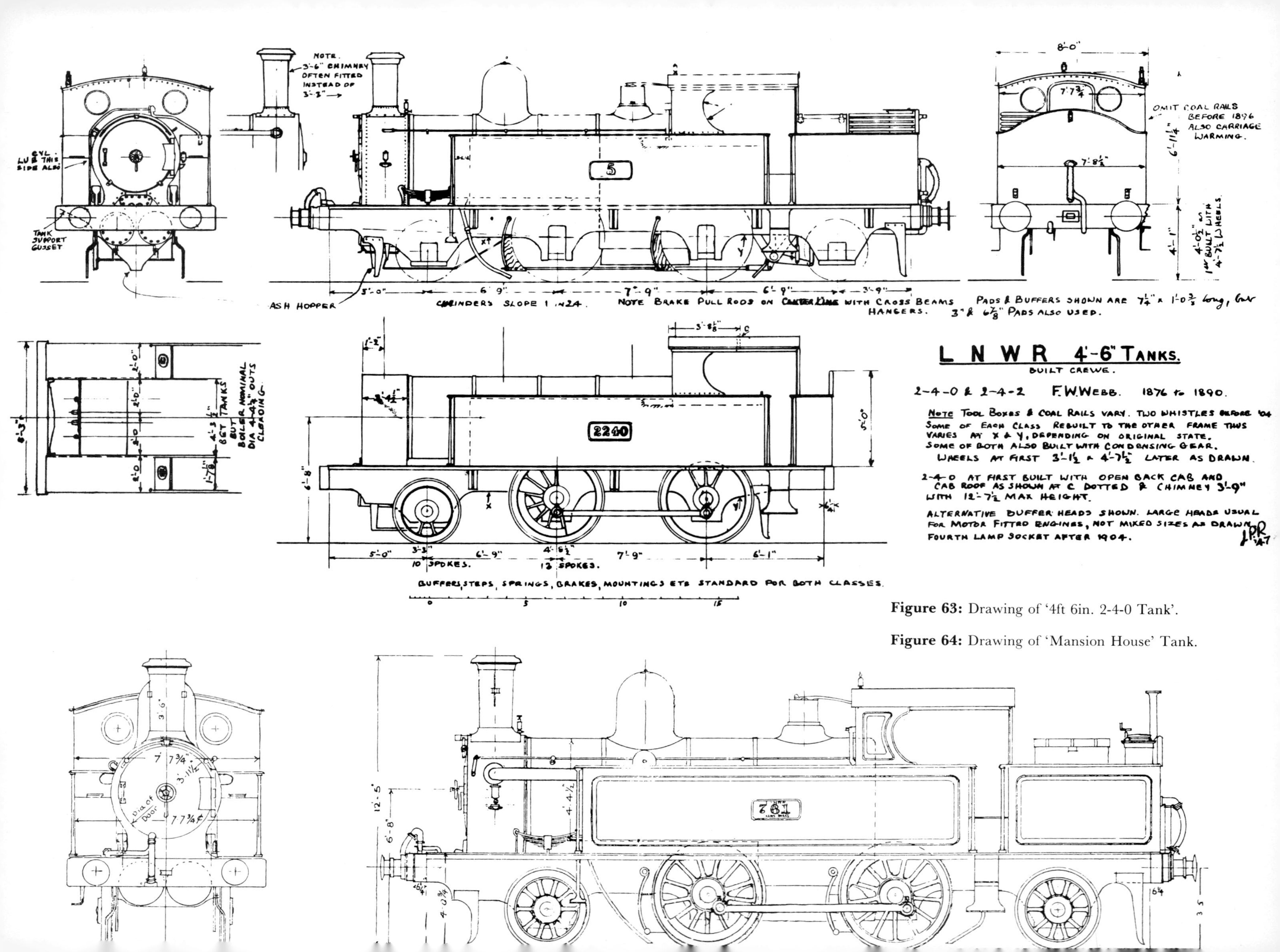

Figure 63: Drawing of '4ft 6in. 2-4-0 Tank'.

Figure 64: Drawing of 'Mansion House' Tank.

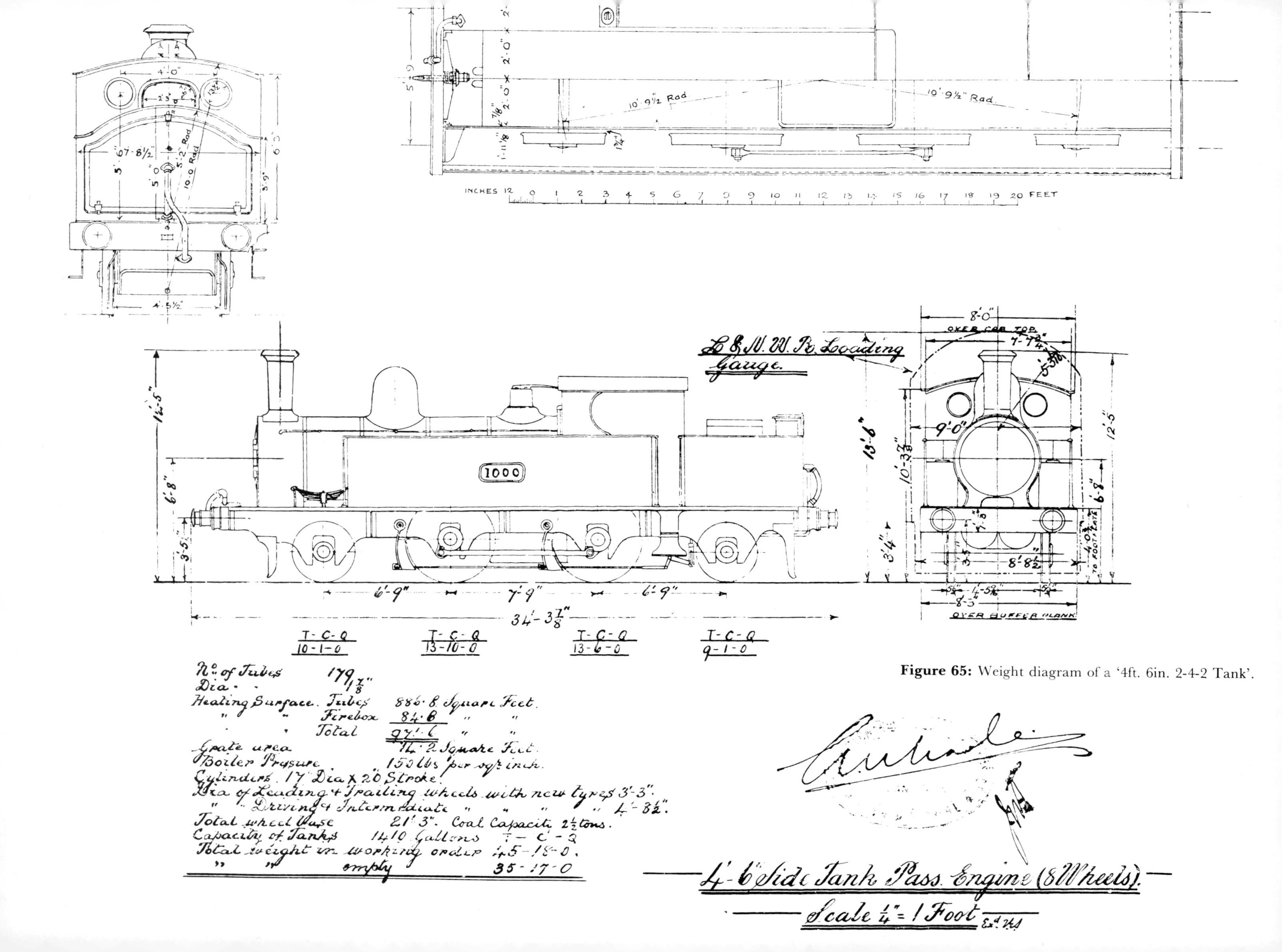

Figure 65: Weight diagram of a '4ft. 6in. 2-4-2 Tank'.

'5ft. 6in. 2-4-2 Tank'

Plate 244: The '5ft. 6in. 2-4-2 Tanks' or '910' class were designed to replace the 'Samson' 2-4-0s on local and branch line passenger work. They were the tank engine counterparts of the 'Precursor' class 2-4-0s and 160 were built in 1890-7, including forty nominal conversions from 'Precursors'. This official photograph shows the first of the class on completion in September 1890. It never ran as No. 1384 but went into traffic as No. 910 in October 1890. It has steel bufferbeams, metal brake blocks, circular smokebox door, rectangular-section coupling rods and no coal rails. The boiler handrail operates the blower valve while above it is the pipe conveying oil pipes from the sight-feed lubricator in the cab to the valves and cylinders. The sandbox is under the running plate in the same style as the 'Jumbos', the filler lid being visible just above the footstep. Behind the chimney is the lubricator for the regulator in the smokebox.

Plate 245: '5ft. 6in. 2-4-2 Tank' No. 427 at Buxton, probably in the 1890s. It was built in February 1894 and is still quite new in this photograph, having rectangular-section coupling rods.

Plate 251 (right): No. 341 at Birmingham (New Street) about 1920.

Plate 252 (left): A view of No. 1754, taken in early LMS days, probably at Rugby. Except for having lost its lined black livery, it is still in much the same condition as in the 1900s. Long-tapered buffers are fitted at the front, but the rear ones are hard to determine. Stowed on the tank top are fire-irons, a bucket and a lamp.

Plate 253 (below): No. 2263 at Peterborough on 30th September 1926, in plain black livery. It has long-tapered buffers and clips on the spring hangers but still retains LNWR lamp sockets.

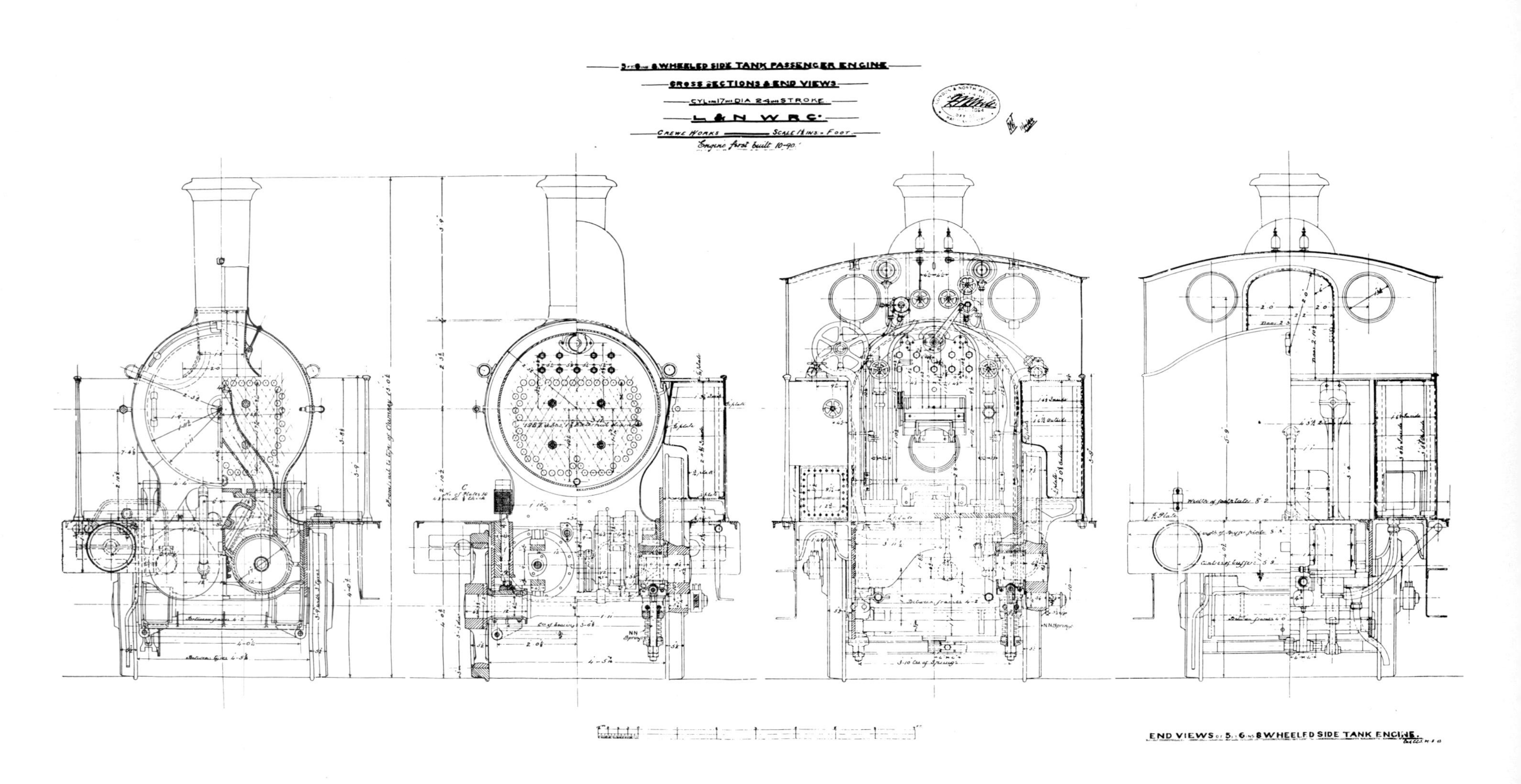

Figure 66: Cross-sectional drawings of a '5ft. 6in. 2-4-2 Tank'.

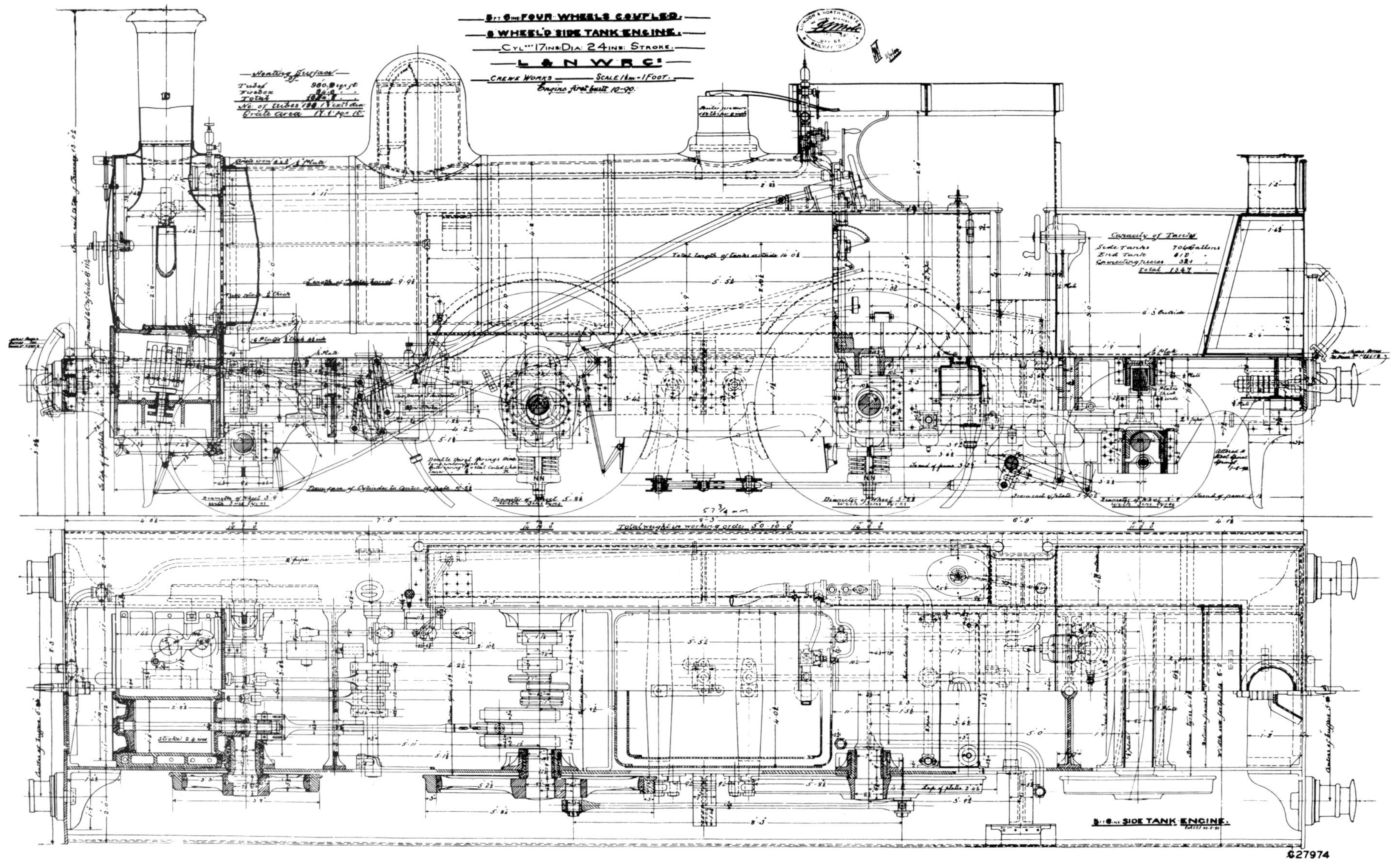

Figure 67: General arrangement drawings of a '5ft. 6in. 2-4-2 Tank'.

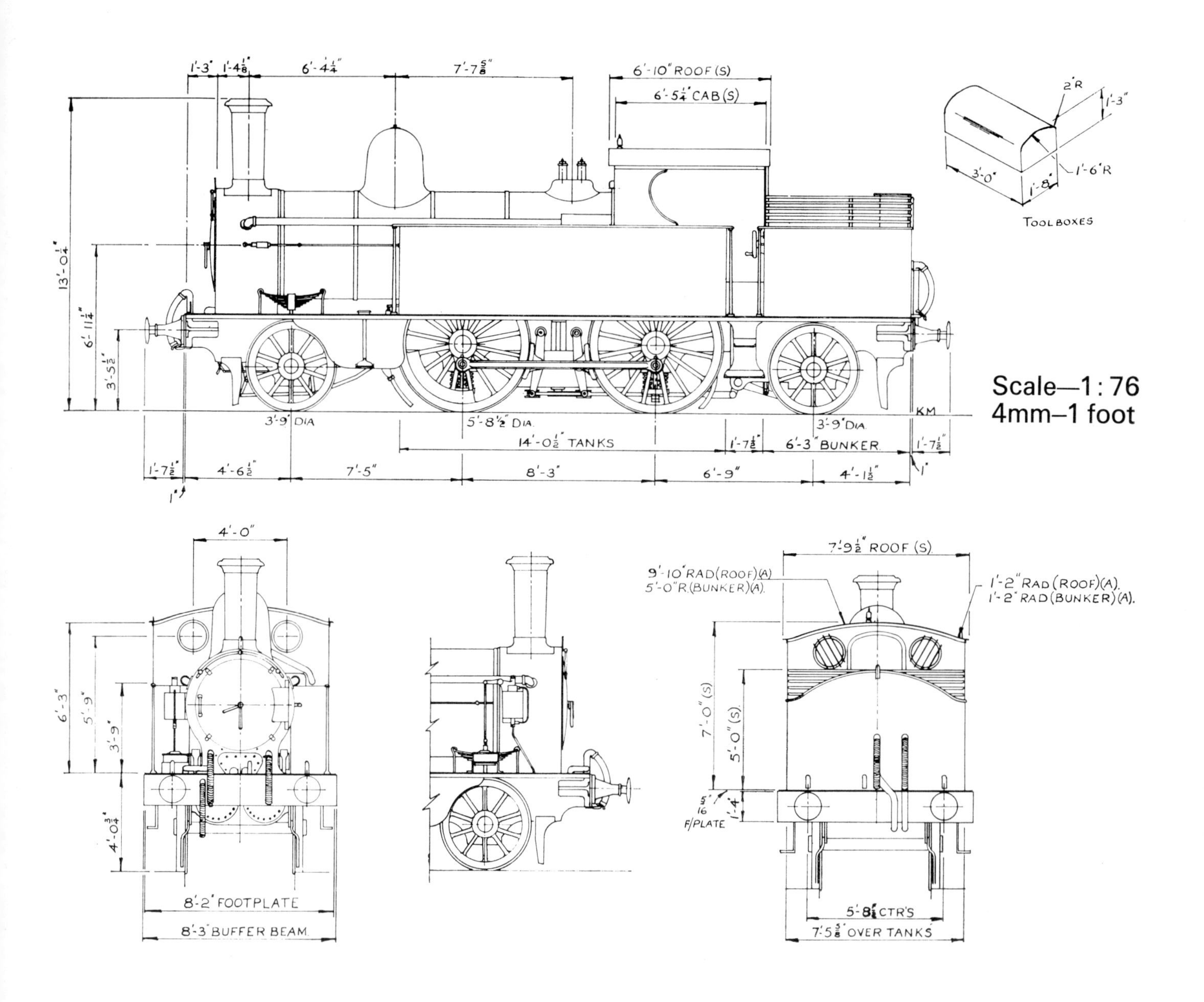

Figure 68: Drawing of a '5ft. 6in. 2-4-2 Tank' in LMS days, fitted for motor-train working and with pop safety valves and lamp irons.

Chapter 8
Three-Cylinder Compound Tender Engines (except Eight-Coupled)

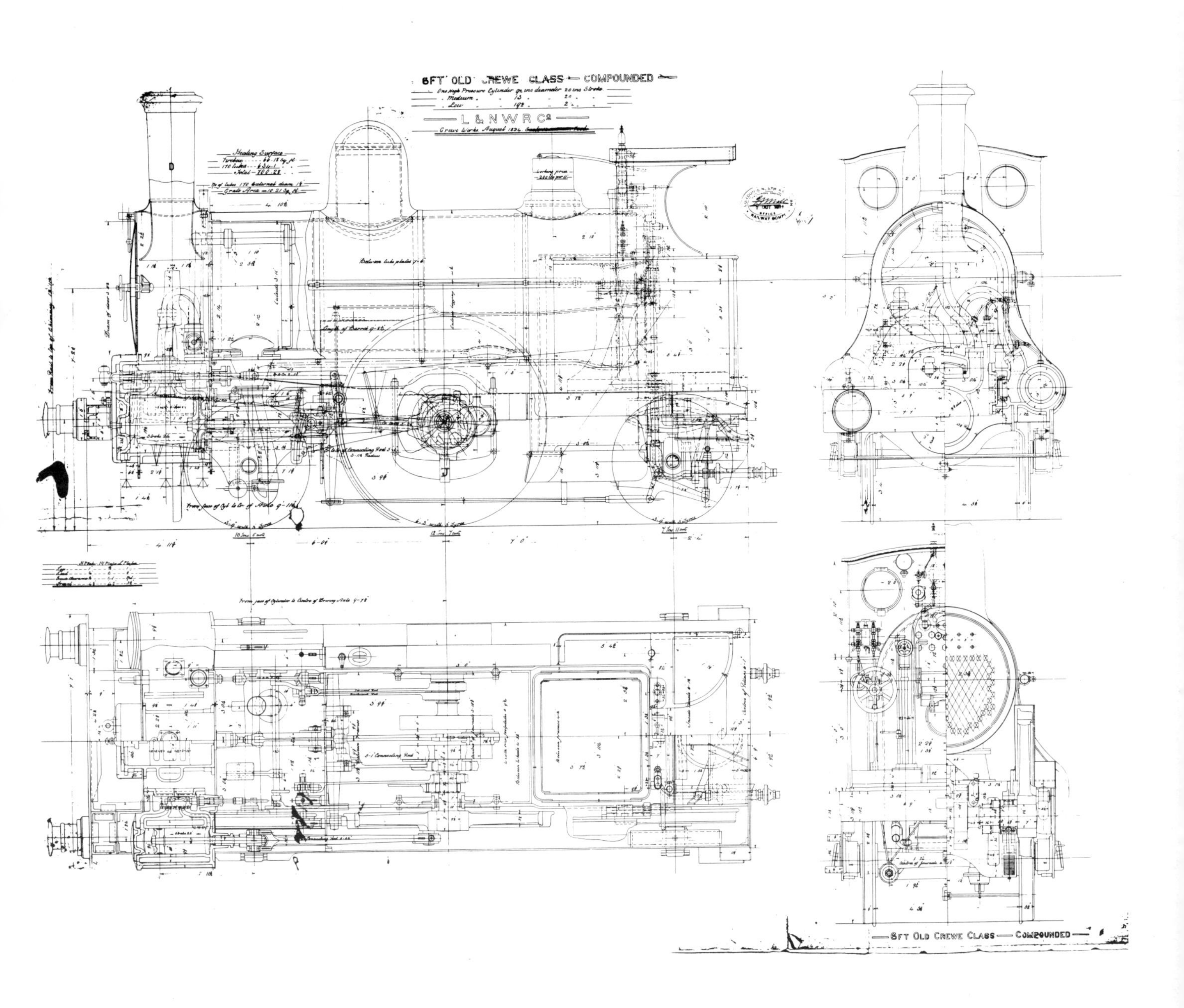

Medusa / Triplex
Figure 69: Mr Webb's first experiment at compounding took place in August 1878 when he converted Trevithick 2-2-2 No. 1874, previously No. 54 *Medusa*, into a two-cylinder compound, with 9in. and 15½in. by 20in. cylinders and a 140 lb p.s.i. boiler. It was the first compound engine in England. In August 1895, then renumbered 3088, it was again converted, to a triple expansion engine and named *Triplex*. This is the general arrangement drawing of *Triplex*.

'Experiment'
Plate 254: The first of the 'Experiment' class three-cylinder compounds was No. 66 *Experiment*, which was completed in January 1882 and used for trials before four more were built in February-March 1883. It is seen here in photographic grey. The outside high-pressure cylinders had Joy valve gear with the valves beneath the cylinders, while the inside low-pressure cylinder had the same gear with the valve above. There were separate reversers for outside and inside cylinders; the reversing rod for the outside cylinder can be seen extending from beneath the round block suspended from the slide bar, and containing the curved slide, to behind the cab footsteps, while that for the inside gear is projecting from behind the splasher. The outside valve gear, slide bars and crosshead were later modified in a number of ways, both on subsequent engines and on *Experiment*. The latter differed from the rest in having narrower footplating, so that the curved side of the cylinder projected beyond it. Otherwise, the engine has the standard Webb features of the day, including a horizontal smokebox door and wooden bufferbeam.

Plate 255 (left): *Experiment* in service about 1890. Steam and vacuum brakes were fitted in August 1883 and the engine also has various other modifications introduced later, including a circular smokebox door.

Plate 256 (left): The second of the class was No. 300 *Compound*, seen here in photographic grey on completion. By comparison with *Experiment,* the outside valve gear has been modified, with a return crank driven off the rear big end and with strengthened slide bars, and the footplate has been widened over the outside cylinders, which are hidden beneath carefully shaped covers. The front coupling is the type introduced by Ramsbottom on the rear of tenders in 1860. It has a bob weight at the end of the bar used for tightening the screw. A more convenient arrangement was introduced on *Dreadnought* in 1884. The bob weight was then done away with and the tommy bar was designed to slip from side to side through a hole in the shank of the screw, to facilitate tightening up.

Plate 257 (right): A rear view of No. 520 *Express*, one of the second production batch built in July 1883, in original condition. It even has the curved plate over the outside cylinder, as on *Compound*. All the 1883 batch had the outside valve gear modified with a return crank. The winch for the Clark & Webb chain brake is secured to the cab side-sheet, and the plate for shed 15 (Crewe) is in position on the rear edge of the roof. The tab can be seen, beneath the plate, carrying mirrors to reflect light from the fire on to the gauges at night.

Plate 258 (right): No. 1120 *Apollo*, one of the last batch built in 1884, at Manchester (London Road) in the late 1880s. The horizontal smokebox door has had two additional clips added at the base but still shows signs of burning. Probably, the fierce blast of the compounds, with only two exhaust beats per revolution, was too strong for this type of door, as the circular type was introduced on *Dreadnought* and was soon fitted to all the 'Experiments'. The valve gear has also been modified. There is no return crank on the rear driving wheel and the anchor link is now positioned in a 'hump' in the running plate behind the leading splasher, while all the slide bars are now the same length. A relief valve for the low-pressure steam chest has been fitted behind the chimney, and the outside cylinder has no shapely covering plate. Vacuum brakes are now fitted.

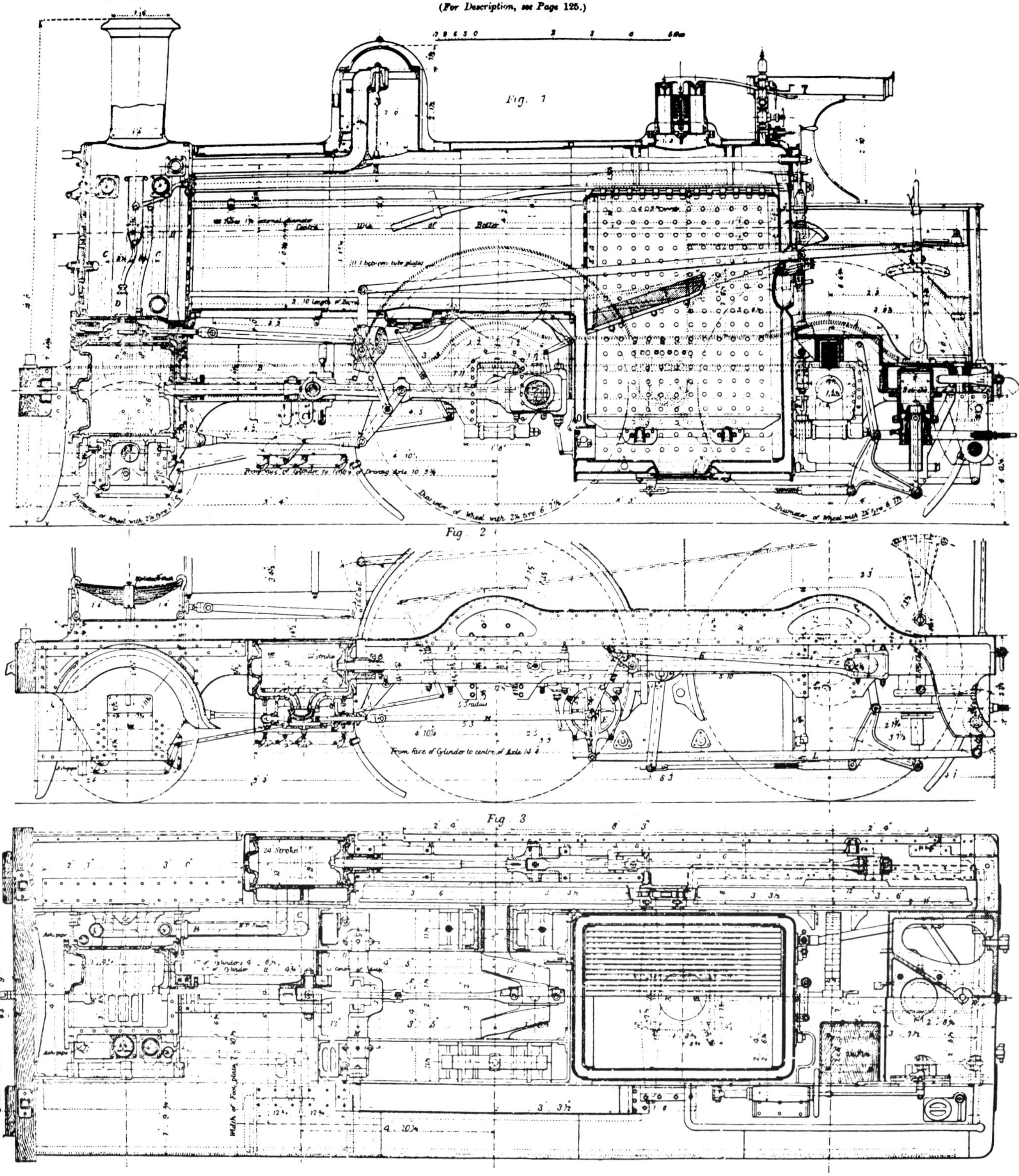

Figure 70 (above & opposite): General arrangement drawings of an 'Experiment' class 2-2-2-0 compound.

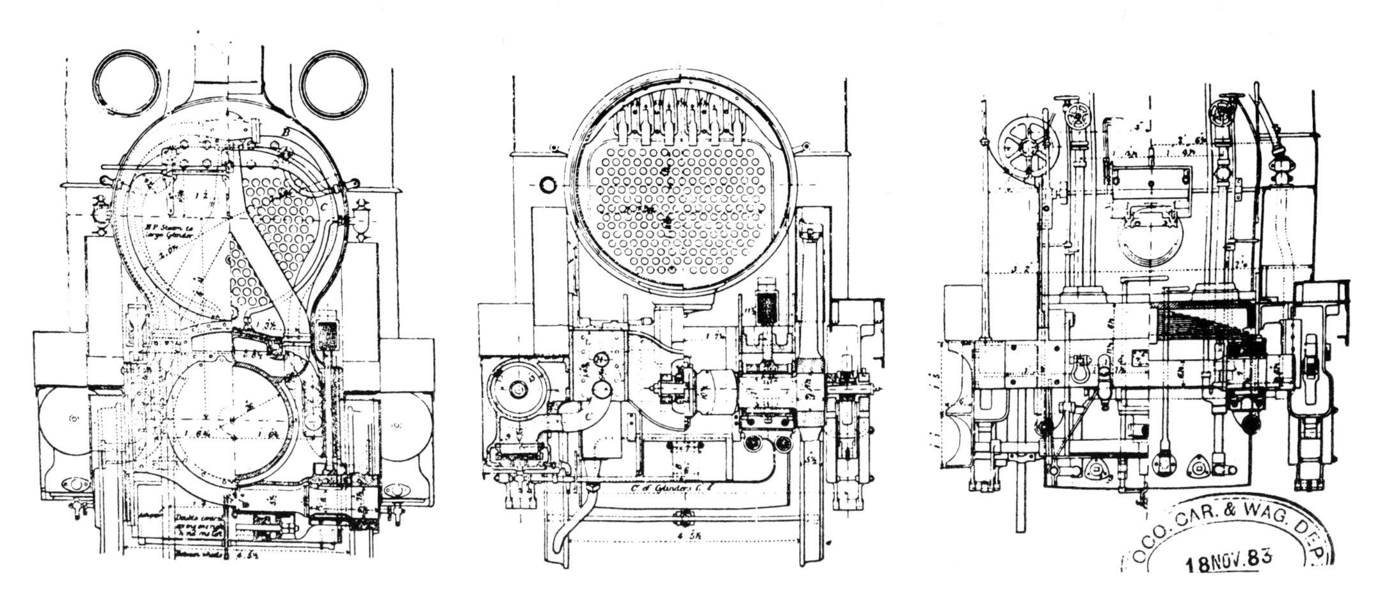

Plate 259: No. 1104 *Sunbeam* at Manchester (London Road) in the late 1880s. An oil box has been fitted on top of the leading splasher, supplying oil to the driving horns and boxes, as introduced on *Dreadnought*. The engine also has a circular smokebox door and is fitted with vacuum brake (the ejector exhaust-pipe is below the boiler handrail) but has no front hose. The handrail on this side operates the blower, while the left-hand boiler handrail operates the 'warming-up valve' which admits live steam to the low-pressure cylinder to warm it up before starting. The nuts and bolts on the end of the inside cylinder are now hidden by a smoothly finished cover, and the width of the block containing the curved guide can be clearly seen beneath the crosshead. Because of this, outside Joy valve gear did not permit the use of coupling rods. There are two whistles, the right-hand one being for connection to the communication cord, while on the front of the tender is an earthenware jar, which probably contains the fireman's drink, perhaps cold tea. These jars were popular with LNWR enginemen because they could be heated up on the 'coffee plate' above the firehole without breaking.

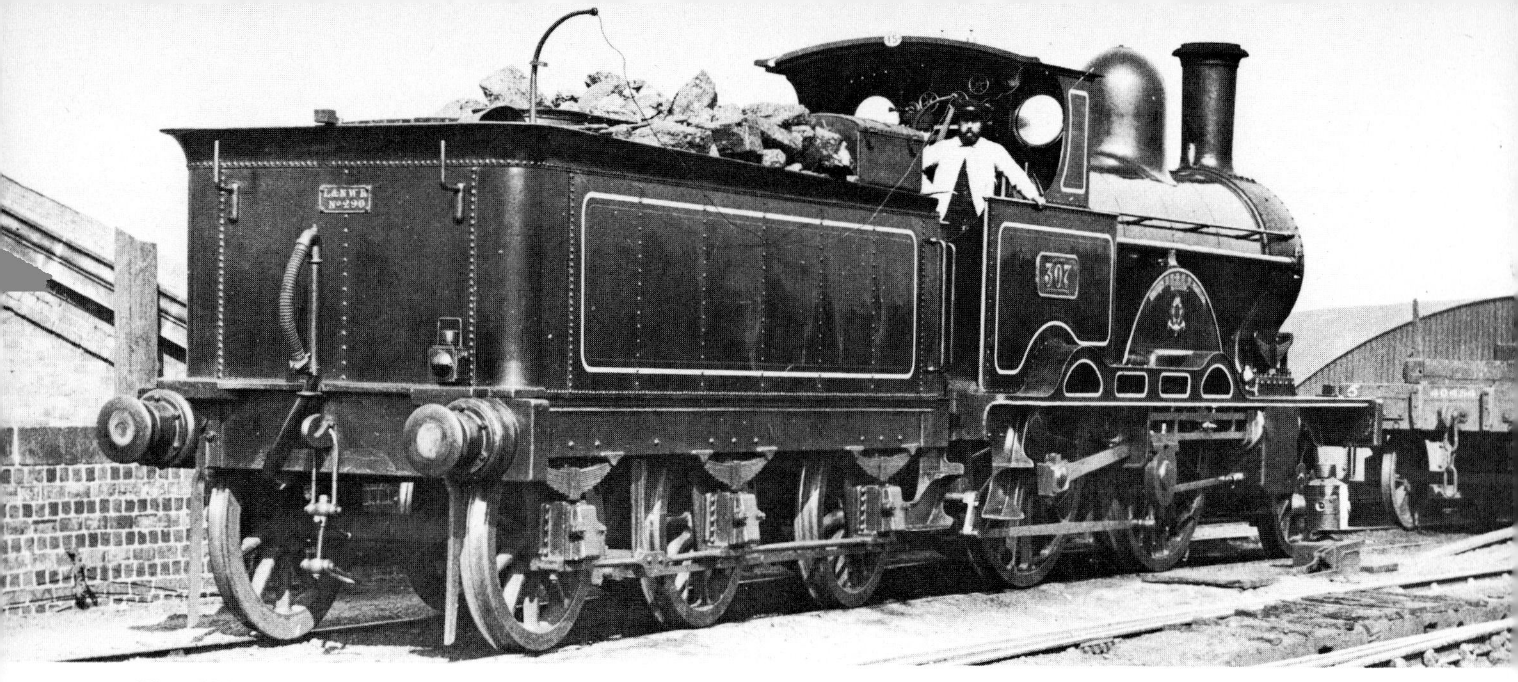

Plate 260: View of No. 307 *Victor* at Crewe Junction, Shrewsbury, sometime between 1889 and 1895, showing interesting detail of the rear of the tender which is No. 290. Photographs taken from this angle are extremely rare. No photograph is known showing fire-irons in position on the fire-iron hooks. They seem to be invariably left lying in the space behind the water filler. Only a top lamp socket was provided on the rear of wooden framed tenders, the two lower positions being served by square holes cut in the timber framing. The tender bufferbeam is painted black, as was always the case on LNWR tenders in the black livery, while both front and rear bufferbeams of tank engines and the front bufferbeam of tender engines were red.

Plate 261: No. 301 *Economist* at the west end of Chester (General) Station in the early 1890's, with Hoole Road bridge in the background. The left-hand handrail operates the 'warming up' valve by means of a handwheel in the cab; this valve admits a small amount of steam (by about a 1in. diameter pipe) from the boiler into the low-pressure valve chest, to warm it up before starting. Because of this fitting, the compounds were the first Webb engines to have the blower valve operated by the right-hand boiler handrail, under the control of the fireman; it was so positioned on all engines after about 1890. The crank and link on the handrail operate the 'bypass' valve when the driver pushes or pulls the handwheel in the cab. This valve allows steam from the high-pressure cylinders to exhaust directly into the blastpipe and was fitted at quite an early stage to make starting easier, by preventing the low-pressure receiver being choked with steam (which negated the power output of the high-pressure cylinders), when the low-pressure engine had come to rest with the cranks in an unfavourable position, with the valve closed or hardly open. Its usefulness was proved on the 'Teutonics' and it was fitted to almost all Webb's three-cylinder compounds in the 1890s. It was, of course, essential on engines fitted with a slip eccentric. Writers often comment that the large steel cover over the end of the inside cylinder was kept polished, but the same is equally true of the outside cylinders.

Plate 262: Official view of No. 310 *Sarmatian* on 19th November 1896, now fitted with all the modifications of the 1890s. No inside reversing rod can be seen, which indicates that the inside cylinder has been fitted with a slip eccentric, a modification introduced after its success on the 'Teutonics' and applied to at least four 'Experiments'. The engine also has a circular die block in place of the original squarish type, a bypass valve, anti-vacuum valves on the inside steam chest cover, and rear sandpipes. Thanks to the clarity of the photograph, the line of small rivets can be seen joining the cleading plates along the top of the boiler. As it is rarely visible in photographs, modellers often omit this detail.

Plate 263: No. 1113 *Hecate* at Shrewsbury shed. It has coal rails on the tender and a centre lamp socket on the bufferbeam, the latter dating the picture as 1903 or later. Again, there is no inside reversing rod, so a slip eccentric must be fitted, and anti-vacuum valves have been removed from the inside steam chest cover. These valves were fitted to many compounds in the 1890s being first tried on *Jeanie Deans* about 1893, but were found to be unnecessary and were removed about 1903.

Plate 264: Front-end view of an 'Experiment' dismantled in a running shed while under repair. The dish under the lubricator on the side of the smokebox was added about 1898 to catch oil drips. Cylindrical lubricators were introduced on *Alfred the Great*, so the date must be about 1902. The steam pipes are lying on one of the short wheelbase (about 2ft. 6in.) trolleys commonly used at steam sheds for removing bufferbeams, which they were designed to slide under.

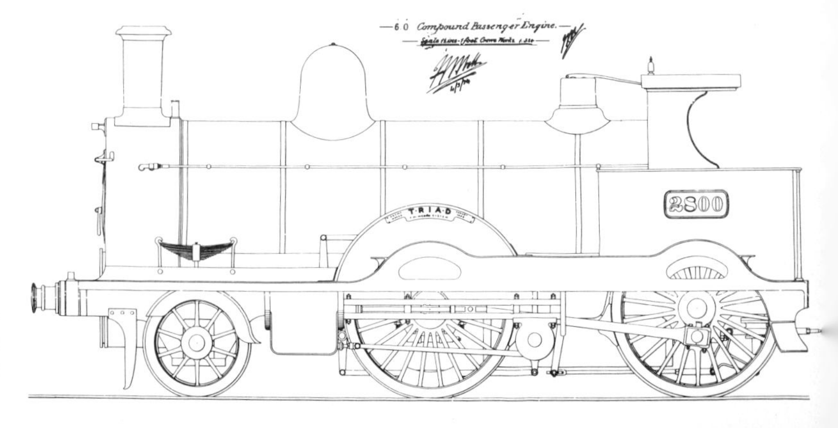

Triad

Figure 71: An official drawing of a three-cylinder compound design, dated 1st March 1884 and bearing the name *Triad*. It was probably an early scheme considered before the design of *Dreadnought* was finalised.

'Dreadnought'

Plate 265: Mr Webb next produced the 'Dreadnought' class, which was basically an 'Experiment' enlarged to produce more power. The boiler was larger, with 175lb. pressure instead of 150lb., and the valve gear was modified. Otherwise, the engine had all the usual Webb features of the day. There is a vacuum-brake pipe on the rear of the tender but not on the engine, while on the left-hand side of the front of the tender is the stanchion for the chain brake. This view shows Mr Webb himself on the footplate of No. 503 *Dreadnought* at Crewe Works on completion in September 1884. In many ways *Dreadnought* was the first modern Webb engine. In addition to a circular smokebox door, tommy-bar screw coupling, oil box on the splasher, ejector, and pipe carrying oil pipes along the side of the boiler to the front end, it was the first engine to have the new 3in. thick tyres, giving what would otherwise have been a 6ft. 1½in. wheel (nominally 6ft.) a diameter of 6ft. 3in. The first batch had the 3ft. 9in. wheels made of steel and the 1886 batch had steel driving wheels also. Despite all this, the 'Dreadnoughts' were the last engines to have splashers on the leading wheels.

Plate 266: A view of the left-hand side of *Marchioness of Stafford*, the fourth 'Dreadnought' to be completed, in March 1885. The upper rod visible between the splasher and the cab side-sheet is the reversing rod for the inside cylinder, while the lower one operates the outside cylinder. In the cab, the upper rod could be locked in any position and the reversing wheel then altered the cut-off in the high-pressure cylinders only. Again, there is no vacuum-brake hose on the front of the engine.

Plate 267: Front end view of *Dreadnought* as built. The 'Dreadnoughts' were almost certainly the first engines to be built new with circular smokebox doors instead of the horizontal type; only twenty 'Coal Tanks' were built at Crewe between the last of the 'Experiments', which had the latter type, and the first of the 'Dreadnoughts'. Pipes are fitted round the low-pressure cylinder to empty char, in place of the hopper used on simple engines.

Plate 268: View of the cab of *Dreadnought* as built. On the left-hand cab side-sheet is the receiver pressure gauge; the vacuum gauge and boiler-pressure gauge are on the left and right of the cab front. The wheel on top of the reverser was used to lock the inside valve gear in whatever position was required by the driver; the use of the reverser then altered the setting of the outside gear independently. The arrangement of the bufferbeam is typical of Webb engines of the time; the drawbar is in the centre, flanked by two links for side chains, which are in turn flanked by rubbing plates for the sprung buffers on the tender. The little pedal on the left-hand side, below the reverser, operates the low-pressure cylinder drain cocks, leaving the driver's hands free for the regulator and 'warming up' valve, the handle for which is hidden by the reverser. Beneath the shed plate is the tab carrying mirrors to reflect the light from the fire on to the gauges at night.

Plate 269 (below): Official view of No. 659 *Rowland Hill* on 18th February 1891. Only one reversing rod can now be seen, which signifies that the inside cylinder has a slip eccentric, all the 'Dreadnoughts' being so modified in the 1890s after the success of the device on the 'Teutonics'. There are now four openings in the valances instead of the two which all 'Dreadnoughts' had originally, and there are vacuum-brake hoses front and rear. A bypass valve, allowing exhaust steam from the high-pressure cylinders to pass directly to the blastpipe, has also been fitted, controlled by the usual lever on the side of the smokebox and operated from the cab by means of the boiler handrail. However, the relief valve behind the chimney (for the low-pressure steam chest) and the lubricator over the outside cylinder were features of the 'Dreadnoughts' as built originally. The other lubricator, low down on the side of the smokebox, was not fitted at first on *Dreadnought* but was on *Marchioness of Stafford*.

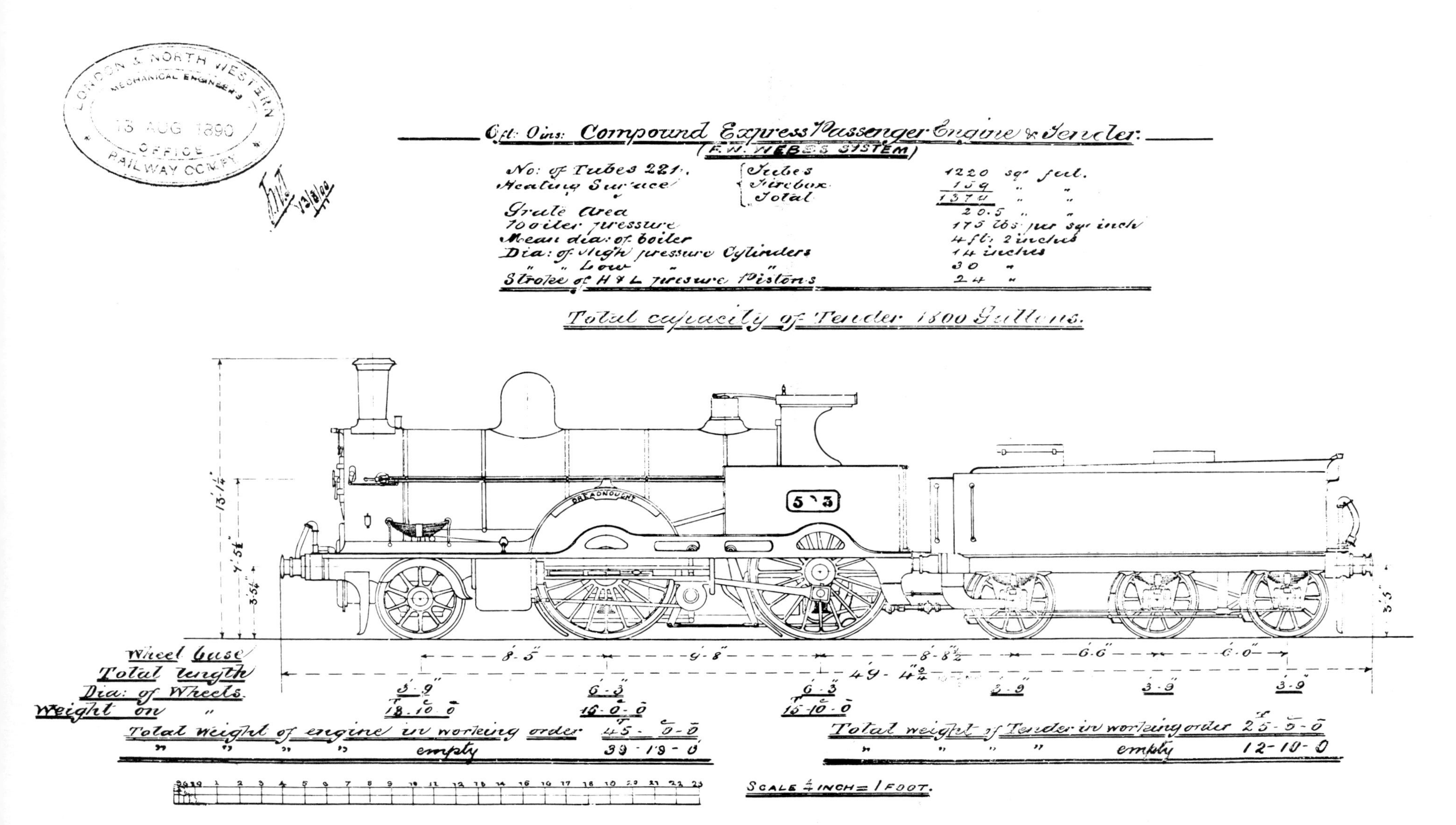

Figure 72: Weight diagram of *Dreadnought*.

Plate 270: No. 645 *Alchymist* at Manchester (London Road) during the early 1890s, a view showing good front-end detail. The outside valve gear is reversed in the usual way by the rod visible between the splasher and the cab side-sheet, but the inside gear has been replaced by a slip eccentric as on the 'Teutonics', there being no reversing rod projecting from behind the splasher. In the centre of the inside-cylinder cover is the tail rod of what is thought to be an experimental piston valve of the type fitted to *Greater Britain* when new, and for which anti-vacuum valves were provided on either side. The new coupling introduced on *Dreadnought* can be clearly seen, with a tommy-bar sliding in a hole through the shank of the screw.

Plate 271: A rear view of No. 2057 *Euphrates*, about 1890.

Plate 272 (right): No. 173 *City of Manchester*, as running in the late 1890s with coal rails fitted to the tender. The valve gear has been modified in the same way as on No. 645 *Alchymist*.

Plate 273 (left): No. 2062 *Herald*, not long before withdrawal in July 1905. Ironically, after being the first engines to have the blower valve on the right-hand side, compounds when fitted with the slip eccentrics had left-hand blowers, though all the simples had by then been changed to right-hand side. The 'warming up' valve was removed, when slip eccentrics were fitted, in case it started the low-pressure cylinder in reverse, so the existing valve on the left-hand side of the smokebox then became the blower and the valve on the other side was removed.

Plate 274 (below): No. 639 *City of London*. Centre lamp sockets were fitted in 1903 and this engine was scrapped in October 1904. Quite a number of engines of various classes had capuchons fitted to their chimneys about 1903. As no reversing rod can be seen projecting from behind the leading splasher and as there is an outside reversing rod as on the 'Experiments', the valve gear must have been modified as on the 'Teutonics', with a slip eccentric for the inside cylinder. Anti-vacuum valves have been removed from the inside-cylinder valve chest cover and the holes blanked off.

'Teutonic'
Plate 275: From the 'Dreadnoughts' was developed the 'Teutonic' class, the largest and most successful of Mr Webb's 2-2-2-0 three-cylinder compounds. Using the same boiler, they had 7ft. 1in. driving wheels compared with the 6ft. 3in. wheels of the 'Dreadnoughts'. This is the official view of No. 1301 *Teutonic*, taken in October 1889, and shows the engine as originally built. The reversing rod for the outside cylinders is arranged as on the 'Experiments' and can be seen extending from beneath the die block housing containing the curved guides to behind the cab footsteps. The one for the inside cylinder projects from behind the leading splasher. In the cab, the two were linked as on the 'Dreadnoughts' so that the driver could adjust one independently of the other. Other features of the compounds which were standard at the time are the relief valve for the inside steam chest behind the chimney, the bypass valve and the 'warming up' valve. There are four openings in the valances, and the front bufferbeam is of steel plate whereas the 'Dreadnoughts' had the wooden variety. The 1,800 gallon tender is of a new type, used only on this class. Instead of side buffers on the front bufferbeam there is a central buffer, through the middle of which is the drawbar. As the distance between engine and tender has been reduced by this arrangement, the tender footplate, fall plate and panel plates are all shorter. The axleboxes are lubricated by oil instead of grease, a feature introduced on the class.

Plate 276 (below): An early view of No. 1302 *Oceanic* at Euston. This engine originally had the same valve gear arrangement as *Teutonic* but had a 28in. low-pressure cylinder. *Pacific*, the third of the class, was built as a 'continuous expansion' or triple expansion compound, but was also capable of working as a three-cylinder simple. Little is known of it except that it was a failure and was soon converted to standard design.

Plate 277: The most famous of all the Webb compounds was the fourth 'Teutonic' to be built, *Jeanie Deans*, seen here on completion at Crewe Works in March 1890. The name was the only one of the class not ending in *-ic* and was specially chosen because the engine was displayed at the Edinburgh Exhibition that year, the rest being named after White Star liners on the Liverpool — New York service. For the same reason the Crewe Works motion number is carried, replaced by 1304 when the engine entered service. Mechanically, *Jeanie Deans* is identical to *Teutonic*, with one important exception. The reversing gear for the inside cylinder has been replaced by a slip eccentric. When this feature had proved its worth, it was applied to all the 'Teutonics' and 'Dreadnoughts' and to some of the 'Experiments'. The lever on the side of the smokebox controls the bypass valve, which allowed exhaust steam from the high-pressure cylinders to pass directly to the blastpipe. It was used only when the engine was re-starting in the opposite direction of travel, and then only for a short time, until the slip eccentric was repositioned for the new direction.

Plate 278 (below left): Front end of *Jeanie Deans* with smokebox door open, March 1890. The long front overhang is due to the tail rod fitted to the large low-pressure cylinder and designed to reduce piston and cylinder wear. In 1896 it was decided that these tailrods not only increased maintenance but were not needed anyway. They were therefore removed and the front ends were cut back. The neat curved cover with inspection flap was later used by Whale and Bowen Cooke on several of their designs.

Plate 279 (below right): Cab view of *Jeanie Deans*, showing the reversing shaft across the rear of the engine, linking the reversing rods for the outside cylinders, and the new arrangement of the rear bufferbeam with the drawbar passing through a central buffer flanked by side chains. This arrangement allowed greater flexibility between engine and tender on curves. The drawbar was secured to the engine by a vertical pin, which was put in place through the hole which can be seen in the cab floor. In general, however, it is a typical Webb footplate. The floor sloping slightly upwards towards the firebox was a feature of many LNWR engines, including Whale's 'Precursors', and caused firemen to complain of uneven wear of the soles of their left boots. Shed plate 15 (Crewe) is carried but the engine was eventually allocated to shed 1 (Camden) for working the 'Corridor'.

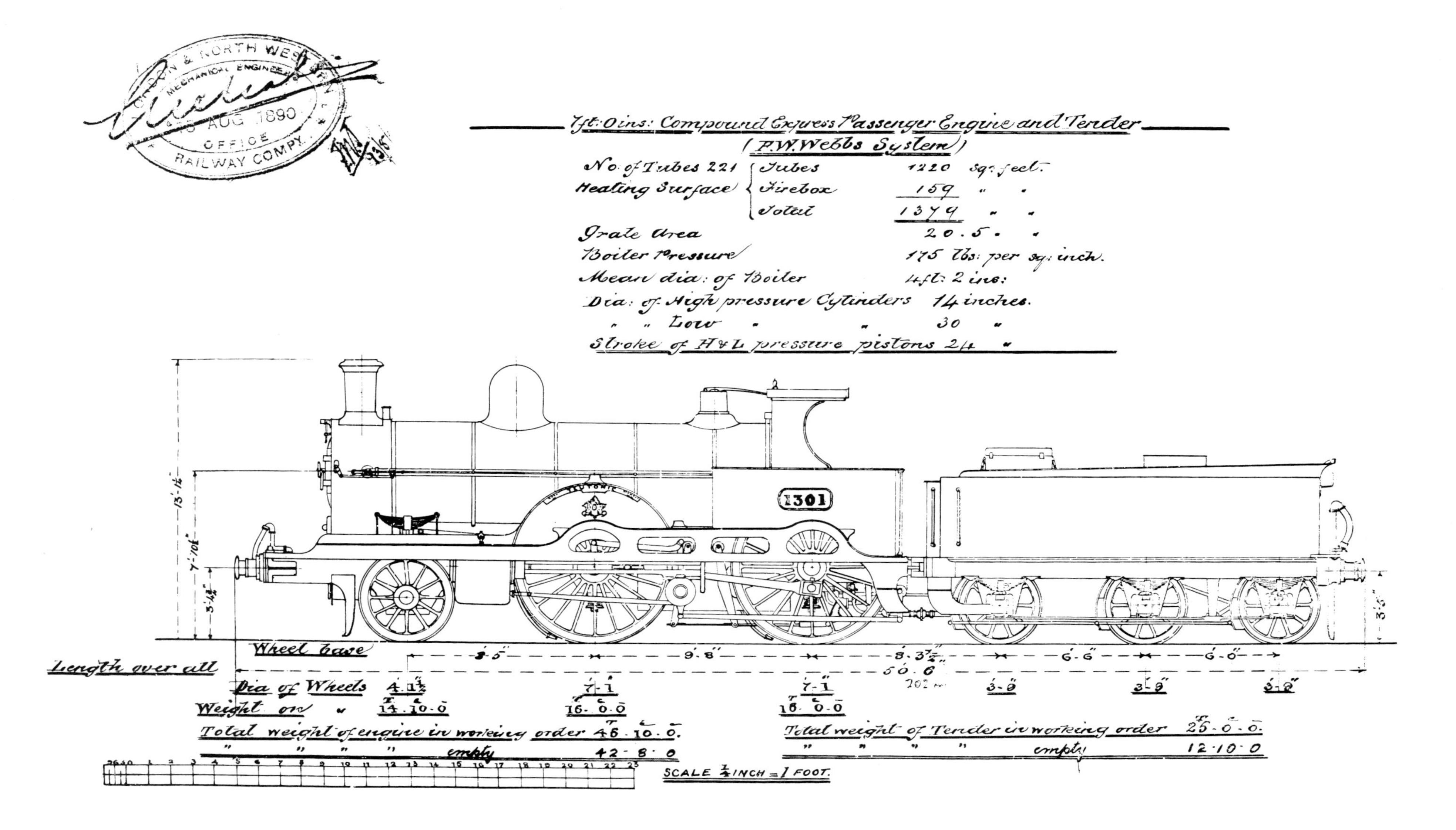

Figure 73: Weight diagram of *Teutonic*.

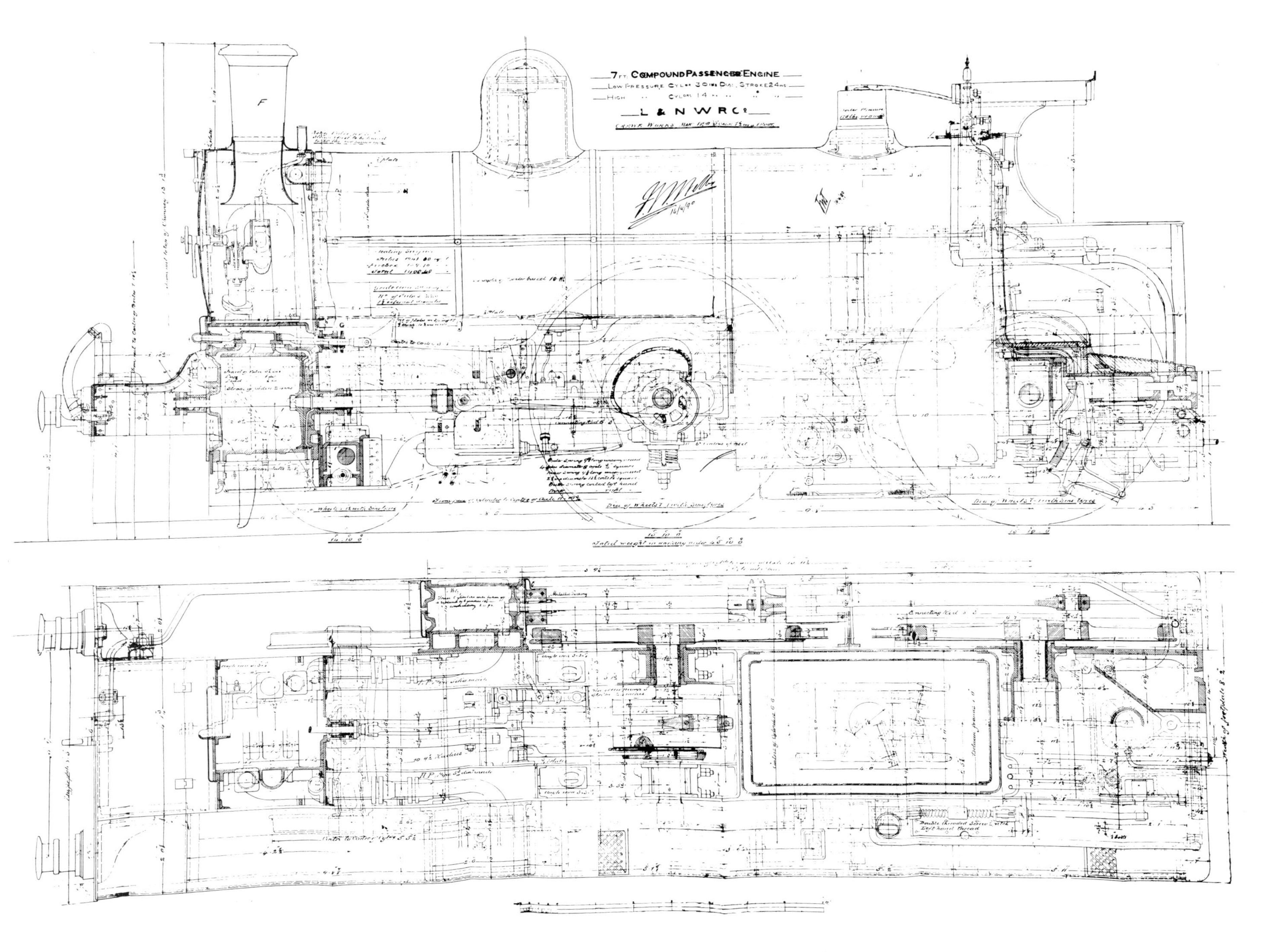

Figure 74 : General arrangement drawing of *Teutonic*.

DORIC
1305

Plate 282 (right): No. 1311 *Celtic*, as running about 1902 with anti-vacuum valves on the inside steam chest cover. The cylindrical lubricator for the outside cylinder is the type introduced on the 'Alfreds' in 1901.

Plate 280 (above left): No. 1306 *Ionic* in original condition, before the front end was cut back and the tail rods removed.

Plate 281 (below left): No. 1305 *Doric* at Crewe in the late 1890s, with anti-vacuum valves on the inside valve chest cover and with coal rails on the tender. The close-coupled tender with shorter side plates can be clearly seen.

Plate 283 (right): No. 1303 *Pacific* in the early 1900s, as running in final condition before withdrawal. Though it can barely be seen, it has a 2,000 gallon tender as used on the 2-2-2-2s; thanks to the deeper solebars of these tenders, the cab floor was now made flat instead of sloping.

'Greater Britain'

Plate 284: In October 1891 the first of the 'Greater Britain' class was completed. The design was basically that of the 'Teutonics' elongated into the 2-2-2-2 wheel arrangement but with two important differences. Firstly, the boiler, which was 7ft. longer, had a combustion chamber in the barrel, so that there were two sets of tubes, one set from the firebox leading gases into the chamber and the other set leading from the chamber to the smokebox; at the bottom of the chamber was a char hopper, which emptied between the frames on to the track. Secondly, Joy valve gear was abandoned; the outside cylinders had Stephenson gear, located between the two driving axles, and the inside cylinder had a slip eccentric as on the 'Teutonics'. This is the official view of *Greater Britain* as built and with the Crewe Works motion number 3292. Behind the chimney is the usual relief valve for the low-pressure steam chest, the lever for the bypass valve is on the side of the smokebox, and there is a tail rod on what is thought to be an experimental piston valve for the low-pressure cylinder. The tender has deeper sole bars to raise the floor to the height of the footplate, but still holds 1,800 gallons. This type of tender was built for the first two 'Greater Britains' and for No. 2524, the first 0-8-0, but the first three-cylinder 0-8-0, No. 50, and *John Hick* had a larger version, which looked similar but had wider tanks holding 2,000 gallons. This was then fitted to all subsequent 2-2-2-2s and to many compound 0-8-0s.

Plate 285: In service *Greater Britain* had the running number 2053 and is seen here at Euston, complete with the L-shaped cab which was fitted to the first two of the class only. Both seem to have been changed to the later style around the time when the rest of the class were built, in April-May 1894.

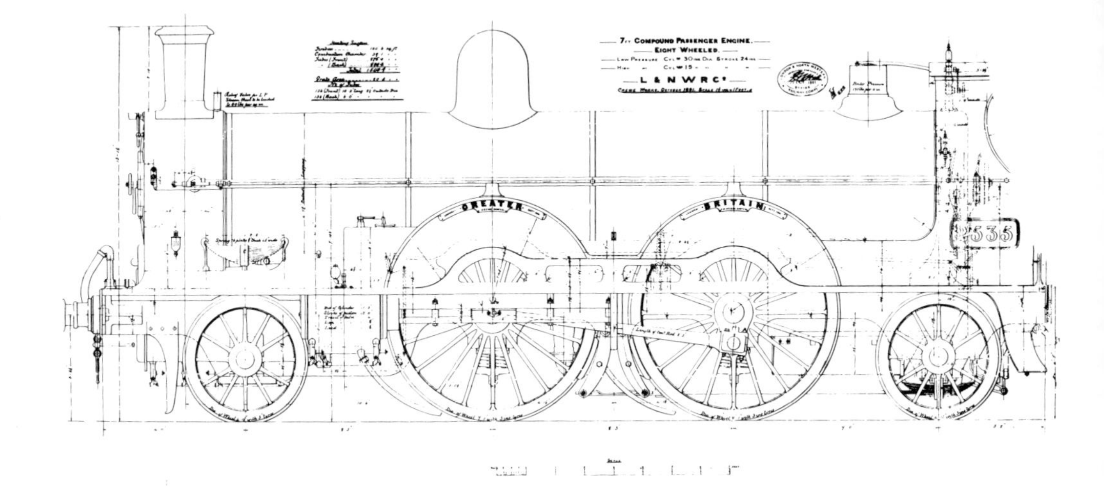

Figure 75: Official drawing of *Greater Britain* as built.

Plate 286: Broadside view of No. 2053 *Greater Britain* in Crewe Works, after running 72,592 miles from 29th October 1891 to 25th April 1893 without heavy repairs. The boiler and cylinder appear to have been painted grey to subdue the reflections from the shiny black paintwork. This was apparently done not on the engine itself but by clever work in the darkroom, which involved touching up and rephotographing a print from the original negative.

Plate 287 (right): The final batch of eight 'Greater Britains' was built in April and May 1894. No. 2052 *Prince George* is seen here when quite new. The location is thought to be Llandudno or Rhyl and the tender has perhaps been taken off to enable the engine to be turned while on a trial trip.

Plate 288 (above left): Rear view of No. 2051 *George Findlay*, probably at Shrewsbury while running in after completion in April 1894. It is fitted with 2,000 gallon tender No. 925.

Plate 289 (left): No. 525 *Princess May* in ordinary service at Crewe in the late 1890s.

Plate 290 (below): A broadside view of No. 526 *Scottish Chief* at Crewe, an angle which emphasises the great length and imposing dimensions of the 'Greater Britains'.

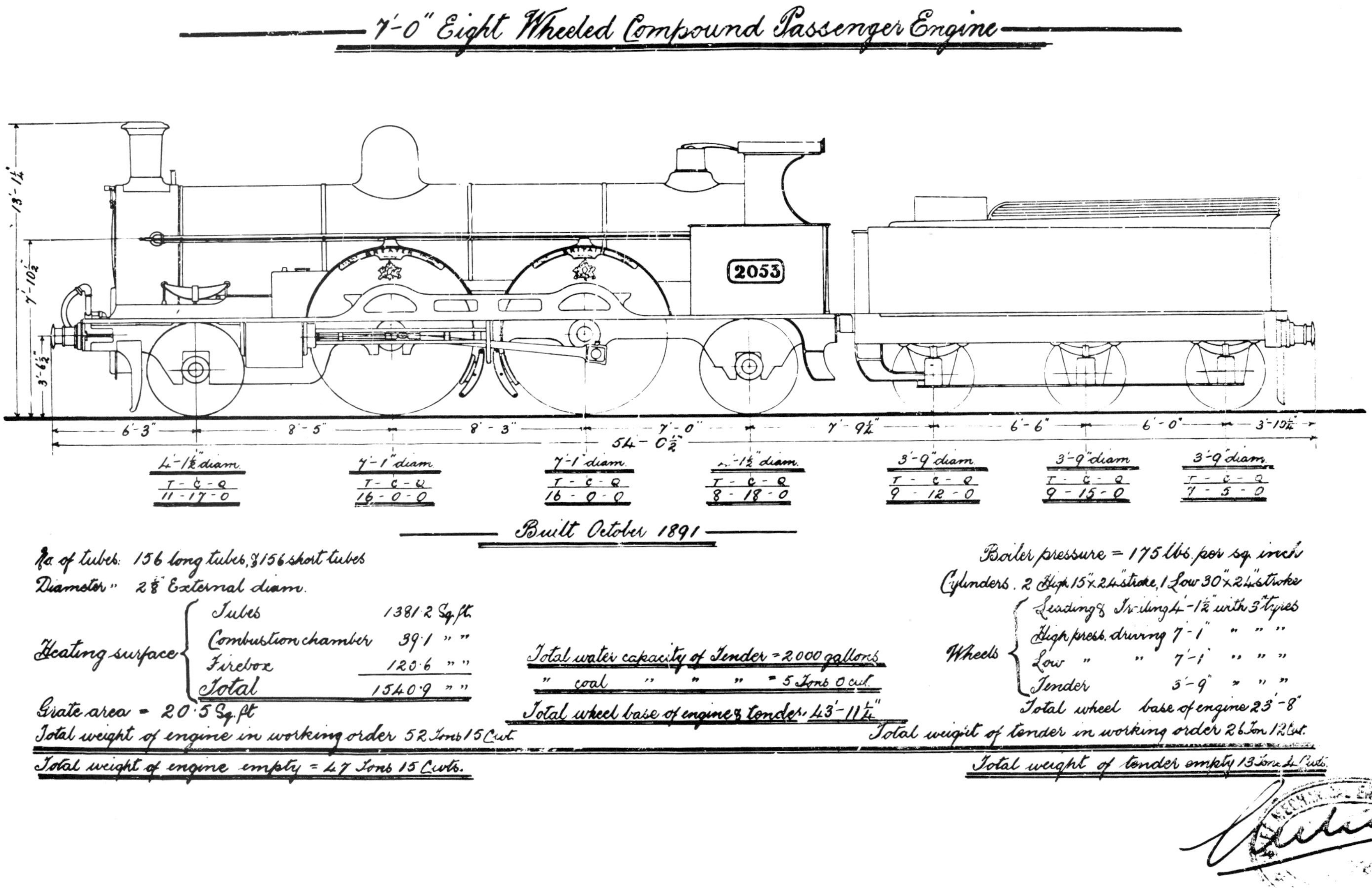
7'-0" Eight Wheeled Compound Passenger Engine
2053
13'-1¼"
7'-10½"
3'-6½"
6'-3"
8'-5"
8'-3"
7'-0"
7'-9¼"
6'-6"
6'-0"
3'-10¼"
54-0½
4'-1½" diam
T - C - Q
11 - 17 - 0
7'-1" diam
T - C - Q
16 - 0 - 0
7'-1 diam
T - C - Q
16 - 0 - 0
4'-1½" diam
T - C - Q
8 - 18 - 0
3'-9" diam
T - C - Q
9 - 12 - 0
3'-9" diam
T - C - Q
9 - 15 - 0
3'-9" diam
T - C - Q
7 - 5 - 0
Built October 1891
No. of tubes 156 long tubes, & 156 short tubes
Diameter " 2⅛" External diam.
Heating surface
Tubes 1381.2 Sq. ft.
Combustion chamber 39.1 " "
Firebox 120.6 " "
Total 1540.9 " "
Grate area = 20.5 Sq. ft
Total weight of engine in working order 52 Tons 15 Cwt.
Total weight of engine empty = 47 Tons 15 Cwts.
Total water capacity of Tender = 2000 gallons
" coal " " " = 5 Tons 0 cwt.
Total wheel base of engine & tender 43'-11¼"
Boiler pressure = 175 lbs. per sq. inch
Cylinders. 2 High 15"×24" stroke, 1 Low 30"×24" stroke
Wheels
Leading & Trailing 4'-1½" with 3" tyres
High press. driving 7'-1" " " "
Low " " 7'-1 " " "
Tender 3'-9" " " "
Total wheel base of engine 23'-8"
Total weight of tender in working order 26 Ton 12 Cwt.
Total weight of tender empty 13 Tons 4 Cwts.

Figure 76: Weight diagram of *Greater Britain*.

Plate 291: In honour of the Diamond Jubilee of Queen Victoria in June 1897, *Greater Britain* and the second of the class, *Queen Empress*, were taken into Crewe Works and given such elaborate and expensive liveries of red and white respectively that they were probably the most magnificently finished locomotives ever to run in this country or indeed anywhere on earth. The scheme applied to *Greater Britain* is seen in this photograph taken on 25th May 1897. The boiler, cylinders, cab, splashers, footplate edging and tender sides were painted scarlet and were lined out with gold-leaf 1 in wide edged with dark blue, ½ in wide on the outside and ⅛ in wide on the inside. Inside this again was a second gold line ½ in wide, edged with ¼ in and 1/16in. dark blue lines on the outside and inside respectively. These lines were placed similarly to those on a normal black engine. The boiler bands were edged with polished brass, on the outer edge of which was a dark blue line; the bands themselves seem to have been dark blue between the brass. Smokebox, frames and wheels were dark blue, and the tyres were white, while the front bufferbeam was lined out in gold, where normally there would be black. The leading splashers and the tender carried the LNWR coat of arms and the trailing splashers had the Royal Arms. The numberplate was of polished brass, as usual, but with a dark blue background. Here the engine has the later style of cab and a 2,000 gallon tender, which being wider matches the cab well. This tender, and that on *Queen Empress*, had the sides specially finished flush, the vertical rows of rivets being countersunk except at the ends.

Plate 292: The second of the class, No. 2054 *Queen Empress*, was completed in December 1892 but rather than being put into traffic was prepared for the Chicago Exhibition in May 1893, the nameplates showing the latter date to coincide; the engine carried its motion number, 3435, for the exhibition. It was awarded a gold medal, replicas of which were subsequently carried on the cabsides, and it returned to Crewe in January 1894, was reassembled and put into traffic in the same month as No. 2054. As built, the engine had an L-shaped cab and an 1,800 gallon tender with no coal rails, but is seen here with the later style of cab and 2,000 gallon tender in its special Diamond Jubilee livery. It was painted white (probably creamy white due to the effect of the varnish) where *Greater Britain* was scarlet and had the same lining but the edges of the panels, the smokebox, the frames above footplate level, sandboxes and footplate edging were of a colour described in various accounts as 'light grey', 'blue', 'mauve', 'lilac' and 'lavender'. The wheels, tyres and front bufferbeam were the same as on *Greater Britain*, and the same coats of arms were carried on the splashers, but one difference was that the front of the cab was lined, a feature unique to this engine so far as the LNWR was concerned. *Queen Empress* was one of the eleven engines experimentally fitted for steam heating of carriages in 1894; it now has drip cups under the lubricators on the side of the smokebox.

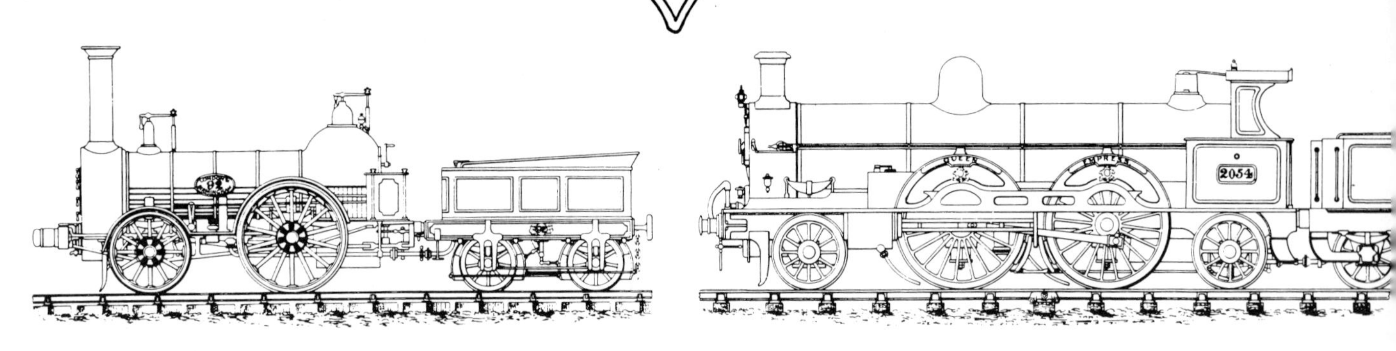

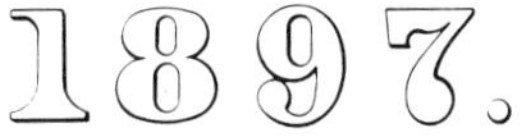

Figure 77: Official drawing of the engraving on the brass plate, of the same size as a numberplate, carried on the left-hand side of the tender of *Queen Empress*. Bury 2-2-0 No. 92 was the first engine built at Wolverton, in 1845. The plate on the right-hand side of the tende showed the same engines facing right, s that the engines faced forwards on bot sides. These engravings were done in thi and thick lines and filled with blac engine stopping like nameplates.

Plate 293 (above left): Another view o *Queen Empress* in the special white livery.

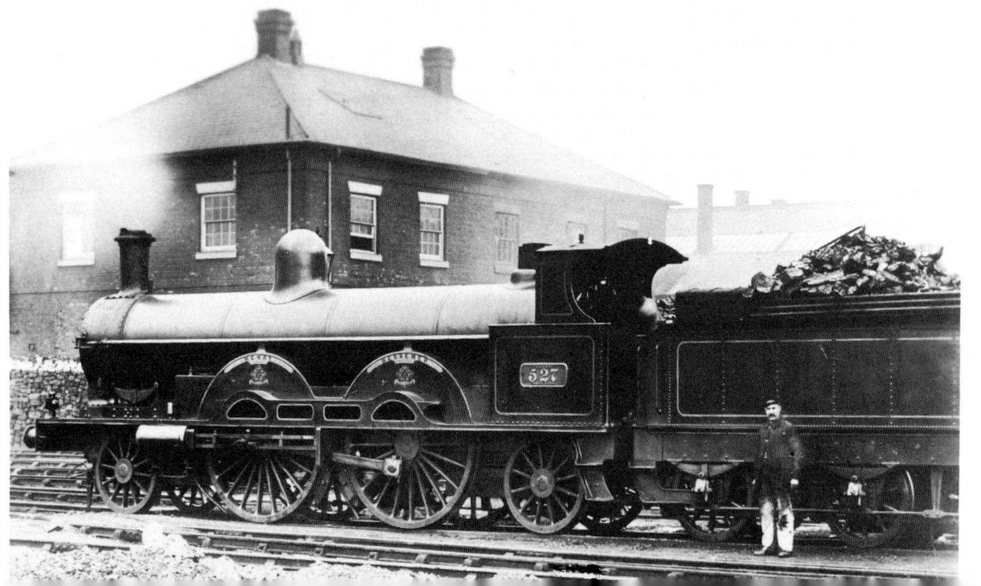

Plate 294 (left): No. 527 *Henry Bessemer* a Shrewsbury around 1904, with capuchon on the chimney.

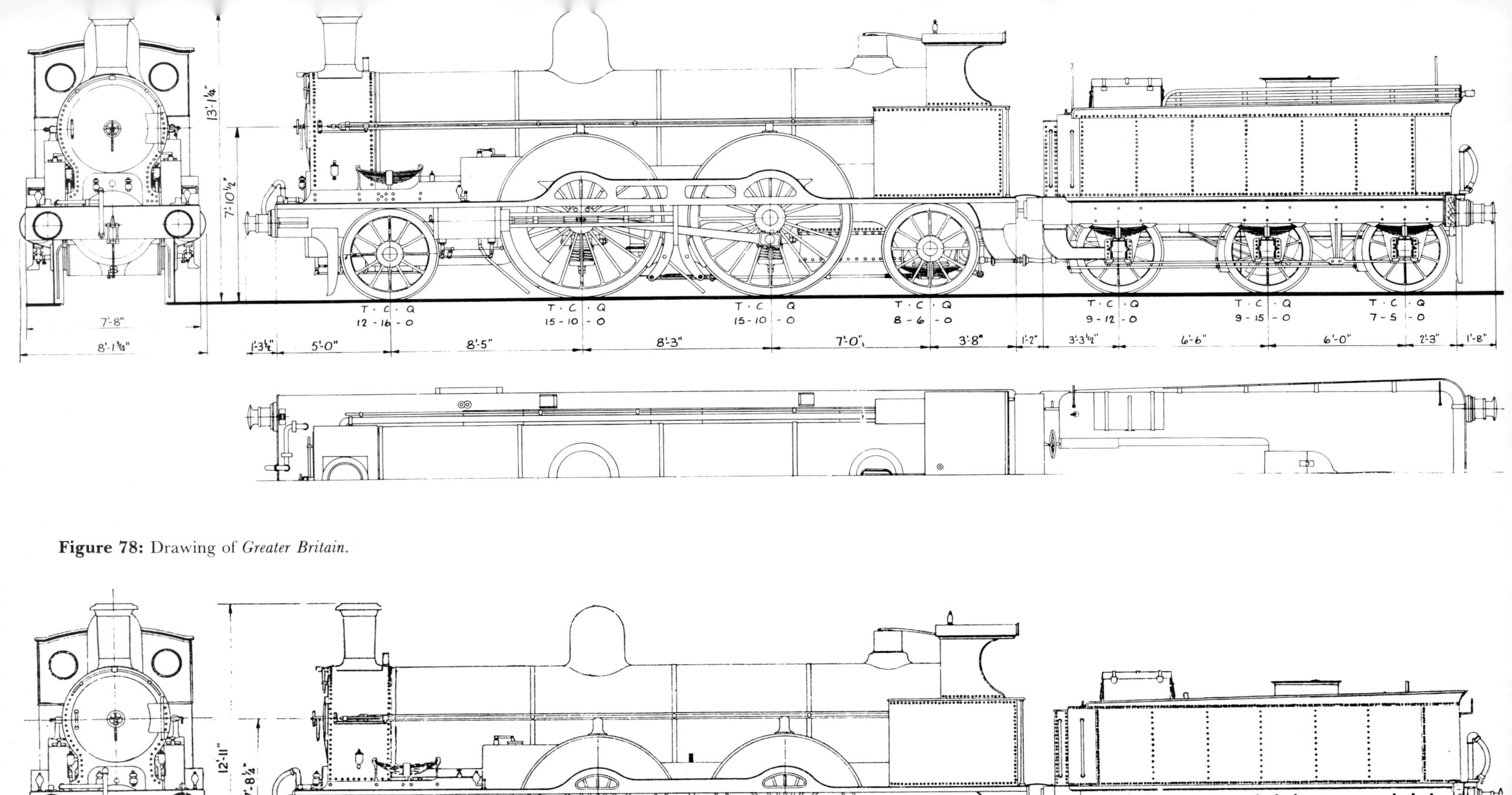

Figure 78: Drawing of *Greater Britain*.

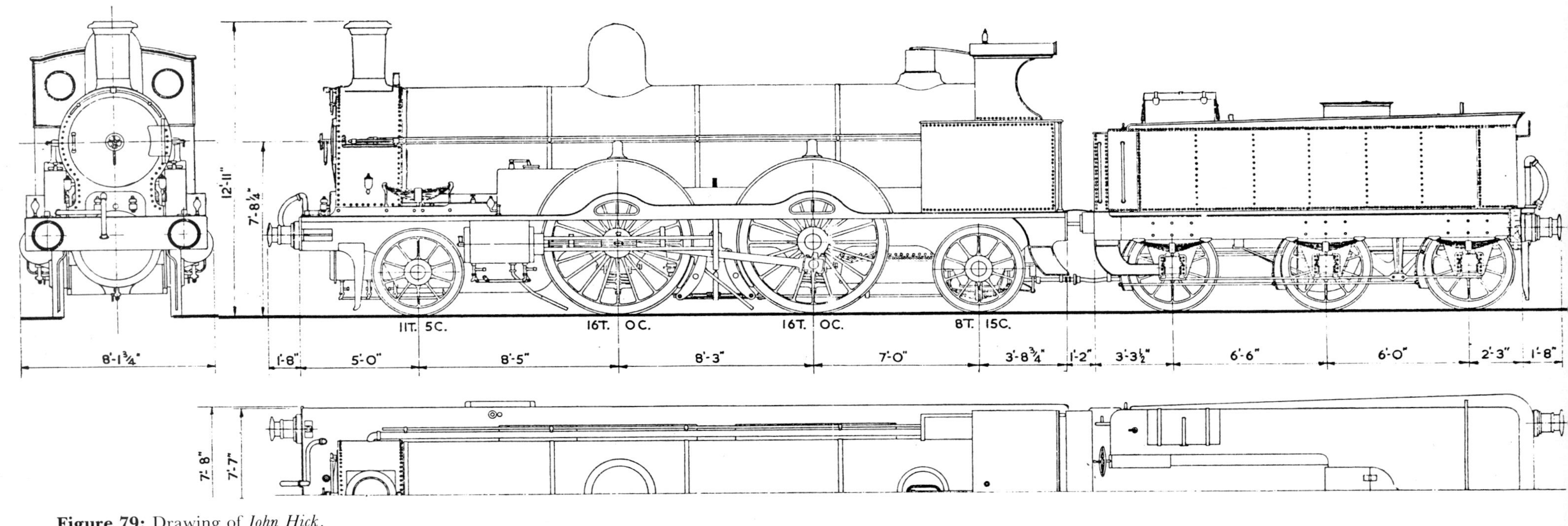

Figure 79: Drawing of *John Hick*.

'John Hick'
Plate 295: It is generally believed that Mr Webb's plan was for the Euston to Carlisle main line to be worked in two sections by large- and small-wheeled 2-2-2-2s. The 7ft. 1in. 'Greater Britains' were for the section south of Crewe and the 6ft. 3in. 'John Hicks' for that north of there. In practice, however, there was no real distinction. The 'Greater Britains' regularly worked the main expresses over the northern section and in its week-long reliability trial *Greater Britain* worked through from Euston to Carlisle. So it may well be that Mr Webb intended the 'John Hicks' to work the heavy secondary expresses and semi-fasts, the duties which they did in fact perform. The first of the class, No. 20 *John Hick*, was built in February 1894, this official photograph being taken on 5th March, and in fact preceded the last eight 'Greater Britains'. Apart from the differences associated with the smaller wheels, the 'John Hicks' were identical to the 'Greater Britains'; they even had the same size of splashers, set lower. The tender seen here is similar to that originally fitted to *Greater Britain*, having the same deep solebars, but holds 2,000 gallons instead of 1,800. It can be distinguished only by the slight overhang of the tank outside the solebar, being 7ft. 2⅞in. wide instead of 6ft 8⅞in.

Plate 296: Another view of No. 20 *John Hick*, taken soon after completion and before the fitting of coal rails to the tender in 1895-6. The location is Carlisle (Upperby).

6'-0" Eight Wheeled Compound Passenger Engine

12'-11" 7'-8¼" 3'-6½"

20

6'-3" — 8'-5" — 8'-3" — 7'-0" — 7'-9¼" — 6'-6" — 6'-0" — 3'-10¼"

54'-0½" 216 mm

3'-9" diam.	6'-3" diam.	6'-3" diam.	3'-9" diam.	3'-9" diam.	3'-9" diam.	3'-9" diam.
T - C - Q	T - C - Q	T - C - Q	T - C - Q	T - C - Q	T - C - Q	T - C - Q
11 - 5 - 0	16 - 0 - 0	16 - 0 - 0	8 - 15 - 0	9 - 12 - 0	9 - 15 - 0	7 - 5 - 0

Built February 1894

No. of tubes: 156 long tubes, & 156 short tubes
Diameter " 2⅛" External diam.

Heating surface		
	Tubes	1381·2 Sq. ft
	Combustion chamber	39·1 " "
	Firebox	120·6 " "
	Total	1540·9 " "

Grate area :: 20·5 Sq. ft
Total weight of engine in working order 52 Tons
" " " " empty 47 "

Total water capacity of Tender = 2,000 gallons
" coal " " " = 5 Tons 0 cwt.
Total wheel base of engine & tender 43'-11¼"

Boiler pressure = 175 lbs. per sq. inch
Cylinders. 2 High 15"×24" stroke, 1 Low 30"×24" stroke

Wheels		
	Leading & Trailing	3'-9" with 3" tyres
	High press. driving	6'-3" " " "
	Low " "	6'-3" " " "
	Tender	3'-9" " " "

Total wheel base of engine 23'-8"
Total weight of tender in working order 26 Ton 12 Cwt.
" " " " empty 13 " 4 "

Figure 80: Weight diagram of *John Hick*.

Plate 297: In the early part of 1898 nine more 'John Hicks' were completed. No. 1535 *Henry Maudslay* is seen here about 1904.

Plate 298: No. 1505 *Richard Arkwright* at Shrewsbury about 1905, with a capuchon on the chimney.

Chapter 9
Three-Cylinder Compound Tank Engines

'The First Compound Tank'

Plate 299: In February 1884, Mr Webb rebuilt 'Met Tank' 4-4-0 No. 2063 as a three-cylinder compound 4-2-2-0 tank on the same basic lines as his 'Experiment' class 2-2-2-0s. It is seen here in the official photograph taken on conversion. The outside Joy valve gear is arranged as on the original 'Experiments', using an eccentric driven off the rear driving wheel and reversed separately from the inside cylinder through the long rod reaching from the curved guides to behind the cab footsteps. The inside steam chest relief valve is behind the chimney. Compared with the original 'Met Tank', the engine has an Adams bogie instead of Bissell truck, Webb chimney, dome and safety valves; the condensing valve is operated by the lever on the side of the smokebox. The smokebox door is the horizontal type and behind the front bufferbeam are brackets holding four destination boards; presumably, similar brackets are fixed to the rear of the bunker.

Plate 300 (left): Another view of Mr Webb's first compound tank, taken at Manchester (London Road) after June 1889 when it was renumbered 3026 on the duplicate list; it was scrapped in March 1897. It has vacuum brake, a toolbox by the smokebox and route-indicator bracket on the chimney, as used on Mansion House services. Otherwise it is much the same as when originally converted.

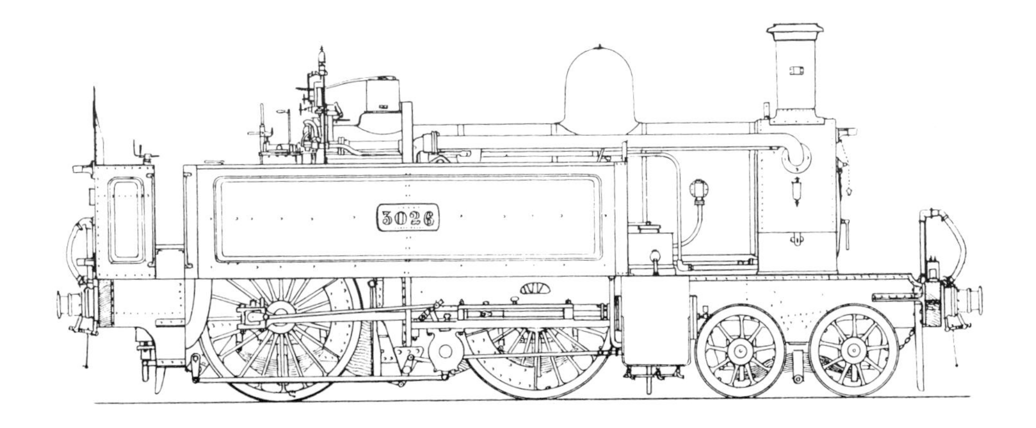

Figure 81: Drawing of No. 3026.

'The Second Compound Tank'

Plate 301: The second compound tank was a 2-2-2-2 with condensing apparatus, and so was comparable to the 4ft. 6in. 2-4-2 'Mansion House' tanks. It was built in September 1885. Unlike Webb's three-cylinder compound tender engines, No. 687 had the valves of the outside cylinders positioned above the cylinder; the curved guides of the Joy valve gear were above the crosshead, carried by the circular block, and the anchor link below. This arrangement was chosen because the driving wheels were smaller, and it was followed on both the compound tanks built subsequently. There were separate valve gears for inside and outside cylinders. This official view shows No. 687 on completion. The condensing gear is as on the 'Mansion House' tanks, with the tall exhaust vent at the rear of the bunker, the linking pipes round the cab to the rear tank, and the condensing valve operated by the boiler handrail. Other fittings are typical Webb at the time including circular smokebox door, wooden bufferbeams and brake blocks, and screw couplings; and the engine is fitted for working vacuum-braked trains. The leading sandboxes are behind the front of the tank side-sheets and the rear ones are under the cab floor between the frames.

Plate 302: Another view of No. 687, at Heaton Chapel in the early 1890s when the engine was shedded at Buxton. It has destination-board brackets on the front bufferbeam and route-indicator brackets on the chimney, having worked on Mansion House trains. The sandbox can just be seen behind the tank side-sheet, below the condensing pipe, and there are fire-irons, a shovel and a jack on top of the tank. The tall exhaust vent in the bunker can be seen above the cab roof.

Figure 82: Official drawing of the 4ft. 6in. compound tank engine.

'The Third Compound Tank'

Plate 303: The third compound tank was a 5ft. 6in. 2-2-2-2 and had the same basic layout as No. 687 except that as the tanks were shorter, the reversing rods for inside and outside cylinders were now clearly visible. It was completed in July 1887 and was officially the 3,000th engine built at Crewe Works, hence the number seen in this official photograph taken before painting in lined black livery; in service it was numbered 600. Changes from No. 687 are the bypass valve, worked by the lever on the side of the smokebox in the usual way, steel buffer-beams, metal brake blocks and the tank filler on the higher centre part of the back tank; the bunker was arranged like a tender, with a U-shaped tank surrounding the coal space and the centre part of it higher than the sides. All Webb tank engines had the same sort of arrangement.

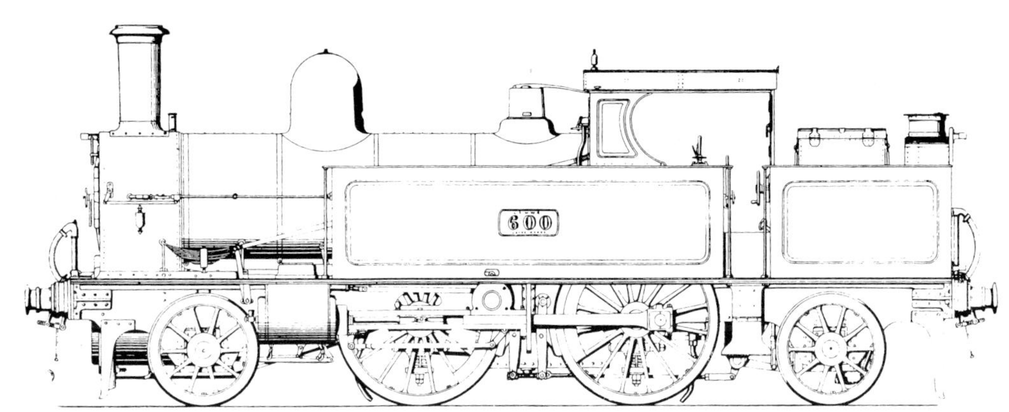

Figure 83: Drawing of 5ft. 6in. compound tank engine.

Plate 303a(below): View of the right-hand side of No. 600 at Manchester (London Road) in the early 1890s when shedded at Buxton.

'The Fourth Compound Tank'

Plate 304 (right): Mr Webb's final design of compound tank had the 2-2-4-0 wheel arrangement and was intended for goods work. It was built in March 1887, before No. 600, and was exhibited at the Manchester Jubilee Exhibition from May to October as No. 2974, its Crewe Works motion number; it did not enter service until November 1887, after No. 600, and presumably for this reason was known as the 'fourth' compound tank. This official view shows it on completion. The outside valve gear is arranged as on both Nos. 687 and 600, while the steel bufferbeams, metal brake blocks, bypass valve and tank-filler arrangement are the same as on No. 600; there are three-link couplings and no vacuum brakes, since the engine is intended for goods work.

Plate 305 (right): In service the 2-2-4-0 tank had the running number 777. Its use on goods work soon ceased and it was sent to Buxton shed, which put it to work on local passenger trains to Manchester (London Road) where it is seen here about 1890. Coupling rods were usually black at this time but on No. 777 they are well polished, like the valve gear and the engine as a whole.

Plate 306 (below): No. 777 at Manchester (London Road) slightly later than in the previous picture. Its status as a passenger engine has now been officially recognised by the fitting of vacuum brakes and screw couplings.

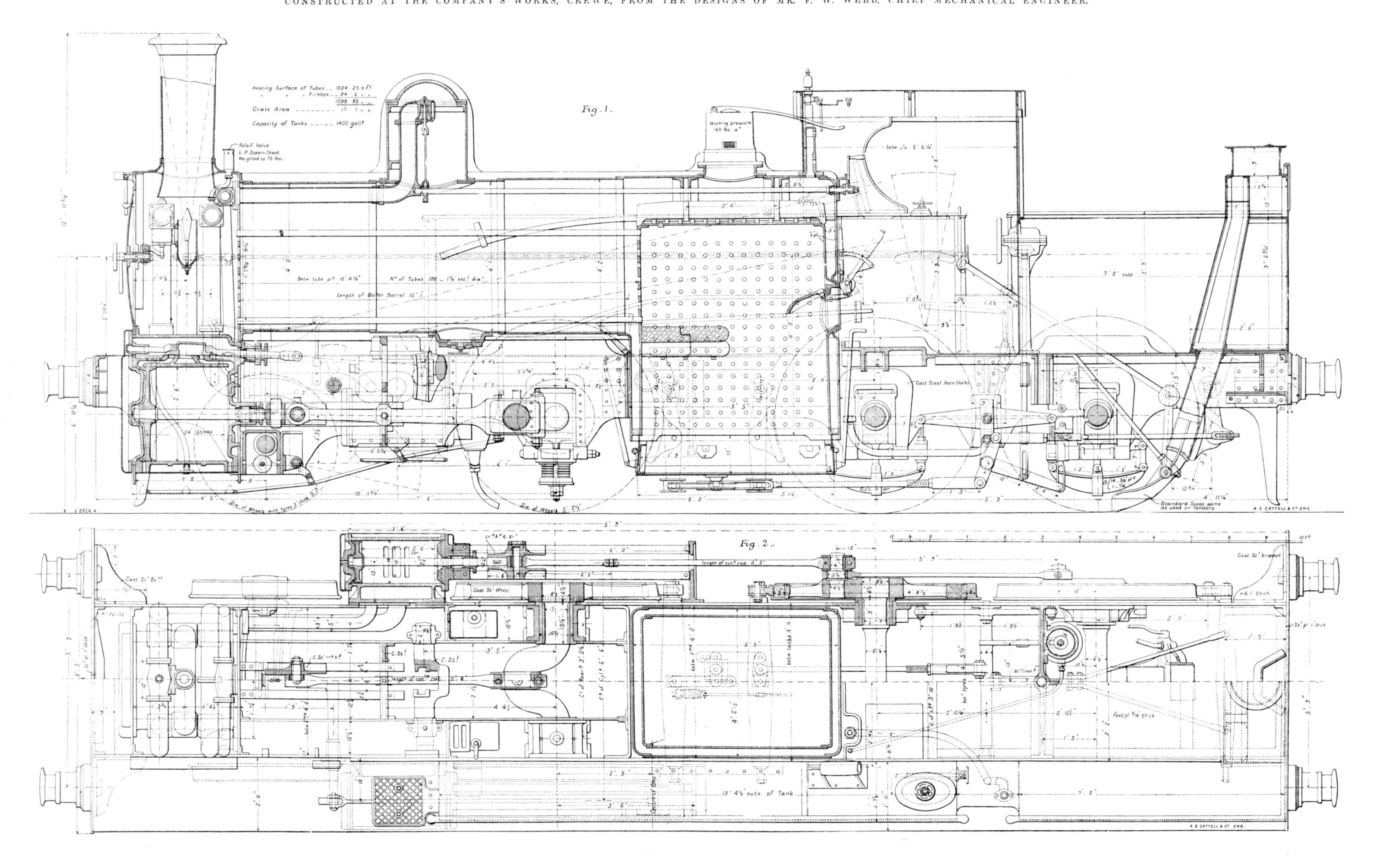

Figure 84: General arrangement drawing of the 2-2-4-0 compound tank engine.

Chapter 10
Four-Cylinder Compounds (except Eight-Coupled)

'Jubilee'

Plate 307: Even before the final batch of nine three-cylinder compound 'John Hicks' had been completed, Mr Webb had already built the first of a quite different type of compound passenger engine. In June 1897 two four-cylinder 4-4-0s were built, No. 1501 *Iron Duke*, which was a simple engine, and No. 1502 *Black Prince*, which was a compound. Not only were the driving wheels coupled but they used some of the longest coupling rods in the country, 9ft. 8in., while at the front end was not strictly a bogie but a double radial truck, the central boss, about which the truck pivoted, being allowed sideways movement radially as in Webb's radial axle. This type of bogie was used subsequently by both Whale and Bowen Cooke for their designs. The valve gear for the inside cylinders (the low-pressure cylinders of the compound) worked the valves of the outside (high-pressure) cylinders by means of rocking levers positioned ahead of the cylinders. So the gear for all four cylinders was notched up simultaneously and the principle of independent control of high- and low-pressure cylinders, which had proved successful in the three-cylinder compounds, was abandoned. Otherwise, the 4-4-0s were really based on the 'Teutonics', the boiler, driving wheelbase and wheel diameter all being identical. Originally trials were held with a double-chimney arrangement, in an attempt to produce an equal draught through all the tubes, and No. 1502 is seen here so fitted at Manchester (London Road). Though coupled to a lined tender, the engine is in plain black or perhaps works grey, while on trial, and will return to the paintshop later for final painting. An earthenware drinking jar can be clearly seen on the front of the tender.

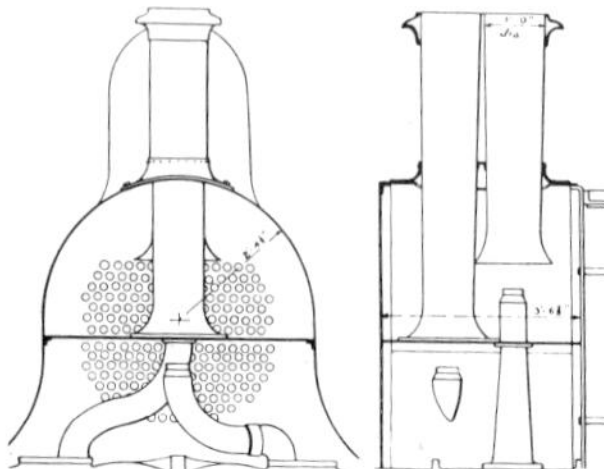

Figure 85: Drawing of the smokebox arrangement of *Black Prince* when fitted with double chimney.

Plate 308: Eventually, No. 1501 was renamed *Jubilee*, and the name was then applied to the class as a whole, though the engine came to be popularly known as 'Diamond Jubilee', because on either side of the name on the nameplate was cut a red diamond; the name of course commemorated Queen Victoria's Diamond Jubilee. At the same time the engine was converted to compound working and renumbered 1901. No. 1502 had its double chimney replaced by a single chimney of standard design and was renumbered 1902. The name *Iron Duke* then passed to the first of the production batch, No. 1903, seen in this official view taken on 30th June 1899. The large driving wheel boss facilitated better casting of the wheel and was designed to contain balance weights, a feature introduced on the 'Jubilee' class and repeated later by Bowen Cooke in the 'George the Fifth' and 'Claughton' classes. The tender is still the standard wooden-framed type of 2,000 gallons capacity and has the wheelbase unequally divided. Tenders of this kind were fitted to all the 'Jubilees' and to the first ten 'Alfred the Greats'.

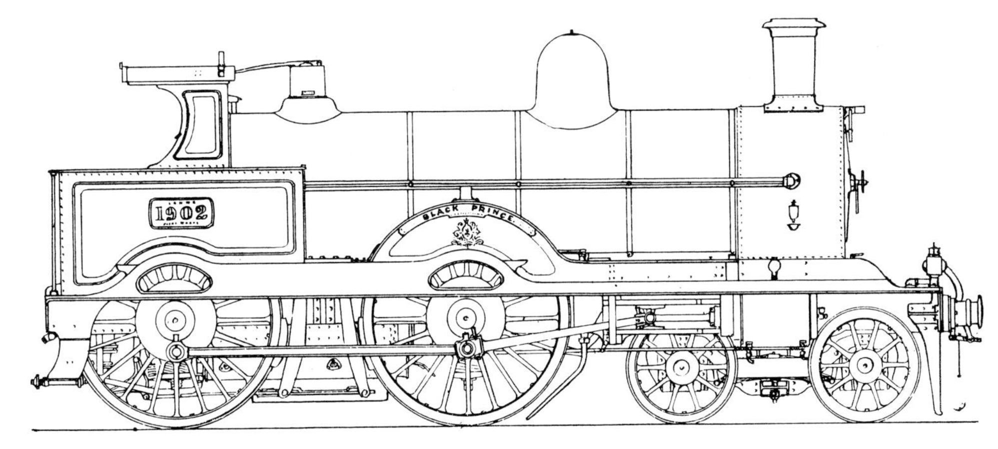

Figure 86: Drawing of *Black Prince* with a single chimney.

Plate 309: An early view (pre-1903) of No. 1908 *Royal George* in No. 3 platform at Crewe, facing north. The communication cord is rigged on the tender, a system which was soon to be abandoned in favour of the modern system operating directly on the brake.

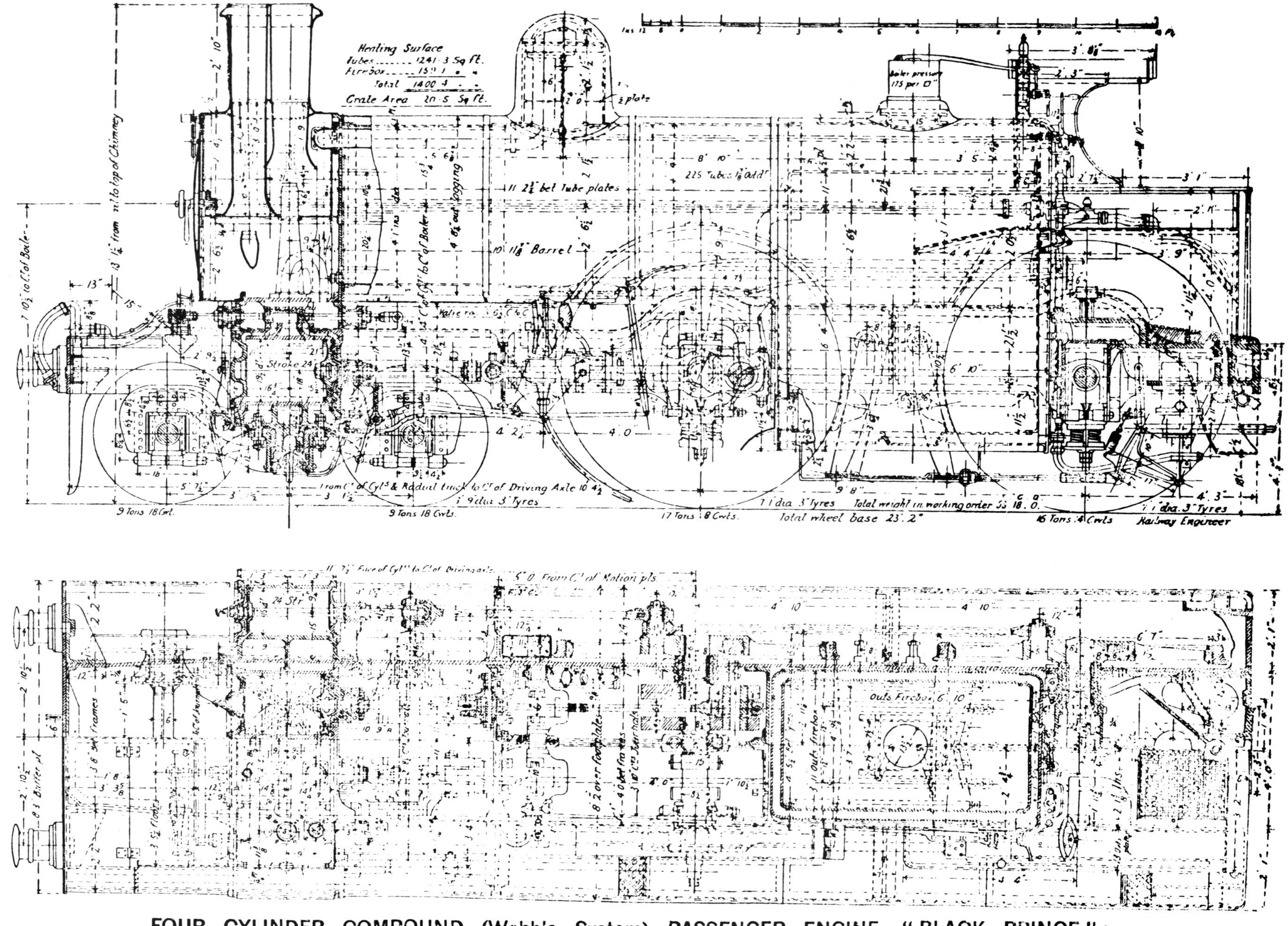

FOUR CYLINDER COMPOUND (Webb's System) PASSENGER ENGINE, "BLACK PRINCE": LONDON AND NORTH WESTERN RAILWAY.

Constructed at the Company's Works at Crewe to the designs of Mr. F. W. Webb, M.Council Inst.C.E., Chief Mechanical Engineer.

Two High Pressure Cylinders 15" × 24". Two Low Pressure Cylinders 19½" × 24". Wheels (new) 7' 1" diam.

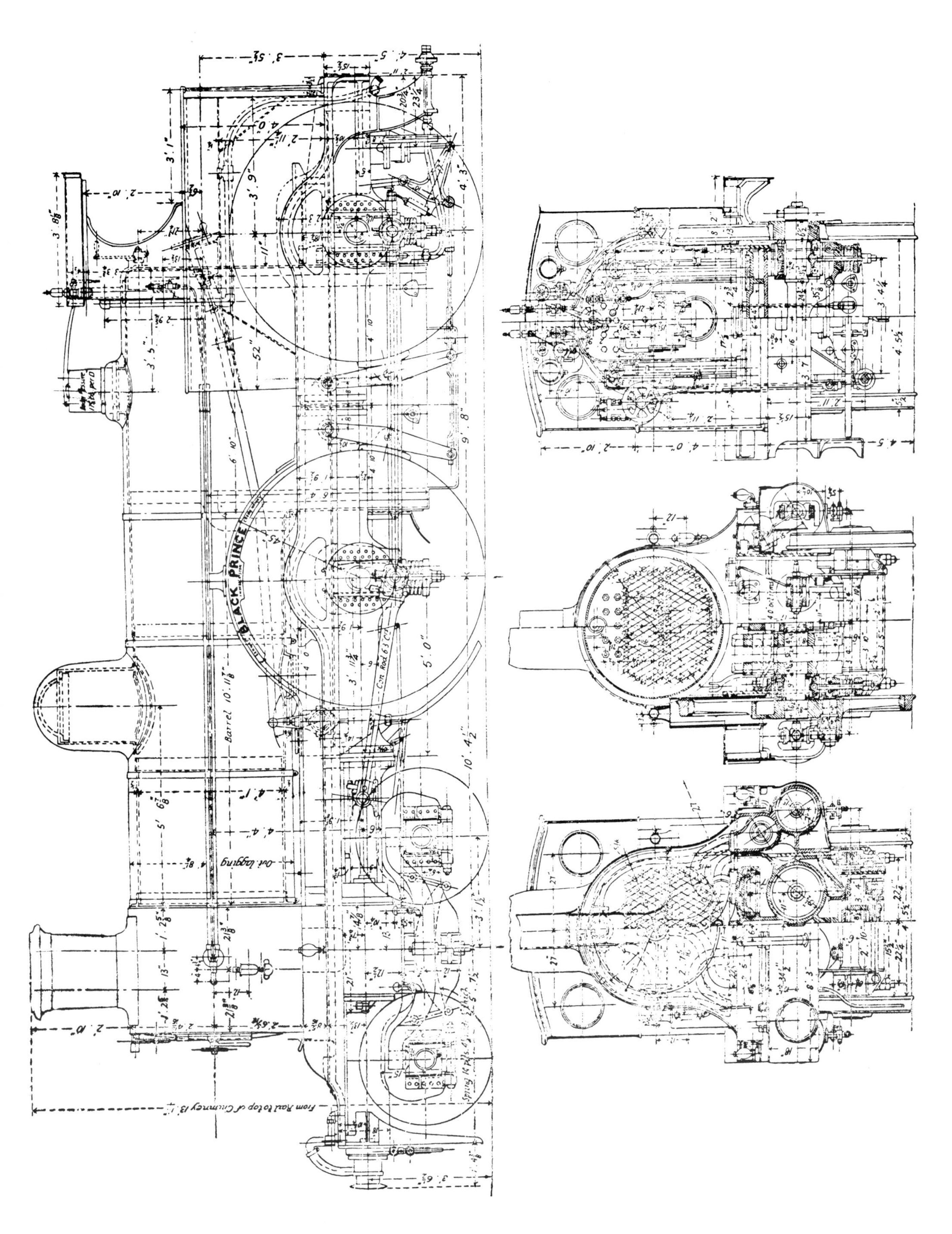

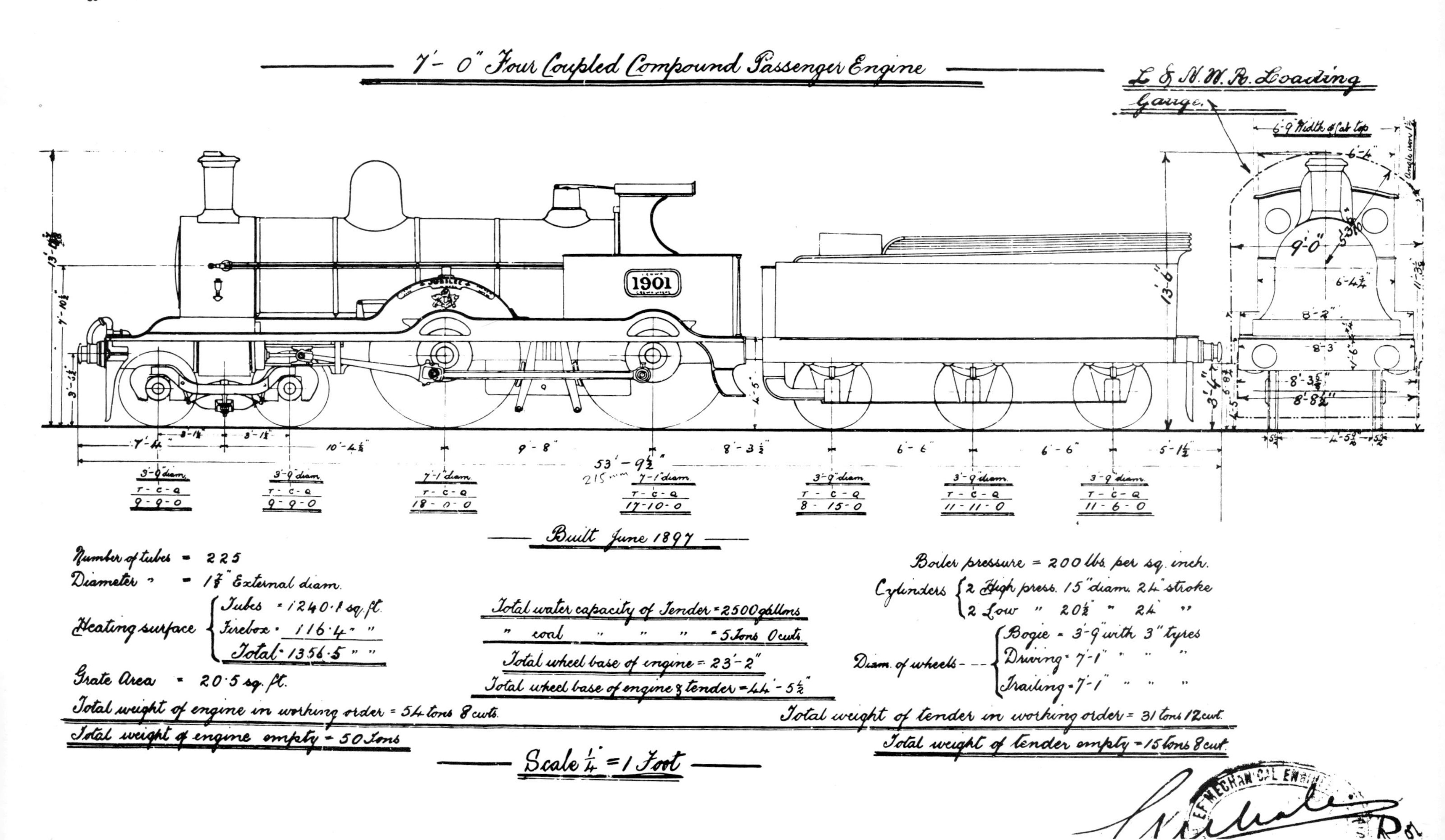

Figure 88: Weight diagram of *Jubilee*.

Plate 310 (right): Another pre-1903 view, No. 1918 *Renown*, thought to be at Bletchley on the up fast line. It now has cylindrical lubricators for the high-pressure cylinders.

Plate 311 (below right): 'Jubilee' class 4-4-0 No. 1907 *Black Watch*, again an early view taken before the fitting of the centre lamp socket in 1903.

Plate 312 (left): A much later view, perhaps about 1915, of No. 1917 *Inflexible* at Llandudno. The chimney has a capuchon and the sandpipes are fitted with shields to prevent the sand being blown off the rails by the wind.

Plate 313: In September 1904 two 'Jubilees' were fitted with boilers having Belpaire fireboxes, the design having been worked out during Mr Webb's superintendence. This view shows one of these boilers fitted to No. 1930 *Ramillies* in the late 1900s. Although the Webb cab is retained, its round front windows have been replaced by ones similar to those on Whale engines, and there is a capuchon on the chimney.

Plate 314: No. 1912 *Colossus*, with Belpaire firebox, long-tapered buffers and sandpipe windshields. The boiler was fitted in 1921 and is supposed to have come from *Ramillies*, one of the two engines originally so fitted, after it was rebuilt to a 'Renown' in 1916. The other Belpaire-fitted 'Jubilee' was No. 1929 *Polyphemus*.

'Alfred the Great'

Plate 315: The last of the forty 'Jubilees' was completed in October 1900 and in the following May the first of an enlarged version appeared, known as the 'Alfred the Great' class. They had boilers 4in. larger in diameter and 16in. high-pressure cylinders, though these were later reduced to 15in. like the 'Jubilees'. The first of the class was No. 1941 *Alfred the Great*, seen in this official view taken on completion at Crewe Works on 30th May 1901.

Plate 316 (right): A head-on view of an 'Alfred the Great', perhaps at Euston. This angle emphasises the greater bulk of the 'Alfred' boiler.

Figure 89: Drawing of the second 'Alfred' No. 1942 *King Edward VII.*

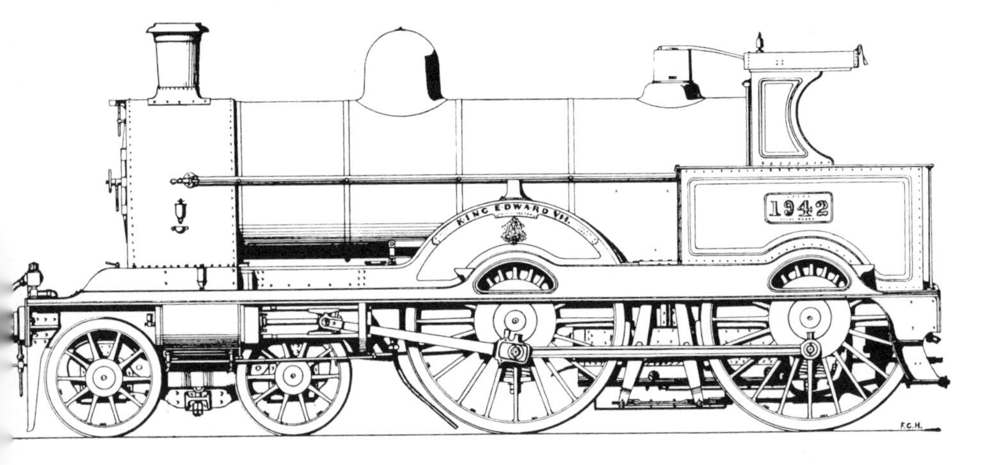

Plate 317: No. 1948 *Camperdown*, an early view taken before the centre lamp socket was fitted in 1903.

Plate 318: No. 1955 *Hannibal* at Euston sometime in 1902 (no centre lamp socket above the bufferbeam), when still quite new. This picture proves that the final type of Webb tender, holding 2,500 gallons and with equal wheelbase and flat tie rods, was introduced with the second batch of 'Alfreds'. The first ten had the 2,000 gallon unequal wheelbase type, as found on the 'Jubilees'.

Plate 319 (right): Another view of *Hannibal*, about 1905. The inspection covers over the rocker arms are open.

Plate 320 (left): No. 1950 *Victorious* leaving Manchester (London Road) about 1904. It has a capuchon on the chimney.

'Benbow'

Plate 321: The 'Jubilees' and 'Alfreds' suffered from not having the valve gear of the high- and low-pressure cylinders independently adjustable, a feature which had been well proved in the 'Teutonics' and 'Dreadnoughts'. This was remedied in September 1903, when No. 1952 *Benbow* was fitted with the so-called 'duplex' reversing gear. The outside cylinders were fitted with separate sets of Joy valve gear and the original gear operated the inside cylinders only, both the outside and inside gears being separately adjustable. This was found to be most successful and all the 'Alfreds' were converted to 'Benbows' by the end of 1907; they generally ran with the low-pressure cylinders in full gear, while the high-pressure ones were notched up as required. The drawings for the modification were prepared in February 1903 and signed by Webb in March before the illness which led to his retirement; but Whale signed the 'Benbow' cab drawing on 23rd July, the actual modification presumably being delayed pending his take-over. For some reason, no 'Jubilee' was ever modified in the same way. This view shows No. 1942 *King Edward VII* after conversion on 29th June 1905. The bulky casing on the running plate ahead of the leading splasher hides the upper part of the outside valve gear, which had to be offset inwards to operate the valves, since they were not directly above the cylinders. The engine also has a Whale cab, with vertical handrail extending to the rear corners of the roof, a Whale tender (fitted to only a few 'Benbows'), Whale buffers front and rear, and a capuchon.

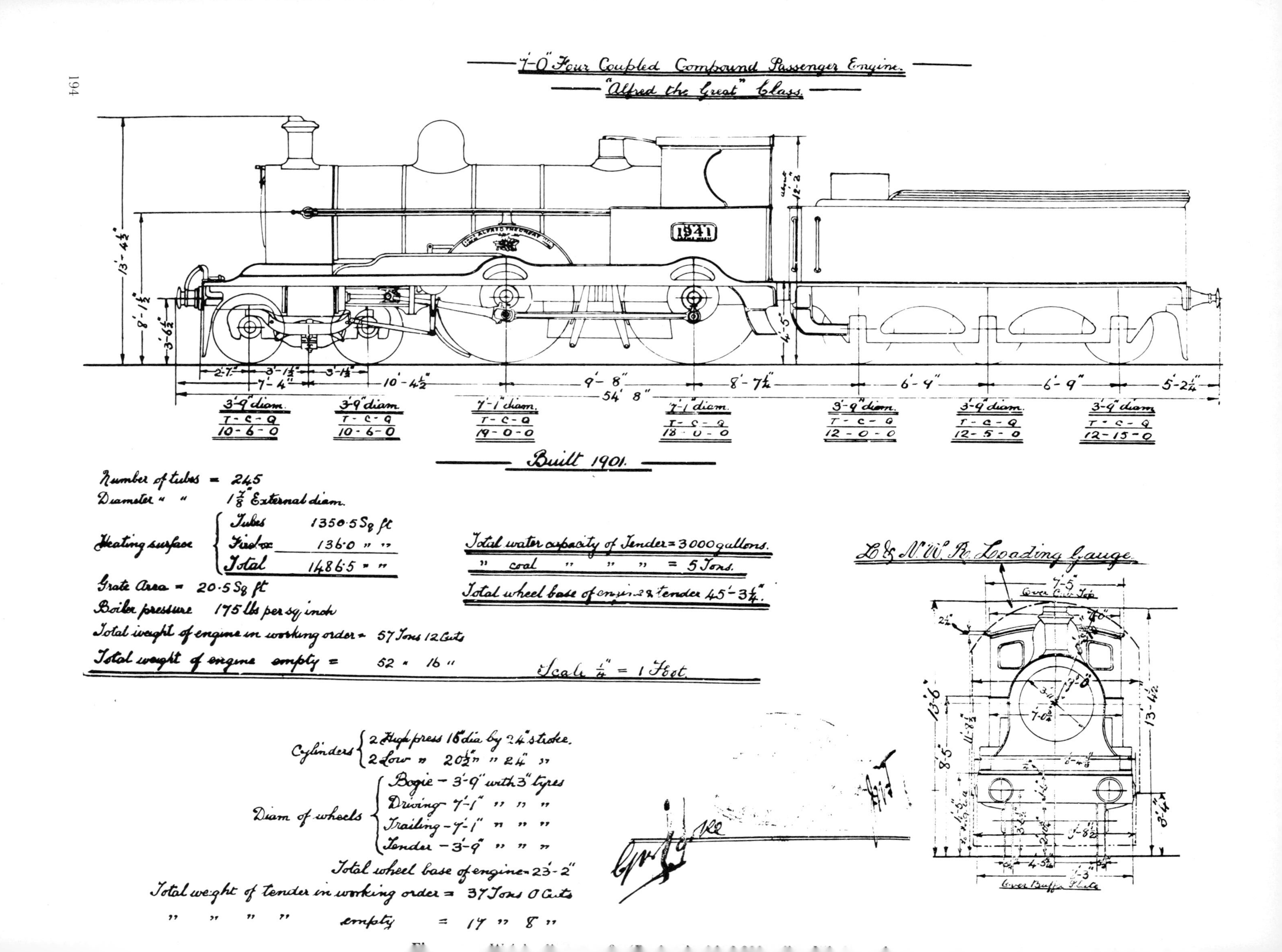

7-0" Four Coupled Compound Passenger Engine.
"Alfred the Great" Class.
1941
13'-4½"
8'-1½"
3'-6½"
about 12'-2"
4'-5"
2'-7"
3'-1½"
3'-1½"
7'-4"
10'-4½"
9'-8"
8'-7½"
6'-4"
6'-9"
5'-2¼"
54' 8"
3'-9" diam. T-C-Q 10-6-0
3'-9" diam T-C-Q 10-6-0
7'-1" diam. T-C-Q 19-0-0
7'-1" diam. T-C-Q 18-0-0
3'-9" diam. T-C-Q 12-0-0
3'-9" diam. T-C-Q 12-5-0
3'-9" diam. T-C-Q 12-15-0
Built 1901.
Number of tubes = 245
Diameter " " 1⅞" External diam.
Heating surface: Tubes 1350·5 Sq ft; Firebox 136·0 " "; Total 1486·5 " "
Grate Area = 20·5 Sq ft
Boiler pressure 175 lbs per sq inch
Total weight of engine in working order = 57 Tons 12 Cwts
Total weight of engine empty = 52 " 16 "
Total water capacity of Tender = 3000 gallons.
" coal " " " = 5 Tons.
Total wheel base of engine & tender 45'-3¼".
Scale ¼" = 1 Foot.
L & N.W. Ry. Loading Gauge.
7'-5" Over Cab Top
13'-6"
13'-4½"
8'-5"
3'-4"
4'-5¾"
Over Buffer Plate
Cylinders: 2 High press 15" dia by 24" stroke. 2 Low " 20½" " 24" "
Diam of wheels: Bogie - 3'-9" with 3" tyres; Driving 7'-1" " " "; Trailing - 7'-1" " " "; Tender - 3'-9" " " "
Total wheel base of engine = 23'-2"
Total weight of tender in working order = 37 Tons 0 Cwts
" " " " empty = 17 " 8 "

Plate 322: A really beautiful picture of No. 1966 *Commonwealth*, taken at Crewe with the 'spider bridge' in the background, after conversion on 13th January 1905. Its condition is more typical of the majority of 'Benbows' than that of *King Edward VII*. All had the modified valve gear and Whale cab, of course, but they probably all originally retained their Webb buffers and Webb tenders. The 2,500 gallon tender, with equal wheelbase and flat tie rods, is seen here to good advantage. Capuchons were also a feature of many of the 'Jubilees', 'Alfreds' and 'Benbows' at this period.

Plate 323 (right): 'Benbow' No. 1947 *Australia* at Stockport in the late 1900s. This engine was renamed *Zillah* in June 1911 when one of the 'British Empire' series of 'George the Fifths' was named *Australia*.

Plate 324 (left): No. 1947 *Zillah* in a view which shows clearly the shape of the windows in the Whale cab.

Plate 325 (right): 'Benbow' No. 1945 *Magnificent*, in typical condition as originally converted, and with a chimney having no capuchon.

Plate 326: 'Benbow' No. 1974 *Howe* was the only Webb compound ever to be fitted with a superheater, in May 1921, and is seen here in superheated condition. The lubricator usually fitted on the running plate above the outside cylinder has been removed and a supply is fed to the same point by a mechanical lubricator fixed to the frames ahead of the splasher. *Howe* also has long-tapered buffers, a capuchon and sandpipe windshields. It was the last Webb compound passenger engine to remain in service, being withdrawn in March 1928.

Plate 327: A view of the left-hand side of *Howe*, showing the oil-feed pipe coming through from the mechanical lubricator on the other side of the engine, to the point above the cylinder where a displacement lubricator was previously fitted.

'1400' or 'Bill Bailey'

Plate 328: In February 1903 Mr Webb's last design appeared from Crewe Works. It was a four-cylinder compound 4-6-0 and was intended as a more powerful replacement for the 'Cauliflowers' on mixed-traffic duties and particularly for fast goods work. The boiler and cylinders were the same as on the 'B' class four-cylinder compound goods engines (except that the high-pressure cylinders were 15in. not 16in. in diameter), the double radial truck was the same as the 'Jubilees' but with smaller wheels, and the wheel centres came from withdrawn 'DXs'. This official photograph shows the first of the class, No. 1400, on completion on 17th March 1903. It has all the usual features typical of the final phase of Mr Webb's work at Crewe: steel front bufferbeam and metal brake blocks, but wooden-framed tender and a capuchon on the chimney. An unusual feature for Crewe is the long continuous splasher. There is a sandbox on the front of the splasher and another on the tender, to help in braking heavy trains.

Plate 329: The second of the 'Bill Baileys', as the class became known, was completed but kept in store at Crewe Works for some months, until trials had been held with No. 1400. It is seen here standing in the works yard awaiting transfer to the paintshop, and with its running number, 2033, chalked on the cabside. The centre lamp socket, a feature introduced in 1903, can be seen just beyond the front vacuum-brake hose, and there are still two whistles on the cab roof.

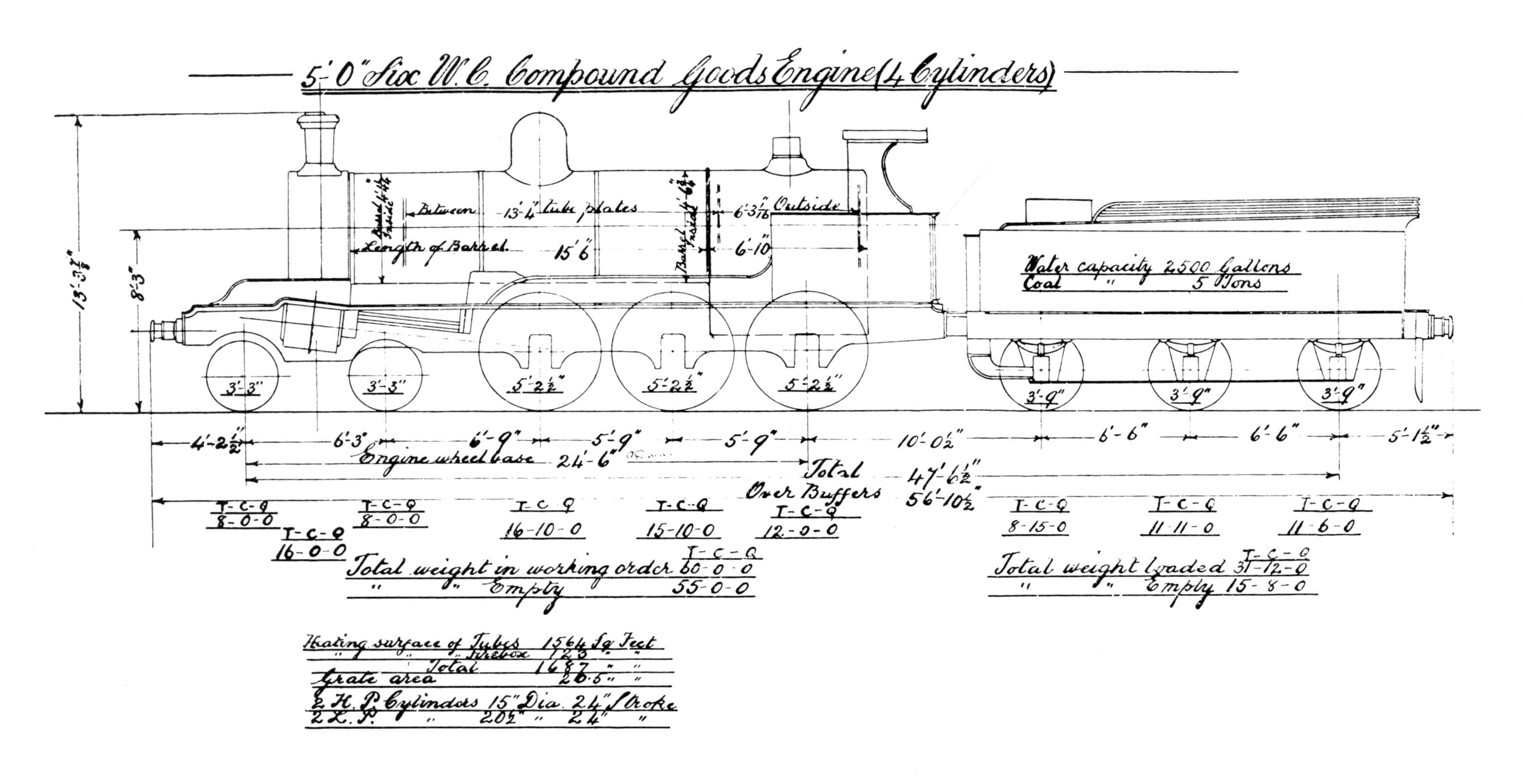

Figure 91: Weight diagram of a 'Bill Bailey' with a Webb 2,500 gallon tender.

Figure 92: Drawing of No. 1400 as built.

Plate 330 (left): Another of the firs batch, No. 1466; it must be an early viev as there are two whistles on the cab roof.

Plate 331 (below): No. 1352 in servic probably about 1905.

Plate 332 (right): The 'Bill Baileys' are generally presented as Mr Webb's greatest failure but in fact only two had been completed before his retirement at the end of May 1903. Eight more, completing the first batch of ten, were built in November and December, and Mr Whale could certainly have stopped construction of the twenty built in 1904-5. This is No. 1729, the last of the first batch.

Plate 333 (above): No. 1414, one of the second batch, at Mold Junction about 1910. It has Whale buffers on wooden bases.

Plate 333a (right): No. 1113, built in September 1904, was one of the last batch and was one of the last to be scrapped, in 1920. It is seen here at Manchester (London Road), fitted with Cooke buffers.

Chapter 11
Eight-Coupled Goods Engines

No. 2524

Plate 334: In October 1892 Mr Webb built the first of the long line of LNWR eight-coupled coal engines, No. 2524. It was basically an enlarged '17in Coal Engine', with two inside cylinders, having valves and motion based on the '18in Goods' but enlarged to 19½in. by 24in., and the 'Greater Britain' boiler, complete with its combustion chamber part way along the barrel. Although various designs of three- and four-cylinder compound eight-coupled goods engines were at first preferred, the eventual line of development was from the basis of No. 2524, through the 'C', 'D' and 'G' class two-cylinder simple 0-8-0s to the superheated 'G1' and 'G2' classes. This official view of No. 2524 as built was taken on 3rd November 1892. Metal brake blocks are used for the first time on a goods engine but otherwise it has the usual Webb features of the time such as steel bufferbeam and wooden-framed tender with wooden brake blocks. The ash chute from the combustion chamber can be seen beneath the boiler, just to the rear of the second splasher. There is one sandbox, alongside the smokebox, for the front of the engine, and another on the tender, just behind the footsteps, to assist with braking and for running in reverse; the latter would be needed especially when shunting a train in bad weather, or when reversing into a siding off a main line to allow a passenger train to pass. The blower valve is on the left-hand side.

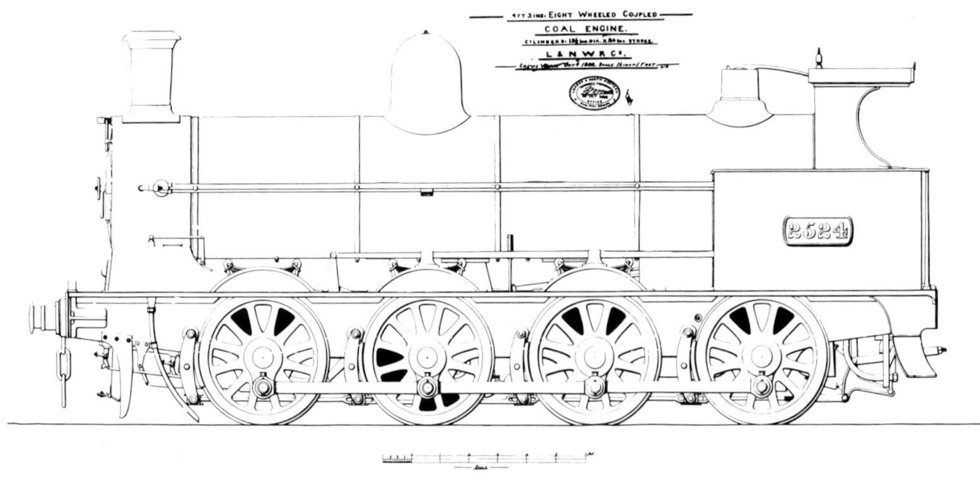

Figure 93: Official drawing of No. 2524.

Plate 335 (above): The number of the engine in this photograph has not been recorded but it seems certain to be No. 2524, since it has no coal rails on the tender and it appears to have no centre lamp socket on the bufferbeam; and no 'C' class were built until long after both these features became standard. The engine is well cleaned in lined black livery and is passing Coleham shed, Shrewsbury, with a northbound freight train. No. 2524 was converted to 'D' class in December 1906.

'A'

Plate 336: In September 1893 Mr Webb built his first three-cylinder compound 0-8-0, No. 50. It was intended as a compound version of No. 2524, with two high-pressure cylinders outside, operated by Stephenson valve gear, and one low-pressure cylinder inside, with a slip eccentric. The boiler was very similar to that of No. 2524 but it had no combustion chamber. Instead the front tubeplate was recessed into the boiler for the same distance as a combustion chamber and the char hopper placed behind and to the right of the low-pressure cylinder. The blower valve is on the left-hand side of the smokebox but there is no linkage for the bypass valve, which on this engine was operated by a complicated linkage passing through the boiler. This is the official view of No. 50 taken on 26th September 1893. Except for features associated with the three-cylinder compound front end, there are no detail differences from No. 2524. The arrangement of sandboxes is the same, one at the front of the engine and one on the tender. The latter was important for the braking of heavy trains and for reversing into a siding off a main line, and was a feature of the 'Bill Baileys' as well as the 'A' and 'B' class 0-8-0s. No. 50 was the first engine to have a 2,000 gallon tender, which must have been built for it, as it has cast H-section wheels. The slight extra overhang can be seen by comparison with the 1,800 gallon tender on No. 2524.

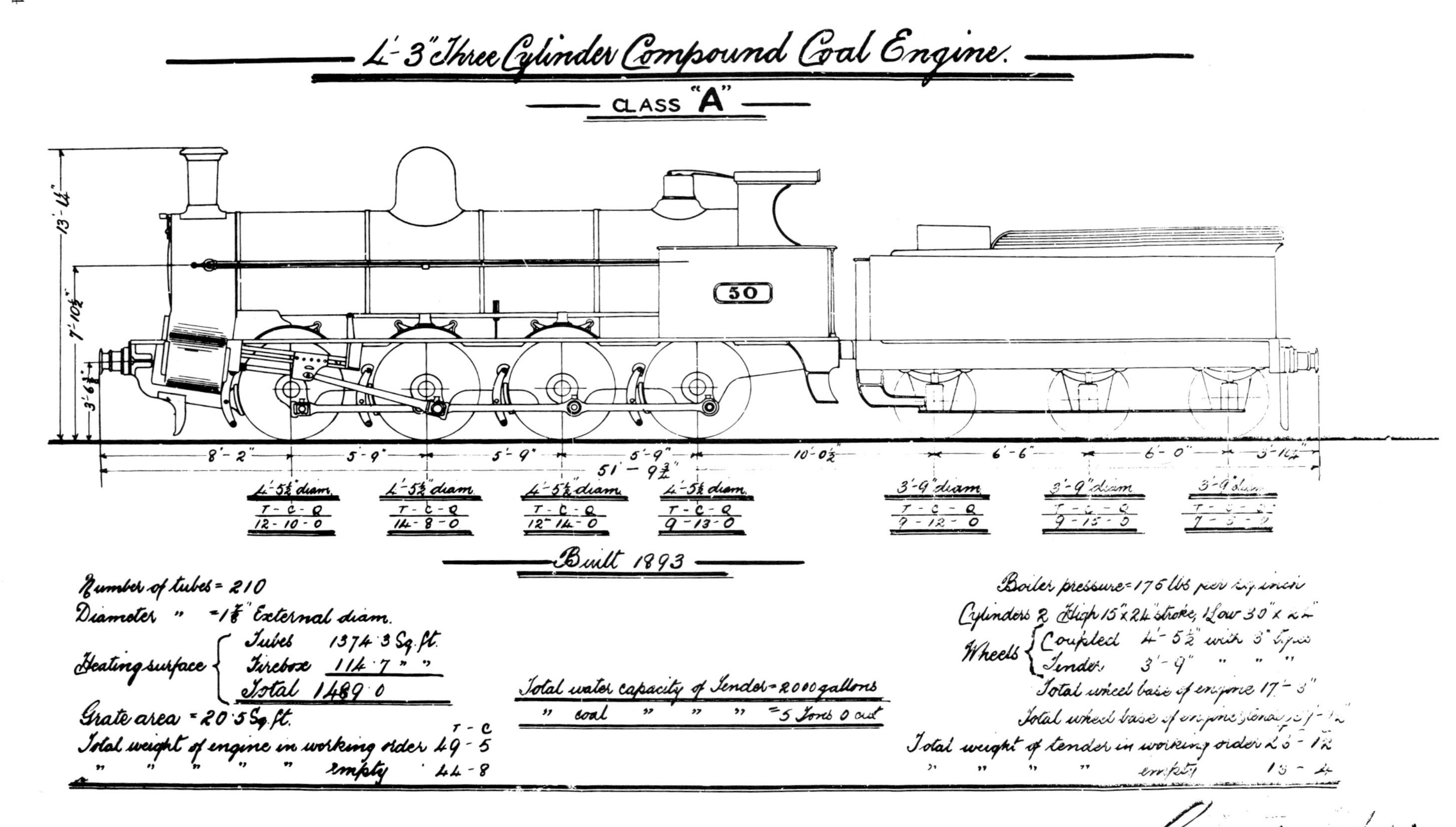

Figure 94: Weight diagram of No. 50.

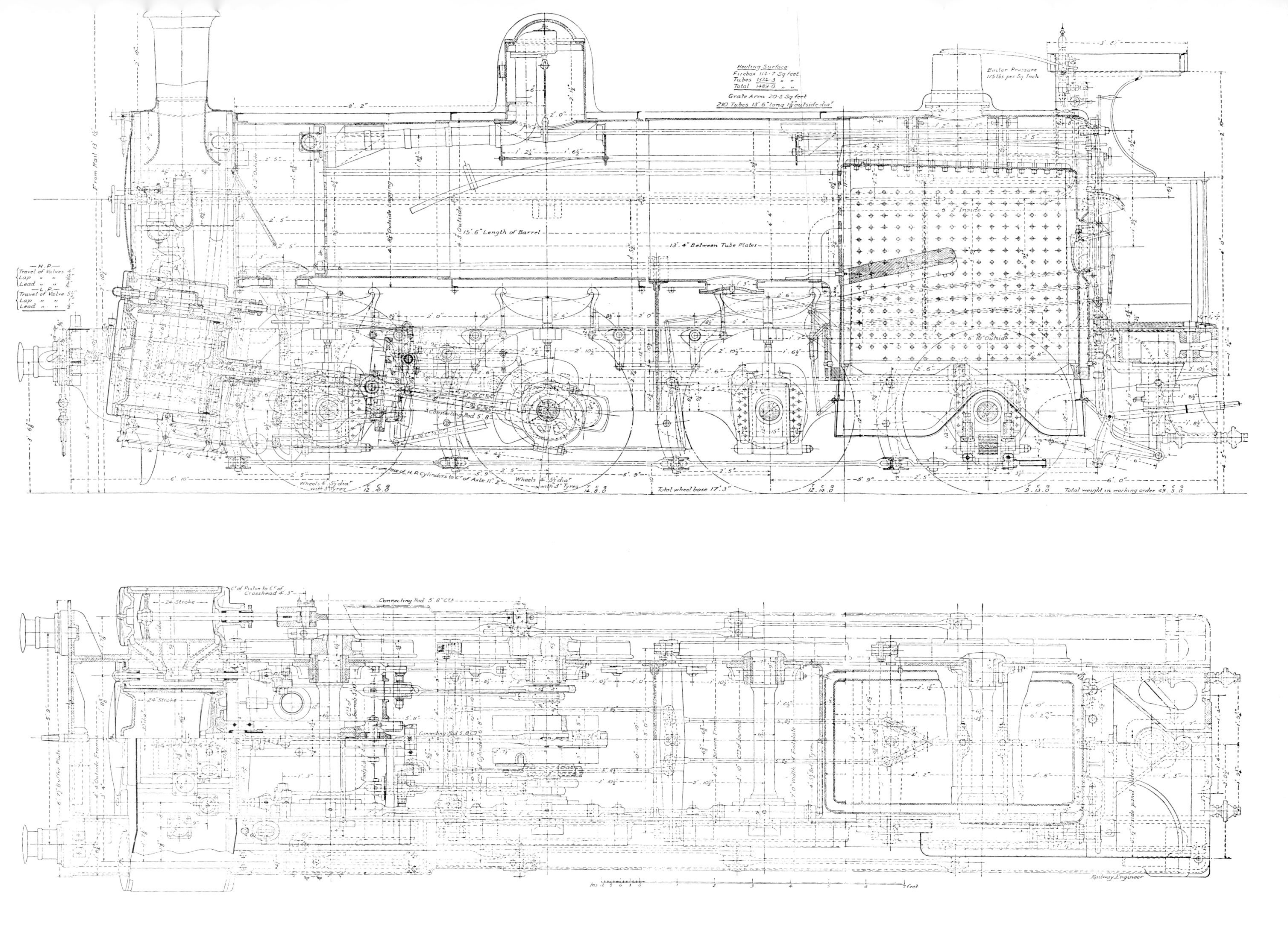

Figure 95: General arrangement drawings of an 'A' class 0-8-0.

Plate 337 (right): After comparative trials between No. 2524 and No. 50, the three-cylinder compound 0-8-0 was chosen as the standard heavy goods engine and 110 were built between 1894 and 1900. The last '17in Coal Engine' 0-6-0 was built in October 1892, after which no more 0-6-0s were built purely for goods work. The last 'Cauliflower' was built in May 1902, being superseded for mixed-traffic duties first by the 'Bill Baileys' and then by Whale's '19in Goods'. So although Mr Webb is sometimes derided for his locomotive policies, both he and the LNWR had abandoned the 0-6-0 type some twenty years before certain much respected railways that built it widely had even come into existence! This picture shows 'A' class 0-8-0 No. 2528. It was probably taken at Shrewsbury, sometime before 1903, as no centre lamp socket is fitted; the tender has coal rails. Incidentally, the system of using letters to denote the various classes of eight-coupled goods engines was not introduced until late in 1911.

Plate 338 (right): An 'A' class 0-8-0 on completion in the paint shop at Crewe Works.

Plate 339 (below): Another official photograph of an 'A' class 0-8-0, No. 1867, taken after completion on 21st September 1899. It has two small but important modifications compared with No. 50. Firstly, the third pair of driving wheels are flangeless, to facilitate negotiation of curves; No. 2528 was the first to have this modification and it was applied to all subsequent eight-coupled engines. Secondly, it has a bypass valve, operated as on a three-cylinder compound passenger engine, by pushing or pulling the handwheel connected to the boiler handrail. This valve allowed exhaust steam from the high-pressure cylinder to escape directly up the blastpipe on starting. Because the 0-8-0 compounds were coupled engines, they did not have the relief valve for the low-pressure receiver behind the chimney, as the low-pressure crank was always in the optimum position. So there was no danger of the high-pressure engine slipping and choking the receiver, as on the uncoupled compound passenger engines. These two modifications were then presumably made to all earlier engines.

Plate 340 (left): 'A' class 0-8-0 No. 1817 in the late 1890s.

Plate 341 (right): View looking down on No. 1843 at Shrewsbury shed, sometime after 1903. The seam of rivets joining the cleading plates along the top of the boiler can just be seen. In November 1904 Mr Whale began converting the 'A' class to two-cylinder simple 0-8-0s; the conversions were to class 'C', 'C1' or 'D' and all had been converted to one or another of these classes by September 1912. No. 1843 became a 'D' class in May 1908.

Plate 342 (below): 'A' class No. 1844, sometime before 1903. The double lamp socket on the bufferbeam was for use over GCR lines in the Manchester area. In May 1910, it was converted to class 'C1'.

'B'

Plate 343: In 1901 Mr Webb produced a four-cylinder compound 0-8-0, later designated as class 'B'. It had two high-pressure cylinders outside and two low-pressure cylinders inside, while compared with the 'A' class, the boiler was 5in. larger in diameter and of 200lb. pressure instead of 175lb. Otherwise, in general appearance and details, it was very similar, with steel bufferbeam, metal brake blocks and wooden-framed tender. At first, it also had the same arrangement of sandboxes, one at the front of the engine and one on the front of the tender. This was changed soon after Mr Whale took over in 1903; a second sandbox was fitted to the engine, on the driving splasher, being worked by rodding from the leading one, and the tender sandbox was abolished. All subsequent developments of the 'B' class, the 'E', 'F', 'G', 'G1' and 'G2' classes, had the same arrangement of sandboxes on the two leading splashers, while developments of the 'A' class, the 'C', 'C1' and 'D' classes, had only one larger one, on the leading splasher. This view shows No. 1881 on completion in August 1901. It later became the only 'B' to be fitted for working vacuum-braked trains. The third pair of driving wheels are flangeless, and there is a boiler support or stay made of steel plate, which was later changed to a casting.

Plate 344 (right): 'B' class 0-8-0 No. 2024 at Buxton about 1910. The arrangement of sandboxes on the two leading splashers can be clearly seen, as can the cast boiler support which looks triangular when seen end-on. The tender wheels are H-section.

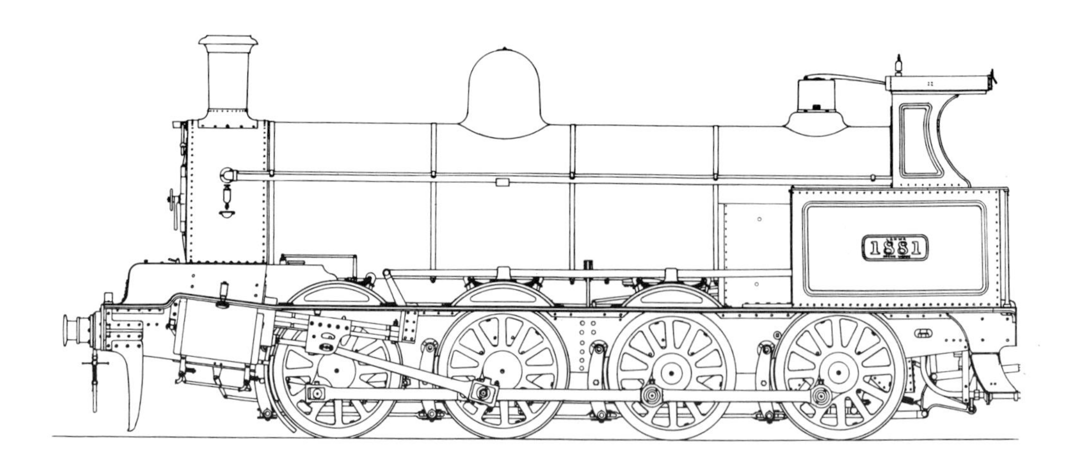

Figure 96: Drawing of No. 1881.

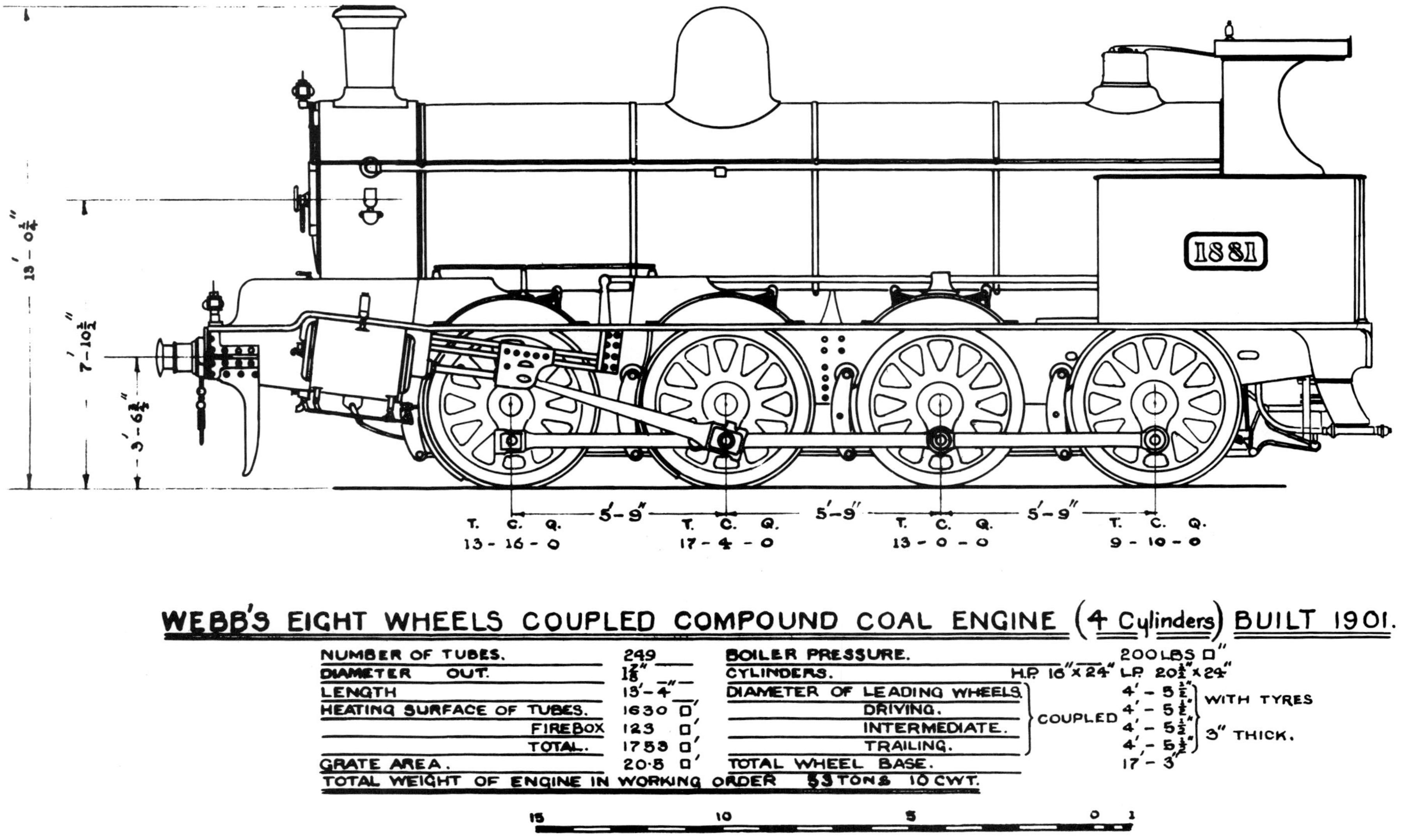

13' – 0¼"

7' – 10½"

3' – 6¼"

1881

	T. C. Q.		T. C. Q.		T. C. Q.		T. C. Q.
	13 - 16 - 0	5'–9"	17 - 4 - 0	5'–9"	13 - 0 - 0	5'–9"	9 - 10 - 0

WEBB'S EIGHT WHEELS COUPLED COMPOUND COAL ENGINE (4 Cylinders) BUILT 1901.

NUMBER OF TUBES.	249	BOILER PRESSURE.	200 LBS □"
DIAMETER OUT.	1⅞"	CYLINDERS.	H.P. 16" x 24" L.P. 20½" x 24"
LENGTH	13' – 4"	DIAMETER OF LEADING WHEELS. (COUPLED)	4' – 5½" (WITH TYRES 3" THICK.)
HEATING SURFACE OF TUBES.	1630 □'	DRIVING.	4' – 5½"
FIREBOX	123 □'	INTERMEDIATE.	4' – 5½"
TOTAL.	1753 □'	TRAILING.	4' – 5½"
GRATE AREA.	20·5 □'	TOTAL WHEEL BASE.	17' – 3"
TOTAL WEIGHT OF ENGINE IN WORKING ORDER	53 TONS 10 CWT.		

15 10 5 0 1

Figure 97: Weight diagram of No. 1881.

Plate 345 (above): 'B' class 0-8-0 No. 859 at Wigan, in full lined livery about 1910. Except for those on the driving axle, its wheels have all come from a withdrawn '17in. Coal Engine' 0-6-0, having only one balance weight instead of the two on wheels made for the class.

Plate 346 (right): On the 'B' class the valves of the outside cylinders were driven from the inside valves by rocking arms which were positioned in front of the cylinders ahead of the smokebox, as on the 'Jubilees' and 'Alfred the Greats'. The rocking arms were hidden by covers shaped like the lid of a piano, which gave rise to the nick-name 'piano-fronts' or 'pianos'. In this view of No. 1047, built in November 1902, two of the covers are raised. It is probably a post-1916 view, as the engine is in plain black livery.

Plate 347 (left): No. 2272 at Bletchley in 1920-1, still in lined livery but with Cooke buffers. It was built in October 1903 and was converted direct to 'G1' class in May 1921. Some 'B' class were converted to classes 'E' and 'F', others were rebuilt to class 'G', and still others were converted direct to 'G1' class.

Plate 348 (right): 'B' class 0-8-0 No. 1282 about 1920, fitted with Cooke buffers but otherwise still much as originally built and in lined livery. This was one of eleven 'B' class which were withdrawn without being converted to any other class.

'E'

Plate 349: Mr Whale disliked the overhang and concentrated weight at the front end of the 'B' class and in August 1904 converted No. 1886 into a 2-8-0 by adding a pony truck. In all, 26 'B' class were converted in this way in four years and were later designated class 'E'. This view shows No. 1886 at Crewe soon after conversion, on 15th October 1904. Except for the pony truck, it is in typical 'B' class condition, though still with steel-plate boiler support. There are two sandboxes on either side of the engine but none on the tender.

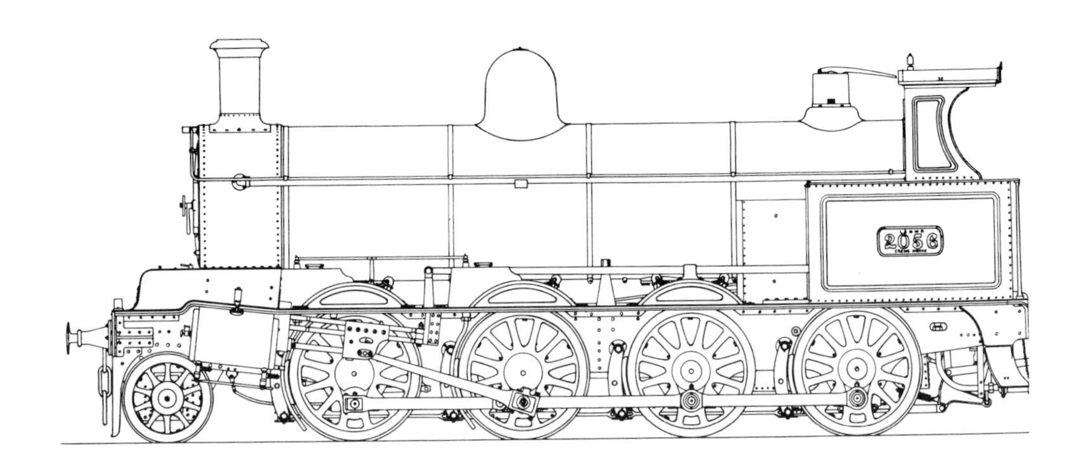

Figure 98: Drawing of 'E' class No. 2056.

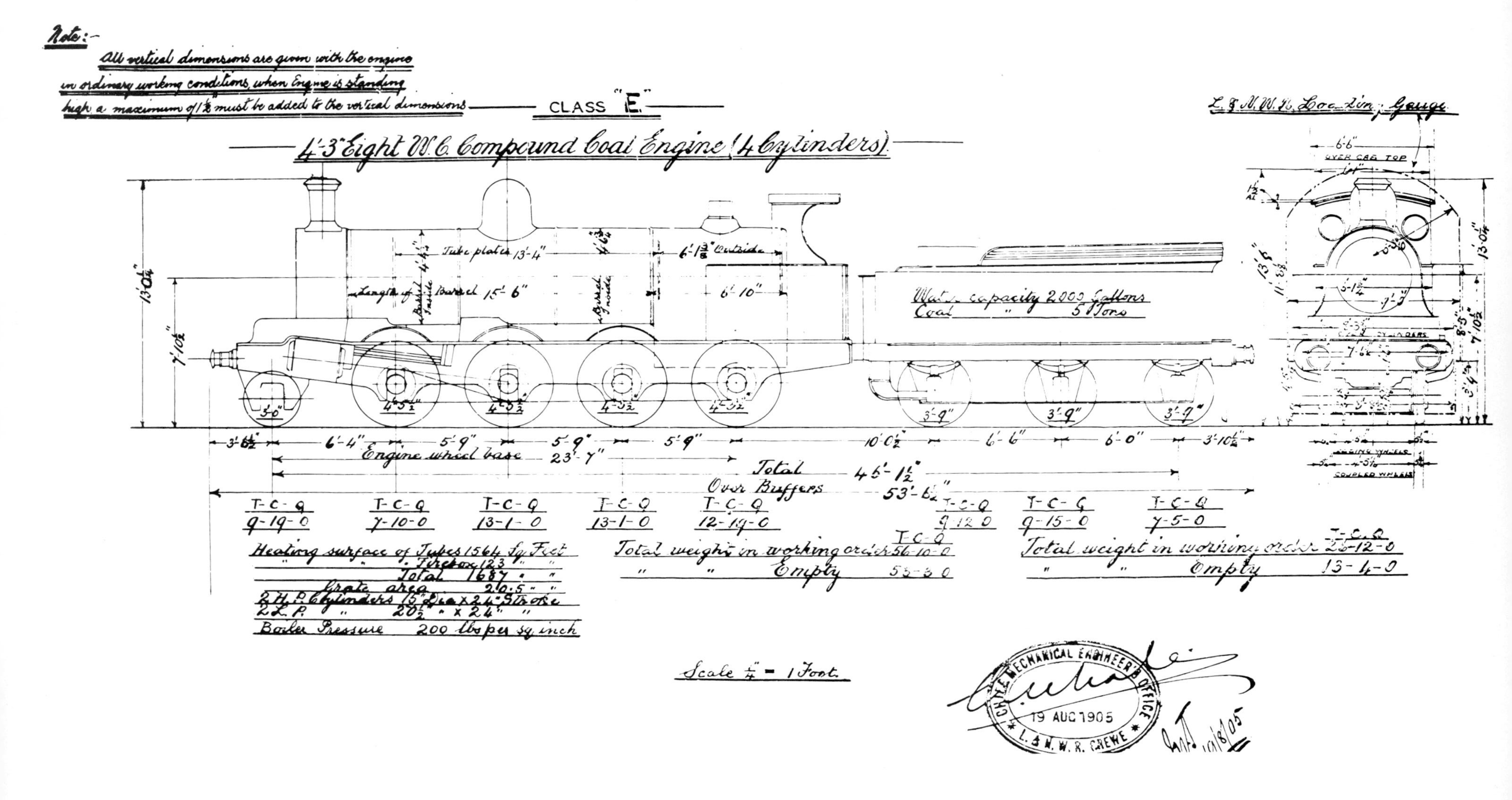

Figure 99: Weight diagram of an 'E' class 2-8-0 locomotive.

Plate 350 (left): 'E' class 2-8-0 No. 18, converted from 'B' class in November 1905, at Willesden about 1920. It still has lined livery and has acquired Cooke buffers but otherwise is little altered, still having wheels from a '17in. Coal Engine'. Most 'E' class were converted to class 'G1', but six were withdrawn as 'Es', one of them being No. 18, in April 1928.

Plate 351 (right): 'E' class 2-8-0 No. 1222, also at Willesden about 1920, still in lined livery and with Cooke buffers. It was converted to 'E' class in May 1906 and withdrawn at the end of 1928.

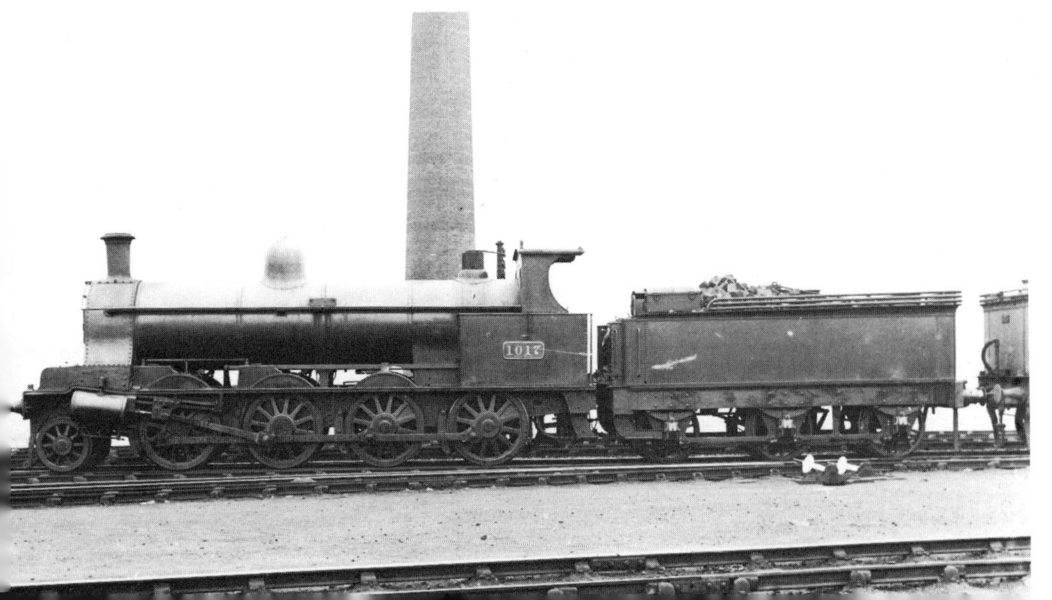

Plate 352 (left): 'E' class 2-8-0 No. 1017, which was converted from 'B' class in January 1906 and withdrawn in November 1927. As well as Cooke buffers, it has acquired a lubricator on the boiler handrail, a Beames feature of 1921-2, and is in plain black livery.

'F'

Plate 353: As well as the 26 'B' class converted to 'E' class 2-8-0s by the simple addition of a pony truck, ten more 'B' class were converted in the same way but also received bigger boilers of the same diameter as used on Whale's 'Precursors' and 'Experiments', and were designated class 'F'; two 'E' class were also fitted with such boilers, so in all there were twelve 'F' class. The first 'F' was No. 1273, which is seen here in the official photograph taken on 16th May 1906, immediately on conversion. It has Whale buffers and a Whale tender, which was almost certainly attached only while the official photograph was taken. In general, rebuilds from compound 0-8-0s to classes 'C', 'D, 'E', 'F' and 'G' had wooden-framed 2,500 gallon tenders, though 'G' class built new had steel-framed tenders; but with Crewe's propensity for changing tenders around, exceptions to this are not hard to find. The tender seen here has long-tapered buffers, which had a parallel portion at the end and were longer than the first type of Whale tapered buffer. They are often referred to as 'Cooke buffers', since they were widely used on many classes of engine during Bowen Cooke's superintendence at Crewe, though they were actually introduced by Whale early in 1906 on the rear of tenders.

Plate 354 (right): Another photograph of No. 1273, taken much later when the engine was painted plain black. It has Cooke buffers, a Webb tender, which is fully lined out, and a sandbox under the cab for working tender first. Most of the 'F' class were converted to 'G1' class but two were withdrawn without being converted, one of them being No. 1273.

Figure 100: Drawing of 'F' class 2-8-0 No. 2573.

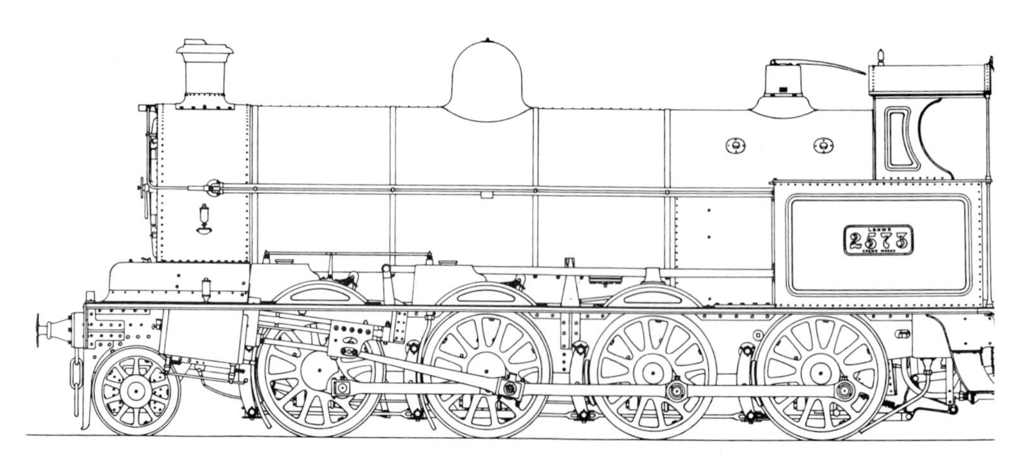

CLASS F.

4'-3" EIGHT W. C. COMPOUND COAL ENGINE (4 CYLINDERS.)

FITTED WITH LARGE BOILERS 5'-2" DIAMETER.

L. & N. W. Ry. Loading Gauge

Length of barrel 14'-6"

Water capacity 3000 gallons.
Coal " 5 tons.

Engine wheel base 23-7"
Tender wheel base 13'-6"
Total wheel base of Engine and Tender 47'-5¼"
Outside buffers 56'-2"

T. C. Q.	T. C. Q.	T. C. Q.	T. C. Q.	T. C. Q.	T. C. Q.	T. C. Q.	T. C. Q.
10-0-0	9-0-0	14-0-0	14-10-0	15-0-0	12-0-0	12-5-0	12-15-0

Number of Tubes 276
Diam " " 1⅞ outside
Heating Surface of tubes 1896.5 sq ft.
" " firebox 146.7 " "
Total 2043.2 " "
Grate area 23.6 " "
Cylinders –
2 High Pressure 15" × 24"
2 Low " 20½" × 24"
Boiler Pressure. 175 lbs per sq inch.

	T. C. Q.
Total weight of Engine in working order.	62-10-0
Total — — — empty.	56-3-0

	T. C. Q.
Total weight of Tender in working order.	37-0-0
Total — — — empty.	17-8-0

Tractive Force. 21810 lbs. at 75% B.P.

SCALE ¼" = 1 FOOT.

Geo. Cooke

Figure 101: Weight diagram of class 'F'.

Plate 355: 'F' class No. 1036, at Manchester (London Road) about 1912. It is in full lined livery and has a Whale tender. The front buffers are the Whale type on wooden bases, and there is a sandbox under the cab. Its driving wheels, with only one balance weight, have come from a withdrawn '17in. Coal Engine'.

'C' and 'C1'

Plate 356: In November 1904 Mr Whale began to convert the 'A' class three-cylinder compounds into two-cylinder simples, the first so treated being No. 2541. New cylinders, 19½in. by 24in., and new motion were provided but otherwise the engines were little changed, the result being very similar to No. 2524 except for the latter's 'Greater Britain' boiler. Fifteen conversions to 'C' class were made, the last being in March 1906 when Mr Whale decided that larger boilers were needed to feed 19½in. by 24in. cylinders. He therefore fitted the large boiler used on the 'F' class to the 'C' class chassis, thus producing the 'D' class; 63 conversions to 'D' class were made, including No. 2524, from March 1906 to March 1909. The fitting of large boilers to 'Ds' left a quantity of small 'A' class boilers unused, so the remaining 'A' class were converted to simples as 'C' class but with smaller cylinders, 18½in. by 24in. They were designated 'C1' class but outwardly, the 'C' and 'C1' classes were indistinguishable from each other. This official view shows 'C1' class No. 2550 after conversion on 3rd January 1910. It has Whale buffers at the front but retains its Webb tender. There is one sandbox at the front, as on No. 2524, and another at the rear of the engine, filled from inside the cab; there is no tender sandbox. As originally built, the 'C' class did not have this arrangement, though they acquired it later. They and the 'D' class originally had one sandbox at the front of the engine only.

Plate 357: View of the front end of No. 2550. No vacuum brake is fitted, as the engine is intended purely for goods work.

Plate 358: View of cab of No. 2550, a quite typical Webb or Whale design. Under the footplate, in the middle, is the cylinder for the engine's steam brake.

Plate 359: 'C' class 0-8-0 No. 1803 at Rugby about 1920 in plain black livery, with Cooke buffers and a lined tender. The original leading crankpin, designed to pass behind the slide bars of the 'A' class outside cylinders, is retained.

Plate 360 (left): 'C' class 0-8-0 No. 1814; the boiler support has been cut away to accommodate a brake cylinder. Five of the class were converted to 'G1' class in early LMS days but the remaining ten, including No. 1814, and all the 'C1' class were withdrawn without being converted.

Plate 361 (above): 'C1' class 0-8-0 No. 1859, converted from 'A' class in March 1911, in plain black livery about 1920.

'D'

Plate 362 : When the 'C' class was found to be under-boilered with the original 'A' class boiler, Mr Whale fitted the large boiler used on the 'F' class to the same chassis and so produced the 'D' class. In all, the 'D' class totalled 63 engines, 62 conversions from 'A' class plus No. 2524, the original Webb simple. The first was converted in March 1906 and the last in March 1909. This view shows the first of the class, No. 1866, after conversion on 12th March 1906. It has the usual Whale features of the day, including Whale buffers, but retains the original 'A' class leading crankpin. There is one sandbox at the front of the engine and no provision for rear sanding. The tender is a steel-framed Whale design, which may have been attached purely for the photograph. Some 'Ds' had these tenders while others had the Webb type.

Plate 363: 'D' class 0-8-0 No. 2526 at Tamworth about 1910, in lined livery and with Whale tender. The single large sandbox, flush with the front of the smokebox, is the easiest means of distinguishing a 'D' from a 'G' class; the rear sandbox is under the footplate.

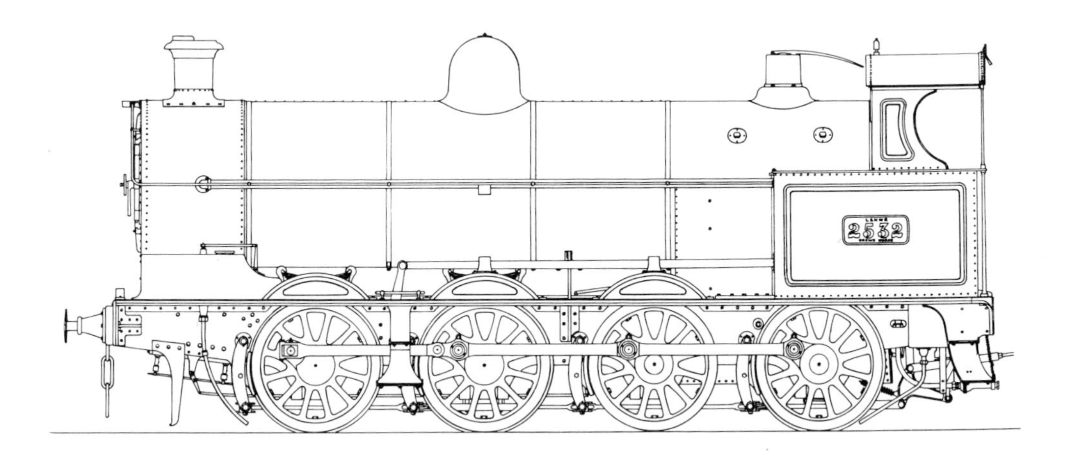

Figure 102: Drawing of 'D' class No. 2532.

Plate 364: 'D' class 0-8-0 No. 2548 taking water in the up platform at Tamworth (Low Level) about 1915. A rear sandbox has been fitted, by the footstep under the cab, and the tender is the Whale type. Because of their great hauling power, the 'Ds' became extremely popular with LNWR enginemen, who for this reason referred to all the superheated 0-8-0s by the blanket term 'Super Ds', whether in fact they were converted from 'Ds' or not.

Plate 365: 'D' class 0-8-0 No. 2532 in lined livery about 1910. It has a Whale tender and Whale buffers on wooden bases.

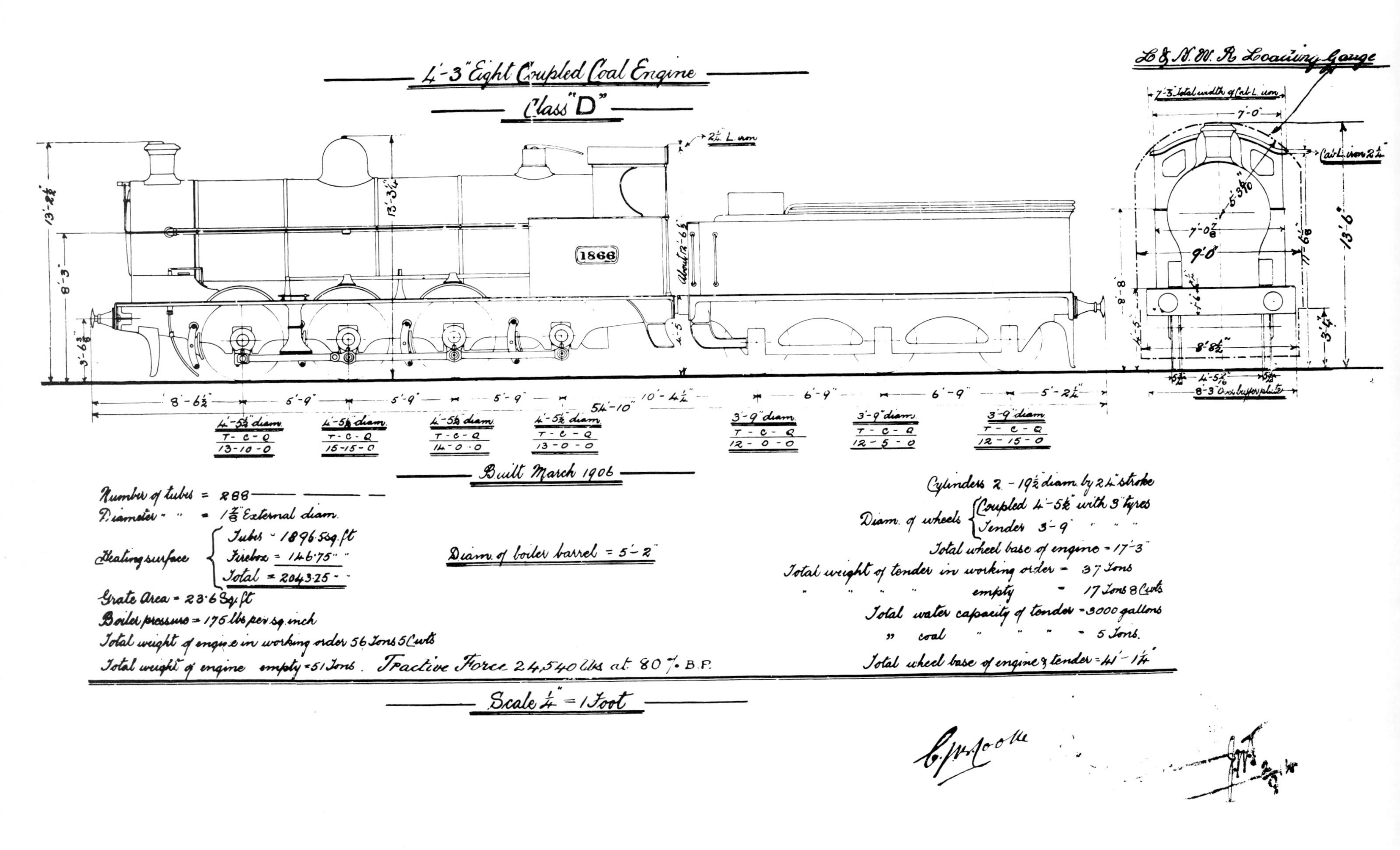

Figure 103: Weight diagram of 'D' class. The drawing is in error in showing a cast boiler support. Being converted from class 'A', the 'D' class retained the steel plate type.

Plate 366 (above): 'D' class 0-8-0 No. 1838 in July 1917 with a chimney having no capuchon. It has been shunted on to the down road to allow an up train to pass.

Plate 367 (right): 'D' class 0-8-0 No. 1819 as running about 1920 in plain black livery, with Cooke buffers but still with Webb tender. The original 'A' class leading crankpin has given way to the more conventional type.

Plate 368 (below right): An early LMS view of 'D' class 0-8-0 No. 1880, fitted with lubricator box on the boiler handrail just to the rear of the dome. It still has its lined livery and original 'A' class leading crankpin.

'G'

Plate 369: After the successful conversion of 'A' class three-cylinder compounds into 'D' class two-cylinder simples, Mr Whale then turned his attention to the 'B' class four-cylinder compounds and produced a rebuild, the 'G' class, that was closely similar. Instead of fitting new inside cylinders as on the 'D' class, the outside cylinders were removed and the former low-pressure ones retained: as these cylinders were 1in diameter larger than the 'Ds' ', the boiler pressure was reduced to 160lb so that the tractive effort would be about the same. The distinctively shaped covers in front of the smokebox were also retained and led to the nickname 'piano front Gs', but actually now had nothing to cover! This view shows the first of the class, No. 1900, which was converted in November 1906. It has a conventional leading crankpin but otherwise is in typical condition, lined out and coupled to a Webb tender.

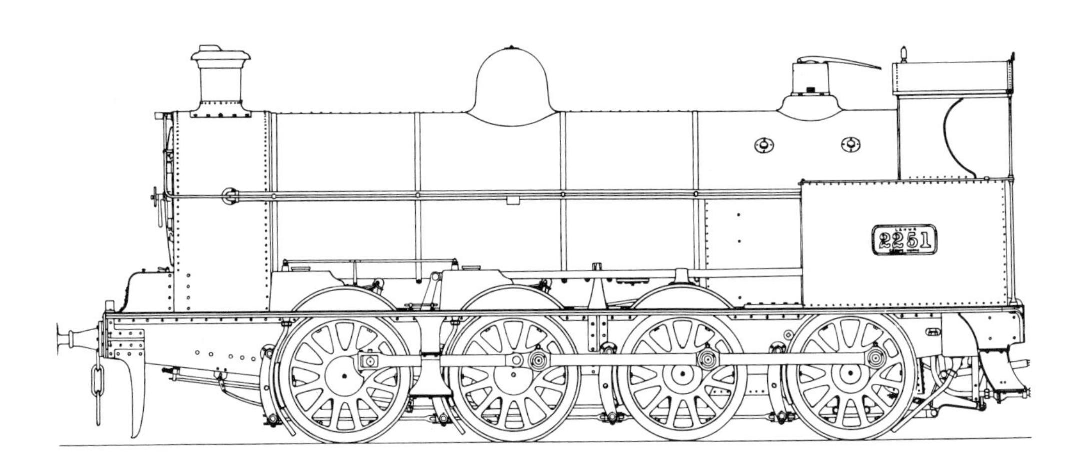

Figure 104 (above): Drawing of 'piano front G' class No. 2251.

Plate 370 (right): 'Piano front G' No. 1229, which was converted from 'B' class in May 1909, at Longsight about 1920. It still has its 'B' class leading crankpin.

Plate 371: 'Piano front G' class 0-8-0 No. 1893, thought to be at Huddersfield about 1920, coupled to a Whale tender. By mid-1917 32 'B' class had been converted to 'Gs' but as by then the superiority of the superheated 'G1' class had been well proved, subsequent rebuildings from 'B' class were made direct to class 'G1'.

Plate 372: Shortly before he retired, Mr Whale ordered sixty new 'G' class to be built at Crewe. They were basically the same as the 'piano front Gs' but had no 'piano fronts'; they also had Whale tenders and conventional leading crankpins. This official view shows the first of the class, No. 2653, on completion at Crewe Works in January 1910. The arrangement of sandboxes seen here, two on the leading splashers and one under the cab, became standard for all 'Super Ds' (classes 'G1' and 'G2'). Similarly, the arrangement of coupling rods — three separate rods, the centre one fitting outside the two outer ones — was followed on subsequent classes until the 'G2s', which had jointed rods; some 'G1s' acquired jointed rods later.

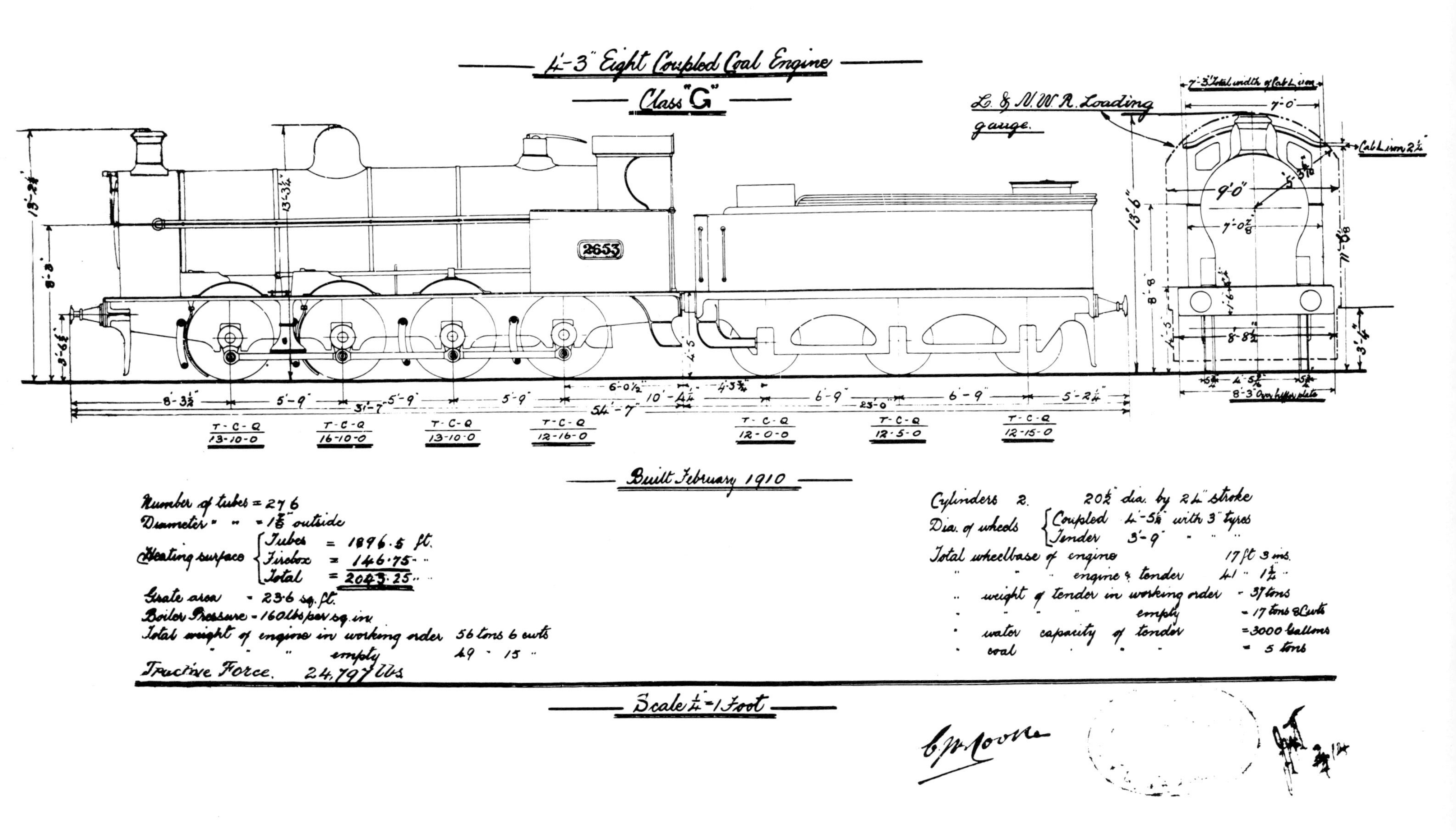

Figure 105: Weight diagram of 'G' class No. 2653. The drawing is inaccurate, showing a combination of 'piano-front G' and new 'G' features. The boiler support should be a casting, as on all new 'Gs' and most rebuilds; only a few 'piano Gs' rebuilt from early 'B' class had the plate type. The sandboxes are the smaller lower type of the rebuilds from classes 'B', 'E' and 'F', but the front overhang of 8ft. 3½in. is that of the new 'G', the rebuilds having an overhang of 9ft. 10½in. Hence the rebuilds were probably heavier at the front, despite the lighter sandboxes. To keep the weight on the front end down, the 'D' boiler as used on the 'D', 'piano G' and new 'G' classes had the front tube plate recessed 1ft. 9in. into the barrel.

Plate 373 (right): 'G' class 0-8-0 No. 1503, built in May 1910. It is still in lined livery and has a capuchon on the chimney.

Plate 374 (right): 'G' class No. 2661, in lined livery and with a plain chimney. It has the longer type of Whale buffers, often referred to as 'Cooke buffers'.

Plate 375 (below): 'G' class No. 1700 in lined livery about 1914. The gentleman on the footplate is the well known railway photographer W. H. Whitworth, thanks to whose efforts so many pictures of LNWR engines exist.

Plate 376 (left): In 1917, 26 'G' class were sent to France with the ROD. Their LNWR numbers were used as ROD numbers and displayed on their Whale tenders, as seen in this view of Nos. 1639 and 2014.

Plate 377 (above): Another view of No. 2014, somewhere in France. All the 'Gs' loaned to the ROD were returned and along with the rest of the class were converted to 'G1' class. Except for No. 2653, which was converted to 'G1' in January 1912, all conversions took place in LMS days.

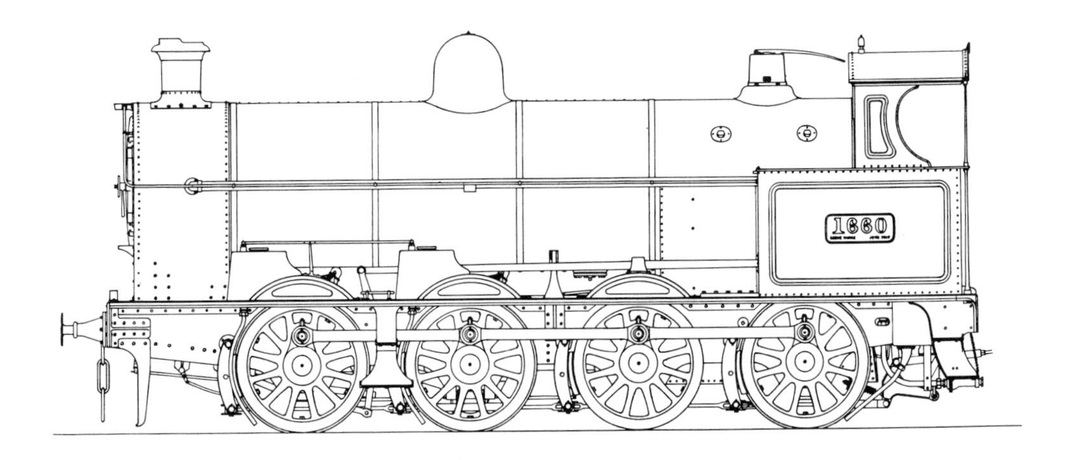

Figure 106: Drawing of 'G' class No. 1660.

'G1'

Plate 378: In January 1912, after superheating had been proved on the 'George the Fifth' class, the first of the 'G' class, No. 2653, was fitted with a Schmidt superheater and reclassified 'G1'. Whether it obtained new cylinders and a new boiler, as then being built for the 'G1s', is not known. Its original boiler, only two years old, could have been re-used on the next 'B' to be rebuilt to 'G'. Or it could have been fitted with a superheater, as with the front tube plate recessed into the barrel 1ft. 9in., there was room to take a header from a 4-6-2 tank, and the original slide-valve cylinders could have been retained. In any case, Bowen Cooke must have been confident of its success, as the first new 'G1' class was completed at Crewe Works the following month, the second of the class, No. 1384, being seen here on completion, and by the end of 1918 170 had been built new. In addition, the majority of classes 'A', 'B', 'C', 'D', 'E', 'F' and 'G' were eventually rebuilt to 'G1' also, totalling 279 rebuilds in all. The main external difference compared with the 'G' class is the longer smokebox, to accommodate the superheater header, though the barrel length of both boilers was the same at 14ft. 10in; internally, inside-admission piston valves replaced the 'G' class slide valves, though the cylinders were the same size. The superheater damper was controlled by the lever on the smokebox, operated by the boiler handrail, while lower down, just above the running plate, is the snifting valve. Superheater dampers were soon found to be unnecessary and were removed. As originally built, the 'G1s' had three-link couplings and steam brakes for the engine only, but the 1914 and subsequent batches were built with vacuum brakes and screw couplings, to enable them to work passenger trains if necessary. Earlier engines were then similarly equipped, though over a period of some years, and when this was done, the engine brakes were converted from steam to vacuum, following the practice with passenger engines which had started in 1913. At some stage, possibly after the war, steam heating was added also, not so much for passenger trains as for working banana specials from Garston Docks. Some 25 specials might be run at short notice when a Fyffe's steamer came in. The tender is the second type of Bowen Cooke tender, having a solid top with a double row of beading, as introduced on *Prince of Wales*.

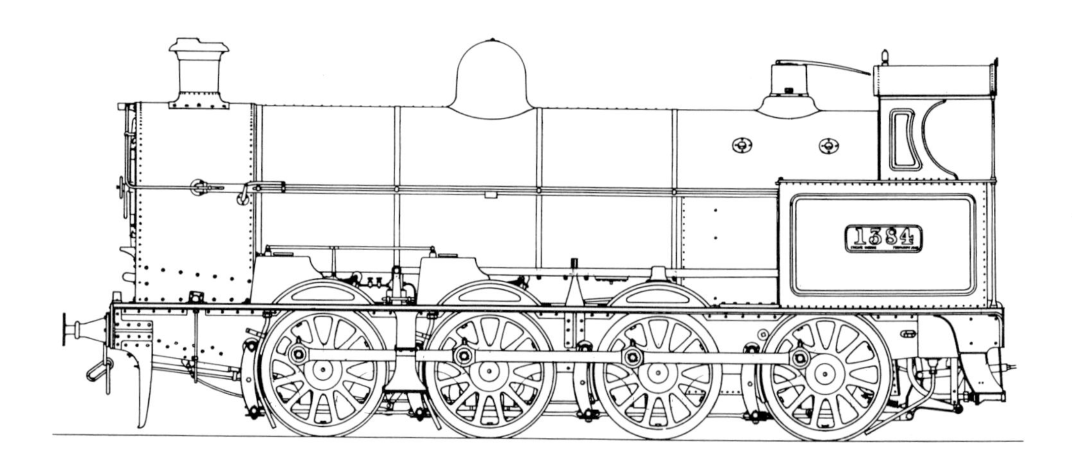

Figure 107: Drawing of class 'G1 0-8-0 No. 1384.

Plate 379: 'G1' class 0-8-0 No. 2246, which was built new as a 'G1' in September 1913. It is in original condition, complete with superheater damper and before the fitting of vacuum brakes.

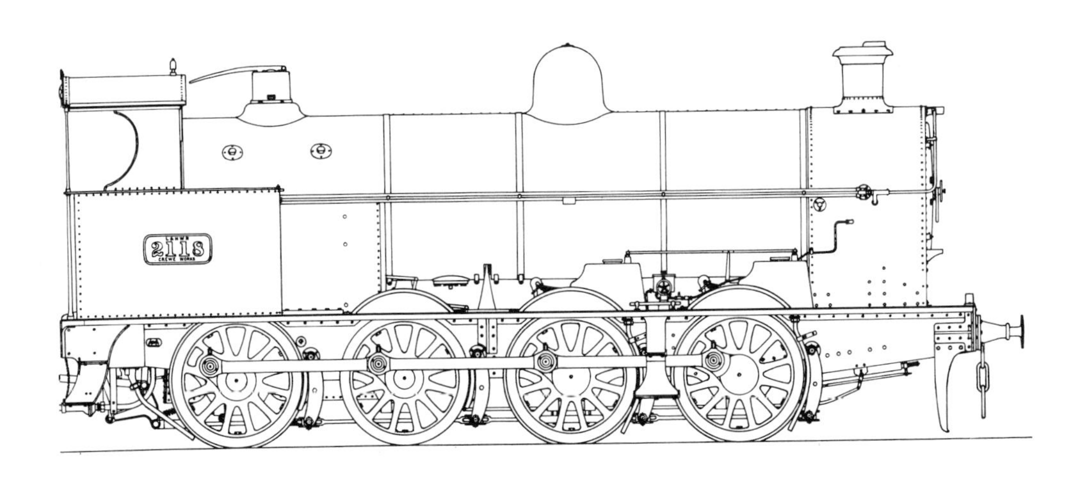

Figure 108 (above): Drawing of 'G1' class 0-8-0 No. 2118, converted from class 'B' in April 1918. This engine, along with No. 410 and two others, retained its old 'B' class cylinders and motion for a few years after conversion.

Figure 109 (below): Drawing of 'G1' class 0-8-0 No. 2057, converted from class 'B' in December 1921.

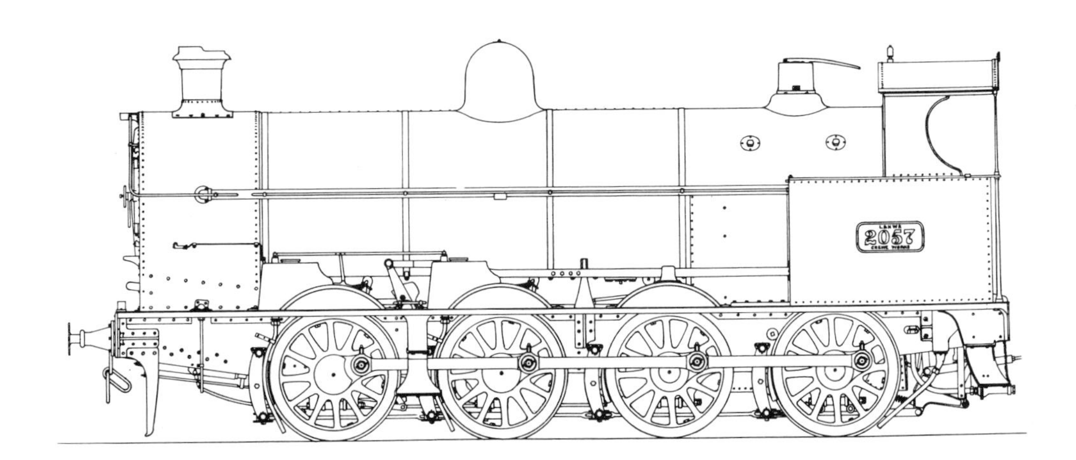

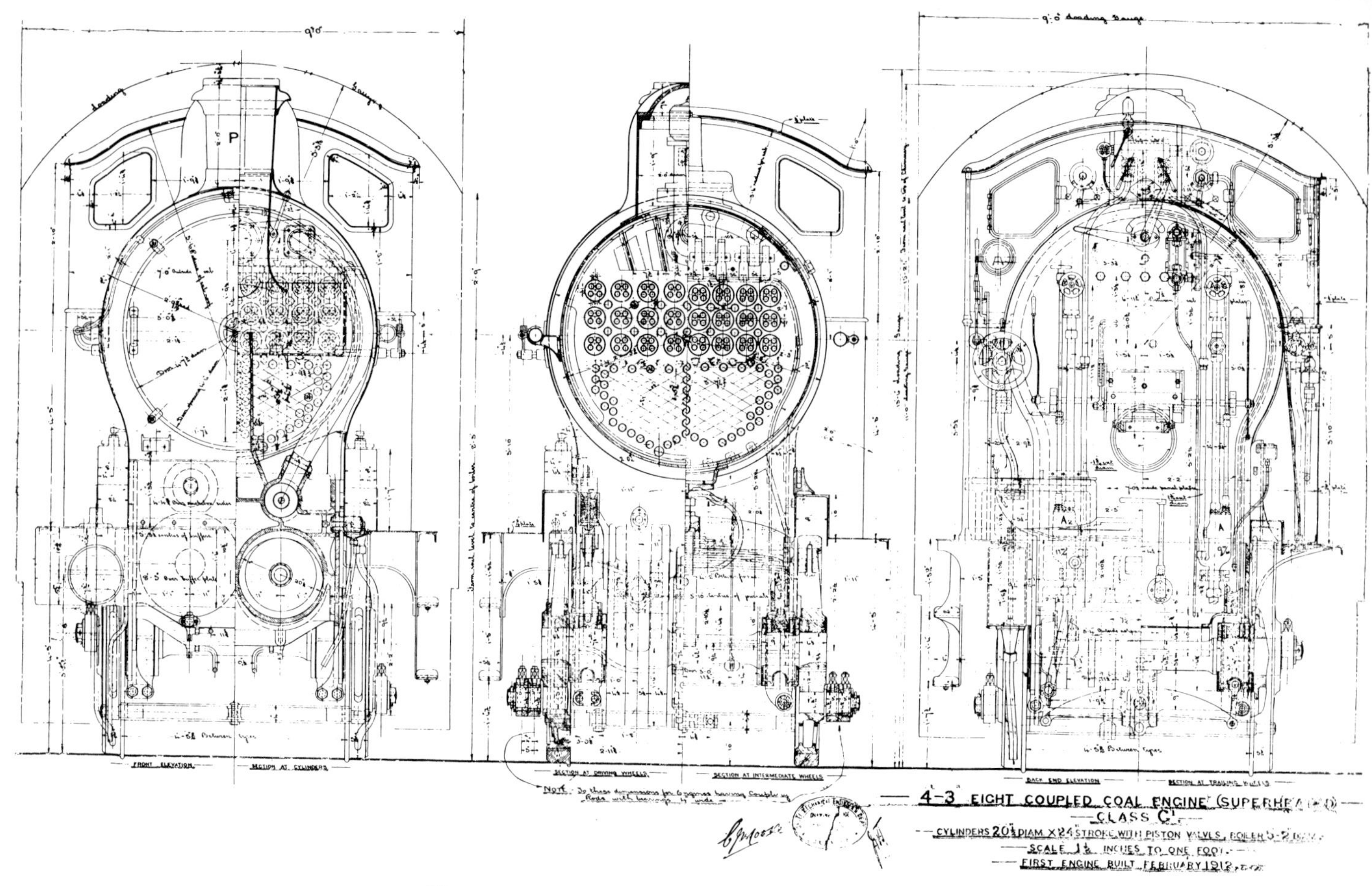

Figure 110: Cross-sectional drawings of class 'G1'.

Plate 380: No. 1568, which was built new as a 'G1' in March 1912. It is still in original condition, except for the screw coupling, and has its original tender. Owing to the policy of having fewer tenders than engines and of fitting any suitable tender to a newly overhauled engine in Crewe Works, 'Super Ds' were likely to be attached to any type of Whale or Cooke tender. The one restricting factor was that an engine with steam brakes had to have a tender with linkage for coupling up to the engine's brake rigging, while a vacuum-braked engine had to have a vacuum-braked tender. The mechanical lubricator can be seen between the two leading splashers.

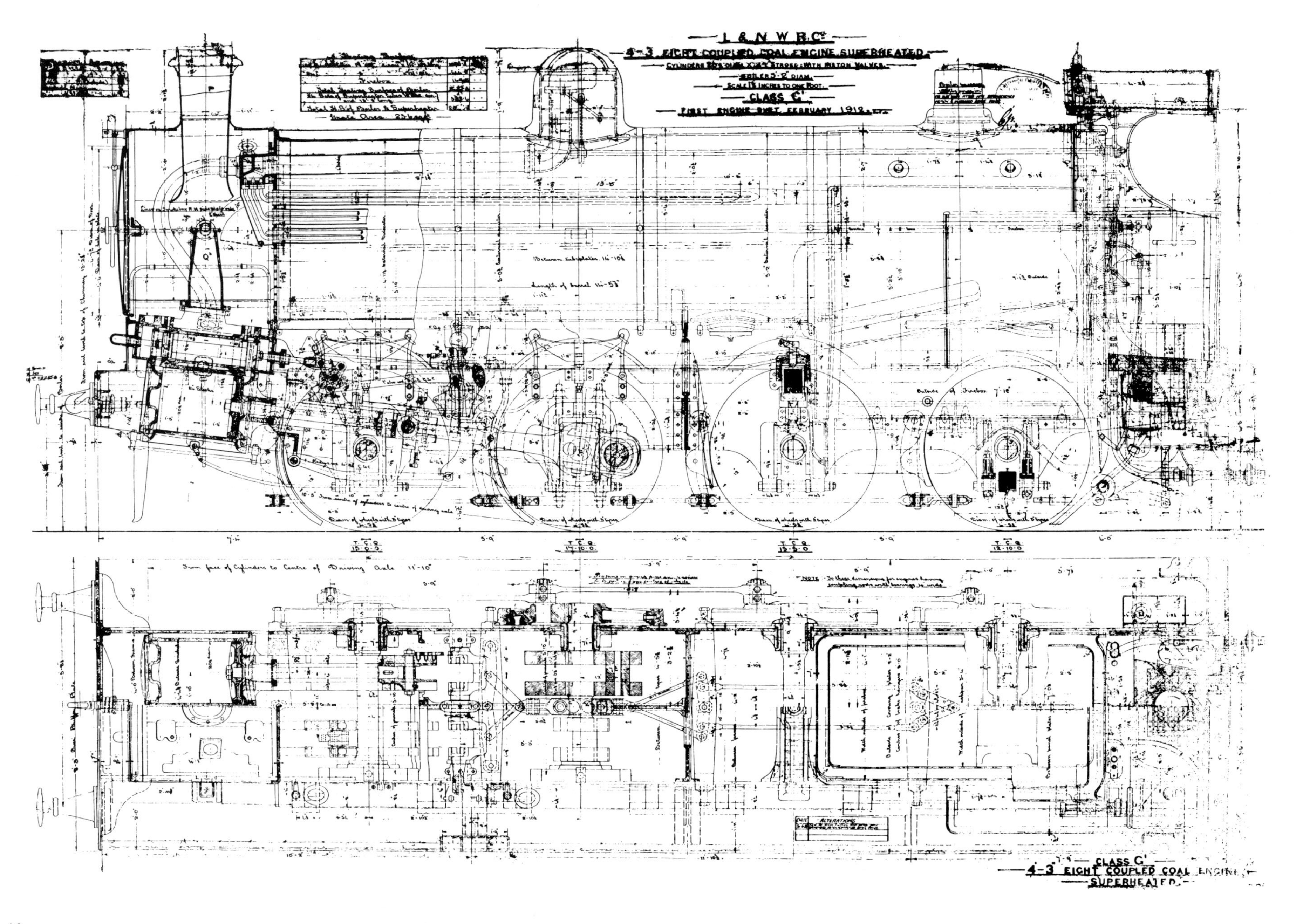

Figure 111: General arrangement drawings of class 'G1'.

Plate 381 (left): 'G1' class 0-8-0 No. 767, photographed from an unusual angle, showing something of the cab. It is still quite new, being in original condition and in full lined livery.

Plate 382 (right): 'G1' class 0-8-0 No. 1181, built as a 'G1' in April 1914, in original condition with vacuum brakes and screw coupling.

Plate 383 (below): 'G1 class 0-8-0 No. 1248, which was converted from 'B' class in March 1923. It is in plain black livery and is fitted to a Whale tender but has no vacuum brake and only a three-link coupling. The lubricator is different from those seen above, as is the arrangement of oil pipes on the base of the smokebox.

Plate 384 (right): An early LMS view of 'G1' 0-8-0 No. 1036, which was converted from an 'F' class in October 1921 and was previously a 'B' class; it still retains its '17in. Coal Engine' wheels. This was one of the 'G1s' which in the 1920s were given 'increased brake power and strengthened motion'. The boiler support has been cut away above the footplate level and an additional brake cylinder has been fitted between the frames for the leading pair of axles, the existing cylinder now braking only the rear pair. The motion has been converted to direct action — indicated by the reach rod, which now curves up behind the second sandbox instead of being straight and has four bolts, between the splashers of the centre pair of axles. The modified engines thus conformed to 'G2' standards except for the boiler pressure; in the 1930s the LMS converted a number of 'G1s' in this way and in addition fitted 175lb. boilers, designating them 'G2a' class. Outwardly, of course, they remained indistinguishable from either the 'G1s' or 'G2s'. The box on the handrail supplies oil to the pipes which lead down inside the frames to the bearings, a Beames modification which was commonly made in the early LMS period.

Plate 385 (above): In 1924 a new standard boiler with Belpaire firebox was produced to the design of H. P. M. Beames for use on both the 'G1s' and 'G2s', the pressure being altered accordingly. It could be used interchangeably with the round firebox type, only the cab front needing modification to suit, and engines entering works with one type were quite likely to emerge with the other. A Belpaire boiler is seen here, fitted to 'G1' class No. 1217. To enable the engine to fit the Midland loading gauge, the sides of the cab roof have been cut back, a modification carried out to all the larger LNWR classes by the LMS.

Plate 386: 'G1' class 0-8-0 No. 2551, which was built originally as an 'A' class in December 1896, converted to 'D' class in October 1907 and to 'G1' in May 1925. It was presumably fitted with the Belpaire boiler on conversion to 'G1', as it was renumbered by the LMS in November 1927. The Bowen Cooke tender is in lined livery and may well have come from a 'Prince', but the engine's Webb compound origins are revealed by the boss of the leading driving wheel, which is shaped to accommodate the 'A' class leading coupling rod.

'G2'

Plate 387: In 1921-2, sixty class 'G2' 0-8-0s were built. They were a development of the 'G1' class with higher boiler pressure, 175lb. instead of 160lb., and were identical to them externally. 'G2' No. 134 is seen here about 1922, as originally built in plain black livery with polished coupling rods, and attached to the final type of Bowen Cooke tender. It has vacuum brakes and a screw coupling, and an additional balance weight on the third driving wheel. The 'G2s' were the only LNWR 0-8-0s which were never rebuilt to some other class and, so far as is known, none were ever painted in the lined livery. This was the engine which replaced the 'B' class compound No. 134, which exploded at Buxton after faulty repair by outside contractors; drivers had reported several pressure gauge anomalies.

Plate 388 (above): 'G2' class 0-8-0 No. 373 in early LMS days. Ross pop safety valves were first fitted in 1924 but apart from these No. 373 is as originally built. It has vacuum brakes, screw couplings and the final type of Bowen Cooke tender.

Plate 389 (right): 'G2' class No. 994, in early LMS days, with LMS lamp irons and a Whale tender.

Summary of the Eight-Coupled Tender Engines

The essential details of the various classes of eight-coupled coal engines are summarised in the table below, which uses the 1911 class letter system but lists the classes in chronological order of introduction.

Class	*Date introduced*	*Details*
2524	October 1892	Two-cylinder simple 0-8-0 with 'Greater Britain' boiler.
'A'	September 1893	Three-cylinder compound 0-8-0.
'B'	August 1901	Four-cylinder compound 0-8-0, with much larger boiler than 'A' class.
'E'	August 1904	'B' class converted with leading pony truck to 2-8-0.
'C'	November 1904	'A' class converted to two-cylinder simple, with new cylinders but original boiler.
'D'	March 1906	'A' class converted like 'C' class but with larger boiler.
'F'	May 1906	'B' class converted to 2-8-0 like 'E' class but with larger boiler.
'G'	November 1906	'B' class converted to simple with original inside cylinders, retaining 'piano front', and 'D' class boiler.
'C1'	March 1909	'A' class converted like 'C' class but with smaller cylinders.
'G'	January 1910	'G' class built new without 'piano front'.
'G1'	January 1912	As 'G' class but superheated; some converted from other classes, others built new.
'G2'	June 1921	Improved version of 'G1 class with higher boiler pressure.
'G2a'	October 1935	'G1' class converted like 'G2', with higher boiler pressure, stronger motion and increased brake power.

The Derivation of the 'G1' Class

All the various saturated eight-coupled tender engines were eventually either converted to 'G1' class or withdrawn, and another 170 'G1s' were built new. In a sense, therefore, the 'G1' class was derived from all the other classes (except the 'C1s') and their rather complicated story is summarised in the diagram below. Beneath each class letter is shown the number of engines in the class and their eventual fate, either being converted to other classes or being withdrawn. All 449 'G1s' were never in service at the same time, as before all conversions to 'G1' had been made in the 1930s, other 'G1s' had already been converted to class 'G2a'. With the sixty 'G2s', the number of superheated 0-8-0s of LNWR origin eventually totalled 509.

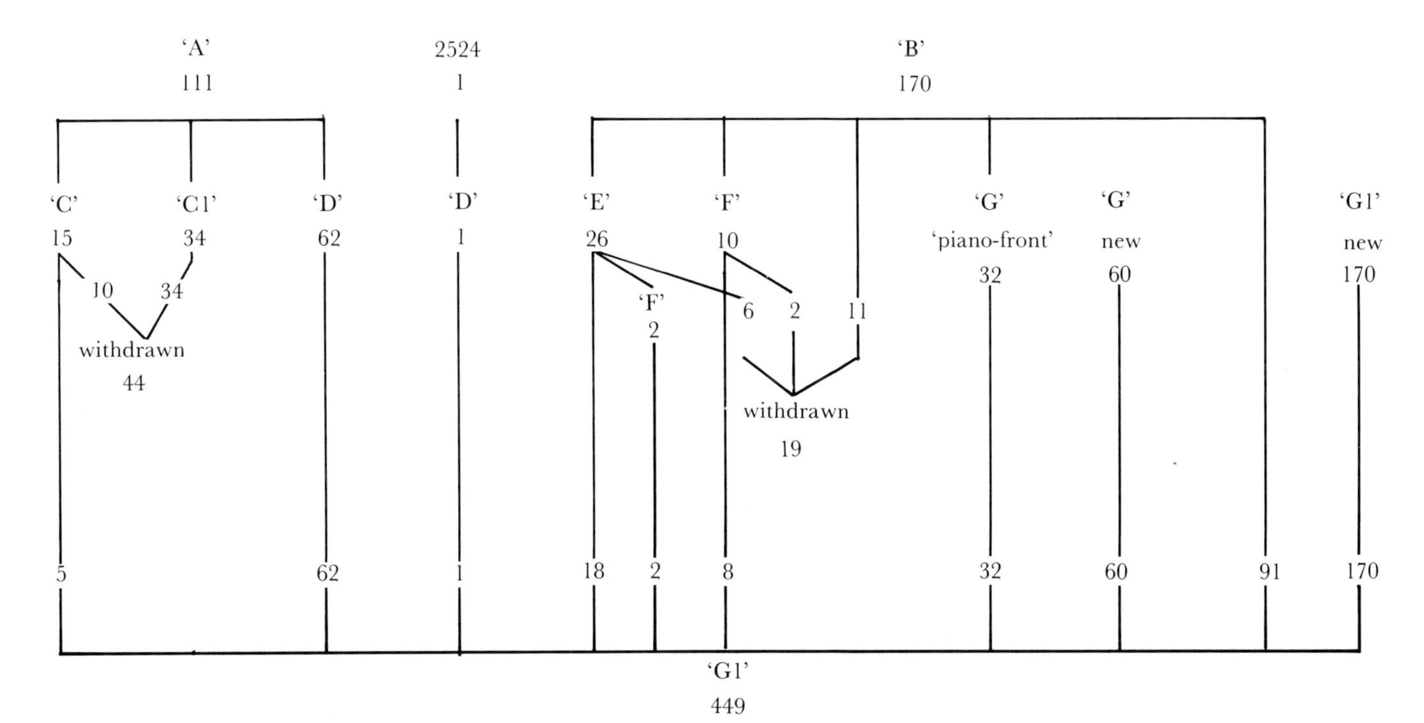

Bowen Cooke's 0-8-2 Tank

Plate 390: In 1911, C. J. Bowen Cooke introduced an eight-coupled tank engine for heavy shunting and thirty were built in 1911-17. The design was basically a tank version of the 'G' class with a rear pony truck; but to make starting easier, the boiler pressure was increased by 5lb. and the valve gear was modified slightly. Some accounts also say the firebox was recessed 6ft. into the barrel, making a combustion chamber. The tube heating surface was less than the 'G' class, possibly due to a few tubes being omitted, but the firebox heating surface was the same, and quite possibly normal 'G' class boilers were used as replacements later. This is the official view, taken in January 1912, of No. 289, the fourth to be built. It has a three-link coupling for handling ordinary goods wagons, vacuum brake for use in emergency on passenger trains and Cooke buffers. In the cab is a lever reverser, preferable in principle to the screw type for shunting engines; these were the first LNWR engines to be so fitted since Ramsbottom invented his screw reverser. As on the 0-8-0s, the third pair of driving wheels are flangeless and there are three coupling rods, the centre one fitting outside the two outer ones, as on the 'G' and 'G1' classes.

Plate 391: No. 1663, one of the first batch completed in 1912, seen here about 1920 with a capuchon on the chimney, probably from an 0-8-0. The standard long-tapered buffers fitted originally seem to have proved unsuitable, probably because of the throw-over on sharp curves in goods yards, and to have been quickly replaced by the standard large Webb buffers with 18in. instead of 13in. heads, as used on 2-4-2 tanks for motor train working and so available from stock.

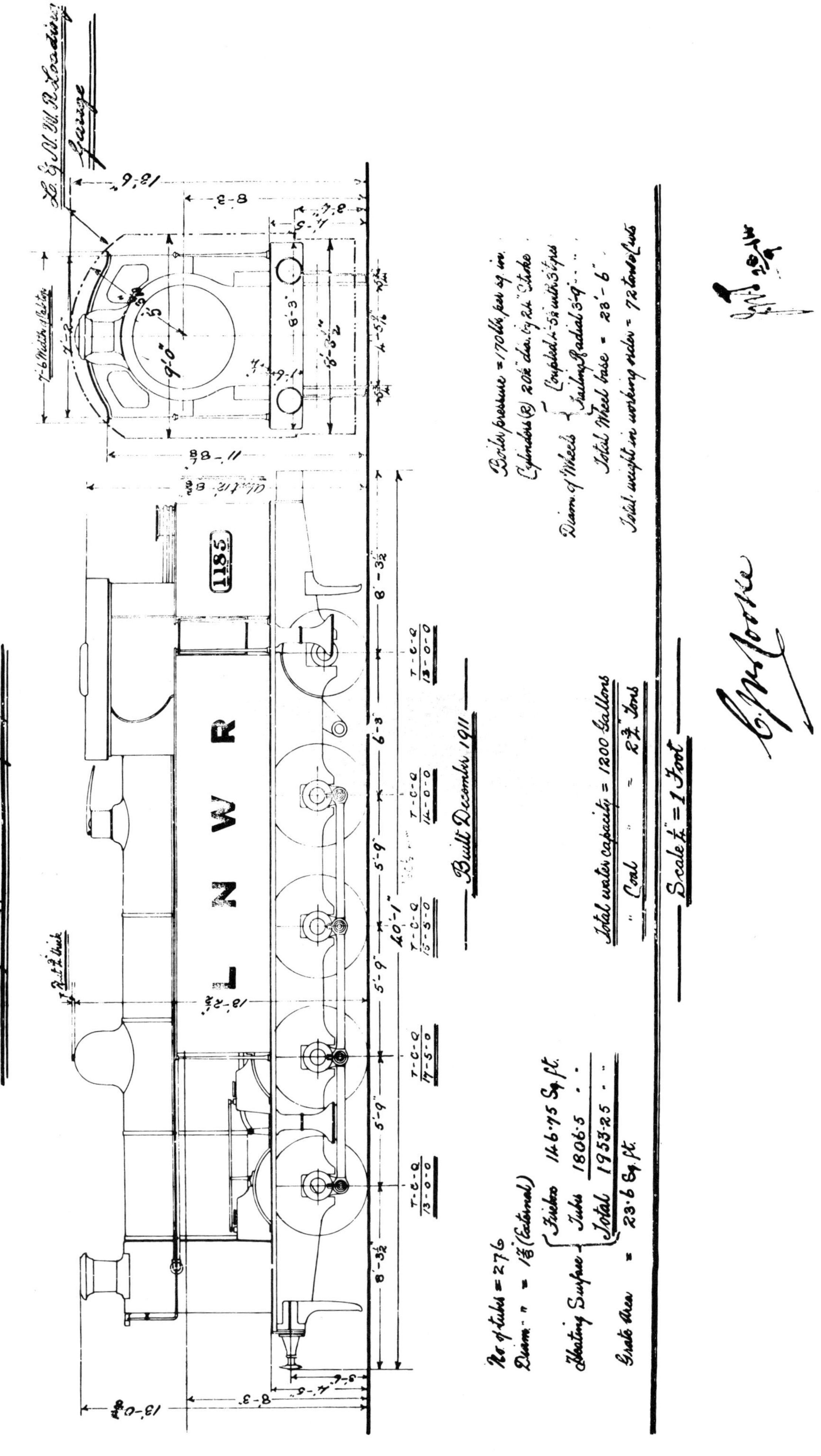

4'-3" Eight Coupled Shunting Engine

L N W R

1185

L. & N.W.R. Loading Gauge

8'-3½" — 5'-9" — 5'-9" — 5'-9" — 6'-3" — 8'-3½"

40'-1"

T-C-Q	T-C-Q	T-C-Q	T-C-Q	T-C-Q
13-0-0	17-5-0	15-5-0	14-0-0	13-0-0

Built December 1911

No. of tubes = 276
Diam. " = 1⅞ (External)

Heating Surface:
- Firebox 146·75 Sq. ft.
- Tubes 1806·5 " "
- Total 1953·25 " "

Grate Area = 23·6 Sq. ft.

Total water capacity = 1200 Gallons
" Coal " = 2¾ Tons

Boiler pressure = 170 lbs. per sq. in.
Cylinders (2) 20½" dia. by 24" Stroke
Diam. of Wheels: Coupled 4'-5½" with 3" tyres; Trailing Radial 3'-9" " "
Total Wheel base = 23'-6"
Total weight in working order = 72 tons 10 cwts

Scale ¼" = 1 Foot

C. J. Bowen Cooke

Figure 112: Weight diagram of 0-8-2 tank engine.

Plate 392 (right): Rear view of the second of the class, No. 1665, at work. The shed plate is 25 (Springs Branch).

Plate 393 (above): No. 1592, also one of the first batch, at Willesden on 3rd March 1922, still in lined livery and with 'LNWR' on the tank sides. Only three classes of tank engine ever displayed the company's initials as normal practice, though 'George the Fifth' 4-4-0 No. 956 *Dachshund* displayed them on its tender for a trial period of a few months in 1911.

Plate 394 (right): No. 1514, one of the second batch. It was probably fitted with parallel buffers when built in September 1915.

Plate 395: Another of the second batch, this time No. 736, at Willesden on 10th July 1921. Except for the buffers and the absence of lining, it is in much the same condition as No. 289 in the official 'as new' picture.

Plate 396: One of the final batch, originally No. 714, is seen here as LMS No. 7892, possibly as late as the 1940s. It has LMS buffers and lamp irons, and the water filler has been raised to allow water to be taken more easily when the bunker was well filled with coal. Otherwise (except for the dirt!) there is little difference from LNWR condition.

Beames' 0-8-4 Tank

Plate 397: The final design of LNWR eight-coupled goods engine was H. P. M. Beames' 0-8-4 tank, which appeared in the first few months of the LMS period. Whereas Bowen Cooke's 0-8-2 tanks had been designed purely for shunting, the 0-8-4 tanks were intended for the haulage of heavy goods trains over short distances, which is why greater coal capacity was provided, and they spent most of their lives in the steeply graded South Wales colliery area. They were essentially a tank version of the 'G2' with higher boiler pressure, 185lb. instead of 175lb. This is the official view of No. 380, taken on completion on 27th April 1923 and showing the engine in full lined LNWR livery but with 'LMS' on the tank sides. As on the 'G2' class 0-8-0s, the centre coupling rod was pin-jointed to the outer rods, and the buffers are parallel ones of the type which had replaced the original Whale buffers on the 0-8-2 tanks. The engine also has vacuum brakes and steam-heating apparatus for working passenger trains, a chimney without a capuchon, Webb safety valves, wire mesh on the rear windows as protection when coaling, a mechanical lubricator between the sandboxes, snifting valves at the sides of the base of the smokebox, and LMS lamp irons. The bufferbeam ends are shaped for greater clearance on platform edges, and the third pair of driving wheels are flangeless. Reversing could be effected by either screw or lever.

Plate 398: Beames 0-8-4 tank No. 468, built in July 1923, photographed at Shrewsbury, possibly while on trial before returning to Crewe Works for final painting. The ventilator in the cab roof is raised to admit more air. Compared with the view of No. 380, Ross pop safety valves have replaced the Webb type used at Crewe since 1874, and there is no mechanical lubricator on the right-hand side.

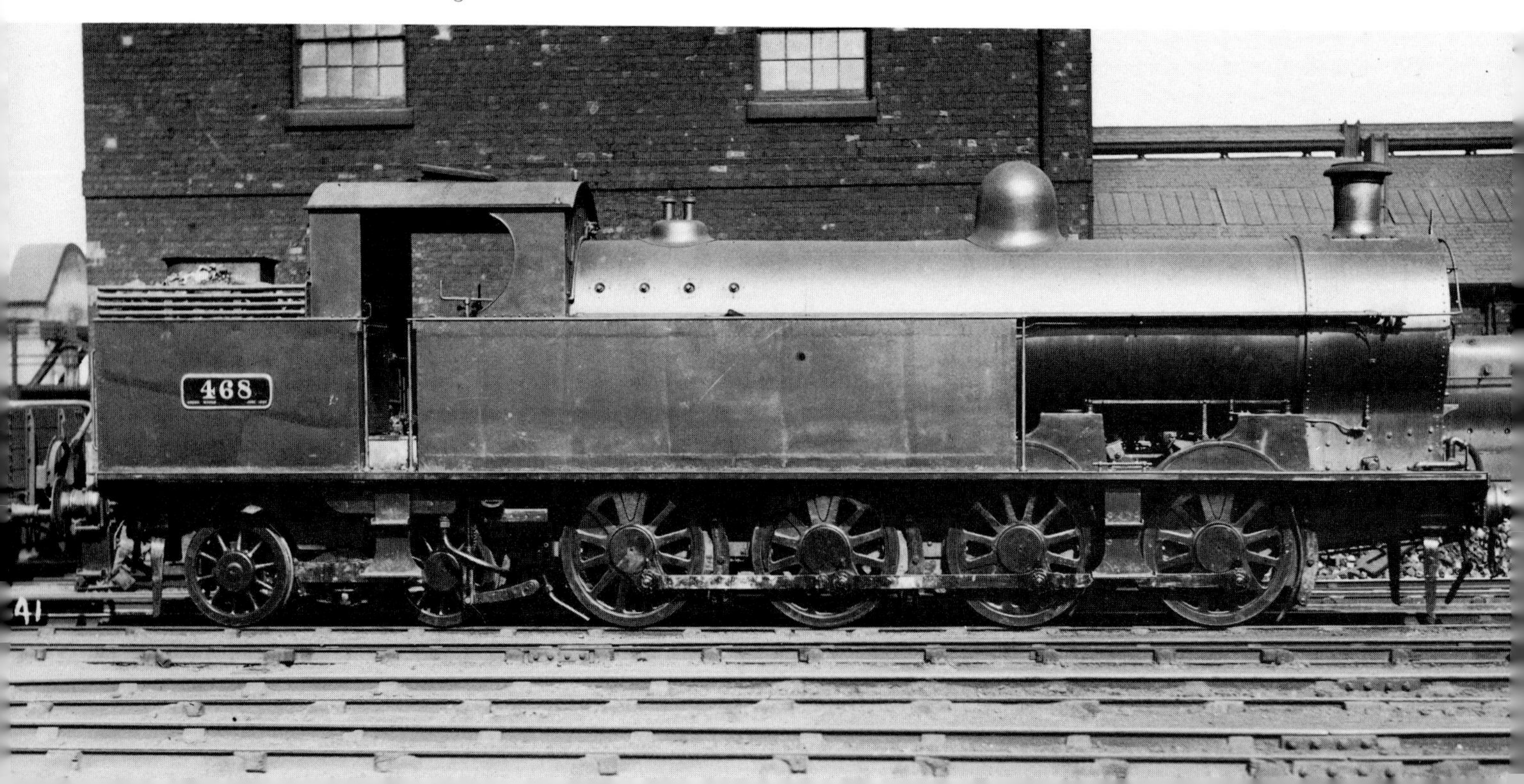

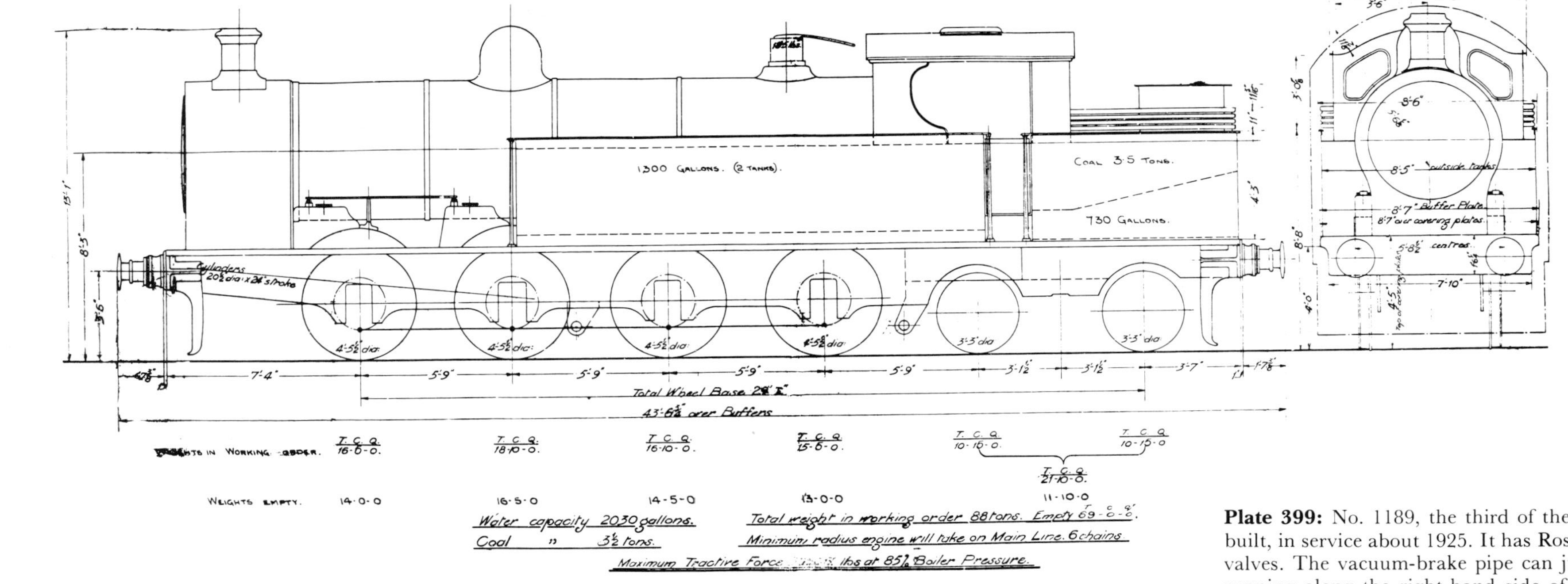

Figure 113: Diagram of 0-8-4 tank engine.

Plate 399: No. 1189, the third of the class to be built, in service about 1925. It has Ross pop safety valves. The vacuum-brake pipe can just be seen, running along the right-hand side of the engine, under the edge of the running plate, tank and bunker, between front and rear connections.

Plate 400: Official view of LMS No. 7957, taken at Crewe Works on 22nd November 1923 before final painting. LMS front numberplates were not tolerated long on LNWR eight-coupled engines. The lid of the water filler in the bunker can just be seen, hinged open transversely.

Plate 401 (above): LMS No. 7953 at Canada Dock, Liverpool, about 1930, in early LMS livery but still very much as built originally.

Plate 402 (right): Rear view of LMS No. 7957 while temporarily renumbered 27957 in the 20000 series by mistake in 1934. No real change from original condition seems to have occurred — there is even an LNWR shed plate on the back of the cab roof.

Plate 403: LMS No. 7938, originally LNWR No. 1908, pictured as running about 1940 with LMS buffers and with carriage-heating hose, snifting valve and front numberplate removed, but otherwise much as originally built.

'MM'

Plate 404: In 1919 the LNWR purchased from the government thirty 2-8-0s which had been ordered for service with the Railway Operating Division on the Western Front during World War I. All except one were built by the North British Locomotive Co. and in fact came to the LNWR as new engines, since the war ended before they could be sent to France. They were classified as 'MM', the name being derived from the Ministry of Munitions which had ordered them, and lead to the adoption of the nickname 'Military Marys' by LNWR enginemen. When the engines were first obtained, they were given numbers in the LNWR ordinary stock list but the purchase was held up and in September 1919 they were numbered in the 2800 series along with 151 other engines of the class on loan. In November 1920 the purchase was completed and they received fresh numbers in the ordinary stock list. This view shows No. 2824, which eventually became LNWR No. 2407, at Carlisle Upperby about 1920. It has neither lamp sockets nor lamp irons at the front end, and so is perhaps in the process of being delivered to Crewe. The Westinghouse pump provided brake power on the engine and so was in constant use when the engine was working; it was not something for use on the Continent only.

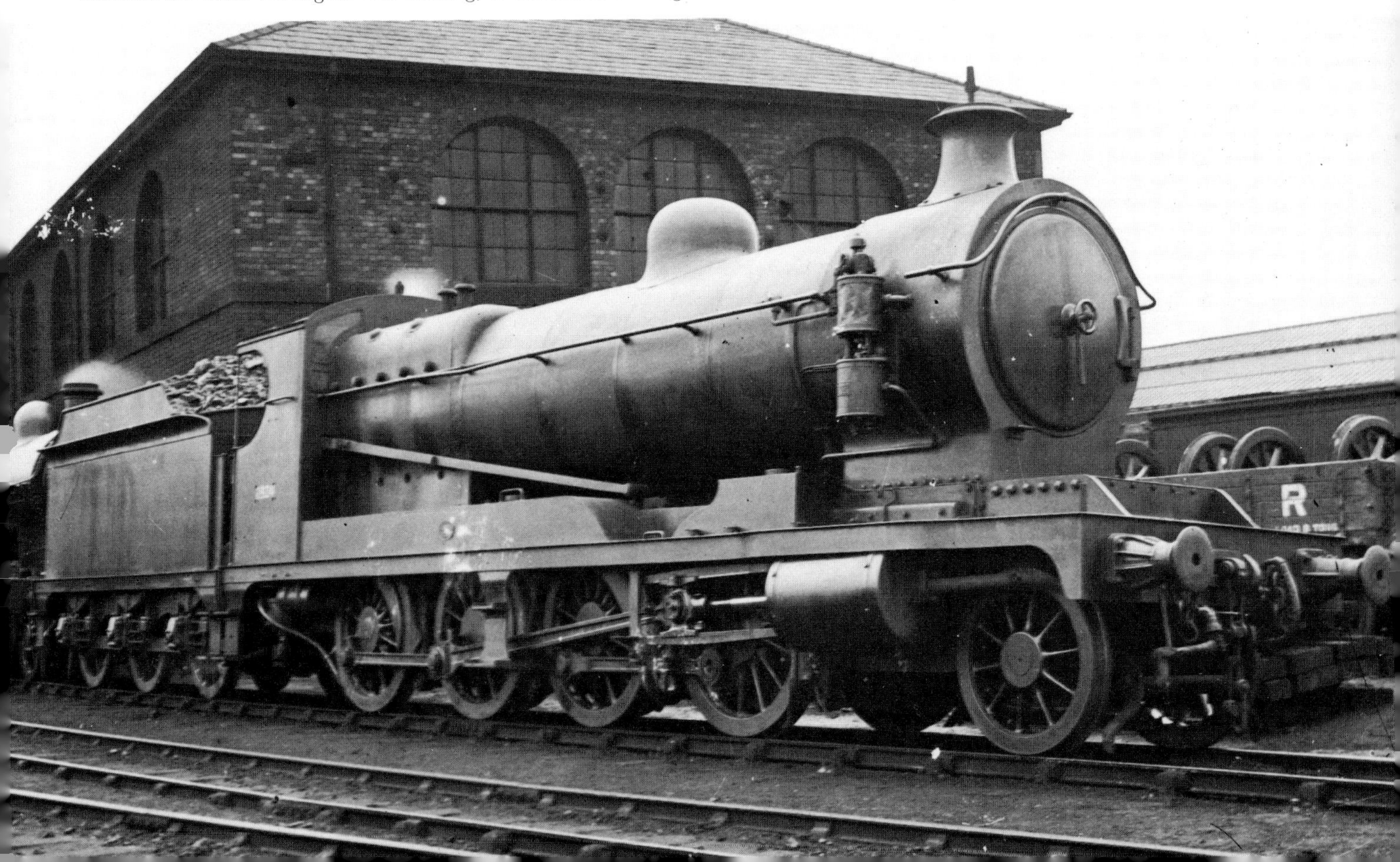

Plate 405 (right): 'MM' class 2-8-0 No. 2100 in 1920, before receiving a proper LNWR numberplate. The NBL (Queen's Park) works plate can be seen on the splasher.

Plate 406 (above): 'MM' class 2-8-0 No. 2400, sometime after November 1920. It has acquired LNWR Cooke buffers and a pre-1906 style numberplate from a withdrawn 'Coal Saddle Tank', which it has replaced in the stock list. Its NBL (Atlas Works) builder's plate is on the middle of the splasher.

Plate 407(right): "MM' class No. 2394 passing Chester about 1922. It still has its side chains for working on the Continent.

centre spring was longer than the other two and, according to the calculations of the chief draughtsman at Vulcan Foundry, the frame was too weak.

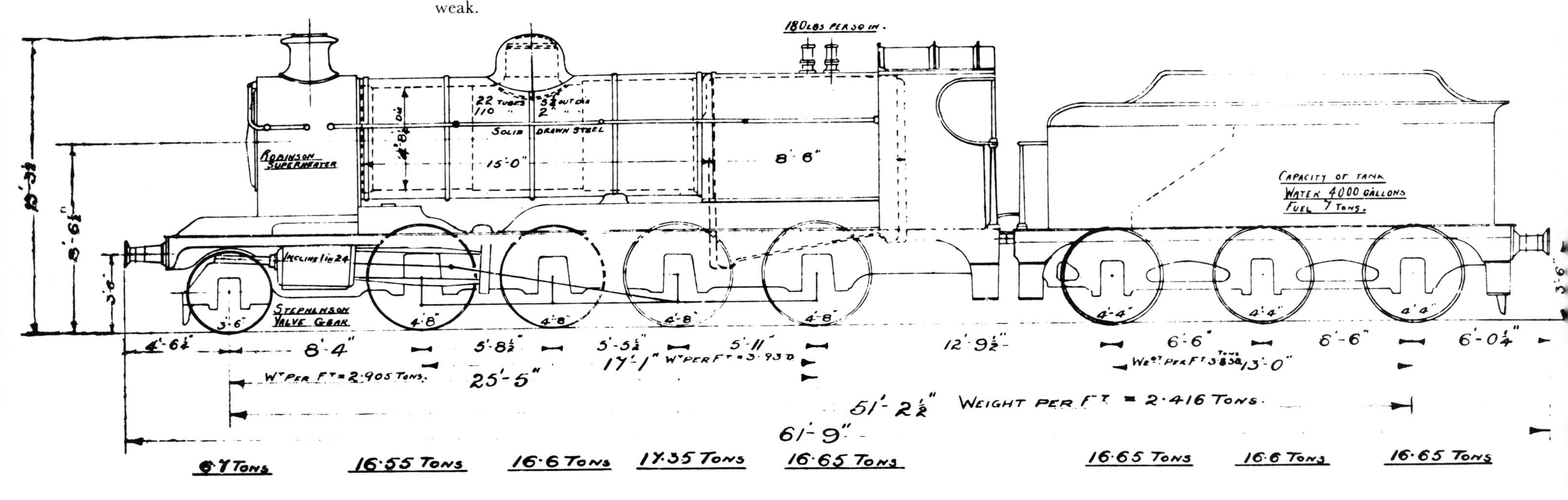

GENERAL PARTICULARS.

CYLINDERS - - - - DIA 21" STROKE 26"
WHEELS - - - - - BOGIE 3'-6", COUPLED 4'-8" DIA.
WHEEL BASE - - - COUPLED 17'-1". TOTAL 25'-5"
BOILER PRESSURE - 180 LBS PER SQ INCH.
HEATING SURFACE — FIREBOX 153 SQ FEET
TUBES - - - 1348 " "
SUPERHEATER 255 " "
TOTAL - - - 1756 " "
GRATE AREA 26·25 SQ FEET.
WEIGHT OF ENGINE IN WORKING ORDER { COUPLED WHEELS 67 TONS 3 CWTS.
TOTAL - - - - - - 73 " 17 "

WATER CAPACITY TENDER 4.000 GALLONS.
COAL " " 7 TONS.
WEIGHT OF TENDER (FULL) 49 TONS 18 CWTS.

TOTAL WEIGHT OF ENGINE & TENDER IN WORKING ORDER } 123 TONS. 15 CWTS.

TRACTIVE FORCE AT 85% 31,326 LBS.

CHAIN LINES LNWRLY LOAD GAUGE
FULL " OVERSEAS

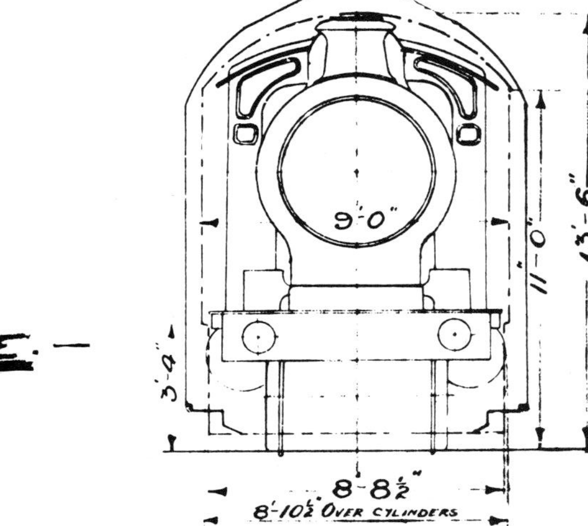

GREAT CENTRAL RAILWAY

DIAGRAM OF 2-8-0 ENGINE. CONSOLIDATION TYPE.

SCALE ¼" = 1 FOOT.

Chapter 12
George Whale's Engines

'Precursor'

Plate 408: Some nine months after Mr Webb's retirement, the first of George Whale's designs appeared from Crewe Works, the 'Precursor' class. It was a large simple-expansion express-passenger 4-4-0 with two inside cylinders. Though typically North Western in general appearance, it seemed outwardly quite different from anything that had gone before but in fact could be regarded as a logical development from the 'Jumbos' and 'Cauliflowers'. This official photograph shows No. 513 *Precursor* as originally built on 16th March 1904. The style of cab, with a handrail from the rear corner of the roof to the footplate and with five-sided windows is Whale's, as is the design of the buffers, but the safety valves and other fittings are typical Webb and the covers over the front of the valves and cylinders are similar to those on Webb compounds. The tender is steel-framed and seems quite modern but has the U-shaped water tank dating from Trevithick's time, and the coal rails and toolboxes as on Webb's engines. This type of tender was used on all Whale's designs, though the spring hangers were changed from the solid type seen here to a hinged design on the 'Experiments' and '19in. Goods'.

Plate 409 (right): *Precursor* at Crewe about 1905.

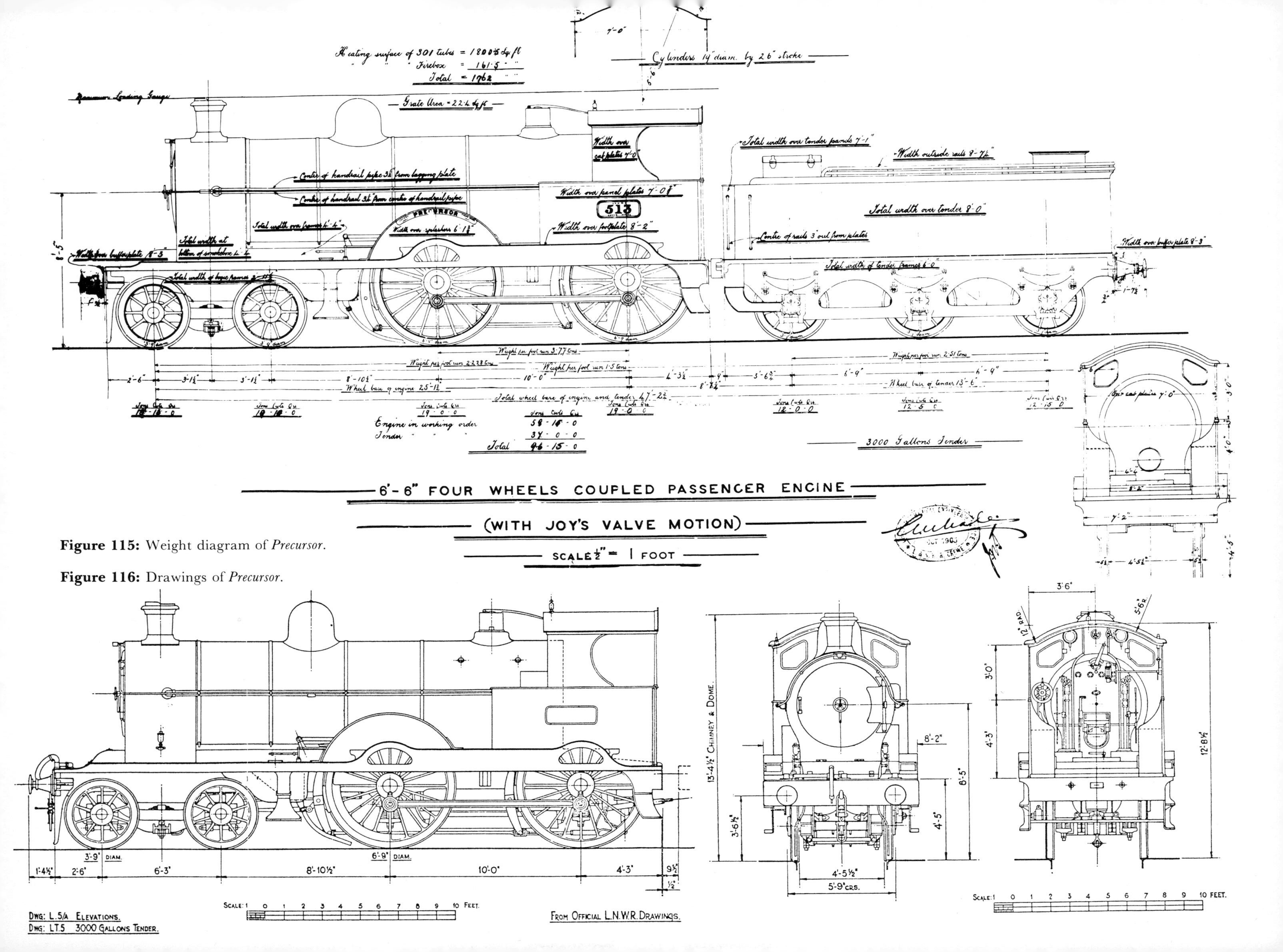

Figure 115: Weight diagram of *Precursor*.

Figure 116: Drawings of *Precursor*.

Plate 410 (above): 'Precursor' class 4-4-0 No. 2582 *Rowland Hill* at Euston about 1905-10, in original condition. The tender has the later type of spring hangers.

Plate 411 (right): 'Precursor' class 4-4-0 No. 1312 *Ionic* at Crewe in original condition. Many of the 'Precursors' took the names and numbers of Webb three-cylinder compounds which they replaced.

Plate 412 (below): 'Precursor' No. 622 *Euphrates* at Camden Shed about 1915. It has the same type of driving wheels as used on the later 'George the Fifths' and derived from Webb four-cylinder compounds, with large centre bosses containing balance weights and with small webs between the spokes and the rim. The sanders have windshields, the original displacement lubricator at the side of the base of the smokebox has been removed, and Cooke buffers have been fitted. Though the tender is the original Whale type, it has 'straight-topped' springs introduced by Bowen Cooke.

Plate 413: When superheating was found to be successful on the 'George the Fifths', many of the 'Precursors' were rebuilt with the same type of boilers, 20½in. cylinders with piston valves and smaller bogie wheels, and so, except for the splashers, became identical to a 'George'. Others were superheated with the original boiler and cylinders. No. 2166 *Shooting Star* is seen here at Manchester (London Road) soon after rebuilding in February 1913. It has a mechanical lubricator on the frames to the rear of the smokebox, Cooke buffers, large-boss driving wheels and sanding-gear windshields. The small pipe high up on the smokebox near the chimney is the connection between the superheater and the pyrometer in the cab. Pyrometers were soon found to be unnecessary and were removed but the circular plates where the connecting pipe entered the smokebox could be seen on many engines for some time afterwards. The front-end covers are open for examination; and the tender is the type introduced for the 'Prince of Wales' class, recognisable by the solid top with double beading.

Plate 414: Rebuilt 'Precursor' No. 515 *Champion* at Manchester (London Road) about 1914.

Plate 415 (above): Rebuilt 'Precursor' No. 1419 *Tamerlane* at Manchester (London Road), probably quite soon after rebuilding in November 1913.

Plate 416 (left): Rebuilt 'Precursor' No. 659 *Dreadnought* about 1917. The lever at the rear of the smokebox operates the superheater damper and is controlled by the boiler handrail. These dampers were found to be unnecessary and were later removed. Below it are the oil pipes leading to the left-hand cylinder from the mechanical lubricator on the other side. The chimney has no capuchon and the driving wheels are the original type, but the tender is the type introduced with the first batch of 'Claughtons', having a solid top with single beading.

Plate 417 (left): Rebuilt 'Precursor' No. 2062 *Sunbeam* at Crewe soon after rebuilding in February 1913, photographed from an unusual angle. The tender is the type introduced with *Prince of Wales*, having a solid top with double beading.

Plate 418: 'Precursor' No. 685 *Cossack* at Crewe, on 28th August 1924. It has the original type of boiler with short smokebox and despite the mechanical lubricator, is not superheated. The box on the handrail contains trimmings for oil feeds to axleboxes. Though the engine is in plain black, the tender is still lined out; it is the final Bowen Cooke type, introduced in 1916 with oval cut-outs in the square-ended frames.

Plate 419 (right): 'Precursor' No. 2202 *Vizier* at Bletchley, on 4th October 1924. The changes from original condition are all minor — the buffers, driving wheels and oil box on the handrail; the tender is the type introduced with *Prince of Wales*.

Plate 420 (below right): 'Precursor' class 4-4-0, formerly LNWR No. 1439 *Tiger*, as LMS No. 5275 in the late 1920s. It was one of eleven of the class which were superheated while retaining slide valves, but it also has a Belpaire firebox as part of Beames' plan for such fireboxes on replacement boilers. The tender is the final type, introduced by Bowen Cooke in 1916.

'Experiment'

Plate 421: With the success of the 'Precursors' established, Mr Whale next produced a 4-6-0 version for the Crewe-Carlisle line, with 6ft. 3in. driving wheels instead of 6ft. 9in. This official view of the first of the class, No. 66 *Experiment*, taken on 3rd June 1905, shows how closely the design followed that of *Precursor*. The only detail differences are the absence of a capuchon on the chimney and the modified hinged spring hangers on the tender. There is only one sandbox, positioned ahead of the leading driving wheels with its filler lid above the footplating, as on the 'Jumbos'.

Plate 422: 'Experiment' class 4-6-0 No. 507 *Sarmatian*, seen at Euston soon after completion in June 1905.

Plate 423: A really beautiful picture of 'Experiment' No. 1455 *Herefordshire*, taken at Crewe North shed during the trials with the Great Western's *Polar Star* in August 1910. The single sandbox on the first engines must have proved inadequate, as both the middle and rear driving wheels now have pipes too. They are supplied by a sandbox very low down inside the frames beneath the ashpan; this was almost impossible to fill (only attempted by two men crouching down and carefully manoeuvring two tundishes, or by flicking sand from a bucket in the required direction!). The driving wheels are the later type with small webs between the spokes and the rim, and four-spoke balance weights for the crank axle.

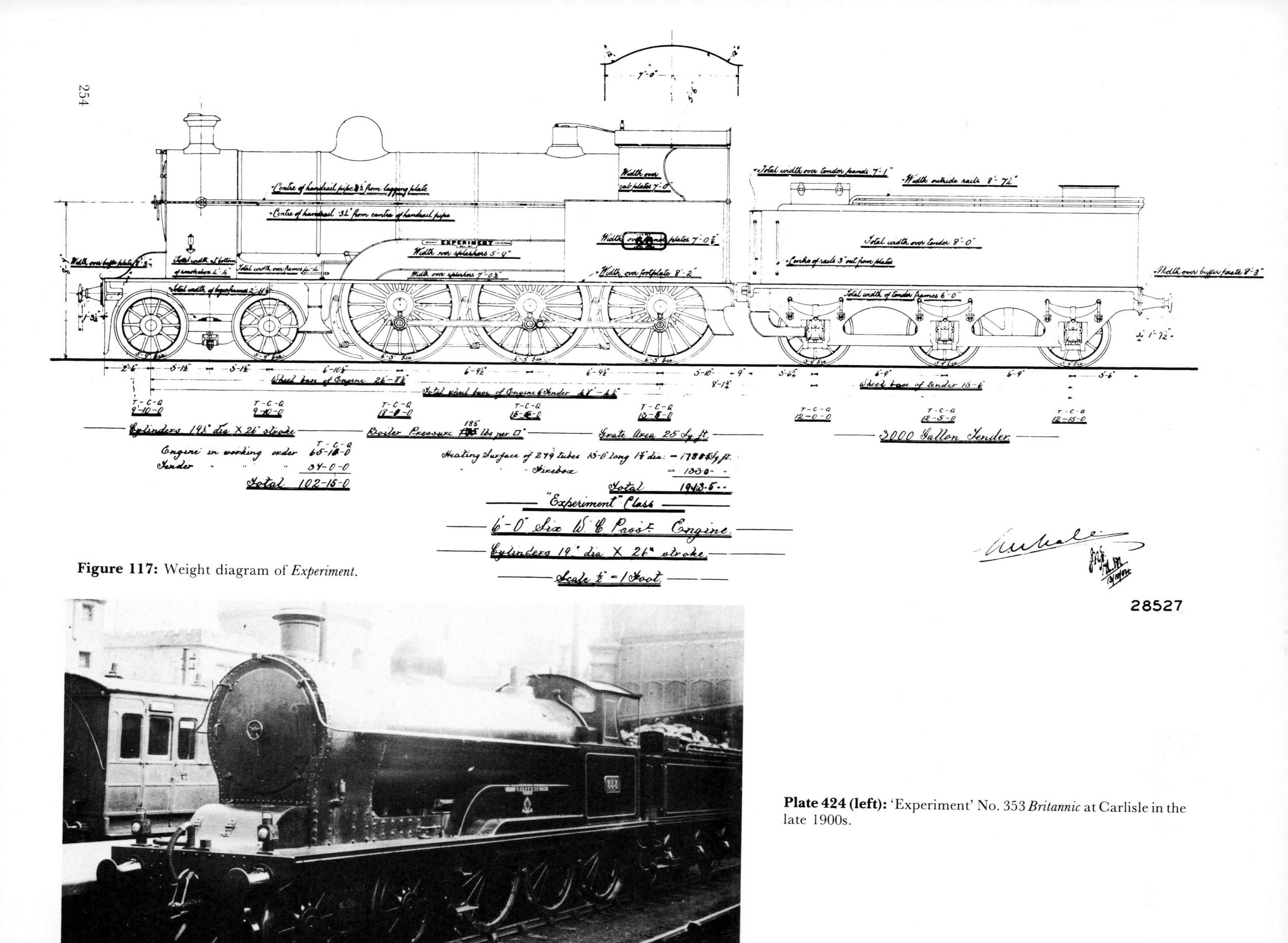

Figure 117: Weight diagram of *Experiment*.

Plate 424 (left): 'Experiment' No. 353 *Britannic* at Carlisle in the late 1900s.

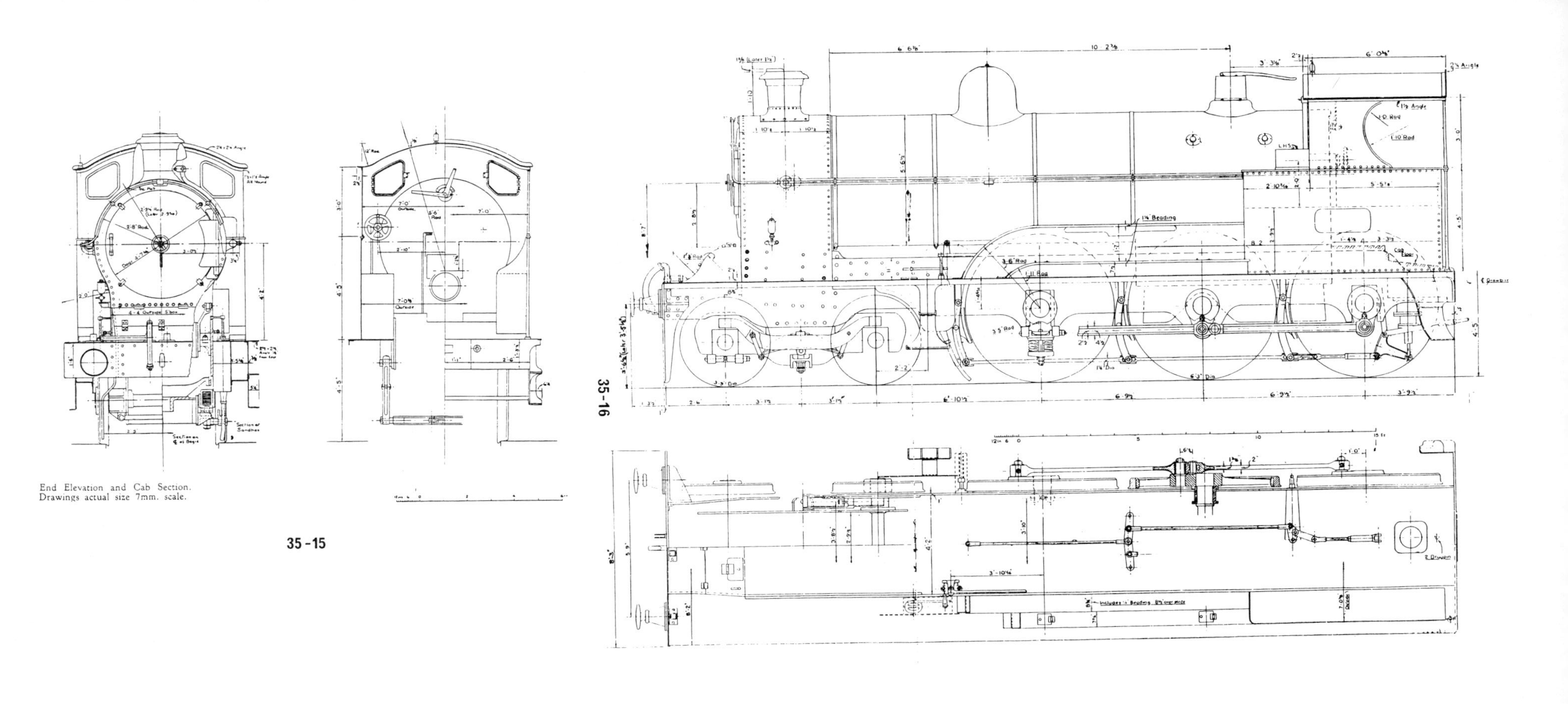

Figure 118: Drawing of an 'Experiment'.

Plate 425 (left): 'Experiment' No. 2027 *Queen Empress* in the late 1900s. Instead of an awkwardly placed sandbox beneath the ashpan it has one in the centre of the driving splasher, supplying a single pipe in front of the centre driving wheels, a much more practical arrangement; the filler lid can be seen above the coat of arms. This placing of a sandbox in the driving splasher was also used on the 'George the Fifth' class.

Plate 426: 'Experiment' No. 61 *Atalanta* at Manchester (London Road) in the late 1900s. The buffers are secured to wooden bases; they are the short-tapered type, which seem to have been introduced in 1906, possibly on the November batch. Presumably, a new type of screw coupling of greater overall length had been adopted for engines, and the wooden pads were used with short-tapered buffers to suit, the long-tapered Cooke buffers eventually replacing them when worn. The wheels are the early Whale type with three-spoke balance weights on the crank axle

Plate 427: 'Experiment' No. 2638 *Byzantium* at Willesden on 10th July 1921. There are only minor changes from the original condition: Cooke buffers, windshield on the leading sander (but not on the centre one, presumably because of the difficulty of fitting one there) and straight-topped tender springs. The driving wheels are the later type with small webs between the spokes and the rim, and three-spoke balance weights on the crank axle.

Plate 428 (above): No. 1709 *Princess May* at Willesden on 3rd June 1922, in plain black livery but with a lined 'Prince' tender.

Plate 429 (right): 'Experiment' No. 353 *Britannic* in the south bay at Rugby in June 1919, fitted with bogie shields to protect the leading axleboxes from water thrown up by a pilot engine when picking up on troughs. These shields were not widely used on the LNWR, being experimental, and were soon removed.

Plate 430 (below): No. 1002 *Warwickshire* at Stalybridge in early LMS days, with an oil-box on the handrail, capuchon on the chimney (not common on the 'Experiments') and Cooke buffers.

Plate 431 (left): 'Experiment' No. 2650 *Buffalo* in early LMS days, fitted with a Belpaire firebox and with a patch on the smokebox!

Plate 432 (above): In 1915 'Experiment' class 4-6-0 No. 1361 *Prospero* was rebuilt with four cylinders arranged on the Dendy Marshall system and with a superheater. The extended smokebox resembled the 'Prince of Wales' class and the outward sweep of the sides of the smokebox resembled a Webb four-cylinder compound. *Prospero* is seen here at Crewe Works on 13th May 1915. It has the usual details of a Crewe superheated engine of the day: mechanical lubricator, pyrometer, snifting valves (on the side of the smokebox) and possibly a damper operated by a lever on the other side. There is an extra small splasher for the connecting-rod big end. Cooke buffers are fitted and a 'Prince' tender.

Plate 433 (left): *Prospero* in early LMS days, with oil-box on the handrail. The left-hand lubricator was probably fitted originally, as four cylinders needed to be supplied.

'19in. Goods'

Plate 434: At the end of 1906 the first of the '19in. Express Goods' or 'Experiment Goods' 4-6-0s appeared. This was simply an 'Experiment' with 5ft. 2½in. driving wheels and the only differences from the 'Experiments' were those resulting directly from the smaller wheels: the long continuous splasher without coupling-rod splashers and the larger cab windows. The '19in. Goods' was in effect the replacement for the 'Cauliflowers' which Webb had had in mind when he produced the 'Bill Baileys', namely a mixed-traffic 4-6-0 for the faster goods trains and the slower passenger trains. This is the official view of the first of the class, No. 285, taken on 3rd January 1907. Minor details are the capuchon on the chimney and the new style of numberplate, stating 'Crewe Works' and the engine building date beneath the number. These plates appeared originally on the first batch of 'Precursor Tanks', which were built immediately before the first '19in. Goods'. All the '19in. Goods' had 3in. wooden pads for the short-tapered buffers, except the last batch built in 1910 which had long-tapered buffers. Some retained their wooden pads until the 1920s. Both sandboxes are of the type that was near impossible to fill! They can both just be seen, the leading one inside the frames behind the brake hanger and leading part of the front driving wheel, and the other one in the same position in relation to the centre driving wheel. Eventually, it was realised that these sandboxes were quite impractical and they were replaced by one behind the footstep, as on the 'Jumbos', and another in the driving splasher, as eventually adopted on the 'Experiments'.

Plate 435: '19in. Goods' No. 2606 about 1910, with original sandboxes.

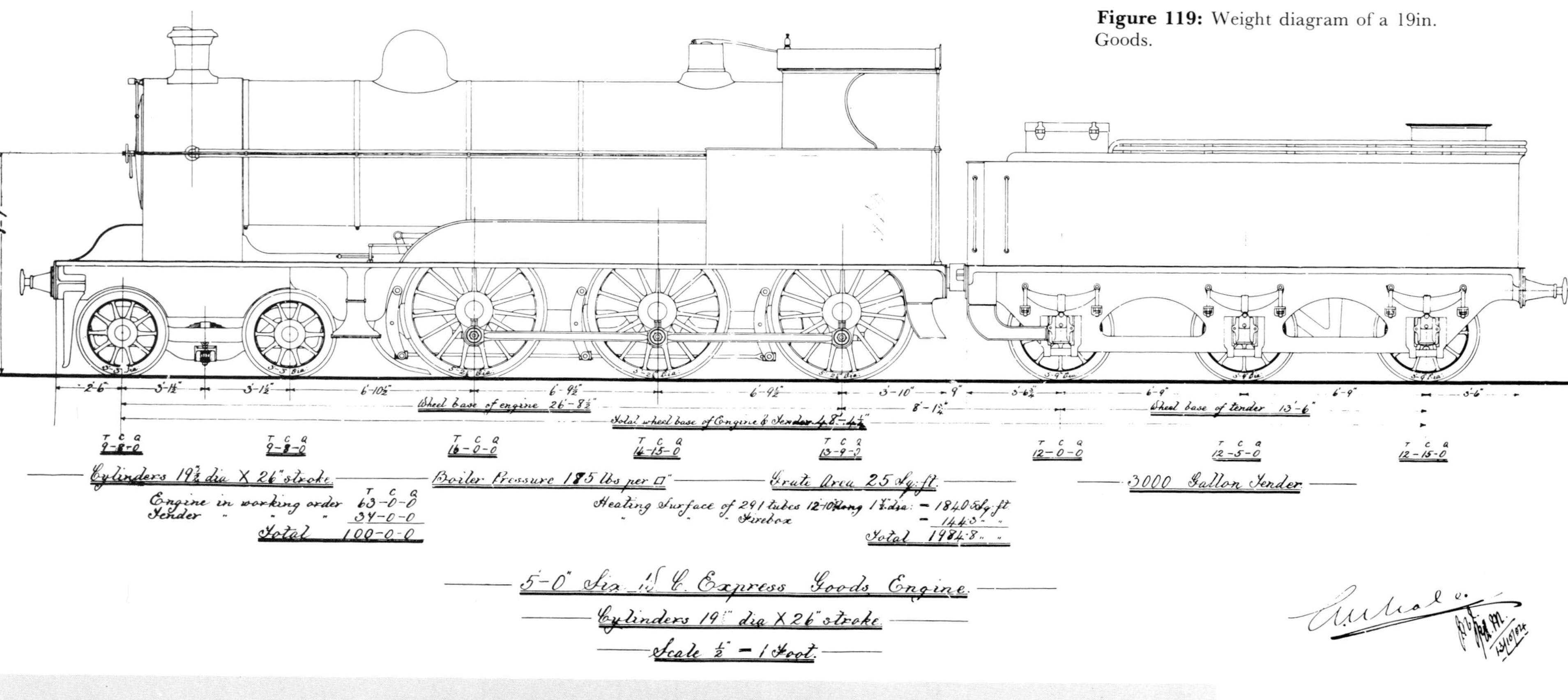

Figure 119: Weight diagram of a 19in. Goods.

Plate 436 (left): '19in. Goods' 4-6-0 No. 1640, as running about 1917 with long-tapered buffers, reversing rod visible above the splasher, chimney without capuchon and the later arrangement of sandboxes.

Plate 437: '19in. Goods' No. 1350, in original condition except for the straight-topped springs on the tender.

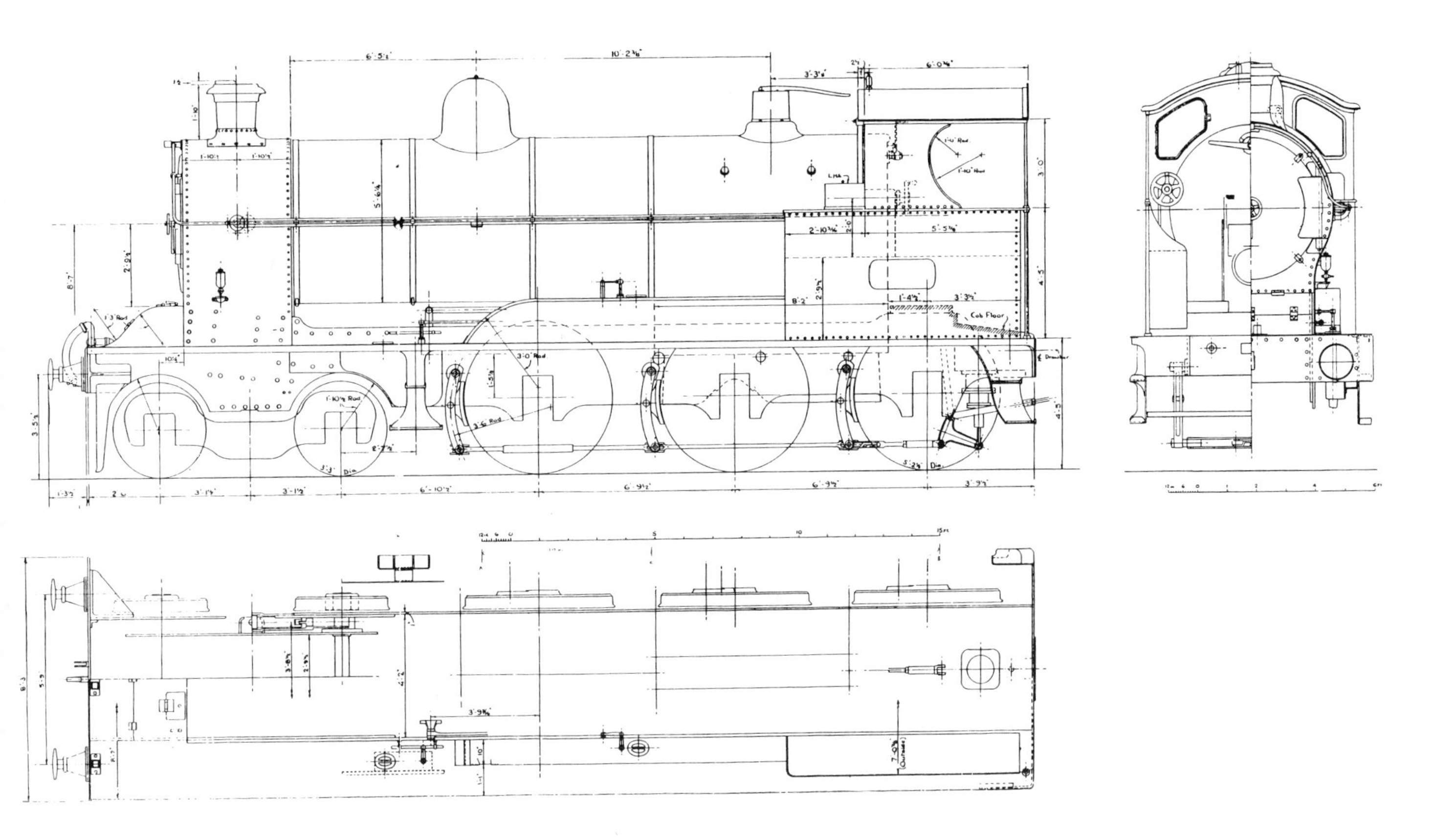

Figure 120: Drawing, to 4mm. scale, of a 19in. Goods.

Plate 438 (left): No. 1625 at Willesden about 1917, with long-tapered buffers, windshields on the sanders, reversing rod visible above the splasher, straight-topped springs on the tender and without a lubricator on the side of the smokebox.

Plate 439 (above right): No. 2270 as running about 1915, in original condition except for the long-tapered buffers.

Plate 440 (right): A '19in. Goods' at Buxton after working the 4.00 p.m. train from Manchester (London Road) in the summer of 1923. It has Cooke buffers, windshields on the sanders and no smokebox lubricators.

Plate 441: No. 1434 at Willesden in early LMS days, with an oil-box on the handrail.

Plate 442: No. 2607 at Manchester (London Road), fitted experimentally with a Phoenix superheater in the smokebox. This device was installed early in 1912 and removed in 1914.

'Precursor Tank'

Plate 443: In May 1906, George Whale brought out the first of his '6ft. Four-coupled Side Tanks'. They were commonly known as 'Precursor Tanks', since they were basically a tank version of the 'Precursor' class with smaller driving wheels, nominally 6ft. but actually 6ft. 3in., and were used on suburban passenger work in the London, Birmingham and Manchester areas. This is the official view of No. 528, the first of the class, taken on 17th July 1906. It has all the usual Whale features of the day, buffers, capuchon, smokebox lubricator and so on, as well as being the first engine to have the new style of numberplate stating 'Crewe Works' and the engine building date. Again, the leading sandbox is the type that was near-impossible to fill, inside and beneath the frames, behind the leading brake hanger. To make things easier, the filler opening has been brought outside the frames — it can just be seen to the right of the upper footstep. The rear sandbox is behind the trailing edge of the rear driving wheel. Both rear sandboxes were filled from a central point in the cab floor as on the 'Coal Tanks' and other tank classes. Two features are typical of Webb tank engines. Firstly, the tank is covered by a smoothly finished side-sheet, with no rivet heads showing, and rising a few inches above the top of the tank itself so as to provide a place for stowing fire-irons and the like. Secondly, toolboxes are provided just inside the bunker coal rails and there are doors giving access to them in the rear of the cab.

Plate 444: The first 'Precursor Tank' derailed twice between the erecting shop and the paintshop. It was found to be too stiff in the wheelbase; there was insufficient bogie clearance and the rear axle was rigid in the frames (Whale had insisted on this though J. N. Jackson, the chief draughtsman, had proposed a radial axle). So more clearance was then provided and a radial axle put in at the rear. The first thirty, built in 1906, had 3ft. 9in. bogie and trailing wheels, but the ten built in 1907 and the ten more in 1909 had 3ft. 3in. wheels, with the frames cut out to accommodate them. The smaller wheels allowed more swing to be provided at the front, and some side play was also allowed at the rear. One of the second batch, No. 762, is seen here at Buxton in original condition.

Plate 445 (above): A rear view of No. 762 and of '18in. Tank' No. 377 at Buxton about 1910, on the same occasion as the previous picture. No. 762 has a shed 16 plate (Longsight). Both engines are vacuum-fitted and have carriage-heating apparatus and screw couplings.

Plate 446 (right): No. 1536, one of the last batch built in 1909, at Carnforth in 1921. It has no capuchon on the chimney but is generally still very much as built.

Plate 447 (below): 'Precursor Tank' No. 803, one of the first batch with 3ft. 9in. bogie wheels, soon after entering service in July 1906. It has a destination board 'Watford' in the bracket just behind the bufferbeam.

Plate 448: Official view of No. 44, the first of the 1907 batch, at Camden on 22nd February 1924. It is still in splendidly LNWR condition with the coupling rods, handrails and smokebox door wheel and handle all finished bright. It has a ventilator in the cab roof and new leading sandboxes like those on the 'Jumbos', behind the leading footsteps; the filler lid can just be seen above the running plate. This improvement to the sandboxes seems to have been made very late on the 'Precursor Tanks', probably not before about 1920. No. 44 also has Cooke buffers and destination-board brackets but there is no capuchon on the chimney and no lubricator on the side of the smokebox.

Plate 449 (left): No. 875 at Birmingham (New Street) about 1910, with destination-board brackets on the rear and Whale buffers mounted on wooden bases.

Plate 450 (right): No. 874, one of the 1906 batch with large bogie wheels, at Birmingham (New Street) about 1910; it is in original condition. None of the original batch was ever modified to take the smaller bogie wheels.

Plate 451 (below): No. 1589, one of the first batch, about 1920, with cab-roof ventilator, 'Jumbo' style sandboxes and Cooke buffers, but otherwise very much as originally built. There is a lamp lodged behind the handrail by the smokebox. No 'Precursor Tank' was ever superheated, which is perhaps surprising in view of the success of superheating on other LNWR engines and of the general usefulness of the class, and also in view of the fact that it was an LBSC 4-4-2 tank which first convinced Bowen Cooke that superheating was worth trying.

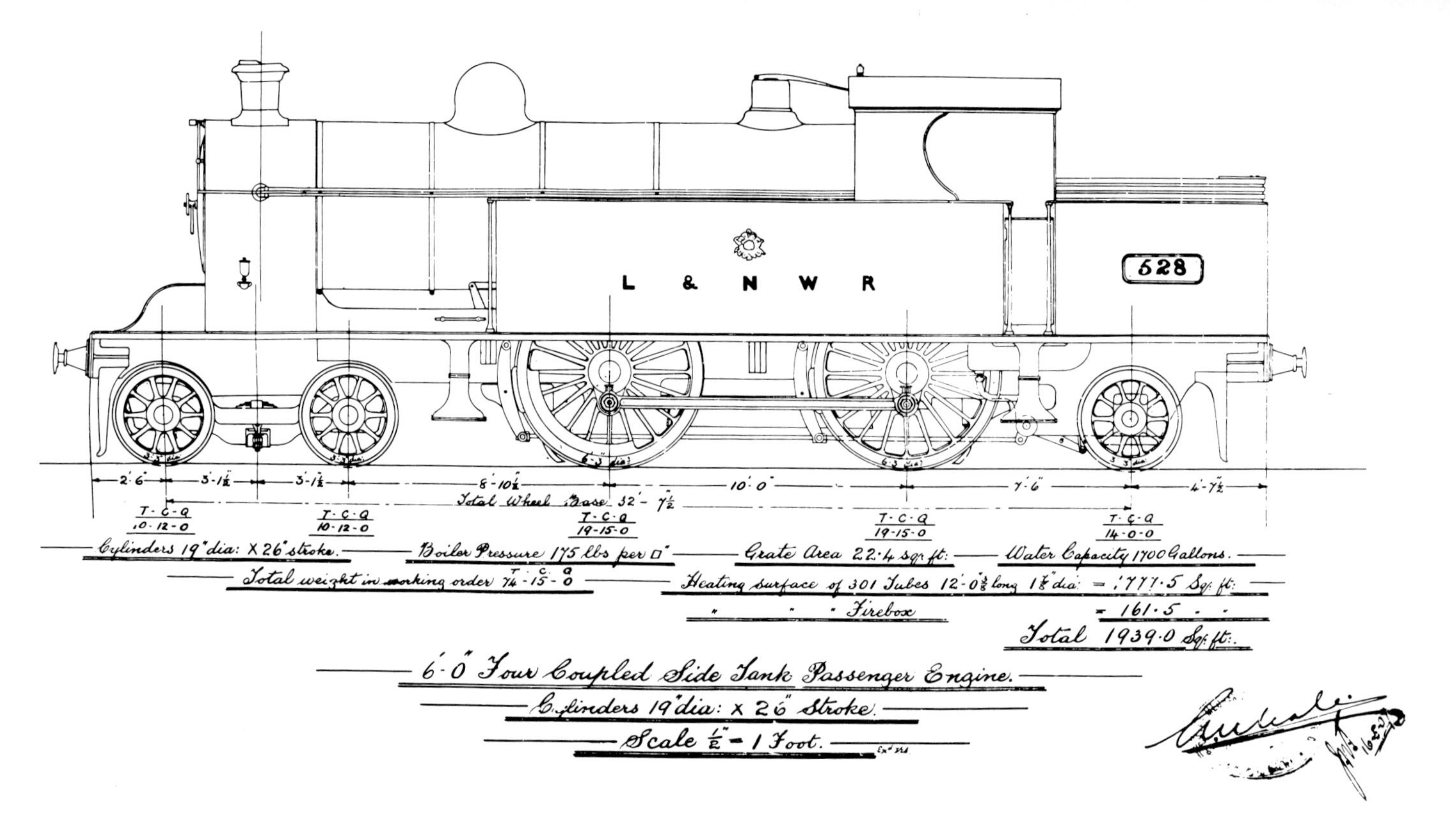

Figure 121: Weight diagram of a 'Precursor Tank'. The engine is numbered 528 but has 3ft. 3in. carrying wheels instead of 3ft. 9in.

Figure 122: Drawing to 4mm. scale of a 'Precursor Tank'.

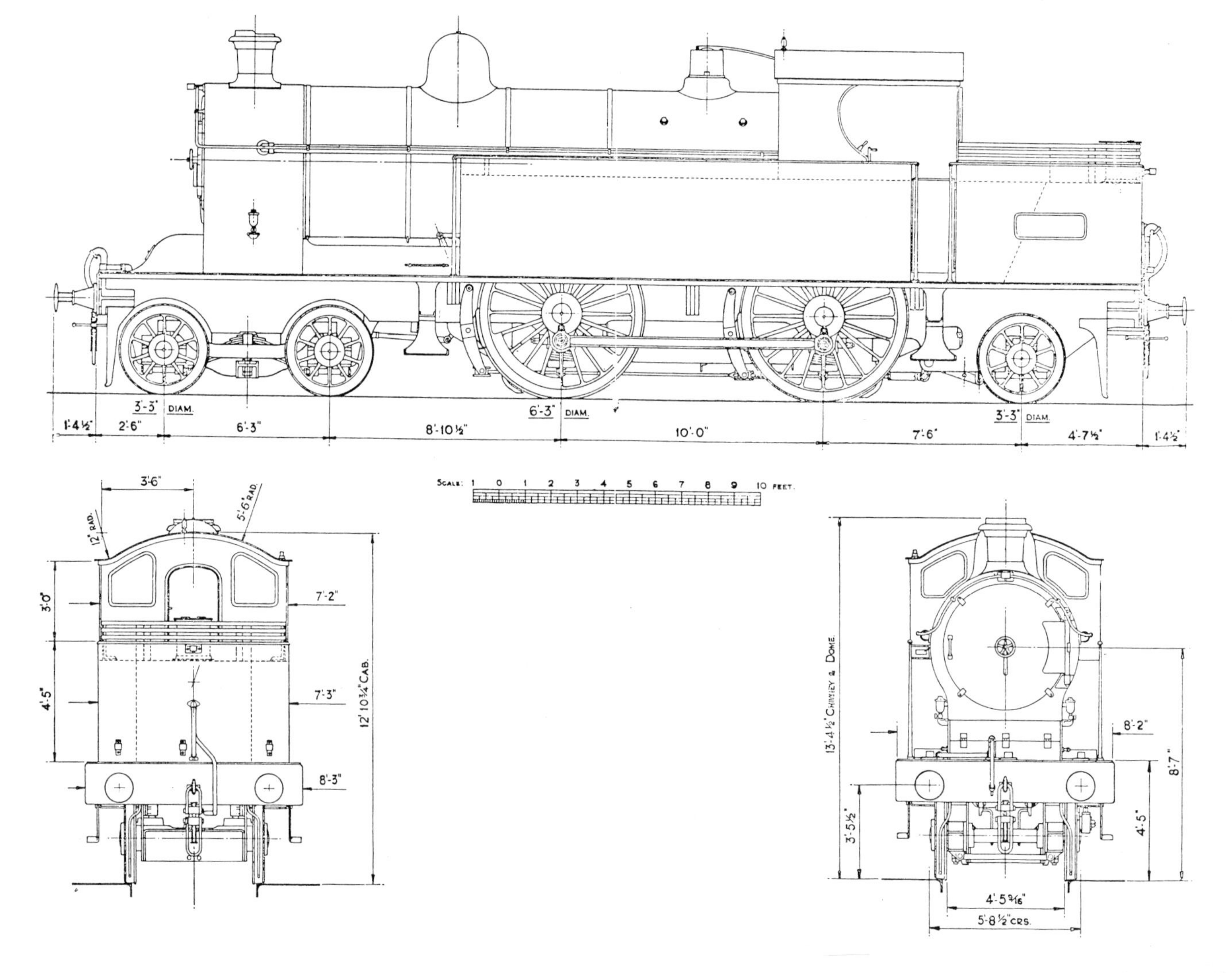

'Renown'

Plate 452: By the end of 1907, all the 'Alfreds' had been converted to 'Benbows' but for some reason no 'Jubilee' was so treated and they all continued to run as four-cylinder compounds until 1908, when Mr Whale undertook a major rebuilding of No. 1918 *Renown*. Basically, the outside cylinders were removed, the inside cylinders lined up to 18½in. diameter and an 'Alfred the Great' boiler fitted, while such Whale features as cab and buffers were applied. The result was in effect a small version of Whale's 'Precursor'. Even then, further conversions were carried out quite slowly. By 1914 only five 'Jubilees' and two 'Benbows' had become 'Renowns' and it was not until after the war that conversions were made in any numbers. Even then, three 'Jubilees' and seven 'Benbows' were never converted. Most 'Renowns' ran with Webb tenders, as fitted to their predecessors, but no doubt a Whale tender was thought more suitable for the official photograph seen here, taken on 18th June 1908.

Plate 453: No. 1943 *Queen Alexandra* was rebuilt in September 1916 and so must have obtained the lined livery after wartime economies ceased and lining out was resumed in October 1921. Apart from minor details such as windshields on the sandpipes, it is in much the same condition as *Renown* on first conversion.

Plate 454 (above): No. 1946 *Diadem*, which was converted to a 'Renown' in October 1914, coupled to a 2,500 gallon Webb tender.

Plate 455 (left): No. 1973 *Hood* was converted to a 'Renown' in September 1921 and is seen here, probably quite soon afterwards, on Crewe South shed in the full lined livery. It has Cooke buffers and a chimney without a capuchon.

Plate 456 (below): No. 1914 *Invincible* was rebuilt to 'Renown' in September 1916 and was renumbered 1257 in April 1920 to allow the war memorial 'Claughton' *Patriot* to be numbered 1914. It is seen here at Willesden on 3rd May 1924 with Cooke buffers, no capuchon and in plain black livery.

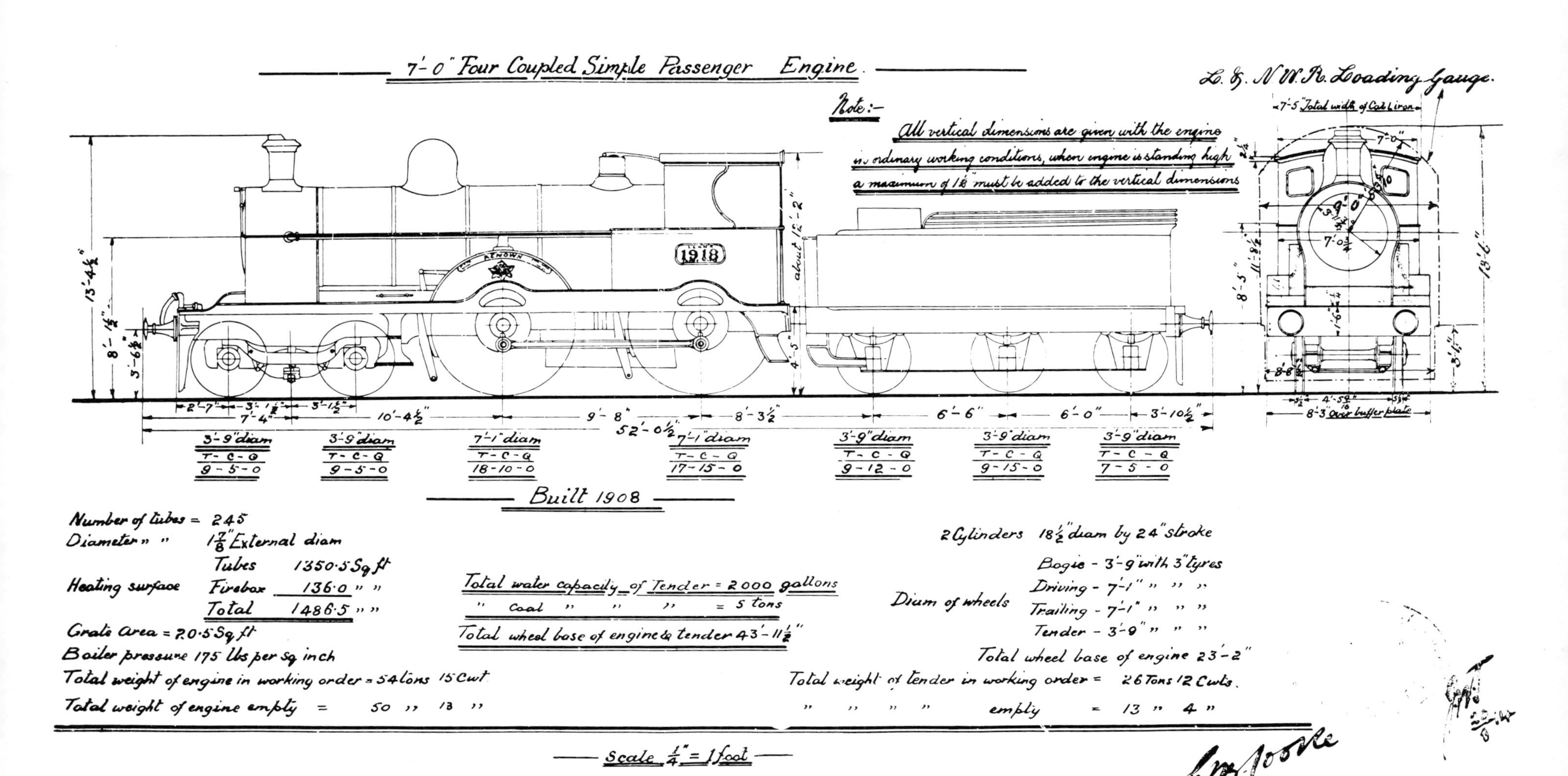

Figure 123: Weight diagram of *Renown*.

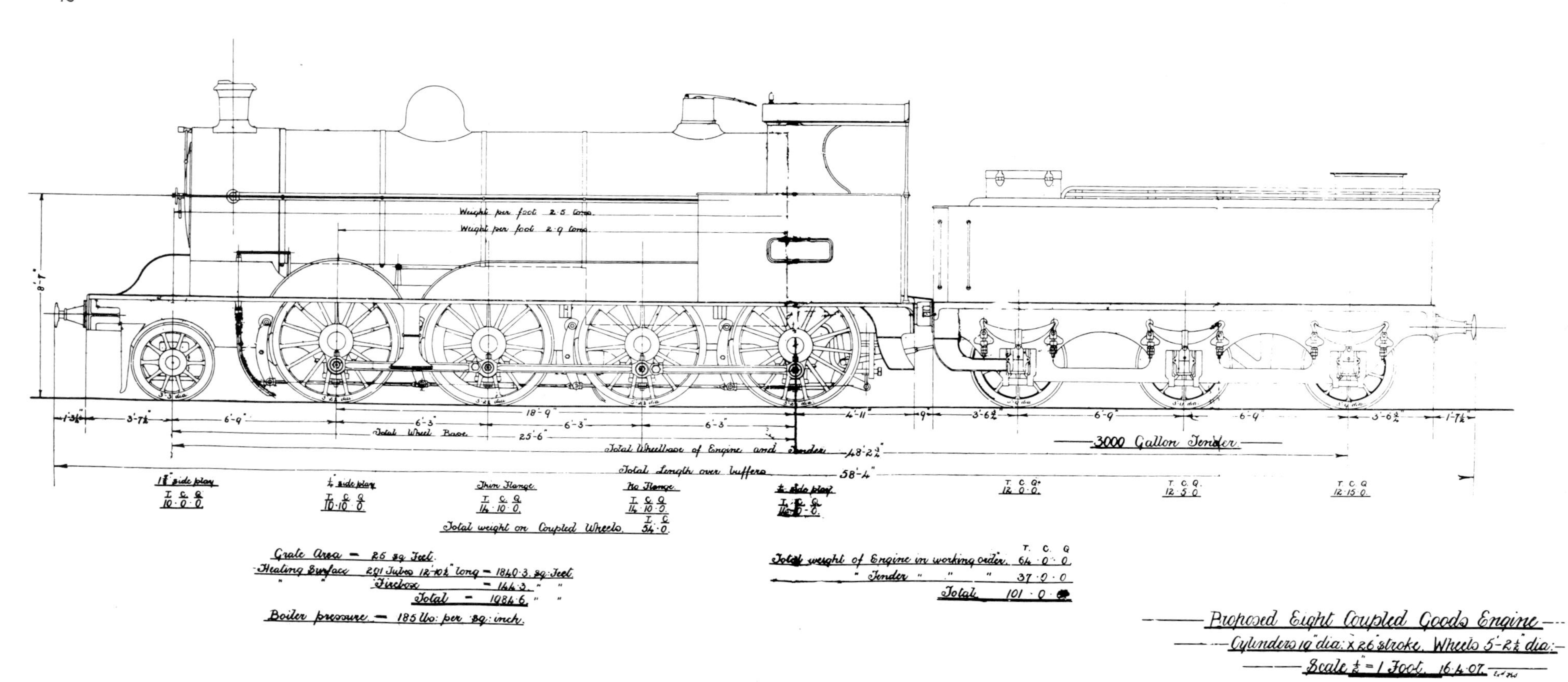

Proposed '19in. Goods' 2-8-0

Figure 124: Over the years an establishment such as Crewe Works must have produced many designs for engines which were never built. This drawing shows a proposed scheme for a 2-8-0 version of the '19in. Goods', with the same boiler, cylinders and driving wheels, and the same overall dimensions. Only the spacing of the coupled wheels has been altered to accommodate an extra driving axle in place of the rear wheels of the bogie. The proposal was presumably intended to examine the possibilities of producing a '19in. Goods' with greater adhesion, which would have been useful on fast heavy freight trains and over Shap and the Pennines. In view of the size of the driving wheels, it was not planned as a new type of heavy coal engine, breaking away from the line of development begun with No. 2524 and the 'A' class compounds. Only one feature can be traced to traditional eight-coupled designs, the flangeless driving wheels on the third axle. The drawing is dated 16th April 1907, only some four months after the first '19in. Goods' appeared.

Chapter 13
C. J. Bowen Cooke's Engines

'George the Fifth' and 'Queen Mary'

Plate 457 (above): In July 1910, two new inside-cylinder 4-4-0s were built at Crewe. They were identical, except that No. 2663 *George the Fifth* had a superheater and No. 2664 *Queen Mary* was unsuperheated. This test of superheating had been suggested to C. J. Bowen Cooke, who had succeeded George Whale as Chief Mechanical Engineer early in 1909, by the successful running of an LBSC superheated 'I3' class 4-4-2 tank between Brighton and Rugby, and by his wide study of current developments in the locomotive world both in Great Britain and abroad. This is the official view of *George the Fifth* on 26th August 1910, after the engine had returned to Crewe Works for final painting, following the completion of trials. The only outward signs of the superheater are the damper lever on the side of the smokebox, which was operated by the boiler handrail, and the absence of a displacement lubricator on the side of the smokebox, instead of which there are three oil pipes to the left-hand cylinder from the mechanical lubricator on the other side. Otherwise, in its details it is a typically North Western engine in the Webb-Whale tradition. There are four sandboxes: the ones for the leading driving wheels are behind the footsteps, shaped like those on the 'Jumbos', and filled from above the running plate; and the rear ones are between the driving wheels inside the splashers and filled from above them. The tender is the first Bowen Cooke type, which outwardly seems little different from the Whale tender but has, in fact, been completely redesigned. It has the same 'curved top' springs and only one coal rail but the separate toolboxes have gone, being replaced by cupboards on the front of the tender. The most important difference of all is that the coal space is no longer formed simply by a U-shaped water tank, but is shaped to help move coal forward and has a shovelling plate. This tender was officially described as having a 'water bottom and sloping bunker'. In service, the 'George the Fifths' were found to be quite outstanding locomotives. For power output in relation to size and cost, they were the most successful engines of their day.

Plate 458 (right): Smokebox view of *George the Fifth*, showing the superheater header.

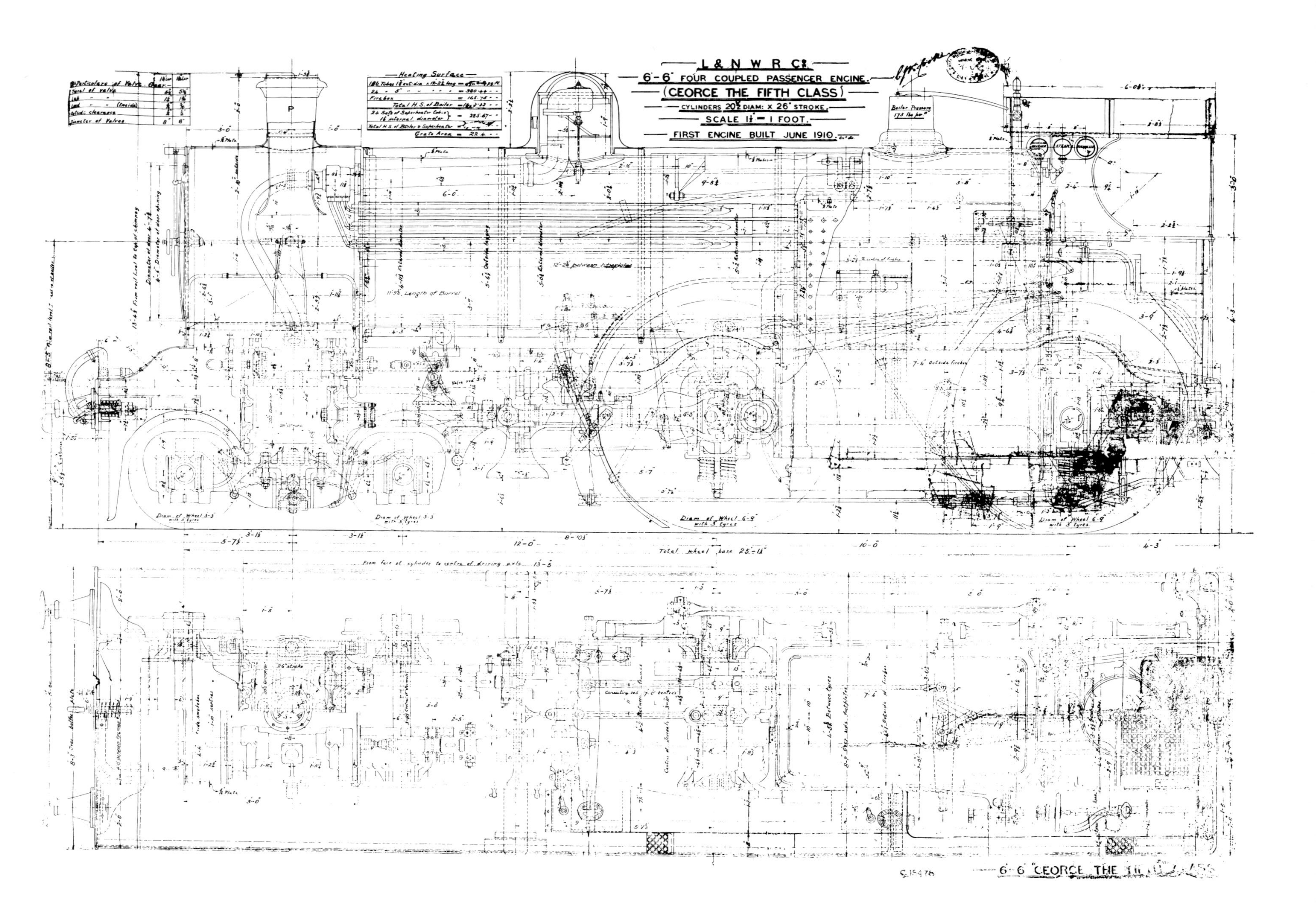

Figure 125: General arrangement drawings of *George the Fifth*.

Plate 459 (above): Official view of No. 2664 *Queen Mary*, also taken on 26th August 1910. The only outward signs that it is an unsuperheated engine are the traditional displacement lubricator on the side of the smokebox and the absence of a superheater damper lever and mechanical lubricator. Nine more 'Queen Marys' appeared in October 1910, as *George the Fifth* was the experimental engine. However, in November, more 'Georges' began to appear and in 1913-14 the 'Queen Marys' were converted to superheating, presumably at their first major overhaul, and so became identical to the 'Georges' in every respect. Careful tests over several months showed that the superheated engine used some 26 per cent less coal. Even so, the 'Queen Marys' were fine engines, being superior to the 'Precursors'.

Plate 460 (right): The second of the 'Queen Marys', No. 238 *F. W. Webb*, at Stockport in original unsuperheated condition but with sandpipe windshields and a Whale tender fitted with straight-topped springs, introduced by Bowen Cooke in 1911. *F. W. Webb* was a most appropriate choice of name and the third of the class was equally well named, *George Whale*.

Plate 461 (below): 'Queen Mary' No. 2507 *Miles Macinnes* in Crewe Works about 1912, with the original type of Bowen Cooke tender introduced on this class. It has short-tapered Whale buffers mounted on wooden pads, presumably to give the same length as the long-tapered type so as to match the length of the coupling.

Plate 462 (above): 'George the Fifth' class No. 82 *Charles Dickens*, built in January 1913, at Manchester (London Road) in original condition. The pipe near the base of the chimney leads from the superheater header to the pyrometer in the cab, and there is a mechanical lubricator on the frames. Driving wheels with large bosses were introduced with the second batch of 'Georges' built in 1911, but originated on Webb's 'Jubilees'. The tender is the type photographed on *Prince of Wales* in February 1912.

Plate 463 (right): *Coronation* running trials as No. 1800 in June 1911 before re-entering the works for final painting in its special livery. It is in original 'George the Fifth' condition except for the large driving-wheel bosses. The name was specially chosen, of course, in honour of the coronation of King George V.

Plate 464 (below): An official view of No. 5000 *Coronation* as first finished for entry into service. The royal coat of arms is carried on the tender and there is special brass decoration on the boiler bands.

Plate 465: No. 5000 *Coronation* in service at Manchester (London Road). The sandboxes have been repositioned on the front of the splashers but otherwise the engine is in original condition.

Plate 466: No. 2664 *Queen Mary* at Manchester (London Road) about 1915, after conversion to superheating with superheater-damper lever and repositioned sandboxes. This engine and *George the Fifth* were built with two rows of eight bolts at the base of the smokebox fixing the cylinders to the frames; later engines had both rows reduced to five bolts only in each, the upper row being slightly higher. In service, this was found to be insufficient and at overhaul the number of bolts was increased to nine in each row, the 1915 batch being so equipped from new. The two original engines, however, remained unaltered. It was the practice in the works that these large hexagon-headed bolts should be lined up neat and straight with each other. They were tightened up and strained with a huge spanner to get them so, even if the threads were nearly stripped in the process!

Plate 467 (above): No. 1550 *Westminster*, originally a 'Queen Mary', as running about 1916 when superheated, with additional smokebox bolts and with sandboxes repositioned on the splashers. The tender is the 'Prince of Wales' type.

Plate 468 (above): No. 1680 *Loyalty* at Manchester (London Road) about 1915. The pipe running along the top of the splasher and disappearing beneath the boiler behind the sandbox connects the brake fittings in the cab with the crosshead vacuum-pump behind the right-hand cylinder, where it was always placed on LNWR engines. The tender is the original type but with straight-topped springs, and has been altered for vacuum braking.

Plate 469 (right): No. 1481 *Typhon* at Rhyl about 1917, with pyrometer removed and with 'Prince of Wales' type tender.

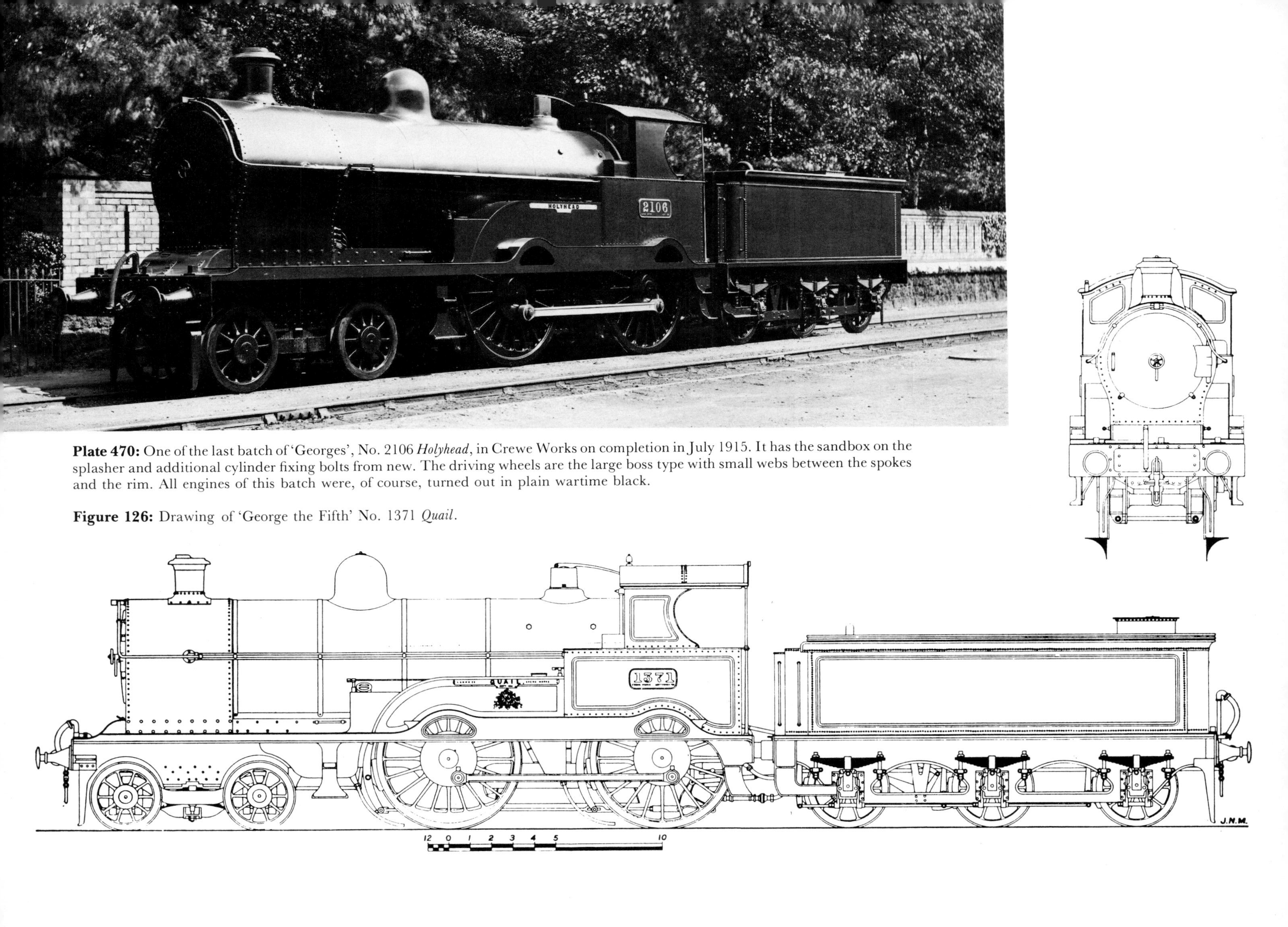

Plate 470: One of the last batch of 'Georges', No. 2106 *Holyhead*, in Crewe Works on completion in July 1915. It has the sandbox on the splasher and additional cylinder fixing bolts from new. The driving wheels are the large boss type with small webs between the spokes and the rim. All engines of this batch were, of course, turned out in plain wartime black.

Figure 126: Drawing of 'George the Fifth' No. 1371 *Quail*.

Plate 471 (left): No. 2663 *George the Fifth* at Willesden on 23rd June 1922, with superheater damper removed and with 'Prince' type tender.

Plate 472 (below right): No. 2495 *Bassethound* at Manchester (London Road) about 1915. Early superheated engines gave trouble with elements burning at the firebox end of the return loops, and *Bassethound* is thought to have been modified with two regulators to combat this. The normal regulator in the dome is now operated by the outside rodding and admits steam into the superheater in the usual way. In addition, a Webb type 'bible valve' regulator in the smokebox admits steam from the outer end of the superheater into the short pipes leading to the cylinders. The chimney has been moved forward to accommodate this regulator, which is supplied with oil by the usual Webb lubricator. A 'bible valve' dealing with superheated steam would be both difficult to lubricate and prone to leak, so perhaps the dome regulator was retained as a safeguard, or perhaps it was to allow a faulty superheater tube to be replaced with the boiler in steam. Superheater dampers were fitted to prevent the burning of elements, but drivers sometimes omitted to use them and they began to be removed about 1917.

Plate 473 & 474 (above & right): Two views of No. 1472 *Moor Hen* when fitted with a Weir feedwater heater and with oil boxes on the boiler handrail. This feedwater heater was first fitted to No. 127 *Snake*, then to No. 2494 *Perseus* and finally to *Moor Hen*, which carried it into LMS days. In both these pictures, the tender is the Whale type, with coal rails and external toolboxes but modified with straight-topped springs.

'Prince of Wales'

Plate 475: In the same way that Whale had produced a 4-6-0 version of the 'Precursors' so Bowen-Cooke produced a 4-6-0 version of the 'George the Fifths'. It was officially described as the '6ft. Six-coupled Prince of Wales' class, after the first to be built. This is the official view of No. 819 *Prince of Wales* taken on 16th February 1912. It is almost exactly an elongated 'George', the only differences being the 3ft. 9in. bogie wheels instead of 3ft. 3in., and the snifting valve above the running plate at the base of the smokebox. The leading sandboxes are in the same place, under the running plate, and the others are under the middle of the splashers. The tender is a new type; the shape of the frames is the same but the springs have straight tops and the top of the tender is solid with double beading instead of coal rails. This type of tender remained standard until the first production batch of 'Claughtons' appeared, on which the top had the same curved coping but with a single row of beading only.

Plate 476: The first batch of ten 'Princes' were built without any preliminary testing of prototypes. They all had particularly fine names, which have puzzled some observers since all were new and were not traditional North Western names; it seems certain, however, that they were taken from warships of the Royal Navy. Third of the batch was No. 1452 *Bonaventure*, seen here at Euston about 1914. The 'Princes' lacked the curved covers over the front end which the 'Georges' had perpetuated but otherwise were identical in details, with a mechanical lubricator on the right-hand side and pipe to the pyrometer near the base of the chimney.

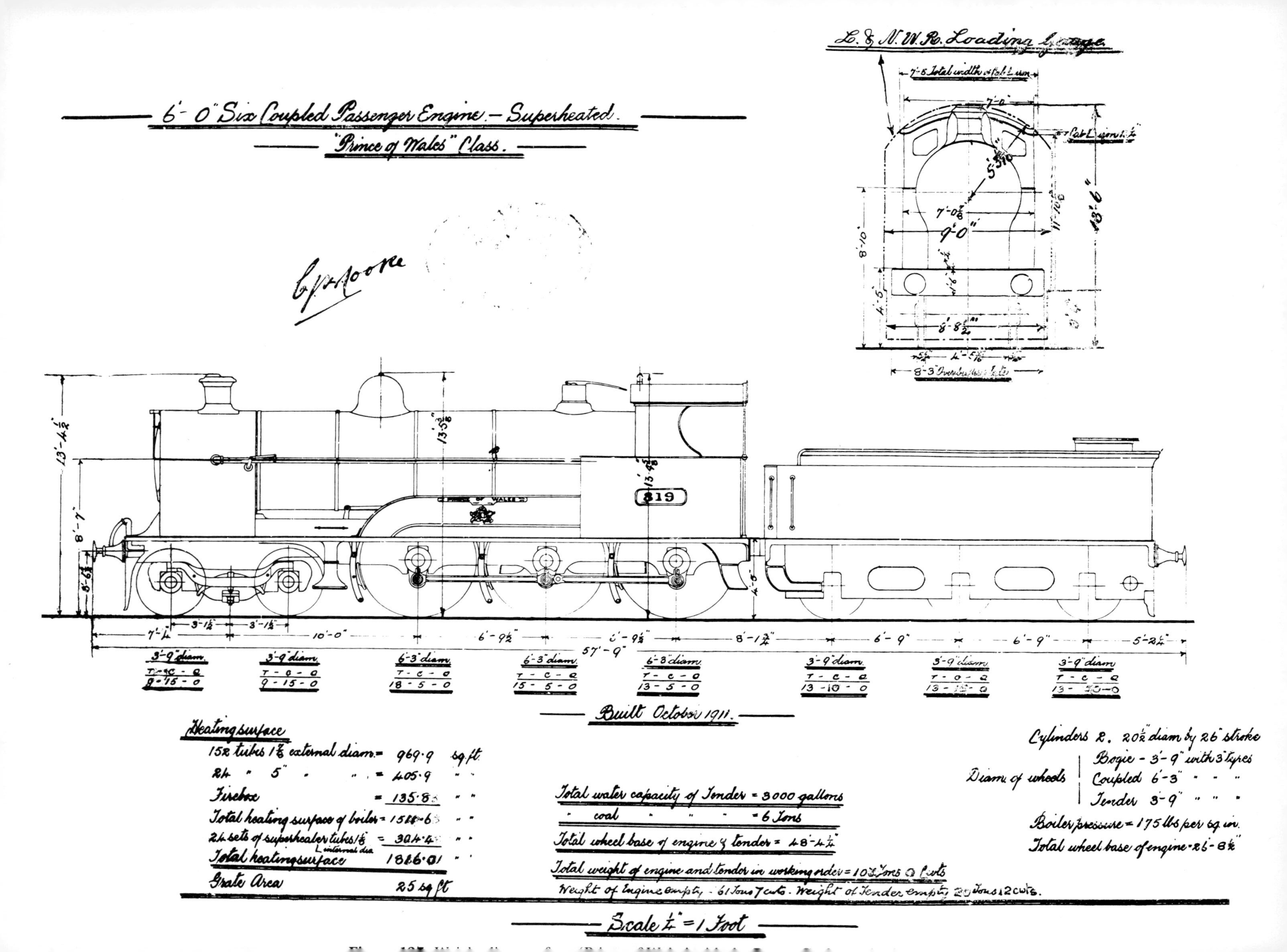
6'-0" Six Coupled Passenger Engine. — Superheated.
"Prince of Wales" Class.
L. & N. W. R. Loading Gauge.
9'-0"
13'-6"
319
Built October 1911.
Heating surface
152 tubes 1 7/8 external diam. = 969·9 sq ft
24 " 5" " " = 405·9 " "
Firebox = 135·83 " "
Total heating surface of boiler = 1511·6 " "
24 sets of superheater tubes 1 5/8 external dia = 304·4 " "
Total heating surface 1816·01 " "
Grate Area 25 sq ft
Total water capacity of Tender = 3000 gallons
" coal " " " = 6 Tons
Total wheel base of engine & tender = 48'-4 1/4"
Weight of Engine empty - 61 Tons 7 cwts. Weight of Tender empty 20 Tons 12 cwts.
Cylinders 2. 20 1/2" diam by 26" stroke
Diam. of wheels
Bogie - 3'-9" with 3" tyres
Coupled 6'-3" " " "
Tender 3'-9" " " "
Boiler pressure = 175 lbs per sq in.
Total wheel base of engine = 25'-8 1/2"
Scale 1/4" = 1 Foot

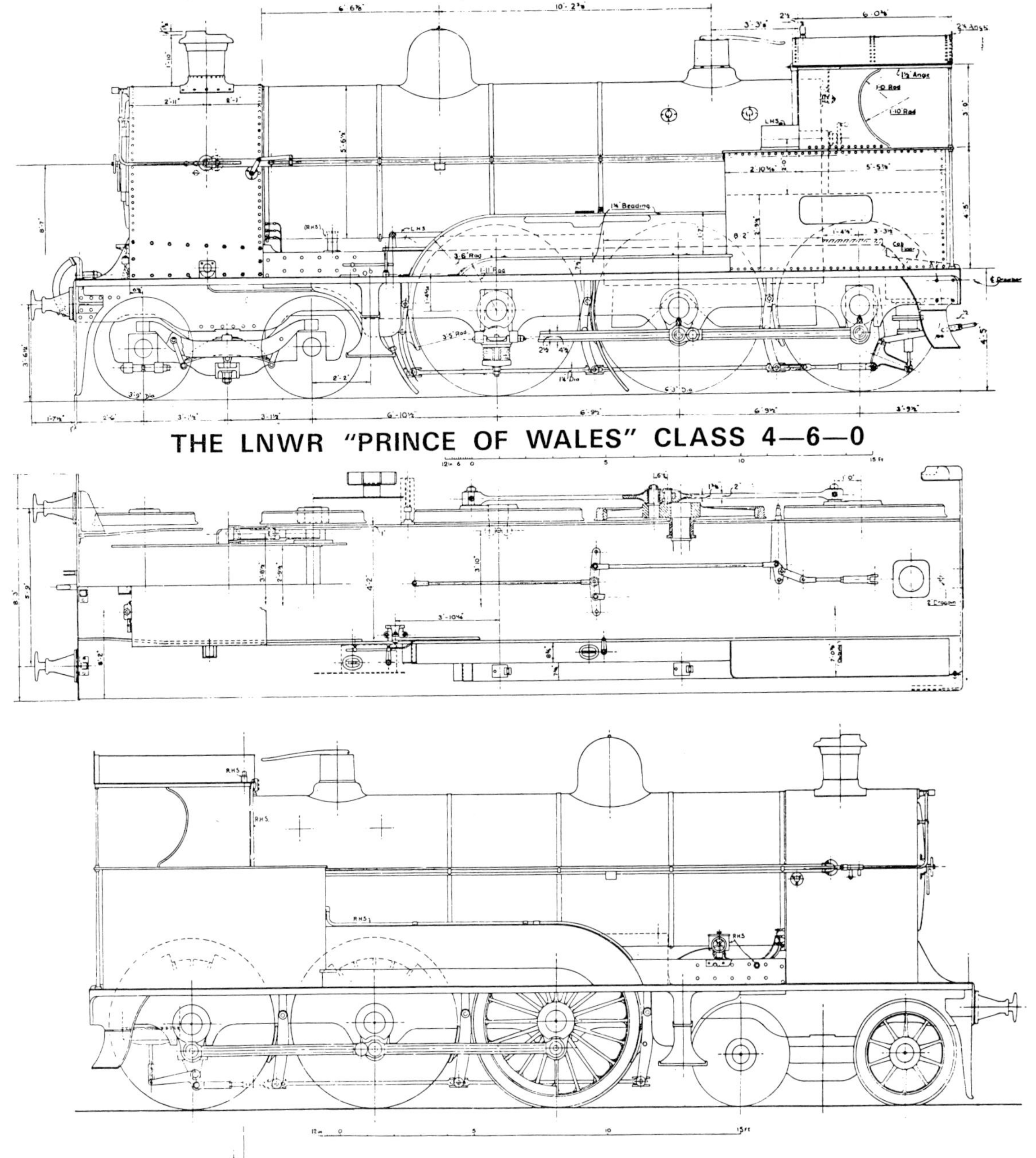

Figure 128: Drawings to 4mm. scale of a 'Prince of Wales' class 4-6-0.

Plate 477: In 1915 twenty 'Princes' were built by the North British Locomotive Co. This is No. 2175 *Loadstone*, one of ten built at Hyde Park Works. It is not coupled to a tender because the tenders were built at Crewe. Except for such minor details as the sandpipe windshields and modified front-end lubricators, it is the same as the earlier Crewe-built engines. The pyrometer is not connected up, perhaps because it is now thought to be not needed.

Plate 478: No. 964 *Bret Harte* at Manchester (London Road) about 1916. The arrangement of lubricators on the front end, the snifting valve and the lever for the superheater damper can be clearly seen. The lubricators supply the tailrods of the pistons; they were removed from about 1916. The 'Georges' had similar lubricators but they were hidden by their 'piano fronts'. There are windshields on the leading sandpipes, and the tender is the type introduced with the first production batch of 'Claughtons'.

Plate 479: One of the North British 'Princes' in service at Stockport about 1917. Though the paint is flaking off the boiler, dome and smokebox, the engine is still well cleaned; there are windshields on the leading sandpipes. The Beardmore 'Princes', built in 1921-2, had their oblong maker's plates in the same position.

Plate 480 (left): No. 1089 *Sydney Smith*, built in September 1913, at Tamworth about 1920. The pyrometer has been removed and presumably the superheater damper also, and there is no capuchon on the chimney; otherwise, the engine is little changed. The tender is the final Bowen Cooke type, with oval cut-outs in the square-ended frames and single beading round the top.

Plate 481 (right): Whereas construction of the 'George the Fifths' ceased in 1915, the 'Prince of Wales' class continued to be built after the war. They had a lower axleload than the 'Georges' and consequently a wider availability, and being overshadowed to some extent by the 'Claughtons', have been discounted by many observers. They were, however, excellent engines and are still remembered as such by enginemen who worked on them in the 1920s, being very economical when in good condition. In 1921-2, ninety were built by W. Beardmore of Dalmuir. They were painted plain black and none were ever named, though some of those built at Crewe at the same time were eventually named. This view shows No. 242 at Willesden on 2nd June 1923. The Beardmore plate is just visible on the smokebox in the same place as the plates on the North British-built engines. Changes from the original 'Princes' are the sandbox on the splasher, as on the later 'Georges' and the 1919 batch of Crewe-built 'Princes', a modified lubricator and lamp irons, which the Beardmore 'Princes' had from new in place of the traditional LNWR sockets. The tender is the final Bowen Cooke type.

Plate 482 (right): Beardmore 'Prince' No. 551 at Camden about 1924. Again, the builder's plate is visible on the smokebox and the condition is generally the same as No. 242.

Plate 483: A magnificent official photograph of No. 88 *Czar of Russia* at Camden on 22nd February 1924 in plain black livery with burnished coupling rods and handrails. It has an oil box on the handrail, modified lubrication details, and the last type of Bowen Cooke tender, introduced in 1916.

Plate 484 (above): In 1923, under the direction of Mr Beames, four 'Princes' were fitted with outside Walschaerts valve gear. Although they were never re-converted to their original form, no others were ever converted like them. This is the official view of No. 964 *Bret Harte* on 2nd May 1923. It has an oil box on the handrail, a 1916 tender and a combined form of lamp iron and socket in the three positions above the bufferbeam, but a socket only at the top of the smokebox.

Plate 485 (below): Another of the 'Tishies', as the outside valve gear 'Princes' were known, at Rugby on 4th June 1924. No. 2340 should be named *Tara* but here has been fitted with one of the *Prince of Wales* nameplates from LMS No. 5845, the engine ordered by the LMS from Beardmore's in 1924 for display at the Wembley Exhibition. It cannot be the plate from No. 819 as that had the usual LNWR subsidiary inscriptions, whereas No. 5845's plate had only the date apart from the name. Why this plate has been fitted is not known but it was perhaps because someone wanted a photograph of it on a 'Prince' in LNWR condition, as No. 5845 was painted LMS maroon from the outset. Here, No. 2340 has Ross pop safety valves and an oil box on the handrail.

Plate 486 (right): Another view of No. 964 *Bret Harte*, this time with a Belpaire firebox and LMS lamp irons about 1925. Many LNWR engines received Belpaire fireboxes during the LMS period as a result of Beames' plans for such boilers, which were drawn up around the time of the Grouping.

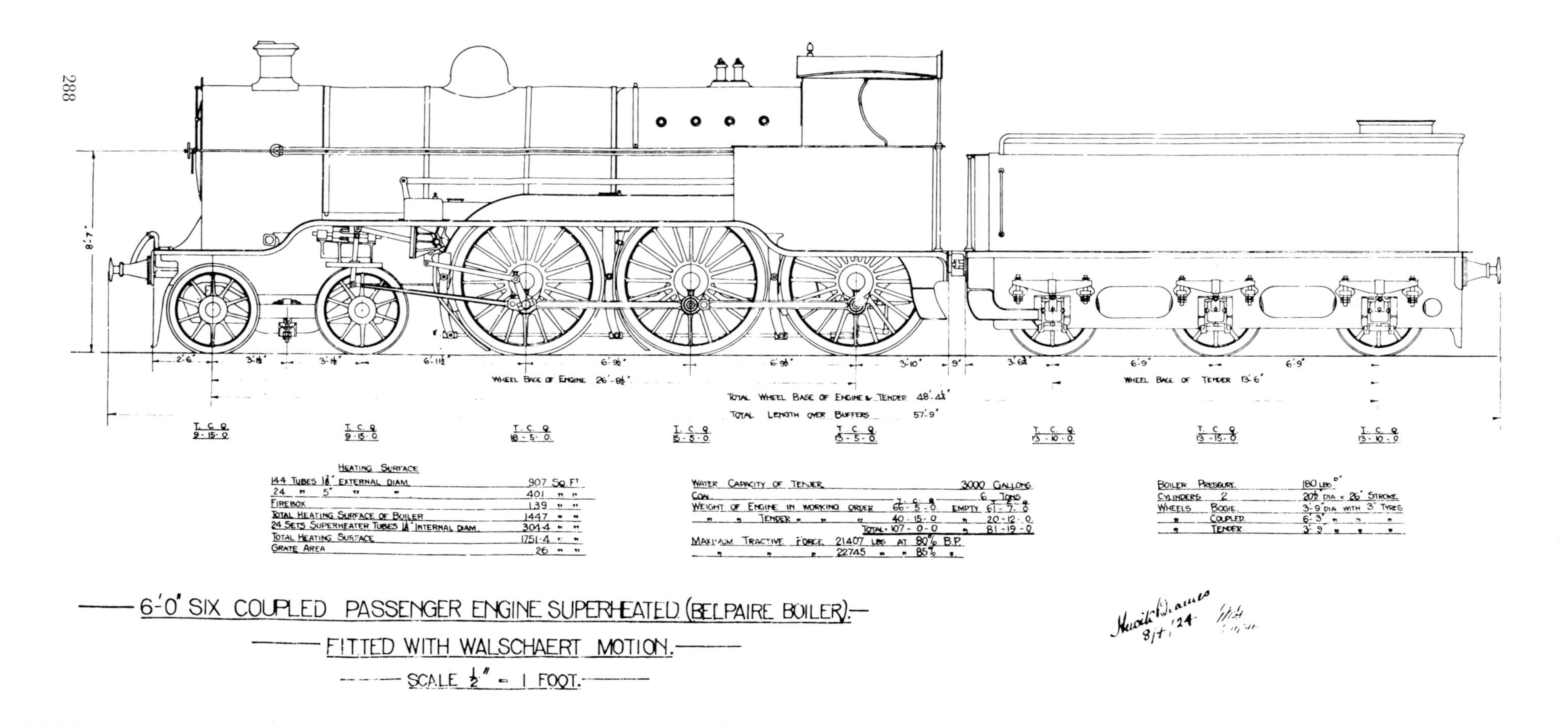

Figure 129: Weight diagram of a 'Tishy', with a Belpaire firebox.

Plate 487: The range of boilers designed by Beames included one which was equally suitable for normal 'Princes' as well as 'Tishies'. 'Prince' No. 497 is seen here about 1925 in lined livery with Belpaire firebox, an oil box on the handrail and a 1916 tender in unlined black. The LMS power classification '4' is painted on the cabside in the upper panel.

Plate 488: The last LNWR engine of all to be built was a 'Tishy' which was specially ordered by the LMS from W. Beardmore & Co. to be the LMS representative at the Wembley Exhibition of 1924. It never had an LNWR number and was painted in LMS livery as No. 5845. It is posed here for the official photograph at Crewe Works on 6th January 1925. Three different types of motion bracket were used on the five 'Tishies'. The builder's plate is on the smokebox and the tender is the 1916 type.

Proposed 2-6-4 Tank

Figure 130: In 1909, design work was taking place on a new suburban passenger tank engine, which eventually culminated in the appearance of the 4-6-2 'Superheater Tanks' in late 1910. One of the proposals which was considered before the design for the latter was adopted is shown in this drawing dated 8th October 1909. It depicts an unsuperheated 2-6-4 tank engine of typical Whale style, with his standard 19in. by 26in. slide-valve cylinders. Presumably, when Bowen Cooke took over, he wanted to at least have the possibility of superheating the engine, and because the latter produced more weight at the front end due to heavier piston-valve cylinders and the superheater, the design was 'turned round' from a 2-6-4 to a 4-6-2. In the bottom right-hand corner of the drawing is the inscription 'Exd T.E.S.', meaning 'examined by T. E. Sackfield', the head of the Crewe design team. The larger initials are those of J. N. Jackson, the chief draughtsman.

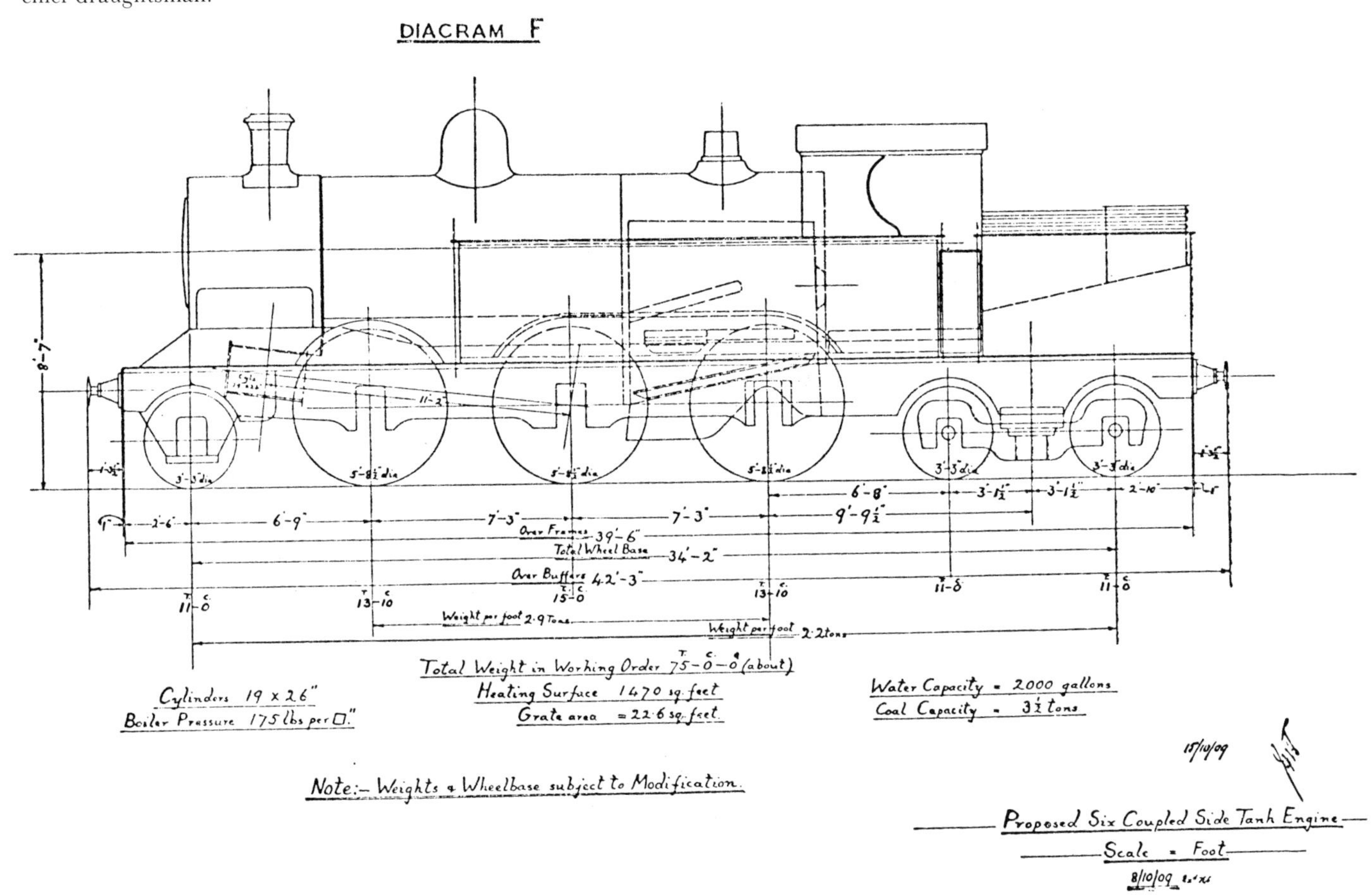

'Superheater Tank'
Plate 489: After the 'George the Fifth' class, Bowen Cooke next produced the 4-6-2 tanks. At first glance, they might appear to have been a tank version of the 'Prince of Wales' class but they in fact preceded them by some months. Initially, some had superheaters and others did not but eventually all were superheated and came to be known as the '5ft. 6in. Superheater Tanks'. As well as being very useful suburban tank engines, they assisted over Shap, both banking and double-heading, and worked on the Central Wales line where 'Precursor Tanks', with their higher axle loading, were prohibited. This is the official view of the first of the class, No. 2665, on 10th January 1911. The lubricator on the smokebox indicates that it was not superheated. Other details are as would be expected at this period: a cab-roof ventilator, 'Jumbo' style leading sandbox and no capuchon. Water pick-up apparatus is fitted — the scoop is visible behind the rear guard-iron. The large letters on the tank were not carried in service but were applied experimentally when the size of letters was being chosen. For some reason, the 'Superheater Tanks' had Belpaire fireboxes, the only entire class to do so before the 'Claughtons'. This was probably because the flanging blocks were already available, from the two Belpaire boilers made for the 'Jubilees' *Polyphemus* and *Ramillies* in 1904, the boiler diameter being the same and the length immaterial.

Plate 490: An official photograph of one of the first batch of 4-6-2 tanks, No. 2670, taken on 11th March 1911. Except for the details associated with superheating, the engine is identical to No. 2665. Again, the large letters were never displayed in traffic.

Plate 491: Front end view of No. 2665, showing how the tank side-sheets were higher than the tanks themselves. This was a traditional LNWR feature, enabling the storage of fire-irons, tools and the like.

Plate 492: Rear view of a 4-6-2 tank. The scoop is visible behind the plate preventing the screw coupling from swinging back into it.

Plate 493: In service, smaller letters, 12in. high, were used for the company's initials on the tank sides, as seen here on No. 1006 at Stockport about 1915. It is fitted with a pyrometer.

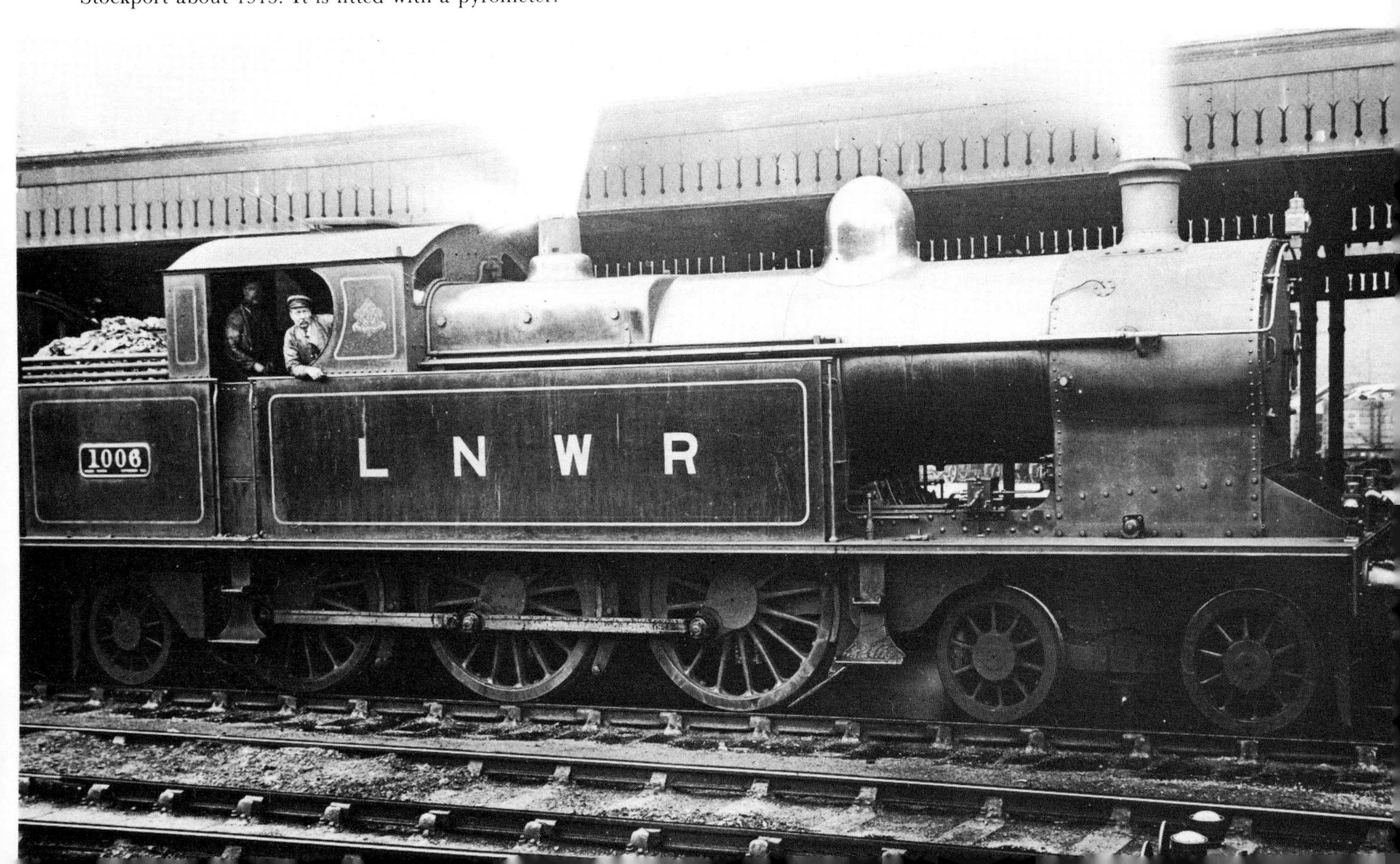

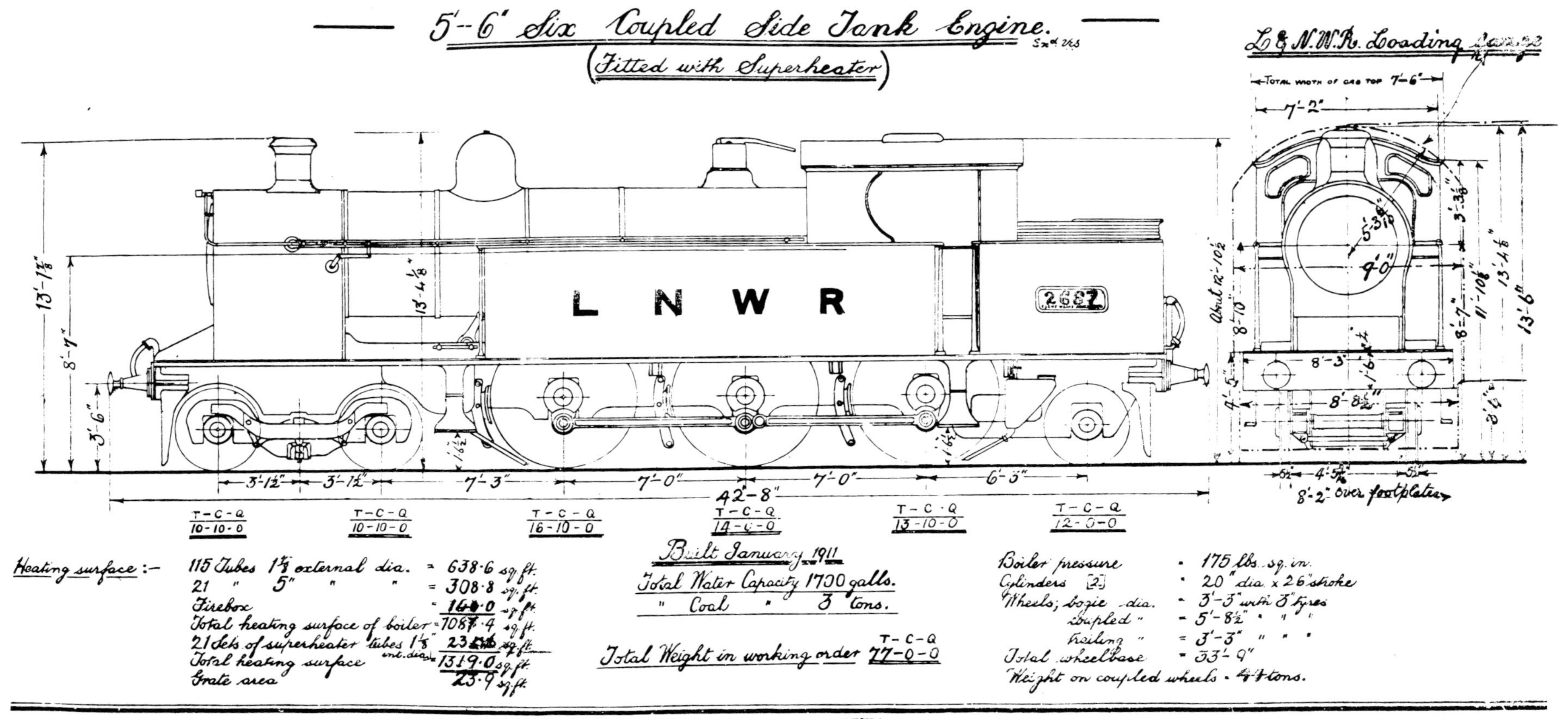

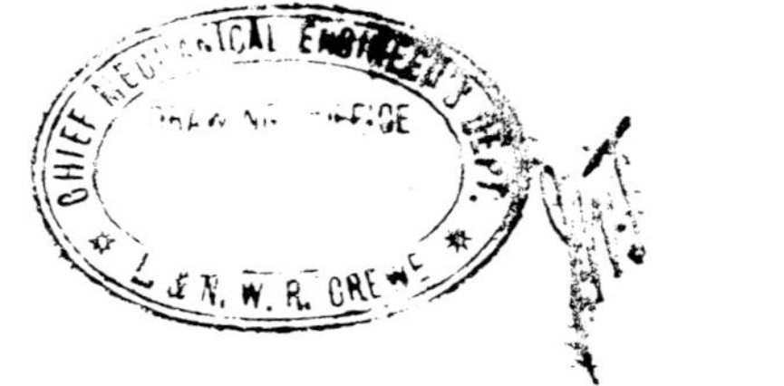

Figure 131: Weight diagram of a 4-6-2 'Superheater Tank'.

Plate 494: Another of the second batch of 4-6-2 tanks, No. 932, pictured at Carnforth in 1921 and still with a superheater damper.

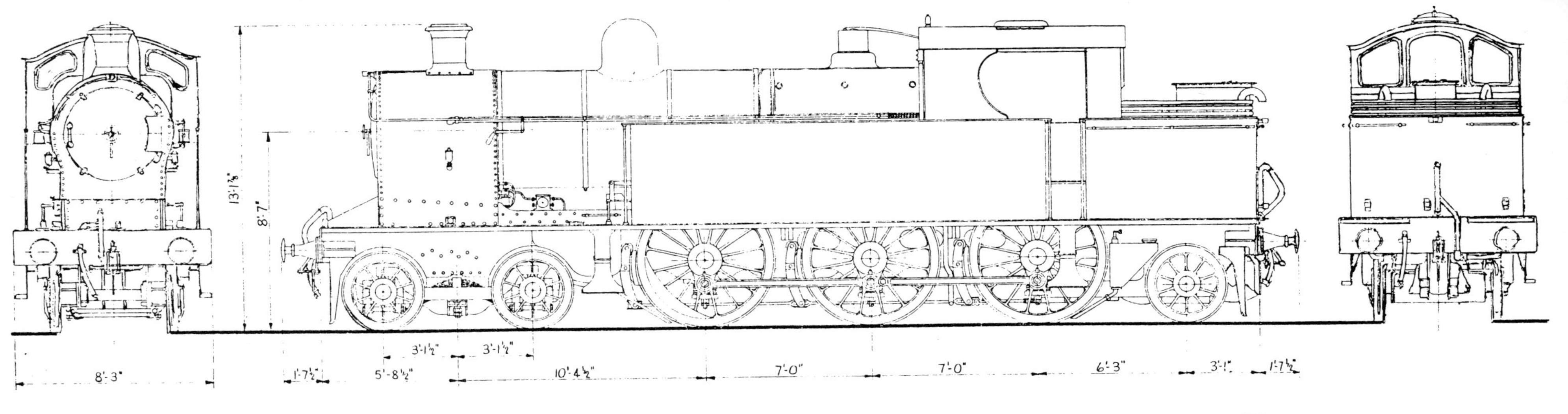

Figure 132: Drawing of a 'Superheater Tank'.

Plate 495: No. 1366 with a London area suburban train about 1916.

Plate 496 (above): No. 2273, one of the third batch of 4-6-2 tanks built in 1916, photographed about 1921. It has the smaller size of letters, 9in. high, on the tanks, as used on the 0-8-2 tanks, and modified rear footsteps. The pipes up the front of the cab, which were associated with two curved pipes over the back of the bunker, were for air release when picking up water and were an addition introduced by Beames in 1921-2. Sandpipe windshields are also fitted.

Plate 497 (above): No. 316, another of the 1916 batch, in the same condition as No. 2273 but with 'LMS' on the tank side in LNWR style.

Plate 498 (right): A rear view of LMS No. 6996 in the late 1930s, showing the curved pipes over the rear of the bunker for air release when picking up water, and the water filler raised to clear the coal. The lamp irons and cylindrical buffers are LMS modifications.

'Claughton'

Plate 499: Although the 'Georges' and 'Princes' were capable of magnificent work, a more powerful engine was needed for the heaviest trains, especially north of Crewe, and early in 1913 Bowen Cooke produced the first 'Claughton' class four-cylinder express-passenger 4-6-0 from Crewe Works, No. 2222 *Sir Gilbert Claughton*. It is seen here at Manchester (London Road) in January 1913 while on trial in shop grey before returning to the works for final painting and fitting of nameplates. As first built, No. 2222 differed in a number of details from what later became usual. It had four windows in the front of the cab (later engines had only two), one set of safety valves (soon changed to two), the brake-valve outside on the left with the train-pipe connection round the firebox in front of the cab (later moved inside like all the others), standard lamp sockets (replaced by lamp irons immediately on No. 2222 but not on the first batch of nine until about 1915) and square lower corners on the front bufferbeam (cut away on the first ten after one fouled Bletchley platform later in 1913). The riveting round the smokebox was also changed on later engines as was the type of tender, and in this photograph there is no cover over the reversing gear, though one was soon fitted.

Plate 500: Official view of No. 2222 *Sir Gilbert Claughton* on 27th February 1913. The lamp sockets have already been replaced by lamp irons front and rear (the one at the top of the smokebox has been accidentally painted out in the darkroom along with the background!) and there is now a cover over the reversing gear. Sandpipe windshields were fitted soon afterwards and appeared on the rest of the first batch and on later engines too.

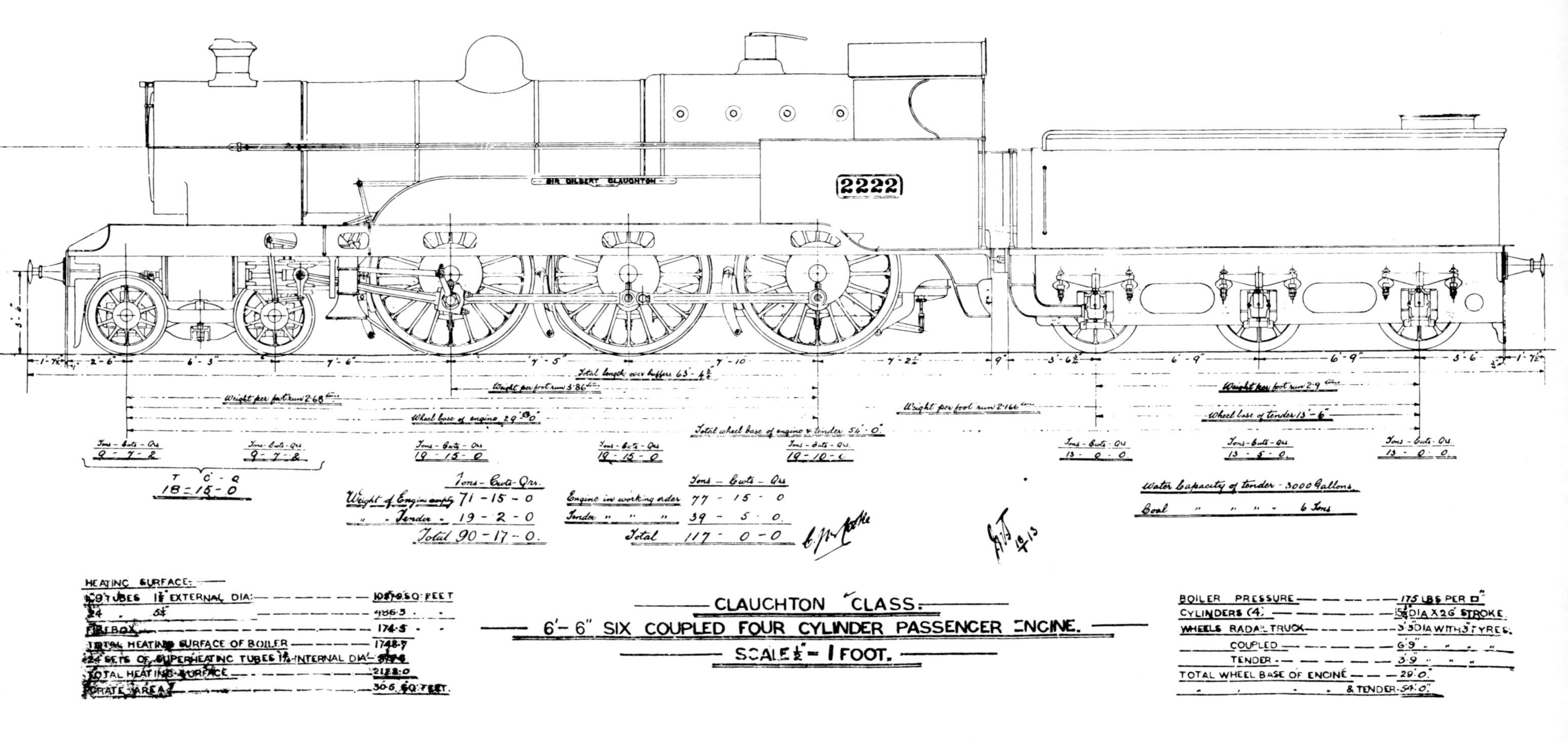

Figure 133: Weight diagram of No. 2222 as built but with tender altered to the final type.

Plate 501 (left): Another early view of No. 2222, at Preston sometime in 1913. The details of the front end can be seen clearly, including the lamp irons and riveting round the smokebox.

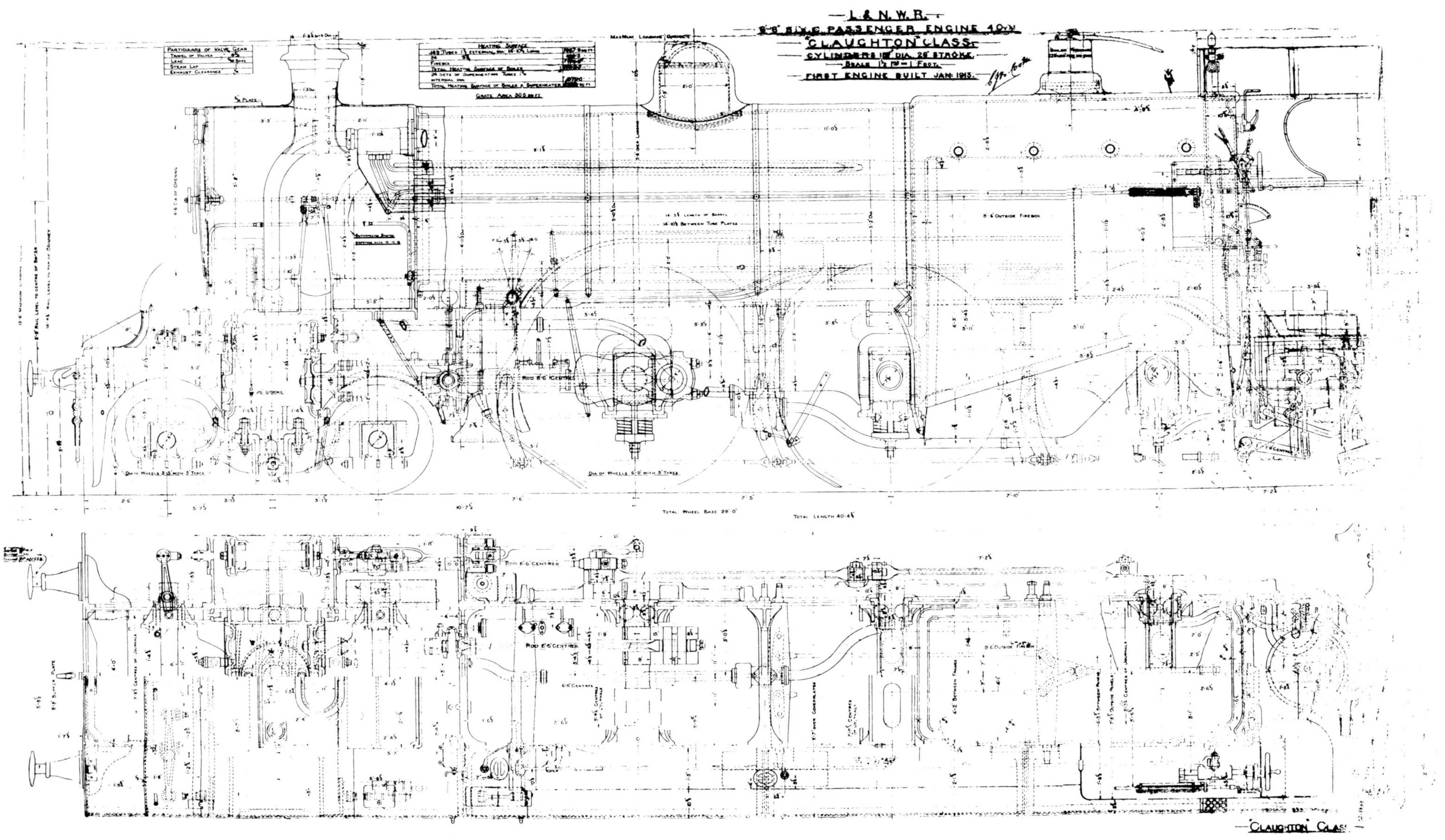

Figure 134: General arrangement drawing of No. 2222.

Plate 502: A truly magnificent sight — 'Claughton' class 4-6-0 No. 1191 *Sir Frank Ree* at Crewe North shed on 7th August 1913. It was one of the first production batch of nine, built in May and June of that year. These engines had two sets of safety valves from new, standard lamp sockets, which they retained until about 1915, and windshields on the leading sandpipes. No. 2222 originally had the same style of tender as was introduced with *Prince of Wales* in 1911 but for the following nine engines the type seen here was introduced, having a curved coping edged with a single bead. All ten tenders had vacuum brakes operated by an independent cylinder, whereas previous Whale and Bowen Cooke tenders had been braked through linkage from the steam brake cylinder on the engine. This type continued to be built until mid-1916 when the final type of Bowen Cooke tender was introduced, with the same sort of top but having square-ended frames with oval cut-outs and slightly modified

Plate 503 (right): Another of the first batch of 'Claughtons', No. 163 *Holland Hibbert*, at Crewe about 1914.

Plate 504 (right): Yet another of the first batch, this time No. 1161 *Sir Robert Turnbull*, again at Crewe in 1914. It still has lamp sockets but the lower corners of the bufferbeam are now cut away. Some of the second batch and all 'Claughtons' built subsequently had the corners cut away to a greater extent than this modification, and all the earlier ones were later altered to conform.

Plate 505 (below): One of the batch of thirty 'Claughtons' built in 1917, No. 2420, which was named *Ingestre* in January 1923 and is seen here at Crewe a few weeks later on 17th March. In addition to a short cabside handrail introduced in 1920, it has lamp irons, cut away bufferbeam corners, two sets of sandpipe windshields and the final type of tender introduced in 1916, and as such is in typical condition for the period up to about 1922. It also has a larger reversing gear cover and two oil boxes on the handrail, both features introduced towards the end of 1922. When built in 1917, it was painted in plain black and was probably repainted in the full lined livery when named, this livery being continued by Crewe Works for a time into LMS days, at which period about a quarter of the class were fully lined. Why lamp irons were fitted to the 'Claughtons' in LNWR days, when other engines had the standard sockets, is not known.

Plate 506 (left): A 'Claughton' in less than immaculate condition, un-named No. 1216 at Camden on 25th June 1922. It was the last but one to be built, only a year earlier, in June 1921. Many 'Claughtons' built in 1917 and after were never named and were originally painted plain black as an economy measure. The catches securing the covers over the rocking arms are undone and the covers are slightly open. There are two small oil boxes behind the handrail, feeding pipes which disappear behind the splasher and supply the axleboxes. No doubt they are the forerunners of the larger boxes which were fitted to many LNWR engines, not just 'Claughtons', in early LMS days. Two pairs of sandpipe windshields are also fitted.

Plate 507 (above): 'Claughton' No. 1407 *L/Corpl J. A. Christie V. C.* at Edge Hill on 3rd April 1922. It was built later in the same batch as No. 1914 and was named in February 1922. There are two small oil boxes behind the handrail and two pairs of sand-pipe windshields.

Plate 508 (left): Another view of *L/Corpl J. A. Christie V. C.*, this time at Camden on 3rd May 1924. It clearly returned to Crewe Works in time to obtain the full lined livery before LMS red took over. Larger oil boxes are now fitted, the reversing cover is larger and the windshields have been removed from the sand-pipes.

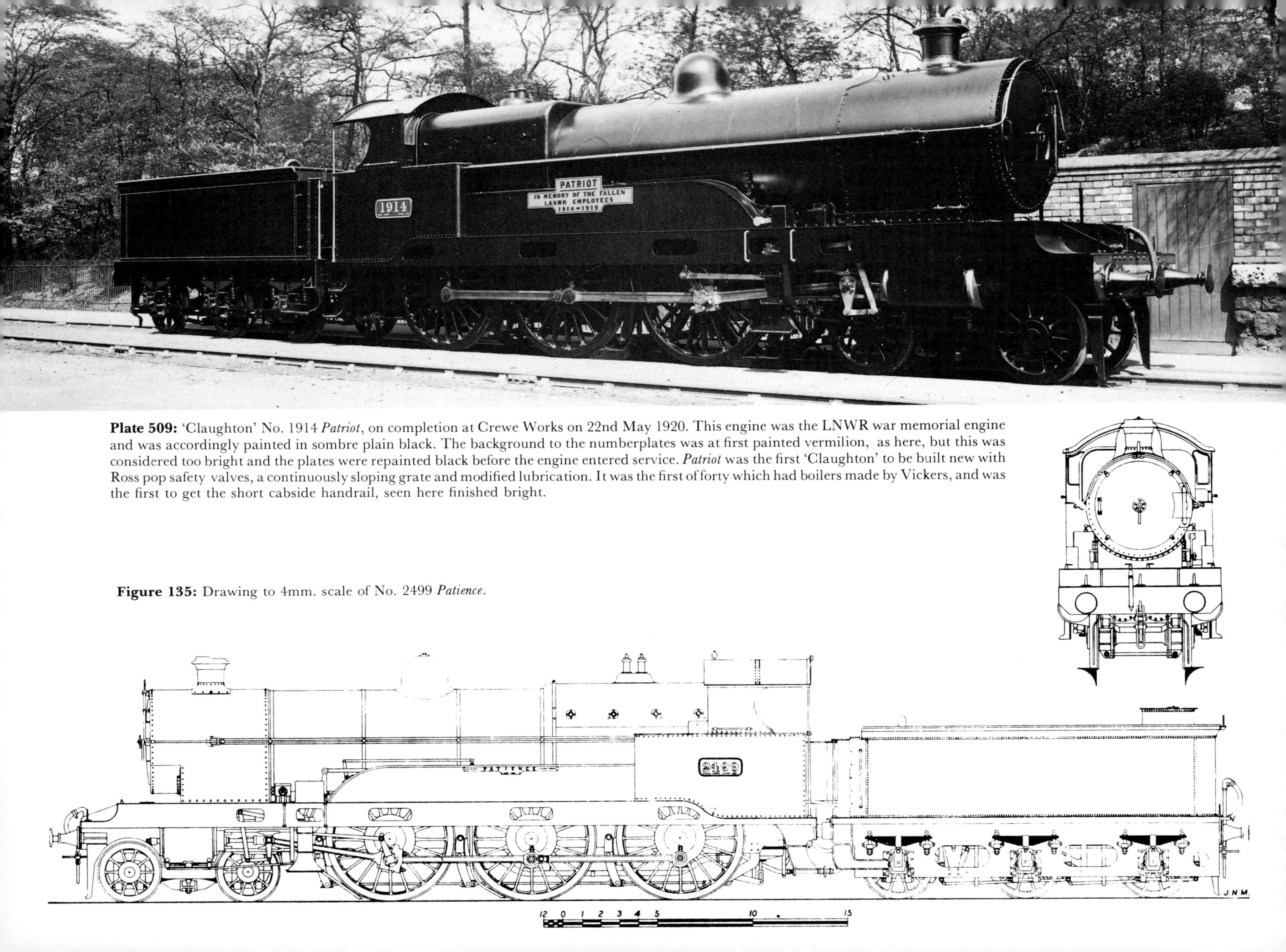

Plate 509: 'Claughton' No. 1914 *Patriot*, on completion at Crewe Works on 22nd May 1920. This engine was the LNWR war memorial engine and was accordingly painted in sombre plain black. The background to the numberplates was at first painted vermilion, as here, but this was considered too bright and the plates were repainted black before the engine entered service. *Patriot* was the first 'Claughton' to be built new with Ross pop safety valves, a continuously sloping grate and modified lubrication. It was the first of forty which had boilers made by Vickers, and was the first to get the short cabside handrail, seen here finished bright.

Figure 135: Drawing to 4mm. scale of No. 2499 *Patience*.

Plate 510 (above): No. 2222 *Sir Gilbert Claughton* at Crewe Works in 1921. It is equipped for oil burning and fitted to a 1916 style tender which is unlined. Because of the height of the firehole, the cab floor of the 'Claughtons' was raised 9in. higher than the normal footplate level of North Western engines and the tender floor was similarly raised to match. This difference can be seen clearly here.

Plate 511 (left): 'Claughton' No. 208 at Camden on 21st August 1926, unnamed and in plain black livery. All the class began to be fitted with Ross pop safety valves from 1923 and 38 of the class were converted to oil firing in 1926.

A 'Claughton' Chronology

During LNWR days the 'Claughtons' remained essentially unaltered in their external appearance but many minor changes were made in detail features and fittings. These are sometimes difficult to date precisely and in some cases may not have occurred to all engines or to all engines at the same time. All these changes are illustrated in this chapter and the information below is designed to supplement the pictures by enabling the detailed state of the majority of the class to be worked out for any particular period.

Date	*Engines*	*Details*
January 1913	No. 2222	completed with: one set of safety valves four windows in front of cab superheater damper standard lamp sockets square-cornered bufferbeam brake valve outside cab with pipe round cab front on left-hand side no cover on reversing gear 'Prince' type tender shop grey paint
February 1913	No. 2222	lamp sockets replaced by lamp irons cover on reversing gear photographic grey paint, fully lined repainted black after photography (probably early March)
May-June 1913	First batch of nine	as No. 2222 except: two sets of safety valves two windows in front of cab lamp sockets brake pipe on left-hand side of cab moved inside; valve remained outside windshields on leading pair of sandpipes new tender having flared top with one row of beading lined black livery
c June 1913	No. 2222	modified with: windshields on leading sandpipes two sets of safety valves
Autumn 1913	First ten	lower corners of front buffer beam cut away
August to October 1914	Second batch of ten	as first batch except: lamp irons fitted not standard sockets bufferbeam corners cut away more on some, and others soon modified to conform only the first one lined; all the rest plain wartime black
c 1915	No. 2222	windows in cab front altered to standard (two not four)
c 1915	First ten	bufferbeam corner cut-away increased as on second batch
c 1915	First batch of nine	lamp irons fitted in place of sockets
July to September 1916	Third batch of ten	as second batch except: windshields on all four sandpipes (perhaps not from new) tenders with square-ended frames and oval cut-outs
Late 1916	All except third batch	windshields fitted to centre sandpipes
February to October 1917	Fourth batch (forty)	as third batch
c 1918-19	Nos. 2222 and 1161	splash shields fitted to bogie for short time
c 1919	All	superheater dampers removed pyrometers removed
c 1920	No. 2222	fitted temporarily for oil firing
January 1920 to June 1921	Fifth batch (seventy)	as third batch except: continuously sloping grate modified lubrication details no superheater dampers or pyrometers first ten had Ross pop safety valves first forty, reportedly, had boilers built by Vickers.
October 1921	All after overhaul	lined black livery resumed
c 1922	Some	fitted with two small oil boxes behind boiler handrail on either side
1923	About a quarter of class	in full lined livery
1923	All	fitted with: two large oil boxes on handrails either side larger reversing gear cover Ross pop safety valves (last LNWR type removed around 1925) sandpipe windshields removed

Notes:

1) At least three of the first batch (Nos. 650, 1159 and 2046) had lamp irons added behind the sockets so as to take both types of lamps about 1914. At least one engine (No. 2239) had such fittings into the 1920s.

2) Large-headed Ross pattern safety valves were fitted to No. 21 in 1915-16 and to No. 2411 in October 1922 (presumably, this was one of the first to get the 1923 modifications listed above).

Appendix 1 Tenders

The first tenders built at Crewe were designed by Trevithick and fitted to his 'Old Crewe' type 2-2-2s and 2-4-0s, but were essentially the direct descendants of the Patentee type of tender which ran on the Grand Junction Railway. They had a U-shaped water tank mounted on a four-wheeled underframe and the coal was carried on the wooden floor between the sides of the tank. Feedwater cocks were positioned one on either side of the tank top at the front, while the handbrake screw worked in a box mounted on the right-hand inner tank side and was operated by a handwheel with four curved spokes. Wooden brake-blocks were fitted, one to each wheel. Apart from the number of wheels, all these features remained standard until the end of the Webb era, and some of them beyond. The outer tank sides were built up of three wrought-iron plates lap-jointed together with rivets at $1\frac{3}{8}$in. pitch, the same pitch as used for the rivets along the top and bottom edges. Between these joints, the plates were fastened to angle-iron frames inside the tank by lines of vertical rivets pitched at $2\frac{3}{4}$in. intervals. Both these pitches remained standard throughout the company's history. Wooden toolboxes were carried on either side of the footplate in front of the tank legs and behind the tank above the rear bufferbeam. Fire-iron hooks were bolted to the back of the tank above the rear toolbox. Stuffed leather buffers were used on the rear bufferbeam, while on the front beam of the tender were two slightly smaller buffers made of square timber baulk, which slid in a square box-like socket stuffed with horsehair. The rear coupling consisted of a shackle bolted to a fixed lug at the centre of the beam, to which were attached two chain links and a hook pointing inwards. Towards the end of Trevithick's reign at Crewe, a six-wheeled version of this tender is thought to have been produced, based on the evidence of a very small number of photographs.

Ramsbottom

In September 1857, one month after Ramsbottom took over, 1,500 gallon tender No. 1 emerged from Crewe Works. It was the first of a standard design built in large numbers until 1874 both for new engines and as replacements for old four-wheeled tenders. The tank was a lengthened version of the previous design with four lap-jointed plates along the sides. Its overall length was 17ft. but the height and width were the same, 3ft. $2\frac{7}{16}$in. and 6ft. $8\frac{7}{8}$in. over plates respectively. It was carried on a six-wheeled underframe which had a wheelbase of 6ft. 6in. plus 6ft. and was 18ft. over headstocks. The solebars were 11in. by 4in. and the longitudes 15in. by $3\frac{1}{2}$in.; the rear beam measured 15in. by 5in. by 7ft. $6\frac{1}{2}$in. long and the front beam was 15in. by $7\frac{1}{2}$in. by 6ft. 4in. (though it was only 11in. deep at the ends to match the solebars). Sprung buffers were used, circular ones at the rear, as on locomotives, but square ones at the front. A large D-shaped tank filler was mounted in the centre of the tank immediately behind the coal space, and behind it was a large wooden toolbox. When the water scoop was added a little later, the U-bend of the delivery pipe was located inside the filler,

Figure 136: General arrangement drawing of the standard 1,500 gallon tender, as fitted to the 'Newtons' supplied to the Lancashire & Yorkshire Railway in the early 1870s.

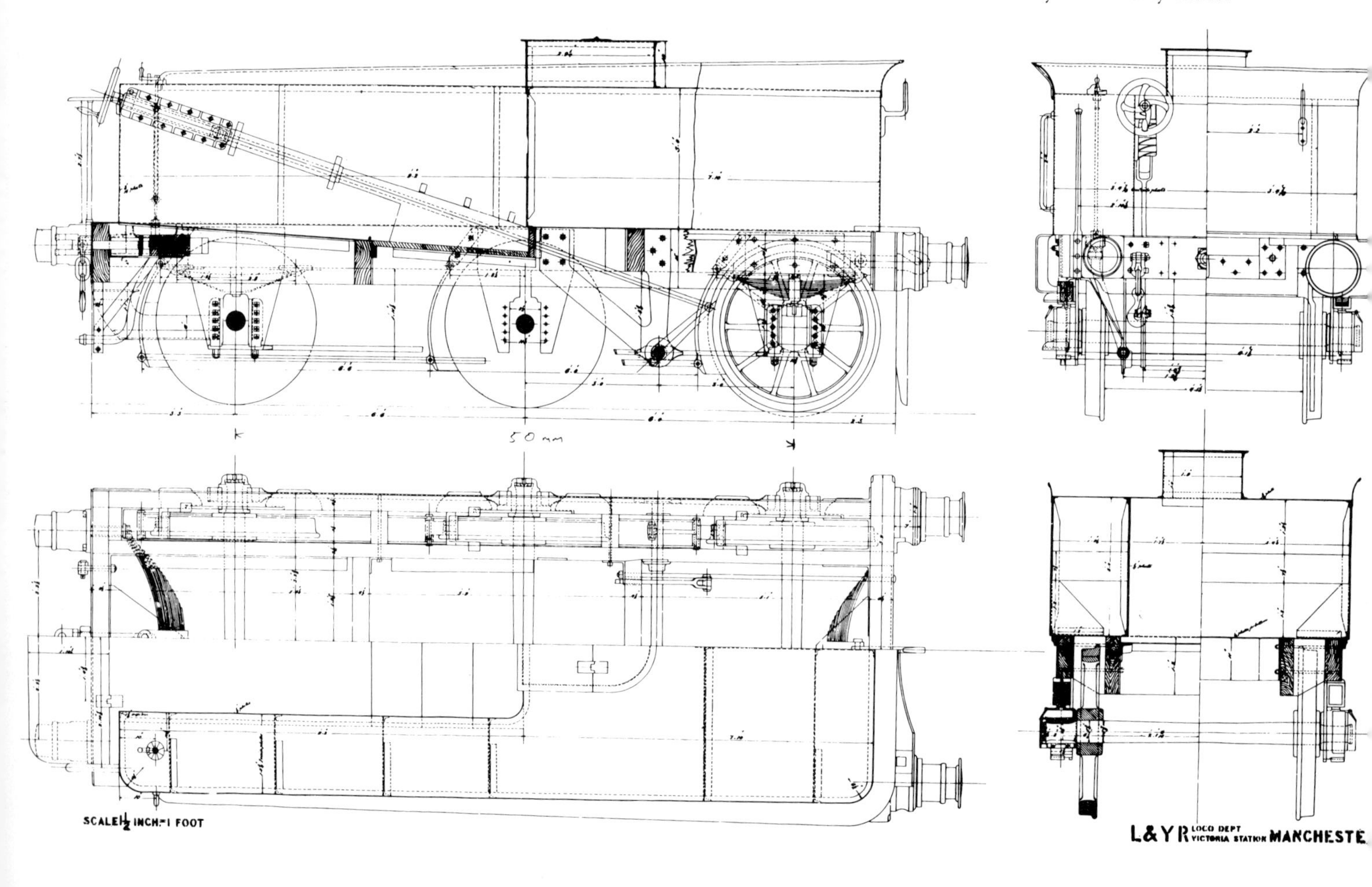

which was often buried when a full load of coal was carried. The weight with a full tank but without the 3 tons of coal was 17 tons 10cwt.

In 1859-60 a number of 2,000 gallon tenders were built but no information about them is available other than a Crewe Works note dated 30th April 1873, which states that the weight, with water but without coal, was 20 tons 7cwt., though Z. Colburn gives 21 tons 8cwt. and 17 tons 10cwt. for the 1,500 gallon tender. These tenders appear in photographs attached to 'Problems' and 'DXs', and were probably necessary for the long non-stop working of the 'Irish Mail' and for certain goods workings. The development of water troughs made them redundant and they were perhaps withdrawn quite early as no photographs seem to exist of them in Webb days.

Webb

A new design of tender was produced in October 1874 for the new express engine *Precedent*. Like the 1,500 gallon tenders built since Webb's succession or thereabouts, it had round sprung buffers on the front beam. These buffers were fitted to all tenders in due course until superseded. The frame and the tank of the new tender were identical to those of the 1,500 gallon type except that the height was increased to 3ft. $8^{7}/_{16}$in. over plates so as to increase the water capacity to 1,800 gallons.

From 1882 new tenders were built with a single side plate 14ft. 3¼in. long in place of the two shorter ones, these long plates

Plate 512: A standard 1,800 gallon tender in the tender shop at Crewe Works about 1892. Although painted on the outside the tank appears to be galvanised, a process widely used at Crewe Works to counter rust.

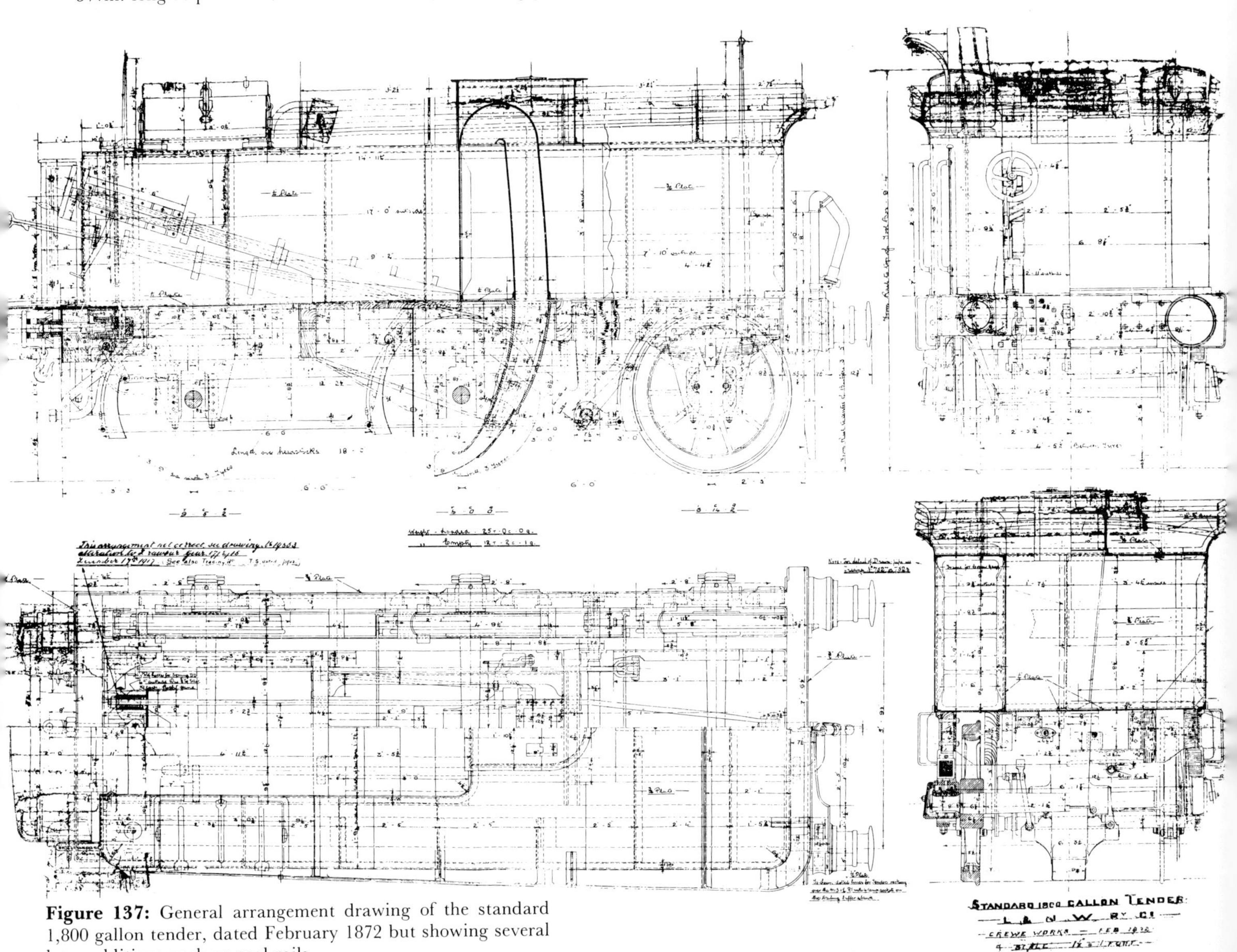

Figure 137: General arrangement drawing of the standard 1,800 gallon tender, dated February 1872 but showing several later additions such as coal rails.

being lap-jointed to shorter ones at either end. The first engine to have this type of tender is believed to have been the first of the last batch of 'Precedents', No. 253 *President Garfield*, which was completed in January 1882. These tenders can be readily identified by the five vertical rows of 2¾in. pitch rivets in the middle of the sides with 1⅜in. pitch riveted joints on either side. A fabricated iron toolbox was carried on either side of the tank top just behind the feedwater cock and was a feature of all tenders until 1910. Another new feature introduced on this tender, and one which lasted until the Grouping, was the panel plate, a vertical side-sheet in front of the tank on each side, which replaced the open stanchion handrail and reduced the draught on the footplate slightly. Some earlier tenders, both 1,800 and 1,500 gallon types, also received panel plates. The weight of the 1,800 gallon tender with 4 tons of coal was 25 tons.

When *Teutonic* appeared in 1889, its 1,800 gallon tender had a number of detail modifications. The axleboxes were lubricated with oil instead of grease, or yellow fat, and the drawgear was improved. Instead of side buffers on the front beam, there was a single central rectangular buffer, through the middle of which was the drawbar coupling to the engine. This modification reduced the distance between the engine and tender from 1ft. 4¼in. to 9⅛in. and correspondingly shortened the tender footplate, fallplate and panel plates. Thus the tenders on the 'Teutonics' were non-standard and as all ten of the class were often on the road at once, the same number of tenders had to be built for them, as is confirmed by a note on the general arrangement drawing.

In this respect, the 'Teutonics' were unique among LNWR engine classes. It was the company's policy to strive constantly for ever greater economy, and the practice of having fewer tenders than engines was adopted at quite an early date, probably in Trevithick's time, since less time was needed to repair a tender than an engine. On arrival in the works for overhaul, the engine and tender were parted, to be repaired separately, and a newly repaired engine was fitted with any suitable tender, which was most unlikely to have been the tender it had arrived with.

The height of the cab floor on the 'Teutonics', with 3in. tyres, was 4ft. 1$^{1}/_{16}$in. above rail level, the same as on previous types, but when the engines were taken off the best expresses around the turn of the century, their cab floors were built up to match the later 2,000 gallon tenders and their special 1,800 gallon tenders were taken off. Whether the latter were then modified to the normal 1,800 gallon type or simply withdrawn is not known, though it seems very unlikely that they would be scrapped.

The basic modifications introduced on the tenders of the 'Teutonics' were adopted as standard. Oil axleboxes were fitted to many of the earlier 1,800 gallon tenders and even to some 1,500 gallon types too. Earlier tenders did not get the central buffer but it was used for all new construction of larger tenders and, in any case, it is doubtful whether many 1,800 gallon tenders were built after about 1895, as the new engines needing them may have had older tenders. Some earlier 1,800 and 1,500 gallon types had their front buffers mounted inboard at 2ft. 6in. centres instead of 4ft. 7in. and the side chains were then attached outside at 4ft. 7in. centres instead of 2ft. 6in. These modified tenders sometimes feature in photographs coupled to goods engines, and the alteration may have been intended to reduce flange wear on sharp curves. This had been shown to be one of the advantages of the central buffer.

The 1,800 gallon tender built for *Greater Britain* in 1891 was identical to that of a 'Teutonic' except that the solebars were 15in. deep, the same as the longitudes, instead of 11in., and the rear beam was 18in. deep instead of 15in. This was so that the footplate level would correspond to that of the engine, which had a higher footplate than standard because of the desire to avoid raised sections over the outside cylinders and leading wheels, and little splashers over the rear wheels. Probably, only two or three examples of this type of tender were built, for the two pioneer 'Greater Britains' and for 0-8-0 No. 2524.

The first three-cylinder compound 0-8-0, No. 50, built in 1893, had a 2,000 gallon tender which was identical to the 1,800 gallon tender of *Greater Britain* except that the tank was wider, 7ft. 2⅞in. over plates, to give greater water capacity. This design was adopted as standard for further compounds, and only the later batches of 'Alfred the Greats', 'B' class 0-8-0s, and all the 'Bill Baileys' had larger tenders when new. The general arrangement drawing is dated 26th June 1894.

Coal rails began to be fitted above the flared coping of tenders in 1895, 2,000 gallon tender No. 295 being recorded as the first to receive them, on 31st May. In the photograph of *Ionic* after the non-stop run in September 1895, the tender has coal rails, and it is highly probable that all three-cylinder compound passenger engines acquired rails very rapidly. Most 1,800 gallon tenders in passenger service had them by early 1896, according to the *Locomotive Magazine* of May of that year, and all new 2,000 gallon tenders, even those for goods engines, seem to have been built with them after May 1895. The fire-iron hooks on the back of the tender were now inaccessible from the top of the tank and were removed, though not necessarily when the rails were added.

A new design of oil axlebox was adopted from 1898 onwards, having a spring-loaded flip-cap on the upper portion of the front, a feature which enables them to be easily spotted in photographs. They were used both on new tenders and as replacements on existing ones, and quite a few of the original 1,800 gallon tenders survived long enough to be fitted with them.

The final development of the Webb tender appeared in 1902, a 2,500 gallon version for the 'Alfred the Great' class. Sources differ as to whether it was first built for the 1902 or 1903 batch, and the subject is further complicated by official photographs showing that, on close examination, the tender has been fitted in the darkroom, and by the general arrangement drawing, which is dated 2nd February 1903. However, a photograph of No. 1955 *Hannibal* at Euston in 1902 *(Plate 318)* proves the type was introduced on the 1902 batch. The tank was 7ft. 7in. wide and 19ft. long over plates, while the height was the same as earlier types, 3ft. 8$^{7}/_{16}$in. The rivets down the side, pitched at 2¾in., were countersunk, and this feature was adopted for all future tenders. The underframe had an equal wheelbase, 6ft. 6in. plus 6ft. 6in., the length being 19ft. 9½in. over headstocks, while the solebars were 15in. deep as before, but 6in. thick, the front beam 7ft. 1¼in. long and the rear one 8ft. 3in. by 1ft. 6in. Other frame dimensions were unchanged from the 2,000 gallon tender. Horns and keeps were made to a more massive design and the hornplates were tied with rectangular section bars 3¼in. deep instead of round ones. The weight in working order with 5 tons of coal was 31 tons 12 cwt. When in later years these tenders ran behind Webb '17in. Coal Engines', the tender was heavier than the engine by almost two tons!

This tender was the last LNWR design to have a wooden frame. In the 1840s wood was used for tender frames by many railways but the LNWR continued to use wooden frames much longer than any other company. Most probably, the reason for this was the concern for economy, because wood was cheaper and lighter than iron. The introduction of water-troughs enabled tank weights to be kept to a minimum, and continuous iron drawbars relieved the frame from tractive stress. Only when the weight carried by the frame became too much for wood to be used was a steel frame adopted.

In the period up to 1903, when engines carried three cast lamp sockets, one above each buffer and one at the top of the smokebox, tenders had one cast socket attached to the centre of the flared coping or, after 1895, to the centre of the coal rails. They also had two 2½in. square holes cut in the wooden plank covering the bufferbeam, to act as lamp sockets one above each buffer. This plank curved out at the ends over the buffer pads but was waisted in the centre to clear the drawhook. At the end of 1902, when the centre socket was introduced on engines, a centre socket was fitted to tenders also and was mounted on the tank 5in. to the right of the centre line. Later tenders, with steel frames, had lamp sockets of similar pattern to those on the rear of tank engines and positioned in the same way.

Whale

A new design of tender was produced in 1904 for *Precursor* and came to be used subsequently for all Whale's engines without major alteration. It had a capacity of 3,000 gallons of water and 5 tons of coal, and although it looked more modern than a Webb tender, it retained the same basic layout of a U-shaped water tank, albeit mounted on a steel frame, with toolboxes on either side of the tank at the front. The coal was still carried between the sides of the tank and had to be shovelled off the floor, but the water filler was moved to the back of the tank directly above the rear axle and behind a coal plate, which served to prevent coal from covering it. Panel plates and coal rails were retained though the latter were reduced from three to two, and the flared coping on which they were mounted was level all round instead of sloping upwards towards the rear. The outside height of the tank was 4ft. 0⅛in. and the width 8ft. over plates, while the outside length was 19ft. 10in. The underframe had an equal wheelbase, 6ft. 9in. plus 6ft. 9in., and was made of steel plates with D-shaped holes cut between the horns. It had a length of 20ft. 6in. between bufferbeams, which were 8ft. 3in. wide both front and rear and were made of steel. The footplate height above rail level remained 4ft. 5¹/₁₆in. and the weight with 5 tons of coal was 37 tons. Road springs and hangers were of the type used on the leading axles of Webb engines. A specimen number for this type of tender is 712.

The brakes were operated through pull rods by the steam cylinder on the engine but after the change to vacuum braking in 1913, with a separate cylinder on the tender, many Whale tenders were converted to vacuum braking. Wooden blocks were used at first, exactly as on Webb engines, but cast-iron blocks were introduced in late 1908, it is thought, during the construction of the '19in. Goods'. All new tenders then had iron blocks but wooden blocks remained in use for many years. The tenders on No. 1918 *Renown* and on a 'Prince of Wales' still had wooden blocks and were steam-braked in 1920.

Among a number of detail changes was the provision of a long pocket on the top of the right-hand side of the tank to hold fire-irons. Not all Whale tenders had this feature, however, as it was later abandoned since about half a ton of coal became trapped between it and the coal rails. Angle extensions were then fitted to the coal-rail brackets to form a rack for the fire-irons. Another change was the fitting of a screw, similar to that for the hand brake, to operate the water scoop. It was located on the left-hand inner tank side and replaced the pull rod and pedal arrangement previously fitted below the brake screw on the right-hand side. On the first batches of Whale tenders the handwheel which worked the screw, and that for the handbrake, had six straight spokes and was 1ft. 2in. in diameter, but on later batches a five-spoke wheel was used. This five-spoke wheel was also used as a replacement in later years for the Ramsbottom/Webb wheel which had four curved spokes. The latter had a long slim handle of similar profile to those on the regulator handle and reversing wheel, but the Whale six- and five-spoke wheels had a short bulbous handle.

Bowen Cooke

When *George the Fifth* appeared in 1910, its tender was outwardly little different from a Whale tender. Its underframe was identical, except for a set of non-standard axleboxes whose design does not seem to have been perpetuated, and the tank had the same overall dimensions. No toolboxes were visible at the front but a single coal rail ran round the tank top in much the same way as the two on a Whale tender. The whole tender, however, had been fundamentally redesigned so as to be more in keeping with the twentieth century. Gone was the U-shaped tank traditional at Crewe from the earliest days and in its place was a 'water-bottom' tender, whose coal well was shaped to make work easier for the fireman. The coal floor sloped gently from the rear full tank height of 4ft. 2⁵/₈in. to a shovelling plate above footplate level, and the plates over the water legs on either side sloped inwards so that on the move the coal tended to shift inwards towards the centre. A coal plate with doors prevented the coal from spilling out on to the footplate, and tool cupboards on either side in front of the tank replaced the separate toolboxes on the top. A specimen number for this type is 870.

All Bowen Cooke tenders remained basically the same as this but over the years modifications were made to the style of coping round the tank top, to the frames and suspension and to the brake gear. The first batch of 'Prince of Wales' engines, which were built in 1911, had tenders of the same type as *George the Fifth* but in February 1912 an official photograph was taken of *Prince of Wales* coupled to a new style of tender which then replaced the previous type. This tender had a double bead attached to the flared coping round the tank top, in such a way as to make, in effect, a solid top in place of a single coal rail. The suspension was also redesigned; the springs were made of thicker plate with a flatter camber than previously and were attached to the suspension brackets by bolts passing through slots in the top three plates. This arrangement was applied in due course to Whale and earlier Bowen Cooke tenders.

From 1913 it was decided that express engines would be fitted with vacuum instead of steam brakes. The first engine to be so equipped is thought to have been the first 'Claughton', No. 2222 *Sir Gilbert Claughton*. All the 'Claughtons' had vacuum brakes from new, as did the 1913 batches of 'Georges' and 'Princes', and earlier engines began to be converted later in the year. At the same time the brake gear on new tenders was redesigned. The brake blocks were positioned behind instead of in front of the wheels and separate slightly inclined pull rods replaced the continuous level ones. One wheel set could now be dropped and removed for attention without the need to dismantle any more than two pairs of pull rods besides the horn keeps. Earlier Whale and Bowen Cooke tenders were subsequently converted to vacuum-brake operation without alteration to the hangers, blocks and linkage, and can be distinguished by the extra cross shaft hangers visible in the front frame openings. Thus double-bead type tenders were eventually in service side by side with three different brake arrangements: steam; converted from steam to vacuum; and built new with vacuum. A specimen number for a tender of the latter type is 624.

The new arrangement can be seen on the tender of No. 2222 (tender No. 472), in the official photograph taken in January 1913. This and all subsequent 'Claughton' tenders were non-standard. Firstly, because the firehole door was higher than on other Whale and Bowen Cooke engines, the footplate was raised 9in. higher than normal to suit, and so the tender footplate was also built up by that amount. Secondly, side doors and stanchion type handrails were fitted to match those on the engines; the handrails were fitted in front of the panel plates, which were set further out than usual, in line with the tank sides. Later 'Claugh-

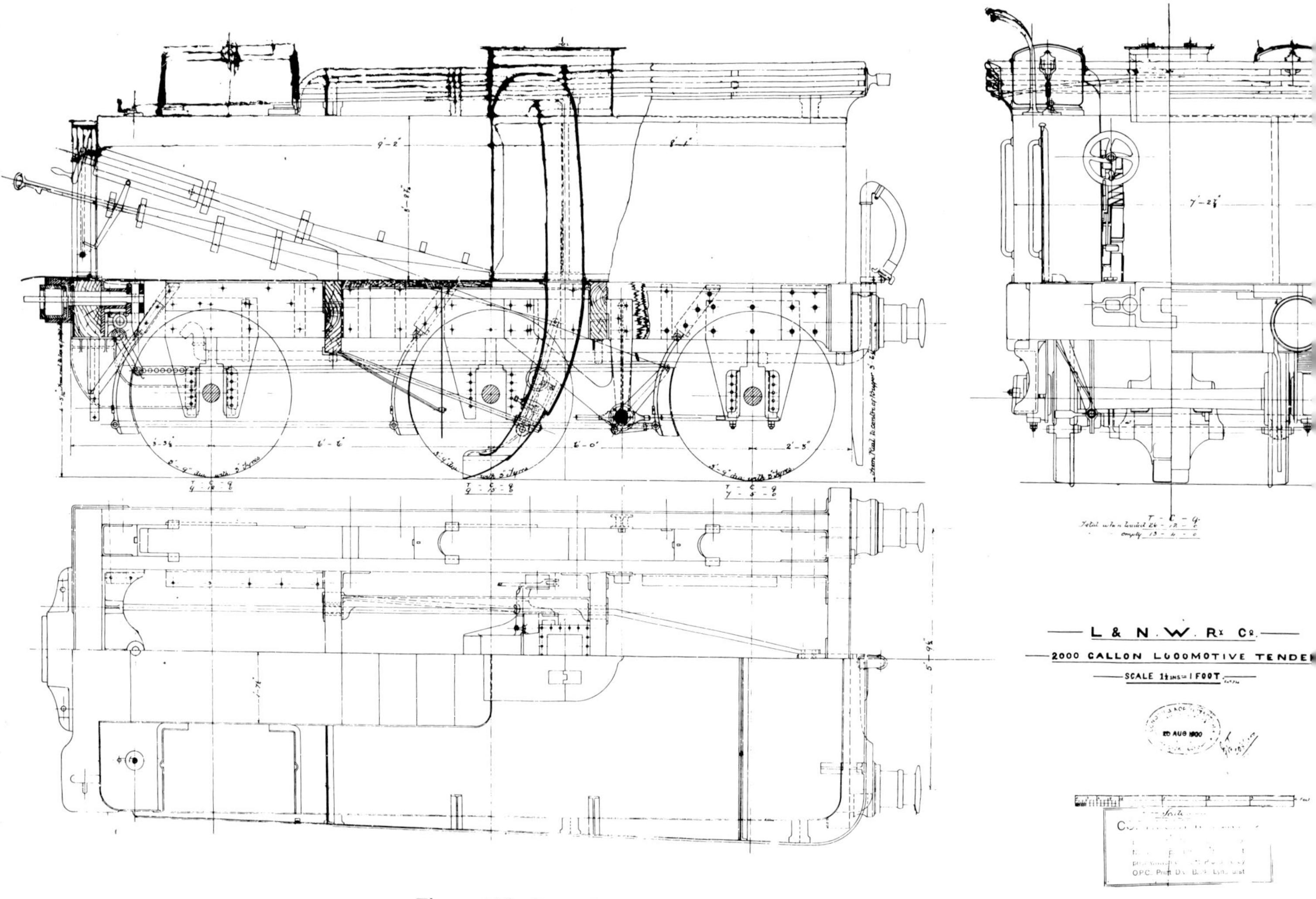

Figure 138: General arrangement drawing of 2,000 gallon tender.

tons' had whichever style of tender was current when they were built, but always with these modifications. 'Claughton' tenders, therefore, were like those on the 'Teutonics' in being exceptions to the time-honoured Crewe principle that tenders were 'common user', and in LNWR days at least were never fitted to other classes.

The tender of No. 2222 was in fact unique since it was the only 'Claughton' tender with double-bead coping. When the rest of the first batch were built in May and June 1913, they introduced a new style of coping in which the flared plate was continued upwards vertically in the manner of a flange, and topped with a single bead. This style of coping then remained standard on all new tenders for the rest of the company's history. A specimen number for a 'Claughton' tender of this type is 1852.

The final development in Crewe tenders occurred in June 1916 when a new frame was designed in which the holes between the horns were a 'square oval' instead of the previous D-shape. All other dimensions and details remained the same. Why the change was made is not known but some authorities suggest it was to give greater rigidity and improved access to brake gear; others, however, say access was in fact reduced and suggest that the 'square oval' may have been adopted for aesthetic reasons, because it matched the valance openings on the 'Claughtons'. The weight in working order with 6 tons of coal is given on the general arrangement drawing as 40 tons 18cwt. (20 tons 12cwt. empty); the weight diagram of the 'Claughton' class gives 39 tons 5cwts. Tender cabs were introduced in 1915. This is thought to have been for 'Super Ds' used for banking 'Jellicoe Specials' in South Wales; or it may have been due to a strike by Midland men at Buxton over tender-first working, which resulted in tender cabs being fitted on Midland engines. Whatever the reason, they were not numerous in LNWR days and only became more common well after the Grouping. Specimen numbers for this type of tender are 21, 213, 1528, with cab 1403 and 'Claughton' 29.

In LNWR days, Whale and Bowen Cooke engines generally ran with Whale and Bowen Cooke tenders respectively, but any type of Bowen Cooke tender could be found on a Bowen Cooke engine. By the end of World War I, Whale engines had begun to be coupled to Bowen Cooke tenders and, vice versa, Bowen Cooke engines to Whale tenders, this becoming quite common in the early 1920s. 'Claughtons', however, were always attached to 'Claughton' tenders and conversely 'Claughton' tenders were only attached to 'Claughtons'. In LMS days the situation of the early 1920s continued, with Whale and Bowen Cooke engines being attached to any type of 3,000 gallon tender indiscriminately. By the 1930s many ROD tenders were in service with the larger LNWR classes, and 'Claughton' tenders, with the floors lowered to normal height but still with stanchion handrails, were then commonly attached to engines of other classes; rebuilt 'Precursors', 'Georges' 'Princes' and 'Super Ds', all feature quite commonly with them. 'Claughtons', of course, still only had 'Claughton' or ROD tenders.

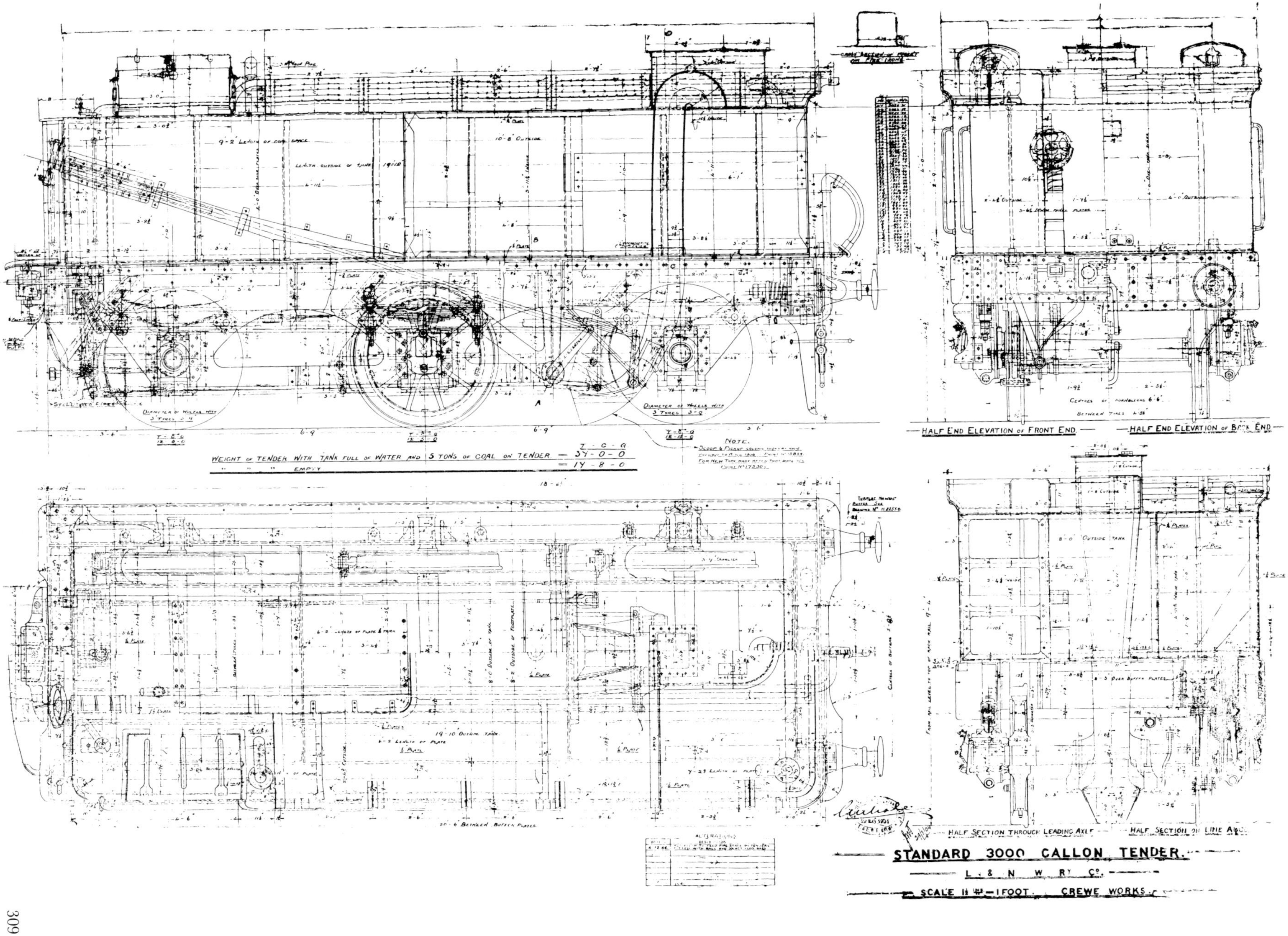

Figure 139: General arrangement drawing of a Whale tender.

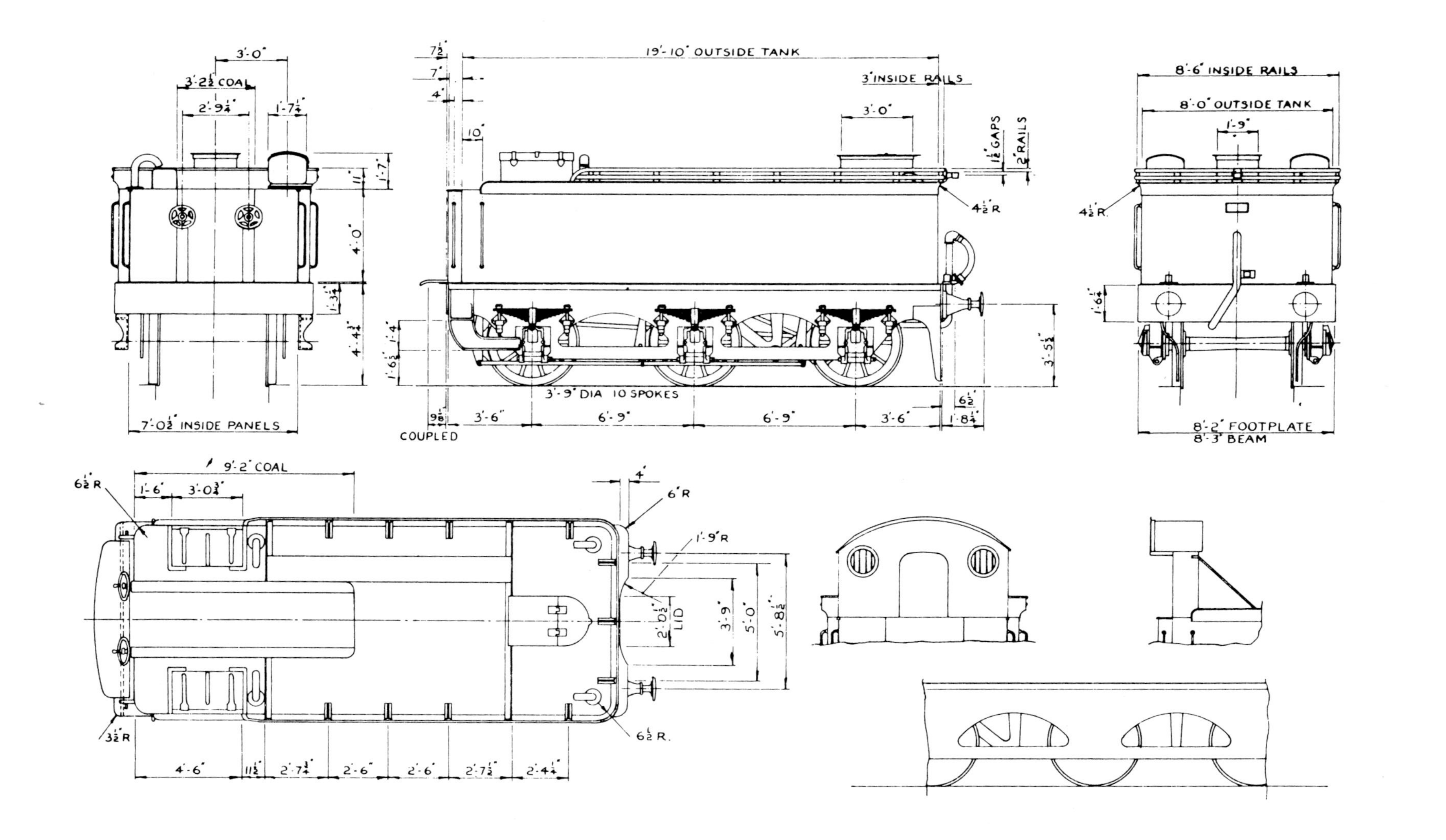

Figure 140: Drawing of a Whale tender to 4mm scale.

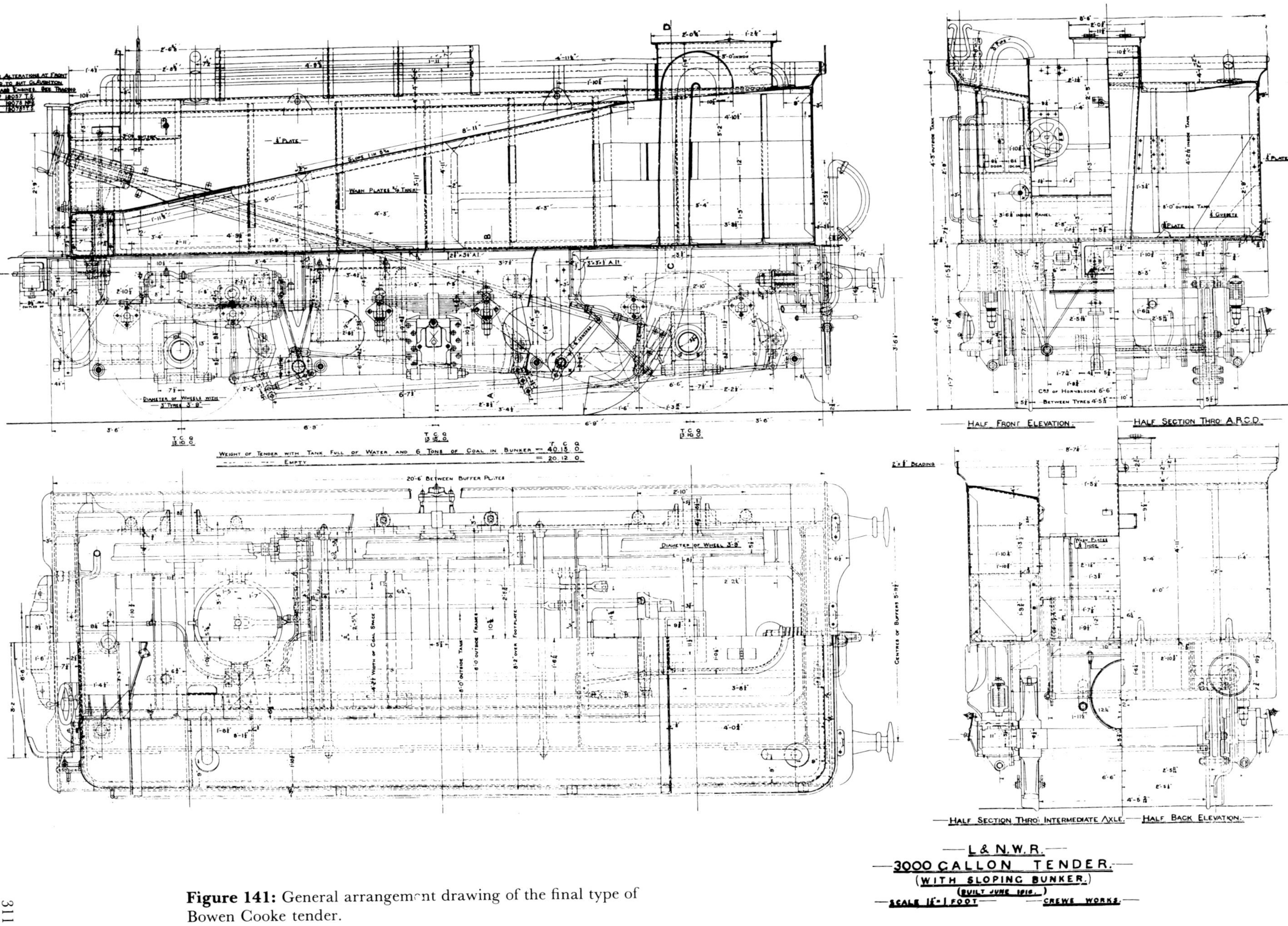

Figure 141: General arrangement drawing of the final type of Bowen Cooke tender.

Figure 142: These drawings are designed to illustrate the detail differences in the Whale and Bowen Cooke tenders. Drawings A, B, C and D show the Whale tender as originally built. The fire-iron tube, stretching from behind the right-hand toolbox to the bulkhead, was eventually abandoned and replaced by a rack formed by vertical angle extensions to the coal-rail brackets, similar to H, I, J, K and N. Drawings E and F show the first type of Bowen Cooke tender. On this, and all Cooke tenders, the coal space was shaped as in K and L, the rear of the tank followed the section as in L, and the front view of the water valves, tool lockers, brake and scoop wheels, vent pipes and coal doors was the same as in I. Vertical angle extensions to the first four coal-rail brackets were later added to form a fire-iron rack, as in H, I, J, K and N. From late 1911 straight-topped springs, as in H, were introduced for all new tenders and as replacements on all Whale and Cooke tenders. Drawing G shows the second type of Cooke tender with double bead, introduced in 1912. At first these tenders had steam brakes as in A but later versions had vacuum brakes with blocks behind the wheels as in G. The third type of Cooke tender is not shown separately, since its frame and brake arrangements were as in G and its flared coping with single bead as in H. Drawing H shows the fourth and final type of Cooke tender. The fire-iron rack and 'tuning fork' brackets were added about 1925 and are shown in H, I, J and K. Drawings G, H, I, J, K and L show the brake arrangements on all tenders built new with vacuum brakes, the brake cylinder being offset to the left as in I; drawings M, N and O show the arrangements on those converted from steam brakes, the cylinder being placed on the centre line. On tenders built new with vacuum brakes, round-bar stays were used, two in I, J and K, and four in H; on conversions the two flat-bar cross-stays remained but the forward one was placed more to the front. As a result of conversions from steam to vacuum brakes and of the replacement of curved springs with flat, different combinations of these features occurred with different tanks, especially after the Grouping. The tank top could be as in A, E or G and the brakes as original or as in O. Some tenders as in E seemed to get new tanks as in H while still steam-braked, and were doubtless converted to vacuum brakes later. In the 1922-6 period some of these tenders still had curved springs.

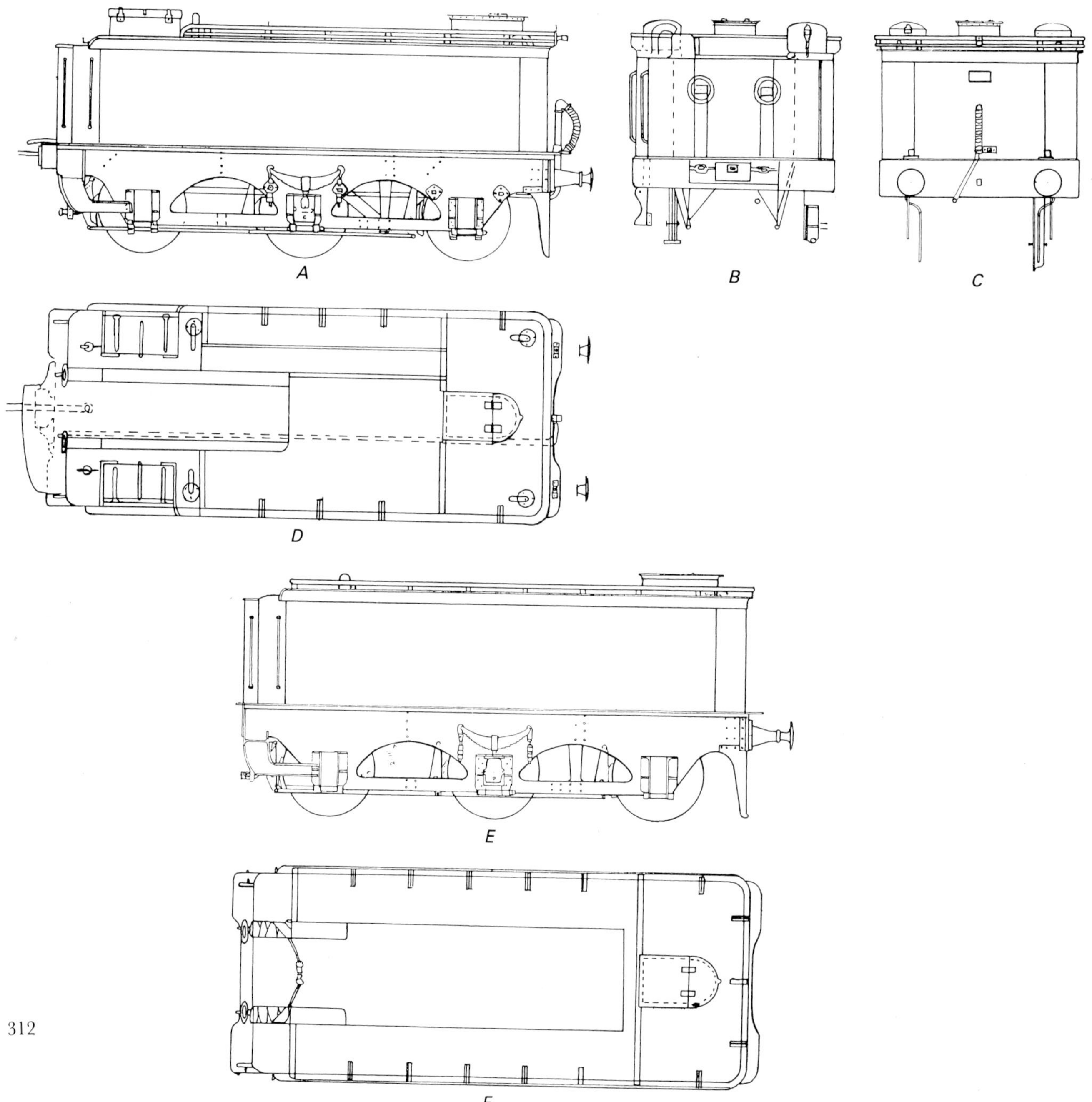

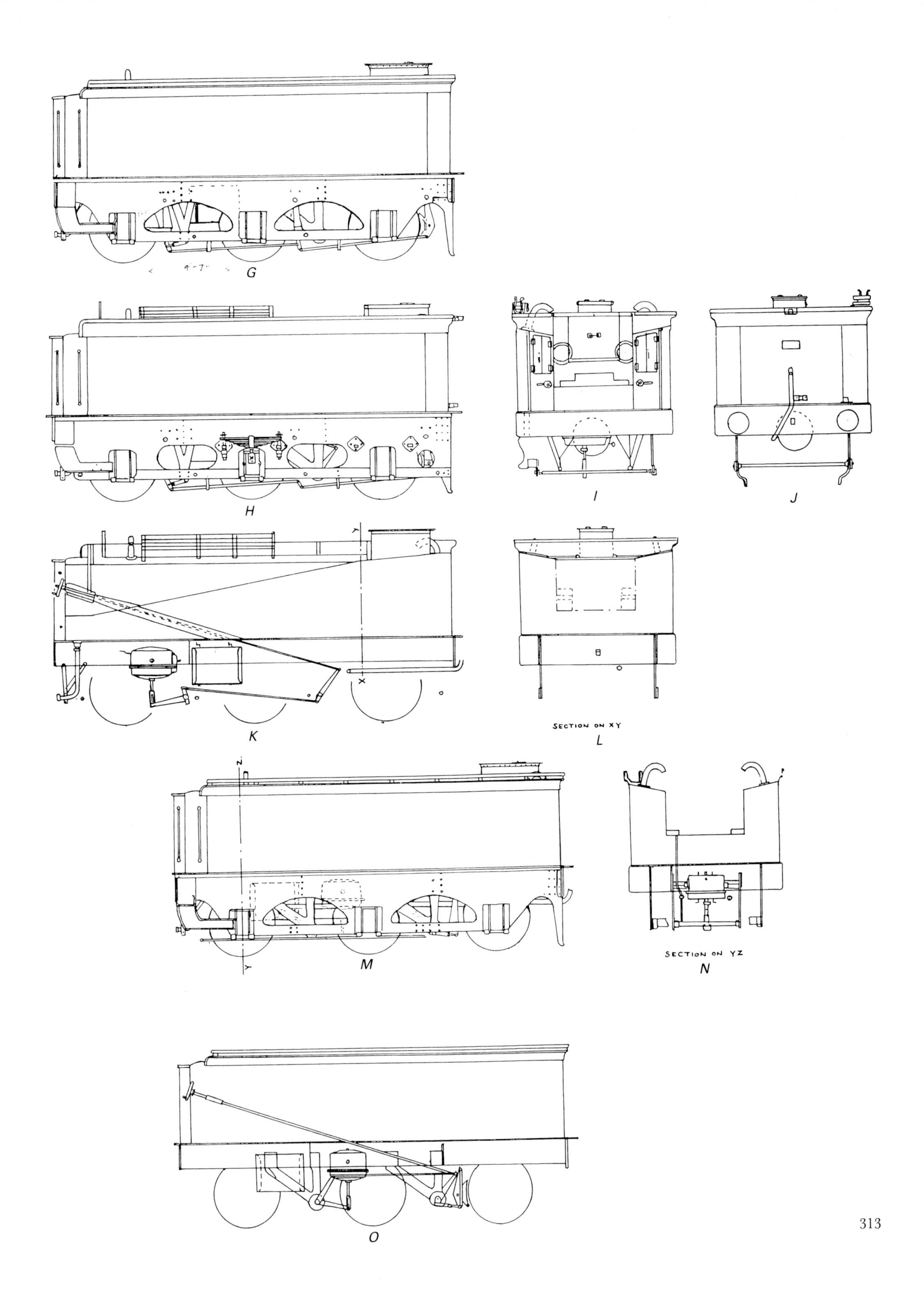
G
H
I
J
K
SECTION ON XY
L
M
SECTION ON YZ
N
O

Plate 513: The drawback of the fire-iron tube is well illustrated in this view of the Whale tender of 'Experiment' No. 1406 *George Findlay* after the Diggle accident of 5th July 1923. Although the tender is tilted at an angle its designer could hardly have envisaged for normal service, a large amount of coal is still trapped between the tube and the coal rails. The shed plate is 17, Farnley and Wortley.

Appendix 2 Fire-irons and Footplate Work

These notes are based on conversations with footplatemen who worked on LNWR engines, though only one of them did so before the Grouping. They were asked to identify the various fire-irons on an official drawing found at an LNWR shed and thought to have been displayed in the stores, and to describe their use. In doing so, various other aspects of working on LNWR engines in the later years were mentioned and are recounted here.

Engine Tools

Most fire-irons were to be found at sheds, for use when engines were being serviced, but at least three were carried by engines as a matter of course: the dart, pricker and paddle. Only the dart features among the drawings of standard fire-irons. The pricker was a long rod which had about eight inches of its end turned at right angles to the rod proper and shaped roughly to a point. It was used to liven the fire up before the start of a run. The driver would tell the fireman to 'run the pricker through it' and he would draw it through from front to rear, either once down each side or just down the middle, as appropriate. This could also be done to break up the fire, if need be, when on a run. The paddle was a sort of long-handled shovel used for shovelling ash, clinker or fire out of the firebox and over the side of the engine. Small engines, of course, also had a short pinchbar. Another fire-iron was the 'bent dart'. This was a dart which had the end, about eight inches or so, bent at right angles and was used for cleaning fire from beneath the firehole door and for cleaning the firebox back corners. Bent darts would be found at ashpits and anywhere where engines cleaned fires, and were possibly carried on engines also.

Some men made their own fire-irons which they considered superior to the standard Crewe versions. For instance, a bar hook might be made from an old coil spring, straightened out and with one end turned up. Many enginemen were quite good fitters and used to do jobs which in later days were done by fitters at the sheds.

Each engine would also have, or rather each crew would draw from the stores at the beginning of a day's work: two headlamps, one gauge lamp, one coal pick, one shovel, one bucket, one box of detonators and one set of spanners. On tank engines and engines with 'married men's tenders', that is, Bowen Cooke tenders which had shovelling plates and sloping bunkers, the shovel would have a short handle. The 0-8-0s were always fired with short-handled shovels too; otherwise the fireman would knock his knuckles on the handbrake or water scoop wheels. Bigger shovels were required for 'Claughtons' and long-handled shovels for 'single men's tenders', which were coal-well types and were 'half a mile from the firehole door'.

Among the spanners was the wheel spanner, one end of which was shaped to fit snugly between the spokes of the smokebox door wheel. Across the smokebox door frame were two horizontal bars, between which the lug of the smokebox door handle fitted when the handle was horizontal. When the door was closed and the handle levered downwards into the vertical position, the door was fast but not tight, or rather airtight. It was tightened by means of the wheel, the spanner being used as a lever to tighten the wheel as required. The other end of the spanner had a sprocket, like two fingers. It fitted the four lugs round the smokebox door and various fittings in the cab, such as small wheels which were generally too hot to adjust by hand.

As well as official company equipment, enginemen commonly equipped themselves with a number of unofficial fittings to make their life on the footplate more convenient and comfortable. The double-beat regulator invented by Ramsbottom and used on many Webb, Whale and Cooke classes gave excellent control and was always very free in operation, so much so that, except when fully open, it tended to work shut unless the driver held the handle continually. Many men therefore carried a regulator clip, one end of which was fastened to the quadrant by a thumbscrew while the other end was hinged to fit behind the handle and hold it in position. Other men used wooden wedges for the same purpose, fitting them between the quadrant and the handle. To improve steaming if necessary, a 'bar' or 'jemmy' was often carried, usually in the driver's food basket where it was out of sight. It would be placed across the blastpipe and held on by a wagon coupling or thumbscrew. To save the driver having to stand up to reach the whistle, he often carried a length of chain which would be attached to the whistle handle. Similarly, because the vacuum-brake handle on the larger Whale and Cooke engines was positioned high up on the top of the firebox backhead, an extension brake handle was sometimes used. Many men also had home-made wooden seats which fitted over the top of the various pipes that were placed where seats ought to have been. Finally, of course, the driver would carry his food or 'snapping' basket, and his stone bottle containing his drink.

Enginemen generally had various tricks up their sleeves and needed to have, to get the job done. At Buxton, for instance, all engines with wooden brake blocks on the tender carried a length of rope, which was tied to the handle of the bucket. When the blocks caught fire, as happened quite often when braking hard on a long down gradient, the bucket was dropped into the tank for water, which was then thrown on to the blocks to put out the flames.

Another important piece of equipment which was regularly carried on the Whale 0-8-0s was half a coupling link. On these engines the brakes on the tender were applied by means of a rod connected to the brake cylinder on the engine; but when the tender was pushed hard up against the engine by the train as on a down gradient, this rod could not function properly and the brakes on the tender were quite useless, just when they were needed most. To overcome this problem, when the engine was pulling hard uphill, as on the climb to Bibbington's Summit, the half coupling was dropped upside down over the drawbar between the engine and tender to ensure sufficient space for the rod to work properly when the engine was over the top. 'Fear Naught' should have been the LNWR enginemen's motto!

Figure 143: Details of the fire-irons are as follows:
A) *Bar Hook* or *Swan Neck*: This was used to lift four or five firebars to one side, so that ash, clinker or, if need be, the whole fire could be dropped into the ashpan.
B) *Tube Cleaner* or *Tubing Rod*: The corkscrew end was used to clear blocked tubes. A piece of rope or cloth was tied in the slot behind it to act as a 'pull through', so as to clean out soot and dirt.
C) Name not known; but used to clean the inside of the firebox, scraping down the rear tubeplate and chipping off bits of ash and clinker that were stuck on. It had to be levered inside the box, because the firehole door was inside the firebox, and had to be raised over the brick arch. When the fire was still in the box, clinker could be removed from the tubeplate by scraping the paddle down it.
D) *Dart*: Used for breaking up clinker. This type was superseded by one with a square end, more like a chisel. But both did the same job.
E) *Bar Tongs*: Used to lift firebars, like bar hooks, both tongs and hooks being in use for this purpose. Firebars had a notch on the under side. They were lifted up and dropped in such a way that the notch engaged on a cross bar, so as to make an opening in the grate. Ash and clinker were then pushed through the opening, and the bars put back in position. Unlike Midland, LMS and BR firebars, which were kept at the required distance apart in the grate by their ends, the latter being wider than the bars themselves, LNWR firebars were the same width all along but rested in a 'comb' — that is, the cross members in which the ends of the bars lay were notched and so kept the bars the required distance apart. This may seem more complicated, but in fact was a good system as the bars could move slightly and so allowed ash to drop through quite freely. On engines with more than one set of firebars, four or five of the front set would be drawn back about 8in. or so. The paddle was then used upside down to push ash and clinker forward, and flicked over to drop it into the gap. When all the ash and clinker had been dropped, the bars were knocked back with the paddle.
F) *Tube Cleaner*: Used for 'rodding' or 'long rodding' the tubes from the smokebox end. This was done during every washout at least and before the Grouping, much more often, probably every night with passenger engines. A trestle was set up in front of the engine and a man standing on the trestle pushed the rod down each tube in turn. He could have stood on the bufferbeam, but because of the length and weight of the rod, it was easier to stand on a trestle. A piece of cloth tied through the slot acted as the cleaner.
G) *Pinchbar*: The purpose of a bar of this length is not known but all small engines (such as 'Cauliflowers', 'Jumbos' and 2-4-2 tanks — presumably, all Webb engines) carried a pinchbar like this but about 4ft. long. It was used to 'shake the bars'; the fireman would get down and put the pinchbar into a square hole in the side of the ashpan, and work the pinchbar up and down, thus shaking the firebars and causing ash to fall into the ashpan. The fireman would often have to stand on the pinchbar to move it sufficiently, especially with the dirty coal prevalent in the early 1920s. A pinchbar would also be used 'to give the engine a start', if it had stopped on dead centre, or by the fitters to move an engine under repair in the shed, or by the coalmen to move a wagon about the coal stage. It was also quite useful generally, for instance to free the reversing wheel if it got stuck. However, the idea that a whole train, engine and carriages, could be moved with pinchbars is surely nonsense, in view of its great weight.
H) *Short Ashpan Rake:* Used to remove ash from the bricked up level base of the smokebox before it was brushed clean, and from the small back ashpan which many engines had and for which the long rake was not suitable.
I) *Long Ashpan Rake*: Before fire cleaning started, this rake would be taken underneath the engine and used to empty the front ashpan of ash that had fallen into it. Then it would be put back in the ashpan, some firebars would be lifted to one side to make a gap, and the fire would be pushed through into the ashpan and so on to the rake. The rake would be pulled out, emptied and put back until all the fire had been removed. On large engines with big fireboxes, especially with the dirty coal of the post-war period, it was 'all go with the rake', forwards and backwards, to keep the clinker and ash from blocking the ashpan altogether.

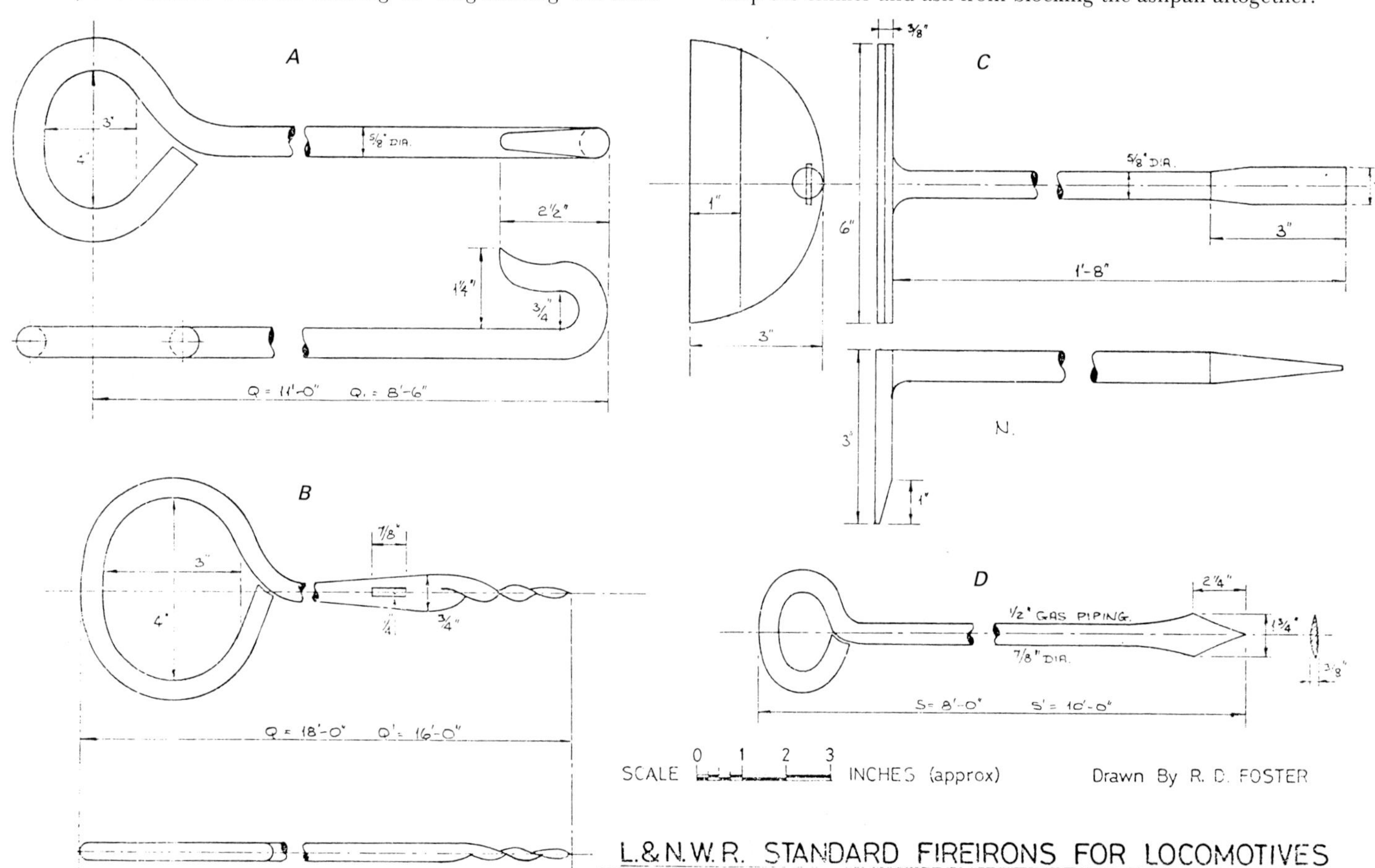

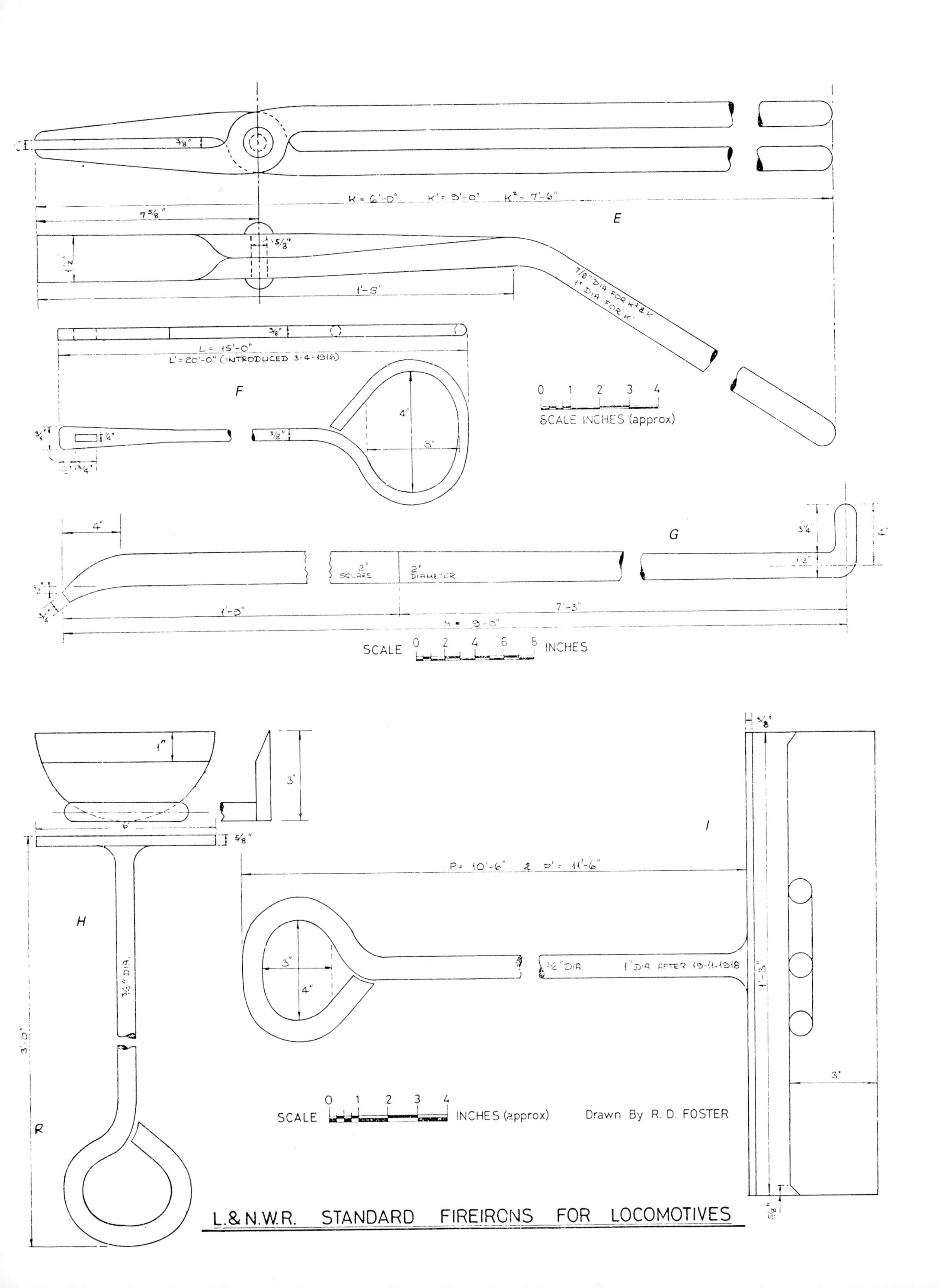
K = 6'-0" K' = 9'-0" K² = 7'-6"
E
7 5/8"
5/8"
1'-5"
7/8" DIA FOR K² & K
1" DIA FOR K'
L = 15'-0"
L' = 20'-0" (INTRODUCED 3-4-1916)
F
4"
3"
0 1 2 3 4
SCALE INCHES (approx)
G
4"
2" SQUARE
2" DIAMETER
1'-9"
7'-3"
M = 9'-0"
SCALE 0 2 4 6 8 INCHES
1"
3"
6"
5/8"
H
3½" DIA.
3'-0"
R
I
P = 10'-6" & P' = 11'-6"
3"
4"
3½" DIA.
1" DIA. AFTER 19-11-1918
1'-3"
3"
SCALE 0 1 2 3 4 INCHES (approx)
Drawn By R. D. FOSTER
L.& N.W.R. STANDARD FIREIRONS FOR LOCOMOTIVES

Appendix 3 Painting

This account of Crewe painting practice is based on the recollections of a painter who was apprenticed in 1921 and so refers to the very end of the LNWR period. Probably by then procedures had been simplified by comparison with the pre-war years and the Webb era, when, it is said, the cost of painting an engine was greater than that of assembling it in the erecting shop. Nevertheless, they were still very laborious and very labour-intensive, by modern standards, and in earlier days can only have been more so.

After an engine had had a general repair in the shops, it passed to the paintshop to be repainted before returning to service. The first job was to strip off all the old paint down to bare metal with caustic soda. Once this treatment was finished, work could proceed on different parts of the engine simultaneously. A special gang of cleaners applied caustic soda using all the old brushes that the painters had finished with. As protective clothing, they wore large aprons of sacking or similar material which went right round them. They also wore sacks round their legs, having tied their working trousers up with string; these were called 'Yorks', but nowadays would more likely be termed 'Gor blimey trousers'! ('Yorks' are leather straps for fastening round working trousers, often cords, below the knee; they were worn mainly by farm labourers and navvies in the early days, to keep out draughts and to prevent vermin causing actual bodily harm, as it were!) Some men wore clogs but those who wore boots or shoes used to tie the upper parts of old shoes above them to protect them.

Caustic soda was applied a number of times, until the old paint was loosened enough to be washed off with water from hosepipes. Where the paint was difficult to remove, as at places where a lot of stopper had been applied previously, it was scraped off with old files from the shops, their ends having been ground to a chisel edge. It was particularly difficult to remove the paint from round the lines of rivets joining the panels on Webb tenders, since the rivets were very close together.

When all the paint had been removed, the foreman examined the engine for loose scale, corrosion and rust. This was often found on the curved rear panels at the corners of tenders (probably because they were often kicked by the boots of enginemen as they were putting lamps on the back of the tender, since there was no continuous step there and not much width, except where the lamp stood). Any rust was removed with coarse carborundum from old grindstones which had been broken up, and then the engine was wiped over with turps, using a round brush called a 'pound brush', rubbed over with emery cloth and wiped off with cotton waste. It was then ready for the painters. Only the boiler, cab front and side panels, splashers and tender sides were prepared in this way. The smokebox, top of cab, tender rails, frames, wheels and all the parts below the angle iron were not stripped. They were cleaned with turpentine substitute and any loose paint was rubbed down with coarse carborundum or emery brick, or in difficult places was removed with old files. The inside of the cab was treated in the same way at about the time when the parts below the angle iron were done.

New engines, of course, did not require stripping as they were, in effect, already stripped to bare metal. However, parts which were inaccessible for painting after the engine had been assembled, were painted in the erecting shops by painters under the control of the paintshop foreman, as the engine was being built.

The first stage in the process of painting was to apply 'lead colour', which was dark grey, to those parts of the engine which had been stripped. This paint was made of zinc white and vegetable black in equal proportions plus paste dryer. Previously, lead white had been used but for health reasons, and perhaps for reasons of cost, zinc white replaced it around 1921.

The next step was 'patching' with 'stopper', which might now be called 'filler', and was applied so as to give a reasonably flat surface. This was needed generally because metal panels did not have the smooth surface of sheet metal today but had water marks, probably from the rolling process in the steel mill. It was also particularly necessary because the process of driving countersunk rivets caused indentations in the metal. For example, a tender tank was riveted by a team of two, a tank lad, or 'tank diver' as he was known, acting as 'holder up' inside the tank for the boilerman outside the tank driving the rivet. The action of driving the hot rivet in the cold sheet metal, followed by the subsequent cooling of the rivet, and the way in which the boilerman finished the rivet more or less flush with the panel, contributed to distortions of the metal which had to be filled by the painters. For some reason, the two rivets holding the numberplate on the panel also needed a lot of stopper. The earlier type of rivets, called 'snap-head' rivets, whose heads stood proud of the surface of the metal, did not need filling. These were used exclusively on almost all Webb tenders, and in many places on Whale and Cooke tenders also.

The stopper powder came in large wooden barrels and was supplied by Kearsley's of Ripon. It was a very fine powder like flour but brown in colour. Each painter mixed his own stopper by adding gold size and copal varnish to the powder until it had the consistency of dough and was very stiff, like cold plasticine. It had to be thick enough for the stick to stand up in it. The more varnish that was added, the harder the stopper dried, and if too much varnish was put in, it was very hard to rub down. The painter then went round the engine with stopper 'patching' the very rough places, such as the 'saucers' or concave spots round snap-head rivets, to produce a reasonably flat surface.

Then a coat of 'brush stuff' was applied all over. This was made with the same brown powder as used for stopper but mixed with best turpentine and gold size, as a drying agent, to the consistency of paint, and was called 'brush filler' or 'brush stuff'. It was usually put on with new pound brushes to break them in. A pound brush was circular, with the bristles fastened round one end of the stale. The bristles were grey or straw in colour and about 5in. long. When new, the bristles were bound up with string, in the same sort of way as some people bind the handle of a potato peeler but with both ends loose and tacked to the handle; as the bristles wore down, the string was unwound to leave the same length of bristle free to apply paint. As the bristles of a pound brush became broken in, that is, more flexible and worn smooth, so the brush was used for successive jobs, the first coat of lead colour, the second coat of lead colour, drop black, and finally, when the bristles were about 3in. long, varnish. In the stale of a pound brush was a hole to take a pin or piece of wire, so that it could be suspended in a can of raw linseed oil after use. Any dirt in the brush could then drop to the bottom of the can. After it had been used for varnishing, there was no need to wash it out when it was needed for use again; the linseed oil would simply be 'worked into the varnish'. If meths had been used to wash the brush it would have made the varnish curdle, because meths is a spirit and is not immiscible. The varnish can was always washed out after use, so that the next lot of varnish would be clean and would not be put into a dirty can. A brush which had been used for paint or filler was left in water. When the painter needed it again, he would just spin the water out of it by working it between his hands.

After brush stuff came 'spreading', with more of the same stopper but mixed to the consistency of soft margarine. This time it was applied with a spreading knife, which was then wiped clean and used again to further smooth the surface. Spreading knives were made from old saws in various sizes to suit different parts of the engine, smaller ones being used for rivets at 3in. centres. The whole process was then repeated, so that there were two layers, and then another coat of brush stuff was applied. Stopper of the same consistency was also used, incidentally, on engine and tender wheels, because when newly cast they had a very rough surface. First they were painted with a primer, which was either brush filler or lead colour, and then the stopper as used for spreading was applied with a pallet knife. The painter then dipped his hand in water and smoothed the stopper on the spokes by hand. When it was dry, it was rubbed down with emery cloth, but dry, not wet as with some modern wet or dry papers.

When the second coat of brush stuff was dry, a stain was applied. This was made from venetian red powder mixed with turpentine, not the best quality but white spirit; it was put on all over and was just sloshed on quickly. The reason for staining was to show which areas had not been rubbed down properly. 'Rubbing down' was done with coarse sponges, a bucket of water, pumice stone and 'brick'. The 'bricks' were about 5in. long and of square section but tapering slightly; they were not building bricks but were reconstituted bricks, specially made for rubbing down. To make them easier to hold, the painter would break them by tapping them on the side of his bucket. Then he would wet the part to be rubbed down with the sponge and use a piece of brick in his other hand to rub down proper. Next he would go over it all again with pumice stone to attain the final surface.

Another coat of lead colour was then applied. This was done by second-grade painters and the lead colour was of a better quality than was applied at first, being made of zinc white and vegetable black in equal proportions, best turpentine and paste dryer. When putting this coat on, the painter had to 'beat it out' — put a small amount on the brush and work it in all directions so as to apply the paint very thinly and leave no brush marks; however, he finished by 'laying it off vertically', that is, with the last stroke vertical, so that if there were any marks, they would be in that direction.

The surface was then rubbed lightly with No. 1 emery cloth, and a coat of drop black was applied. Drop black was the same as vegetable black, which was a cheap black paint made from some vegetable source, but with the addition of a chemical to give it a better colour and superior hiding power. It was bought in ready-made and had the consistency of butter. Before it could be applied, it had to be thinned with best turpentine. It was very easy to put on, had good hiding powers and dried with a matt finish. Its colour was not so intense as japan black but was rather a greyish black. Sometimes gold size was added to drop black to produce what was called 'over bound' black. This was slower to dry but had better adhesive powers and was used in areas which were likely to be greasy, such as the underside of the boiler.

When the paint was dry, it was rubbed very lightly with used emery cloth, and a coat of varnish was applied. This was mainly done with a pound brush which was well worn in, but other brushes were also used for certain parts. A 'No. 9 tool', which had a wooden stock of about 1¼in. overall diameter, was used for varnishing round rivets, and a 'fitch' or 'No. 3', which was about as thick as a man's finger, was used for windows and for the numberplate.

After varnishing, the engine was then 'flatted'. There was no rubbing paper in those days or teepol to be used as a wetting agent. It was done with hard soap and 'pummy powder'. The painter took a coarse cotton sweat cloth, soaked it in his bucket of water, squeezed it out, dipped it in powder, put on a bit of soap to help it slip, and then rubbed the panel with a certain amount of pressure. This acted as an abrasive and removed any knibs. Passenger engines were then ready to be lined but goods engines received another coat of varnish and their painting was then complete.

While all these jobs were going on, lower grade painters were painting the other parts of the engine. The smokebox and chimney were painted with chimney black, a mixture of japan black, which was glossy, and oil black, which was a cheap vegetable black. The frames behind the wheels, the brake gear, the tender frames and axleboxes, the buffer heads and shanks, the coupling hooks and chains, the vacuum pipes, the top of the cab roof, the firebox 'front' (or 'backhead' in enthusiast jargon), the inside of the splashers in the cab, the footplate floor and the toolboxes on the tender were all painted oil black. Wheels were done in wheel black, which was a glossy black similar to chimney black but with oil black and japan black mixed in different proportions. The mixing was done by the paint mixers to formulae which had been developed over the years, the japan black and oil black being bought in. Inside the cab, the side panels, the spectacle plate and the underside of the roof were painted indian red, which came as a paste and was reduced with raw linseed oil. Alternatively, boiled oil could be used, which made it shine but dried more slowly. The inside of the frames were painted by the lads or by semi-skilled painters, who made themselves special long handled brushes called 'reachers' for the purpose. Red frames were an LMS innovation, black being the rule in LNWR days. They also painted the cranks white but generally had to wait for the engine to be moved slightly before they could reach to complete the job.

The front bufferbeam, and both bufferbeams of tank engines were given two coats of red, one undercoat and one fairly glossy, with a black edge. Passenger engines had a ¼in. black line forming an oblong with rounded corners between the buffers, but the buffers themselves were black and where they met the bufferbeams, were edged with a ½in. black line. This latter probably arose because the painters found it easier to do it that way. The same red was used for the inside of the frames as well, and for the background of the numberplate, but the numbers and the rim were a straw shade of yellow. The whole of the rear of the tender was black, including the bufferbeam. When the paint was dry, the painter dipped his middle finger in white paint and 'pathered' (presumably a corruption in Cheshire dialect of 'puddled' or 'paddled') the letters and rim of the tender numberplate — that is, dabbed paint on them to pick them out. This method was quicker than using a brush. The inside of the tender, where the coal went, was tarred with gas tar, which came in barrels; it was applied with a 'turk's head' on the end of a stick. The coal rails were also tarred in the same way, both inside and out.

The lads also polished the handrails, with turps, rags and emery cloth, and the outside motion, smokebox door handle (but not the wheel) and the stanchion handrails to the cab. They also polished various fittings in the cab, including the boiler gauge glass frame and the handle of the ejector. The whistle was polished by the painter who went on top of the firebox to flat it. On some engines, the reverser scale was painted white all over and then wiped off, so as to leave white paint in the notches and figures.

When they had been flatted after the first coat of varnish, passenger engines were lined. Corners were drawn with compasses and had a radius of about 4½in. Straight lines were struck with a chalk line. A length of No. 22 crocheting cotton was chalked, and one end was held by the painter and the other by the lad assisting him. When the painter was satisfied that the line was positioned correctly, he plucked it with his finger and it marked the paint accordingly. To help him paint the lines straight, the painter used a mahogany straight edge, which had brass lugs at each end, so that the edge itself stood away from the newly painted surface. With the brush between his thumb and forefinger, and the tip of his middle finger roughly at right angles to them and resting on the straight edge, he drew the brush along the chalk line. He also had a little platform, which could be hooked over the coal rails, for example, to hold his paints when he was doing the upper lines on the tender, because he could not hold his pallet, brush and straight edge, and paint, all at the same time!

The grey paint was made from ochre, white lead, paste dryer and a touch of black. Because it was a 'dirty black', that is, slightly greyish, it may have given the grey a bluish or greeny tinge; but because of the ochre, it was certainly a warm colour, a sort of dove grey. The yellow was made from lemon chrome, with a bit of ochre, which was a 'dirty yellow' (slightly drab), to take the brilliance off, white, to make it less intense, and paste dryer. It was definitely a pale yellow, a straw rather than cream, because of the ochre.

The grey and yellow were made by the paint mixers to formulae of long standing but the painter made the red paint himself. He used a stone slab about a yard square and 2in. thick, whose surface was as smooth as glass; it may have been marble. He put some vermilion red powder in the middle of the slab (it was a brilliant red colour and slightly coarser than flour) and then added some paste dryer and a spot of linseed oil. He then mixed it all up with his pallet knife until all the powder had been absorbed – it looked like red mud but was slightly coarse. He then took his 'muller' (presumably a corruption of 'miller'), which was a stone about the size and shape of a hand bell, and ground the 'mud' on the slab. The operation took a long time but eventually the 'mud' acquired the consistency of butter. This paint went on beautifully. When the painter dipped his brush in it and drew it along the straight edge, the paint was just as strong at the end of the stroke as it was at the beginning. No join could be seen where the next stroke began but the paint did not run or level out like a modern gloss paint, and the brush marks could still be seen in it. It had a thickness and quality which cannot be achieved with modern paints, nor can the colour be precisely matched today either despite the advances of modern science and technology. This is the only paint which would genuinely 'cover in one coat'!

As a rule, the men made their own lining brushes using a swan's quill which they got from the foreman. Each brush was made to the required width for the line it was to produce by putting into the quill the appropriate number of hairs; it was then tapered down by use on rough surfaces or sometimes with very fine sandpaper.

After lining, passenger engines were varnished again and their painting was then complete. All engines which had not received general overhauls in the works were simply cleaned with turpentine substitute and their paintwork was touched up where necessary. The dome on *Cornwall*, which was polished brass at this time, was also varnished. First it was polished with metal polish. Then to remove any residue of the polish, it was wiped over with meths, and the varnish was applied immediately.

Around the turn of the century and probably up to World War I, painting an engine took one month. The actual working time was two weeks, with the men starting at 6.00 a.m. and working a six day week. The process was basically the same as that used after the war but with more attention to achieving a perfect surface for the paint and with more coats of varnish. The renowned blackberry black paintwork of the golden age of the LNWR was achieved in some nineteen stages, as follows:

1) Chipping, wire brushing and then emery stone down.
2) White lead priming coat.
3) Knife filling of bad patches with slate powder (mixed with mixing varnish or gold size to suitable consistency in the paintshop).
4) Knife spread all over with slate dust (as in 3).
5) Brush filling with slate dust (mix thinned with best turpentine).
6) Dry emeried down.
7) Knife spread and brushed with slate powder as above.
8) Stained with venetian red powder in best turpentine (mixed in paintshop).
9) Rub down all over with pumice stone.
10) Second coat of lead white applied (white lead ground in oil in the paintshop and mixed with best turpentine and gold size with addition of sun driers. The effect of this was to allow it to dry slowly and naturally).
11) Checking of all surfaces and touching up if necessary, knife patched.
12) Thin coat of drop black applied (this was milled in the paint shop using drop black, gold size and best turpentine).
13) After drying, all surfaces were glass papered.
14) First coat of varnish applied. This was usually an elastic coach varnish.
15) Flatted with felt pad and moist pumice powder.
16) Lining and transfers applied.
17) Second coat of varnish applied.
18) Flatted again with felt pad and pumice powder.
19) Final coat of varnish applied. However, if the foreman was not satisfied, the surface was flatted again and a fourth coat of varnish was applied.

Appendix 4 Liveries

Basic information on the liveries used by the Northern and Southern Divisions is well established but precise details are now impossible to ascertain as there is really no concrete evidence as to exactly how engines were painted and lined before the early 1860s, when the first official photographs were taken at Crewe. The earliest photographs of engines in normal service date from the late 1860s and so any account of liveries before that time must contain a considerable element of speculation. Moreover, in the very early days of railways, the concept of a 'standard livery' had not been developed and variations in painting styles on engines from different makers were accepted as being quite normal.

Southern Division

For most of its existence the Southern Division continued to use the green livery of its predecessor, the London & Birmingham Railway. The engine boiler, wheels, footplate side-sheets, firebox lagging, bufferbeam ends and probably the front also were painted green and the smokebox, chimney, frames, boiler bands, and lining (on the tender frames and in three oblong panels on the tender sides) were black; the firebox top (domed on Bury's engines), chimney cap and various steam pipes were polished copper, while the dome, safety-valve covers and other fittings were polished brass. By the late 1840s the black panels on tenders, and on some footplate side-sheets and outside cylinders, also had reversed corners. This livery continued throughout the McConnell period right up to 1862 and a few photographs have survived showing engines in this scheme: green paint generally, with black lining having reversed corners on panels, and with domes, safety-valve covers and splasher rims polished brass and chimney tops polished copper or possibly painted. The green itself is believed to have been a medium shade with a slightly bluish tinge, like the Southern Railway's malachite green.
McConnell's 'Patent' 2-2-2s had a much more elaborate scheme. The cab side-sheets and tender sides were lined in panels having corners with three steps. This lining is also shown in a photograph of 'Bloomer' No. 249 as first built. Another style of lining is shown in the photograph of 'Small Bloomer' No. 103, built in May 1857 *(see Plate 43)*. In this, the tender and side-sheets are lined in dark and light tones in such a way as to suggest a panel with reversed corners on a dark surround with a raised rectangular frame. At a guess, the engine is green with red and yellow lining, as this scheme was described by Frank S. Hennell; the bufferbeams were also green with a panel in red and yellow lines in the same style as on the side-sheets and tender.
The famous 'red' livery seems to have been introduced only in late 1861 and it appears in only one photograph, of No. 381 taken in December of that year, in which the actual shade of red seems to be very dark. However, film in those days was insensitive to red, and so the paint could have been as dark as it seems or much lighter, even vermilion. The lining is again different. As on No. 103 there is a recessed panel effect, with reversed corners, but the arrangement of the light and dark lines is different; there is an extra light line within the panel and elaborate lining outside the boiler bands. The lining is possibly in black, white and grey.
After Ramsbottom took over, Southern Division engines were painted in the same style as those of the Northern Division. Chimney tops and domes, which had hitherto been polished, were now painted over, to save cleaning, but there was probably little real change in the case of most engines.
Up to 1862 Southern Division engines carried their numbers in cut-out brass numerals on their chimneys, latterly in a bold square-serif style, as first introduced on the London & Birmingham Railway in 1837. From 1856 the number was shown on the bufferbeam also, in numerals of the same size and style, preceded by 'Nº'. London & Birmingham engines had had brass oval numberplates on the boiler sides but McConnell's engines had a variety of styles of numberplates. The early 'Small Bloomers' had a keystone-shaped plate at the top of the splasher but later 'Bloomers' had elliptical plates on the side-sheets. Another variant was the combined number and maker's plate on No. 371, express goods of 1861, which was situated on the centre coupling-rod splasher, and there were probably other variants also.

Northern Division, North Eastern Division and Ramsbottom Period up to 1871

The Northern Division green livery, as used by Ramsbottom from 1857 and for the whole of the LNWR after 1862, is believed to date from the formation of the company in 1846, and indeed was quite probably the original colour of the Grand Junction Railway. Nothing is known of the original livery of the North Eastern Division in the eleven years of its separate existence up to 1857 but it seems possible that it was basically the same as that of the Northern Division.
In the early days of the Northern Division the whole of the engine and tender was painted green, including the bufferbeams and wheel centres; the tyres, buffers, smokebox, chimney, tender axle guards, boiler bands and lining were black; and the dome, safety valves, chimney top, certain cab fittings, connecting rods and driving axle ends, were all polished metal, copper, brass or iron as appropriate. Early drawings indicate that the lining on the tender and side-sheet panels was in two parallel black lines with reversed corners, and an excellent illustration of this livery appears as the centre spread in *Loco Profile No. 15 The Crewe Type*. However, all photographs of engines in service in the 1860s and 1870s show a single black line only. The only photograph showing double lines is that of *Lady of the Lake* outside the Old Works at Crewe some time in the 1860s *(Plate 161)*. In this picture, the outer and inner lines are about ¾in. and ¼in. wide respectively. It seems possible that the livery was simplified at some stage, from double to single lining, possibly when Ramsbottom took over, but that *Lady of the Lake* had the more ornate style for some special reason, perhaps for display at the 1862 exhibition.
The other official photographs outside the Old Works all show engines specially prepared for photography, with complicated white lining in many places where no black lining can be seen in pictures of engines in normal service. It must be assumed, therefore, that in these official views, the white lining was applied for photographic reasons, perhaps to make the various features of the engine stand out better on the emulsion of the day, and does not represent the black lining applied to engines for everyday service. Here again the photograph of *Lady of the Lake* is puzzling, since it shows black lining corresponding to that in the 'white lining' pictures, on many parts of the tender such as axleboxes, spring pads and buffers but there seems to be no lining at all on the engine, nor are the painted numerals shaded in black. Similar problems are presented by several models which have survived in museums and show complicated lining in black, white and yellow; these should not be taken as being representative of engines in service, certainly not in Ramsbottom's day at least, though their green paint may well be a guide to the correct shade and in one case is known to have been the actual paint used by Crewe.
All the evidence therefore points to the fact that at some stage, the livery was simplified and indeed photographs of engines in

service in Ramsbottom's day show a livery scheme which was really quite austere. The shade of green is variously described as 'medium green', 'medium green with a slight tendency to blue' and a 'deep chrome green'. All these descriptions incidentally have been applied to Southern Division green also and indeed paint scraped from old tenders in the 1960s showed no difference between the two. When *Loco Profile No. 15 the Crewe Type* was in preparation, the authors arranged for the artist drawing the colour plate to match the colour with paint scraped from the preserved Ramsbottom '4ft Shunter' No. 1439. The colour in the plate corresponds to BS381C of 1964 No. 221 'brilliant green'. This green was applied to the whole engine including the buffer beam and wheels, only the tyres, smokebox and chimney being black. The black lining was about ¾in. wide. On footplate side-sheets it was positioned about 4½in. from the edge, with reversed corners of about 4in. radius, to form a panel. The inner edge of the splasher beading had a similar line and the splasher slots were also edged with black. On the 'DX' class the coupling-rod splashers had the lined beading also but there was no black edging round the openings. The boiler bands had a ½in. black line along each edge. On the 'Problems' and Trevithick engines, the sandboxes on the driving splashers had the ¾in. line forming a simple panel, without reversed corners and following the shape of the sandbox, while the 'Problems' also had the leading wheel splasher lined in a similar way.

Tenders were lined in the same way as the side-sheets, in panels matching the plates which made up the tender sides, and with the front and rear panels carried round the curved corners on Ramsbottom tenders. The rear panel of the tender was also lined in the same way. No photograph of a 'Special Tank' in this livery exists but from photographs of other tank engines, including McConnell engines, the same principles of lining were followed on panels and in general.

The engine number was painted on the footplate side-sheet or on the tank side of tank engines, in either yellow or possibly gold-leaf; by the late 1860s the numerals were shaded to the right and below in black but before then at some stage they may very well have been unshaded. The number was also displayed on the front bufferbeams of tender engines and on both front and rear bufferbeams of tank engines, in both cases with 'No' to the left of the drawhook. Some photographs certainly show this number to have been enclosed in an oblong black panel, as used later in the black livery but without the number. In this case it may be assumed that the bufferbeam was painted green with a black line forming the panel and with the number in yellow.

All Northern Division engines were named originally but Ramsbottom ceased naming goods engines in 1859-62. Then engines which were not named had numberplates in the same style as nameplates on the centre splasher but this too was discontinued at the end of March 1872.

Shed plates were fitted to the top of the rear of the spectacle plate and had white letters on a dark ground. Tender numberplates are believed to have gone unchanged throughout the company's history and to have been green at this period with the letters and numerals picked out in white.

There was little brightwork, except for the brass columns of Ramsbottom's safety valves and the exposed copper parts of Trevithick fireboxes, which were polished. Domes were painted and coupling rods were black, either painted or perhaps chemically blackened, though outside connecting rods were always polished.

The Transition to Black 1871-3

The first engine to be painted black was the first of Webb's 'Special Tanks', No. 2045, when completed in November 1871. Whether it was lined is not known though it seems very unlikely, but it was certainly an experiment as engines continued to be painted green until April 1873, after which all engines turned out from the works were black.

The first changes which can be determined from photographs concern engines in green livery but with Webb chimneys, and so may be assumed to have occurred after Webb took over. Several can be seen with the livery as before except that the lining has rounded corners, not reversed. Another photograph *(Plate 195)* shows an engine in this condition (green, Webb chimney, rounded corner lining) but without a number on the front buffer beam, which has a panel, as used on Ramsbottom engines, but is probably painted red, not green. Perhaps the change to red bufferbeams, but still with a black line forming a panel, was a general one made at this time.

An ex-works photograph of the first Webb 'Newton' *(Plate 193)*, No. 1211 *John Ramsbottom*, completed in March 1872, shows open splashers but Webb cab and chimney. As the engine is in photographic paint the colours of the livery are difficult to determine, but it seems to be a green engine with painted numerals and black tyres, as in the standard green livery, but lined out in red, cream and grey.

The second Webb 'Newton' No. 1212 *Pioneer* (which was in fact the first to enter traffic, perhaps because No. 1211's special livery required more time in the paintshop) was painted 'invisible green', which looked like black but in good light was seen to be very dark green. Soon after No. 1212, 'DX' No. 1536 was painted black and it seems quite likely that the next step was to combine black paint proper with the lining of No. 1211.

The first cast numberplate is thought to have been made for the first '17in. Coal Engine', completed in February 1873, while the last engine to be turned out in green is thought to have been No. 502, the eighth of that class, in April. If this is so, the first eight of the class were the only engines which were green with cast numberplates instead of painted numbers. What colour these early numberplates were painted is not known, but possibly they had yellow numerals on a black ground. The ninth '17in. Coal Engine' was turned out in plain black with cast numberplates.

The first passenger engine in black lined red, cream and grey is not known but it may well have been 'Problem' No. 806 when temporarily renamed *Shah of Persia* in June 1873 *(Plate 162)*. The first new engines to have the livery were probably the last batch of Webb 'Newtons', the first of which, No. 1141 *S. R. Graves*, came out in August. However, until the change to black was made around April 1873, all engines put through the works were probably outshopped in green, except for the two experimental liveries, and it was not until March 1880 that all the company's engines were black.

'Blackberry Black' 1873-1922

After 1873 LNWR engines were painted black as a matter of course. At first passenger engines were lined and goods engines were plain black. All engines had cast numberplates except Trevithick engines on the duplicate list, which had painted numbers in yellow with blue shading. Later on, duplicate list engines also had cast numberplates.

In June 1878 passenger engines were adorned with the company coat of arms on the driving splasher, the first being 'Precedents' *Amazon*, *Balmoral*, *Meteor* and *Penrith Beacon*. The 'Cauliflowers' had the coat of arms from their introduction in 1880 and were also lined, being mixed-traffic engines rather than goods engines, and the 'Special DX' class began to be lined for the same reason around 1881. Lining out of goods engines began about 1890, and from the first 0-8-0s of 1892-3 goods engines in general were fully lined, the only exceptions being the Trevithick 2-4-0s and the '2ft. 6in. Shunters'. Even then goods engines as a rule did not carry the coat of arms.

In August 1914, all lining out ceased as a wartime economy measure; the last engine to be lined was the first of the 1914 batch of 'Claughtons' No. 250 *J. A. Bright*, and the first to be unlined was the next of the batch, No. 260 *W. E. Dorrington*. Twenty 'Prince of Wales' class 4-6-0s built by North British in 1915-16 were delivered fully lined but it is believed that no lining out at all was done at Crewe during the war. The wartime livery was plain black with no lining and no coat of arms, and many engines were unvarnished also. Some engines, notably 'Benbows', can be seen in photographs without the black line forming a panel on the front bufferbeam, while others were even put into traffic for a time in shop grey without being painted black. In October 1921 the directors resolved that the 'pre-war practice of lining and varnishing engines and naming passenger engines be resumed', and this continued uninterrupted by the merger with the Lancashire & Yorkshire Railway and the Grouping well into LMS days.

Colour of Paints

The phrase 'blackberry black' is an excellent description of the overall effect of the shining black paintwork of a clean LNWR engine on a sunny day. This effect was the result of a combination of two factors, the high quality of finish attained in the paint shop and careful cleaning at the sheds. The actual paint used was known as 'drop black', and this was applied only after a perfectly flat and smooth surface had been prepared by a most thorough and painstaking process using filler and frequent rubbing down; varnish was then applied, then lining, and then further varnish, two or more coats in Webb's day and up to World War I, which may account for the descriptions 'ivory black' and 'glossy black', commonly found in contemporary literature. This carefully painted surface was cleaned at the sheds with equal care. As a general rule, only water was allowed to be used for cleaning those parts which were varnished. A 'little cleaning oil' was permitted exceptionally for particularly dirty engines but paraffin was totally prohibited as was grease, other than the elbow variety, which was no doubt needed in large quantities.

The lining colours of red, cream and grey are similarly descriptive of the effect but not of the paints used. The red can more accurately be described as scarlet (less yellow than vermilion and less blue than crimson lake); the cream is described in early accounts of the 1890s as 'white' and may have appeared cream due to varnish but in later years was definitely a very pale cream, resulting from mixing flake white with a touch of yellow ochre. The grey was a bluish grey or dove grey, resulting from mixing flake white with ultramarine blue, yellow ochre and crimson lake.

Lining Details

On tender engines lining was applied to the cab panels, cab sides, boiler bands and footplate edging, including coupling-rod splasher openings. There was no lining on sandboxes, footsteps, wheels, frames or below footplate level in general. Tank engines were lined in the same way and the tanks and bunker, including the back of the bunker, were also lined. On tenders, however, only the sides were lined; the back of the tender was plain black, including the bufferbeam, which was never red as on other railways. The footplate edging of tenders was lined as on engines and the frames of steel-framed tenders had their lower edges and cut-outs lined also.

The lining consisted of a broad grey line, ⅝in. wide, with a fine cream line, ⅛in. wide, on its inner edge and a red line, ¼in. wide, 1½in. in from that. These are the official thicknesses, and measurements of engines painted in LNWR days approximated quite closely to them but there are greater variations on preserved engines painted in the 1930s and subsequently. Variations occurred in any case at certain points, on corners, for instance, where lines were 'swelled' so that they would appear to maintain the same thickness throughout, and round splasher slots, so that all the lines could be fitted in. On panels in general the grey line was set 5in. from the edge, except for the top line on tender sides, which was only 3in. from the lower edge of the coping. At corners the radius to the outer edge of the grey line was 4in. On the upper part of cab sides the lining was only 3in. from the sides and roof angle, and 3½in. from the bottom edge. The radii of the corners was 1½in. to the outside of the grey line and ¾in. to the red.

Boiler bands at first had the full lining with a central red line on the band flanked by cream and grey on either side. From 1876 this was changed to two parallel red lines on either edge of the band. In the early days of the black livery there were other variations. On some engines there was lining on the bottom edge of the tender frame and spring pads, and on the engine footsteps, and on some too there was a red line round the tyres. These features probably occurred because the new livery had not yet been settled in all its details and was still influenced in some respects by previous practice. *Shah of Persia* also had the tender footsteps lined, and it is not impossible that the rear of the tender was lined too, as in Ramsbottom's livery.

The front bufferbeams of all engines, and the rear bufferbeams of tanks engines, were painted red while rear bufferbeams of tenders were all black. The standard red bufferbeam had a black border, ¾in. wide, all round the edge, and a narrower black line, about ½in. wide, round the base of each buffer or of the wooden pad on which some buffers were mounted. Between the buffers was a black line about ¼in. wide, forming an oblong panel with rounded corners of 1½in. radius. The panel was 10½in. high on 15in. high bufferbeams and 13in. high on 18in. high beams, and its ends were located between the two lines of bolt heads inside each buffer, that is, opposite the centre lines of the frames. All engines, even those painted plain black, had lined bufferbeams and this seems to have been generally maintained during the wartime economy period, so far as is known, with only a few exceptions, mainly 'Benbows'.

Cab Interiors

In Webb days and after, the inner surface of the cabside panels, spectacle plate and cab roof were painted indian red, a reddish brown. The firebox backhead and the inner surface of splashers in the cab were black. According to Max Dunn, the cab colour was changed to 'dirty putty', possibly by Bowen Cooke with his 'George the Fifth' class but certainly most engines, Webb, Whale and Bowen Cooke included, had indian red cabs up to the Grouping. When full lining was resumed in late 1921, a grained oak finish for the cab is thought to have been introduced on newly painted 'Claughtons', and was perhaps applied to other new engines from then on also, such as the 'G2' 0-8-0s and 0-8-4 tanks, and possibly some repainted 'Princes' and 'Georges'.

Frames

The frames were painted black both inside and out. When the first ten 'Precursors' appeared in 1904, they had red frames at first as an experiment but they soon reverted to black, and frames were then black for the rest of the LNWR period. Parts inside the frames, such as motion brackets when built up from plate and angles, were also black but when made of cast steel were painted red. Certain classes such as the 'Coal Tanks' originally had built up fittings, but many received the cast type later. Painting the inside of the frames red was an LMS innovation and though this may seem surprising the fact that frames were always black in LNWR days is well authenticated.

Lettering

The only engines which normally carried the company's initials were three classes of tank engines in the early twentieth century. Whale's 'Precursor Tanks' had 'L & NWR' in letters of gold leaf 6¼in. high on the tank sides; Bowen Cooke's 4-6-2 tanks had 'LNWR' in yellow ochre letters 12in. high and his 0-8-2 tanks had the same inscription but in letters 9½in. high. All these were block letters and were shaded in red below and to the right. Some photographs show larger letters on the 4-6-2 tanks but they were applied only to test the effect and were never carried in service, though some of the class later received 9½in. letters as on the 0-8-2 tanks. The only engine to carry 'LNWR' on its tender was 'George the Fifth' class 4-4-0 No. 956 *Dachshund*, which did so for about six months in 1911 as an experiment. The letters are believed to have been 9½in. high, from a very poor photograph, and may even have been applied because this engine was one of a batch of 'Georges' and 'Princes' which were turned out of the works in undercoat to meet the demands of greatly increased traffic in the spring, summer and autumn of 1911, and were returned to the works for full painting during the winter.

Numberplates

The numberplates introduced in 1873 were made of cast iron. Above the number was the legend 'L&NWR' and below it 'Crewe Works'. The numerals and the border of the plate were painted yellow and the background, along with the subsidiary legends, was vermilion. In style, incidentally, the numerals followed those of the painted numerals used on Ramsbottom engines and before. In 1877, starting with the first of the second batch of 'Precedents', No. 890 *Sir Hardman Earle*, numberplates were cast in brass and had all numerals, border and subsidiary legends polished, with the background painted vermilion. Cast-iron plates, painted as before, continued to be used for duplicate-list engines. These Webb plates were all the same length, irrespective of the number of digits.

In May 1906 a new style of numberplate, showing the date when the engine was built but omitting the company's initials, was introduced on the 'Precursor Tanks', though the last engines to have the old style of plates were some, if not all, of the 'Experiments' built from September to December of that year. As before, all characters and the border were polished, the background was painted vermilion and the overall dimensions remained the same irrespective of the number of digits.

In 1915 numberplates were again made of cast iron for economy and through an error in the drawing office, the numbers '6' and '9' were interchanged, the former being an upside down version of the latter and vice versa. Nevertheless, a few numberplates were made exceptionally with the old correct numbers, an example being 'George the Fifth' No. 226. After the war brass plates are thought to have been produced again but details as to when and how many are not known. Cast-iron plates, painted in the standard manner, were fitted initially to 'Claughton' No. 1914 *Patriot* but Bowen Cooke thought them too bright and they were replaced by polished brass plates with black backgrounds before the engine entered traffic.

Tender Numberplates

Tender numbers were carried on a small cast-iron plate which was attached to the rear of the tender with square-headed bolts, and painted black. Sometimes, the characters and border of the plate were picked out in white, but quite often they were not. This style of plate went unchanged from Ramsbottom's time if not before, to the end of the company's existence. A variant of this plate, with smaller block numerals, was also in use in the later LNWR period.

Shed Plates

The shed number was displayed on an oval plate of white enamel with black numerals and border. The plate was 5in. long by 3½in. high, with numerals 2in. high. It was fastened to a tab of sheet iron which was inserted in a holder fixed to the angle iron at the rear of the cab roof. When this type of plate was introduced is uncertain, but it was in use in mid-1878 and might well date from the introduction of cabs by Webb in 1872. The style of numerals seems to have followed that used to display the shed numbers on Ramsbottom engines. Under the LMS up to 1935, LNWR-style shed plates were fitted to the smokebox doors in Midland style and the range of numbers was increased to include several sheds which had not belonged to the LNWR.

Figure 144: A typical numberplate of the type introduced by Webb.

igure 145: A typical numberplate of the .ter type introduced by Whale.

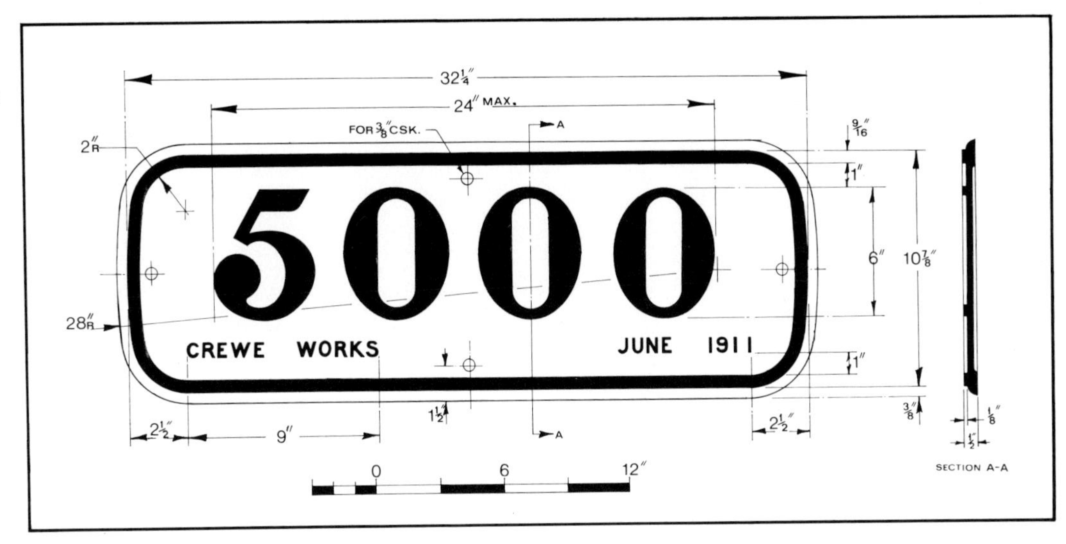

Figure 146: Numerals used for all engine numberplates. The painted numerals used before plates were introduced were of exactly the same style except that they were shaded to the right.

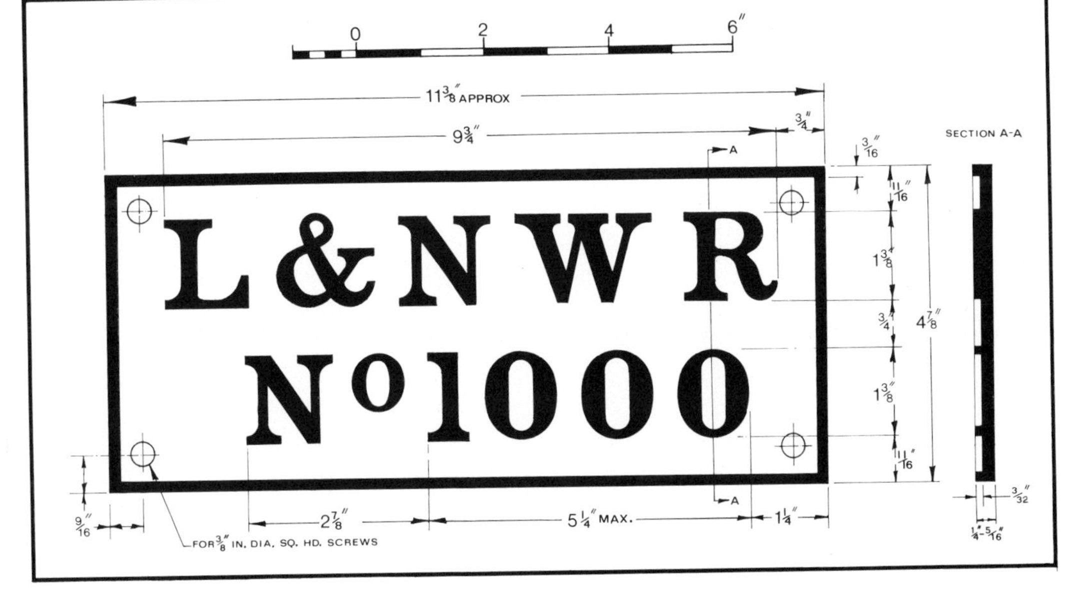

Figure 147: A typical tender numberplate.

Figure 148 (top left): Numerals used on tender numberplates.

Plates 514-517 (above): Examples of shed plates: 8C, Coventry (sub to shed 8, Rugby), 10, Aston, 15, Crewe, and 16L, Lees (sub to shed 16, Longsight).

Plate 518 (right upper): Tab of sheet iron, fitting into the holder on the cab roof, and to which the shed plate was attached (this is a rear view of plate 15 in *Plate 516*). This tab was presumably made in Crewe Works.

Plate 519 (right lower): A much more roughly made shed-plate tab, presumably cut from sheet metal at one of the sheds.

Appendix 5 Nameplates

Engraved Plates

The traditional LNWR nameplate consisting of a brass strip with the letters of the name engraved into it, originated in the earliest years of the company if not on one of its constituents. By about 1860 a standard design had been evolved and changes thenceforward can be chronicled quite accurately, thanks to the wealth of photographs available and to the many plates which have been preserved by collectors. Before that time, however, there is little reliable information, though it is certain that the style of lettering changed at least three times.

The earliest description of LNWR nameplates is found in the notes of F. H. Clarke, preserved in the Science Museum: 'Early Crewe engines had name spread all over the plate until about 1852/3, 164 was about last like this, then heavier type normal until about 1852/3, then closer spacing and in 1856 lighter type again'. The repetition of the date '1852/3' makes this virtually meaningless, but as No. 164 *Sun* was built in May 1847 the first '1852/3' should most probably read '1847'. There is also the difficulty of deciding exactly what is meant by such phrases as 'name spread all over the plate', 'heavier type' and 'closer spacing'. Nevertheless, the note confirms that the style changed from time to time in the early years of the company and, since it mentions this but makes no mention of any change in the way the plates were made, it implies that they were always of the brass strip type.

Indeed, in the same way that the 'LNWR tradition' of engine naming can be traced back to the Grand Junction Railway and even to the Liverpool & Manchester, so it seems quite probable that the brass-strip plate originated on the Grand Junction. C. Williams, the well known LNWR enthusiast, was once told by an old driver, who had worked on Grand Junction *Prince Albert*, that the nameplate was in exactly the same style as LNWR plates except that the name of the company was Grand Junction. However, an old man's recollection of what he had seen in his youth is not necessarily the best of evidence and there are several indications that early Crewe plates showed the name only and not the owning company as well. From drawings in contemporary publications and the model of *Wildfire* now in the National Railway Museum, it seems certain that at one time the Grand Junction used straight cast plates, fixed to the boiler. The brass-strip type of plate may have been introduced in the 1840s, perhaps by the then new works at Crewe, but that is really a matter of conjecture.

Early Styles

The earliest known illustration of an LNWR nameplate seems to be Allan's drawing of *Velocipede*, which was built in November 1847. This shows the nameplate to be in the style which later became traditional, both in the letters making up the name and in the shape of the plate itself, with incurved corners. Only the name is shown, the other familiar details such as the building date being absent, and so perhaps this is an example of the name being 'spread all over the plate'.

By great good fortune, a named engine from this period has survived, *Cornwall*, and there seems good evidence for assuming that its nameplates are the originals, made in 1847. At first glance the plates are identical to the standard curved plates of later years; but on closer examination two significant differences emerge. Firstly, the plates are larger than later plates, being 3in. wide instead of 2¾in., with letters 2½in. high instead of 2¼in. Secondly, at some time the plates have had extensions dovetailed to the ends and brazed up to carry the subsidiary legends which were later standard; not only can the lines of the joints be seen but the ends are of slightly different-coloured metal, more noticeable when tarnished than when the plates are polished. From this it may be assumed that the original *Cornwall* plates were identical to those in the drawing of *Velocipede*, that 3in. wide plates were standard at that period, and that at some time plates of this kind still in service were altered to carry the subsidiary legends when they became standard. The plates of *Cornwall* are, of course, the oldest surviving nameplates. None others like them are known. However, one photograph exists which seems to show a plate of the same kind as *Cornwall*'s plates were originally, the view of the Trevithick 2-4-0 No. 89 *Bela* after the Watford tunnel accident of 1866. There is no inscription on the plate except the name, and the letters seem to be the same large size as on *Cornwall*.

Another early illustration is D. K. Clark's drawing of a Trevithick 2-4-0, which he named *Crewe*. This drawing was completed by about mid-1853 and was published in his *Railway Machinery*; it is reproduced in *Railways of Cheshire down to 1860* by H. J. Hewitt and also in *The Crewe Type* by Stuart and Reed. It shows the name, in the same style of letters as became traditional but slightly larger, flanked by the legend L&NWR C$^{\underline{o}}$ on the left and AUG$^{\underline{T}}$ 51 on the right; these subsidiary legends are in smaller letters and the date, both month and year, is abbreviated. Since the date falls in the period when F. H. Clarke says 'heavier type' was in use, this may well be an example of it.

A number of photographs exist showing engines with the same type of plate as *Crewe* but with letters of traditional size, and with the year of building unabbreviated. Examples are: No. 155 *Ousel* (1854), No. 365 *Vesta* (1855), No. 179 *Nun* (1857) and No. 159 *Adjutant* (1857). On the other hand, photographs of No. 31 *Pegasus* (1853) and No. 1848 *Sefton* (1857) show double-row subsidiary legends as was later standard but of course these plates may have been altered like those of *Cornwall*. However, two photographs exist of the second 'Problem', No. 229 *Watt*, built in November 1859, showing the nameplate bearing the name only, with no subsidiary legends at all, but apparently of the same size as was later standard and not of the same dimensions as *Cornwall*. These photographs of *Watt* were presumably taken in the early 1860s.

The earliest photograph showing the standard type of plate with double-row subsidiary legends is probably that of 'DX' No. 568 *Stewart*, which was taken apparently when the engine was new in August 1861 outside the Old Works at Crewe; photographs of other Ramsbottom engines at the same location show the same type of plate. This seems to date the introduction of the standard plate fairly precisely, and certainly by the early 1860s a style of plate had been evolved that was to be used for the rest of the company's existence. It seems likely, however, that for a time different styles of plates were in service side by side and that plates of the older styles were altered to the new style when engines were in works for overhaul.

The Standard Curved Plate

The standard LNWR nameplate consisted of a strip of brass 2¾in. wide into which the letters of the name, 2¼in. high, were engraved to a depth of about ⅛in. (officially, 3/32in.). In the early days, the letters are thought to have been cut out by hand using a hammer and chisel but from 1871 a nibbling machine was used. This machine made both plates for an engine at once, its operator guiding the cutters by tracing pattern letters with a pointer; the inner surface of the letters was cross-hatched to enable the filling material to be retained more easily.

When engines were painted green, this material was a bright emerald green shade but when the black livery was introduced,

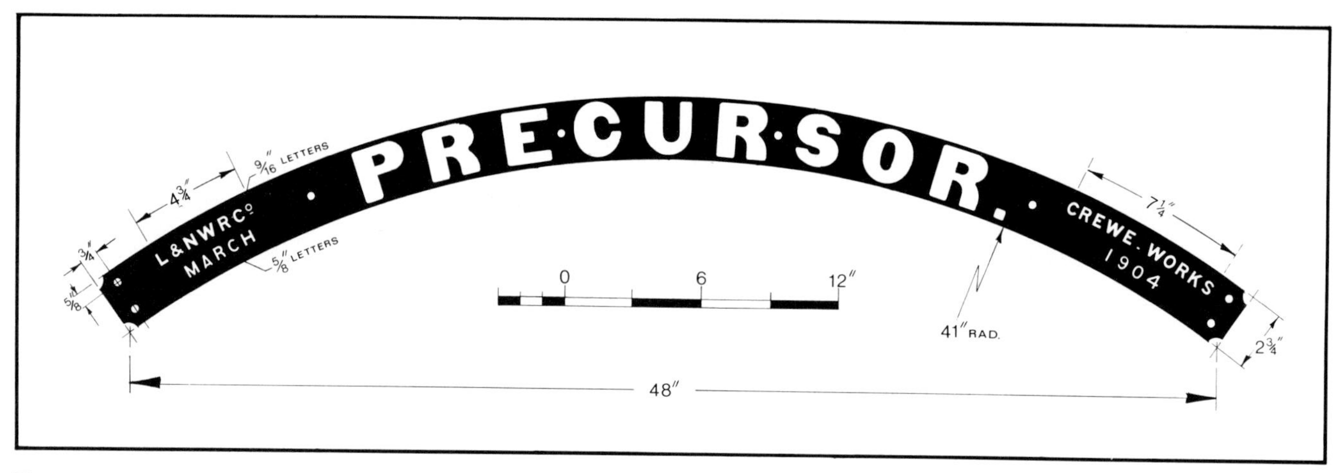

Figure 149: A typical standard curved nameplate.

black filler was used accordingly, and plates with green letters were refilled with black. The green can still be seen on one or two preserved plates, where the later black material has worn through. In many published accounts, the filler material is described as 'black wax', which perhaps conjures up visions of the letters on a hot engine in the heat of a summer's day gently melting and slowly dripping into black pools on the footplating! However, an official drawing dated 1911 of the nameplates of *Prince of Wales*, has the words: 'Letters cut 3/32in. deep & filled in with black engine stopping & coated with black japan'. Confirmation of this has come from a Crewe-trained painter, who saw the job done in the 1920s. He describes the material as a kind of stopper or filler resembling black putty and made from vegetable black powder and gold size, mixed very stiff. It was put into the letters by a first grade painter with a small knife and the first layer was left rough and porous, in the same way as a plasterer leaves his first coat rough. The painter kept adding stopper until it was no longer rough and porous and was proud of the surface of the plate. Then he rubbed it down with brick and water until the black stopper was flush with the brass; he also rubbed the brass itself with the brick or with pumice powder to get a good polish.

Except for the Crewe Works 18in gauge shunters, all engines before the 'Experiments' of 1905 had nameplates curved to fit inside the beading on the outer edge of the driving wheel splasher. One of the few exceptions to this was *Cornwall*, whose plates were shaped to fit above the splasher slots. Even when some of the Trevithick 2-4-0s were converted to tank engines, the curved nameplates were retained, being transferred from the splashers to the tank sides. At least this seems to have been the case, on the evidence of the one surviving photograph of one of these engines, that of No. 37 *Hawk* at the opening of the Kirkburton branch in 1867; whether the named engines which were built new as 2-4-0 tanks also had curved plates is not known, as no photographs have survived. All standard curved nameplates had inscribed upon them, in letters 5/8in. high, certain legends additional to the name itself. To the left of the name was L&NWR Cº and below that the month of building while to the right of the name was CREWE-WORKS and below that the year of building. Some of the months were written in full and others were abbreviated as follows: JANY, FEBY, MARCH, APRIL, MAY, JUNE, JULY, AUGT, SEPR, OCTR, NOVR, DEC. On curved plates, the engine name was followed by a full stop.

The 18in. gauge Shunters

The Crewe Works 18in. gauge shunters were the first engines to have straight, rather than curved, nameplates. Straight plates were obviously decided upon because they were made to be attached to the casings, these engines having no splashers to take curved plates. The nameplates of these engines were also exceptional in a number of other ways. Firstly, they were smaller overall than standard plates, so as to be more in keeping with the smaller engines, and had letters 1⅜in. high. Secondly, they had the legends additional to the names positioned as on the standard curved plates; they were the only straight plates on which this was so. Thirdly, some of the names were followed by full stops as on curved plates, but others were not: *Nipper* (built 1/67), *Topsy* (1/67) and *Billy* (7/75) had full stops; *Tiny* (5/62), *Pet* (6/65), *Midge* (11/70) and *Dickie* (5/75) had no full stops. When standard straight nameplates were introduced for Whale's 'Experiments' some forty years later and were subsequently used on the various Bowen Cooke classes, they differed from those of the works shunters in all three respects: they were larger (naturally enough); the legends were positioned differently; and there were no full stops after the names.

Webb Compounds

When the first 'Experiment' class compounds appeared, they had nameplates of the usual curved style but with the centre portion widened downwards to carry another line of inscription: F. W. WEBB'S PATENT. With the first of the 1884 batch, No. 311 RICHD FRANCIS ROBERTS, this was changed to F. W. WEBB'S SYSTEM, though the earlier engines seem to have run with PATENT until withdrawal. The precise reasons for this alteration are not known. Incidentally, at least two of the Webb compounds built by private firms for overseas railways carried the name of Mr Webb. The 2-2-2-0 built by Sharp Stewart in late 1884 for the Western Railway of France was named *Compound* (in separate brass letters, not a plate, fastened to the splasher) and had an oval cast plate on the same splasher reading WEBB'S PATENT, No. 2, while the engine built for the Pennsylvania Railroad of the USA by Beyer Peacock in 1888, *Pennsylvania*, had the name on a typically North Western plate with F. W. WEBB'S SYSTEM underneath.

All the nameplates of the Webb compounds had widened centre portions but those of the 2-2-2-2s, the 'Greater Britain' and 'John Hick' classes, were non-standard in a number of other respects also. These engines had two-word names displayed on separate plates, one on each of the two driving wheel splashers. Naturally enough, there was no full stop after the first word of the name, that is, on the left-hand plate, but there was a stop after the second word, on the right-hand plate, in the usual manner. Because there were two plates on the same side of the

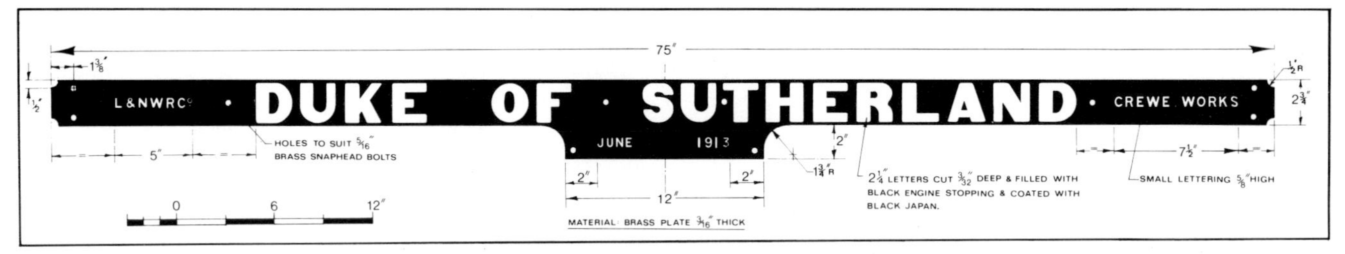

Figure 150: A typical standard straight nameplate. This plate actually measures 6ft 3in. long instead of the more usual 'Claughton' standard of 6ft.

engine, the legends additional to the name were repositioned by comparison with the standard curved plate. On the left-hand plate, the widened centre portion contained the words CREWE-WORKS, while on the right-hand plate it read F. W. WEBB'S SYSTEM; on both plates, L&NWR Cº appeared to the left of the name and the date of building, month and year, to the right. The 'Dreadnoughts', 'Teutonics', 'Jubilees' and 'Alfred the Greats' all had the inscription F. W. WEBB'S SYSTEM, but when the engines of the latter two classes were rebuilt to 'Renowns', their nameplates had the wider centre portion cut off. At least, that was the general rule; photographs exist of two 'Renowns' (No. 1951 *Bacchante*, rebuilt 10/13, and No. 1971 *Euryalus*, rebuilt 4/13) with unaltered plates, and conversely of one 'Alfred the Great', No. 1947 *Zillah*, with an altered plate. There may well be other examples too.

The Standard Straight Plate

After the 'Precursor' class, no more new LNWR engines received curved nameplates. Since all subsequent named classes had long continuous splashers over the driving wheels, they had straight nameplates to suit the splashers and the positioning of the various legends was altered slightly. Unlike the standard curved plates, all these straight plates had widened centre portions like the Webb compounds but containing the month and year of building while to the left of the name was L&NWR Cº and to the right of it CREWE-WORKS. Even the 'Prince of Wales' class engines built by the North British Locomotive Co. during World War I had plates inscribed CREWE-WORKS; an example, *Scott*, is in the Birmingham Science Museum.

A small number of 'Prince of Wales' and 'Claughton' engines were named after the Grouping. Those named in 1/23 had plates inscribed L&NWR Cº in the usual way: the 'Princes' *Marathon* and *Scotia* and 'Claughtons' *Talisman** and *Ingestre**. But the 'Claughton' *Breadalbane** (named 3/23) had LMS instead of L&NWR Cº as did all the rest of the class named subsequently, *Llewellyn**, *Thalaba** (4/23), *Lady Godiva*, *Illustrious** (5/23), *Croxteth** (6/23), *Baltic** and *Bevere** (7/23). Otherwise, all these plates were of the standard LNWR type. Of course, like the builders' plates put on to pre-Grouping engines by the LMS, they showed contradictory information — the LMS initials with pre-1923 dates.

The last 'Prince' to be named was the 'Tishy' built by Beardmore's for the LMS in 1924 especially for display at the Wembley Exhibition. It was numbered LMS 5845 and carried typically LNWR straight nameplates *Prince of Wales* with the date MARCH 1924 in the widened centre portion, but with no other inscriptions at all. The nameplates for this engine are sometimes said to have been taken from the original *Prince of Wales* but this is not so. Firstly, the plates of the latter had the standard inscriptions L&NWR Cº and CREWE-WORKS, which were missing from those of No. 5845; and, secondly, the spacing of the letters on the two plates was quite different. These points can be clearly seen on photographs. Incidentally, when the original *Prince of Wales* was built, despite the fact that it was the first of a new class, new nameplates were not made for it. With customary LNWR economy, the plates from 'Experiment' No. 1676 were taken and the new date brazed in, OCT^{R} 1911. This can still be seen on the plate today.

The use of the full stop

Another minor curiosity concerns the use of the full stop after the name. While it is generally true that curved nameplates had full stops and straight ones did not, there are exceptions in both cases. Two curved plates without full stops are *Glow-Worm* (now displayed in the National Railway Museum, York) and *Puck* (in the Science Museum, London), the former plate carrying the date OCT^{R} 1869 and the latter NOV^{R} 1880. These dates show that the plates were not made for or carried by the Ramsbottom 'Samsons' of those names, but were new plates made in 1914 and 1913 respectively when the 'Improved Precedents' No. 1745 *John Bright* and No. 514 *Lawrence* were renamed *Glow-Worm* and *Puck*. The principle was that the nameplate showed the building date of the engine which carried it. When possible in such circumstances, the original plates would be re-used with the dates modified for the new recipients; but in this case, new plates had to be made because of the difference in the radius of the splashers. The fact that these plates were made when straight plates without full stops had been in vogue for some years probably accounts for the absence of full stops, even though the plates were curved. Another interesting feature is that these new plates also show the date of 'rebuilding' from 'Newton' and 'Precedent' to 'Improved Precedent', in accordance with the practice followed with all the 'Jumbo' replacements. Normally, the new engines took the old nameplates of the engines they replaced, the plates being stamped REBUILT 1893 or whatever, in letters about ¼in. high. It is thanks to this practice, incidentally, that a number of Ramsbottom plates, such as *Bee*, have survived.

Conversely, a number of straight plates are exceptional in having full stops after the names. Examples are 'Queen Mary' *Miles Macinnes* (10/10), 'George' *E. Nettlefold* (1/11), 'Princes' *G. P. Neele* (3/14) and *Richard Cobden* (1/19), and 'Claughtons' *Duke of Connaught* (1/22), *Buckingham* (3/22) and *Bunsen* (3/22). The variations on this minor point can perhaps be explained by individual choice on the part of the drawing office junior told to draw each batch of plates, or even on the part of the workman cutting the letters out.

Splasher Numberplates

The practice of naming all engines as a matter of course ceased in 1859-62, the first new engines to appear without names being 'DX' class 0-6-0s. Those engines of this class which were not named were fitted with curved numberplates, in the same style as nameplates, on their centre splashers until the end of the Ramsbottom period. Apart from showing the engine number instead of a name, they were identical to standard curved nameplates, with the same subsidiary legends positioned in the same places. According to the *S. L. S. Journal* of January 1955, 'Prob-

*checked from photographs or actual plates.

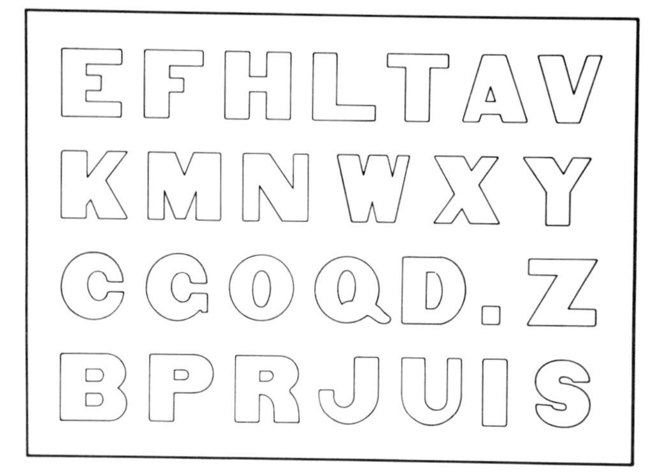

Figure 151: Alphabet of letters used on all standard engraved nameplates.

lems' Nos. 561-5 also had such numberplates for the first two years of their lives until they were named, but an 'as built' photograph of one outside the Old Works shows no such plate. A drawing by F. C. Hambleton shows a similar numberplate on the driving splasher of the first 'Special Tank' No. 1750 but a later Hambleton drawing does not, and it seems highly unlikely that these engines had them. Unfortunately, no photograph of one in Ramsbottom condition exists.

Minor Variations

As a general rule, the vast majority of the many hundreds of nameplates made at Crewe followed the standard types very closely and any variations from those types were of a very minor nature. 'Problem' No. 806 temporarily carried the name *Shah of Persia* in Arabic letters in June 1873, in honour of the visit by the Shah to Crewe Works. The 'Jubilee' compound No. 1901 *Jubilee* had two diamond shapes engraved into the plate and painted red, one on either side of the name, and so came to be known as 'Diamond Jubilee'. During World War I, the names of certain engines were struck through with a single red line and other names mounted above. There were three instances of this: No. 372 *Germanic* became *Belgic* and No. 956 *Dachshund* became *Bull-dog*, both engines running in that condition until 1921 when the defaced plates were removed and new plates showing the replacement names were fitted in the usual position; and No. 2583 *Teutonic* became *The Tsar* at the same time as the other two, but both its plates were removed in December 1915 and replaced by *Moonstone*. 'Claughton' No. 2059 *C. J. Bowen Cooke* was named when built in May 1920 but new plates were made later to read OCT$^{\underline{R}}$ 1920, the date of Bowen Cooke's death.

Certain minor variations concerned the actual inscriptions on the plates. Sometimes, the letters of certain words were smaller than normal as in the 'and' of VICTORIA AND ALBERT, and sometimes, the final letter of an abbreviated word was smaller, for example, S$^{\underline{T}}$ GEORGE and S$^{\underline{T}}$ PATRICK ('Jumbos' but the 'George the Fifth' was ST. GEORGE), JOHN o' GAUNT ('Jumbo' and 'Jubilee'), JOHN o' GROAT ('Jumbo' and 'Claughton'), L/CORP$^{\underline{L}}$ J. A. CHRISTIE V.C. ('Claughton') and RICH$^{\underline{D}}$ FRANCIS ROBERTS ('Experiment' compound). At least two engines had the ligature, the 'Precursor' *Antaeus* and the 'Benbow' *Caesar*.

Another small variation concerns the colour of the metal of some plates. Although the vast majority of all plates were made from brass of the usual colour, some 'Precursors' had plates of a reddish coppery-coloured brass — examples are *Medusa* (5/05), *Hydra* (8/05), *Rowland Hill* (12/05), *Watt* (1/06), *Richard Trevithick* (5/06), *Clive* (6/07) and *Phalaris* (8/07) — and one or two 'Experiments' such as *Yorkshire* (1/10), had plates of a very white or silvery colour.

The Length of Nameplates

During the Ramsbottom era and before, the length of nameplates varied according to the length of the name but from early in the Webb period nameplates were generally of a standard length for each class. Perhaps batches of plates were made at one time to be engraved later, or perhaps standard lengths were adopted to simplify work in the erecting shop. The lengths of the standard straight plates, subject to minor variations, were: 'Experiment' 4ft. 7½in., 'George the Fifth' 4ft. 9in.; 'Prince of Wales' 5ft. 1¾in. and 'Claughton' 6ft.; but there were numerous exceptions, mainly because names were sometimes too long for the standard length. The 'Precedent' *Duchess of Lancaster* had nameplates which were made in two sections and brazed together, and others which were longer than standard were 'Precursor' *Richard Trevithick* and 'Prince of Wales' *Queen of the Belgians*; the original *Prince of Wales* plates were, of course, of 'Experiment' length. One plate is known which is unaccountably shorter than standard, 'Claughton' *Sir Francis Dent* being only 5ft. 6in. long instead of 6ft.

Figure 152: A typical cast departmental plate. On all the double-row plates the word ENGINEER was spaced the same. Even when the second word had the same number of letters, as here, it was spaced more closely and so appeared shorter.

Non-Standard Engraved Plates

The one major example of a non-standard engraved plate was that of the war memorial 'Claughton' No. 1914 *Patriot*. This engine had nameplates which were basically in the same style as the standard plates but were enlarged to incorporate beneath the name the legend: IN MEMORY OF THE FALLEN L&NWR EMPLOYEES 1914-1919. These plates did not have the usual subsidiary legends. Sadly, both the nameplates from this engine are thought to have been destroyed in a fire in Crewe Works.

Cast Plates

During the time of Mr. Webb, plates cast in iron or brass were introduced for use on departmental engines. They were not strictly nameplates as such but rather were intended to show the department to which the engine was allocated, and very often its location also. Cast plates were used because, like duplicate-list numberplates, they could be unbolted and transferred from one engine to another, perhaps from a withdrawn engine to one replacing it from capital stock. Soon, however, other cast plates were produced which were never intended to be transferred from one engine to another and which were more strictly nameplates in the proper sense of the word. After a time these plates were no longer cast in iron but in brass. The change probably occurred, as with numberplates, in 1877. Probably also, they were generally painted like numberplates, the iron ones being yellow with red backgrounds and the brass ones being polished with red backgrounds.

Departmental Plates

The majority of cast plates were fitted to engines allocated to the various engineers' departments and plates showing the inscription in a single row were: *Engineer*, *Engineer Bangor*, *Engineer Crewe*, *Locomotion* and *Maintenance*. Where two or more words were used and would have resulted in a plate too long to fit on the cabside, two rows of inscription were used, as follows: *Engineer Lancaster*, *Engineer Liverpool*, *Engineer Manchester*, *Engineer Northampton*, *Engineer South Wales*, *Engineer Stafford*, *Engineer Walsall* and *Engineer Watford*. All these plates are believed to have been made of brass with letters polished and backgrounds painted red, but some enthusiasts remember the backgrounds as being black.

Similarly, a number of tank engines allocated to the carriage and wagon departments carried cast plates. The carriage department plates were unusual in two respects. Firstly, they did not, with one exception, incorporate any number or means of identifying the individual engine carrying the plate. They merely showed that the engine belonged to the carriage department and where it was allocated, Crewe or Wolverton. In LNWR days, at least some engines had separate brass numbers, quite large and stylish, on the cabsides, but they were later removed, perhaps by the LMS. Some, possibly all, engines originally had small cast plates that were similar, if not identical to tender numberplates, on the back of the bunkers, stating for example, L&NWR No. 6. Secondly, there was considerable detail variation among the plates themselves, no standard form of lettering being followed. It is not known for certain whether these plates were of iron or brass, but since they were all made after 1877, they were probably brass; certainly that of No. 7, which is now in the National Railway Museum, is brass. This plate has a different style of lettering from the others, much smaller and simpler, and was made in 1911, some ten years after the rest. As restored by the National Railway Museum, it has polished letters on a red background.

The Wagon Department had only one engine, a 'Special Tank' which worked at Earlestown wagon works. After a time, it was transferred to the Carriage Department, becoming No. 8 at Wolverton, but despite that it retained its name, *Earlestown*. It never acquired a Carriage Department plate as such and in BR days the only sign of its number was a large 8 painted at the top of the back of the bunker.

In trying to establish the details of the Carriage Department plates, it is sometimes difficult to establish which plate was carried by which engine because of the absence of numbers. In any case, there can be no guarantee that the same plates were used for the same departmental numbers when transfers occurred between capital and service stock, as happened with C.D. 4 and 5 in the 1890s, or even that the same plate was carried by the same engine throughout its life. For these reasons, the details below may not be correct for all periods but they are as accurate as information now available permits.

CD 1 CAR DEP^{T} WOL^{TN}
CD 3 CARR DEP$^{\underline{T}}$ WOL
CD 4 CAR DEPT CREWE
CD 6 CARR$^{\underline{E}}$ DEP$^{\underline{T}}$ WOL$^{\underline{N}}$
CD 7 CARR DEP$^{\underline{T}}$
WOL N$^{\underline{O}}$ 7

(No. 2 is thought to have had a plate identical to No. 3, and No. 5 one identical to No. 6.)

Nameplates Proper

In the same way that there were departmental engines with engraved nameplates, so there were two groups of engines in ordinary service with cast nameplates. Firstly, there were the two 'Special Tanks' which were named for working the boat trains to Liverpool Riverside, *Euston* and *Liverpool*. Probably, their plates were cast in brass but whether the letters were polished or were painted yellow is uncertain. Photographs seem to offer conflicting evidence, so perhaps the answer is that they were both, at different times in their careers. Secondly, there were the six engines built for the Dundalk, Newry & Greenore Railway. They had cast plates of the usual type, the first five (built 1872-6) having cast-iron plates, *Macrory*, *Greenore*, *Dundalk*, *Newry* and *Carlingford*, and the last one, *Holyhead* (1898), having brass plates. Restored examples in the National Railway Museum have letters painted yellow with a red background, while the letters and rim of *Holyhead* are polished with a red background.

Finally, the one major example of a non-standard cast plate on a North Western engine was that produced for *Coronation* the 'George the Fifth', which was the 5,000th engine built at Crewe Works and which was named in honour of the coronation of King George V. Above the name on this plate was a crown, while below it ran the legend 5,000TH ENGINE BUILT AT THE LOCOMOTIVE WORKS CREWE JUNE 1911. The background was painted red. This nameplate was perhaps the most impressive ever to be carried by an engine of the Premier Line.

Appendix 6 A Chronology of LNWR Engines

In 1857 John Ramsbottom became Locomotive Superintendent at Crewe responsible for all locomotive matters on the Northern and North Eastern Divisions. His first new design appeared in the following year, the 'DX' class, and although it was not until 1862 that Southern Division locomotives also came under Ramsbottom's control, the 'DXs' may be regarded as the first class to be built for the LNWR system as a whole, since they were built in large numbers throughout Ramsbottom's tenure of office. For that reason, and also because locomotive details before the 'DXs' are difficult to determine accurately, the class is taken as the starting point for the chronology below, which aims to list the dates on which various improvements and new fittings first came into use.

In their original condition, the 'DX' class had horizontal smokebox doors, castellated chimneys and green livery lined in black. All these features are often attributed to Ramsbottom but there seems to be no documentary evidence that he, in fact, originated any of them. The 'DXs' also had coupling rods with split ends and wedge adjustment, Ramsbottom safety valves and screw reverser, and couplings consisting of three links with a hook at the end, both front and rear. On the front bufferbeam, which was made of wood, were two square lamp sockets, one at either side, and there was no cab. The tender was the standard 1,500 gallon type.

1859 Giffard injector, indicated by large handwheel of steam-valve on side of firebox, fitted to tenth 'Problem' to be built, *Star*, and subsequently to all Ramsbottom engines.

1860 13th September-Locomotive Committee Minute: 'Mr Ramsbottom to provide all passenger engines with a screw shackle'. This was on the rear; hook-type couplings remained in use on the front.

c 1860 2,000 gallon tenders built for 'Problems' working the 'Irish Mail'.

1863 Cast-iron wheels and solid-end coupling rods on '4ft. Shunters', though previous type of rods remained in use for many years.

1871 November, first new engine to be painted black but green continued in general use.

1872 Cab and different chimney top introduced by Webb. Two whistles on cab roof, right-hand one for communication cord.

c 1872 Round buffers replaced square at front of tenders. Webb injectors replaced Giffard type.

1873 February, cast-iron numberplates instead of painted numbers. April, all engines painted black, passenger engines lined out, goods plain.
Lamp socket added in front of chimney, for revised head-code brought into use about January 1874.

1874 Webb's modified version of Ramsbottom's safety valves, contained in one casting to prevent tampering, and 1,800 gallon tender introduced on *Precedent*.

1875 Three-link couplings on goods engines.

1877 February, brass numberplates instead of cast-iron.

1878 June, coat of arms displayed on driving wheel splasher of passenger engines.

1879 Screw couplings on front of tender engines.

1880 Tender engines fitted with brakes on engine, first on October batch of 'Precedents'. Metal blocks used on passenger engines, wooden on goods, but some 'DXs' and '17in. Coal Engines' still without brakes in 1901.

1882 Tank sides of tenders made of single plates, so no longer have three prominent seams; side-sheets at front and two standard toolboxes fitted as regular practice.

1883 Simple vacuum brake adopted; tender engines had rear hose only at first.

1884 Circular smokebox door, hinged on left, on *Dreadnought*.

1886 Cast steel used for driving wheels on 'Dreadnoughts'.

1887 Steel, instead of wooden, bufferbeams on 5ft. 6in. compound tank No. 3000.
Automatic vacuum-brake adopted; both the simple vacuum and chain brake were extinct by the end of 1892.

1889 Steel bufferbeams and front vacuum hose fitted on 'Teutonics'; oil axleboxes instead of grease on tenders, also first on 'Teutonics'.

1890 Tall vertical smokebox regulator lubricator instead of T-shaped plug type, positioned behind chimney on '5ft. 6in. 2-4-2 Tank'.

1892 Metal brake-blocks fitted to goods engines, first on No. 2524, but wooden blocks in use for many years on goods engines other than eight-coupled. Goods engines lined out.
1,800 gallon tender with deeper side frames on *Greater Britain* and No. 2524.

1893 2,000 gallon tender on same deeper frame for compound 0-8-0s.

1894 December, eleven engines ordered to be fitted for experimental steam-heating of carriages.

1895 Coal rails fitted to tenders, very soon on main-line passenger engines but later on others, and on tank engines probably only in 1900s. Fire-iron hooks no longer fitted.

1896 Fluted coupling rods instead of rectangular section on 'BissellTank' No. 317 and a 'Jumbo', and polished not black.

1899 Steam heating becoming more widespread on passenger trains, so carriage warming reducing valve on right-hand front corner of cab roof.

1902 Last 'Jumbo' with rectangular-section rods, *Marquis Douro*. 2,500 gallon tender with equal wheelbase, flat tie rods and flush sides supplied to 'Alfreds' from No. 1951, 'Bill Baileys' and 0-8-0s.

1903 1st January, centre lamp socket on front bufferbeam (except some departmental engines) came into use (ordered in October 1902).

1904 Whale's steel-framed tender with flush sides (counter sunk rivets) and curved-top springs introduced, but still with wooden brake blocks, on *Precursor*. Tapered buffers, short type for engines and long type, with parallel end portion for tenders. Latter type used widely in Bowen Cooke's time and so sometimes called 'Cooke' buffers. From 1st July, communication cord replaced by modern system acting on train brakes; supports removed from tenders at sheds, right-hand whistles removed at Crewe during general repairs.

1908 Motor fitting of certain tank engines, especially '4ft. 6in. 2-4-2 Tanks', using rodding under carriages.

1909 Cast-iron brake blocks used on steel-framed tenders.

1910 Superheating tried on *George the Fifth* and soon widely adopted. Also first engine to have Bowen Cooke tender with 'water bottom and sloping bunker' instead of U-shaped tank; toolboxes replaced by cupboards; curved-topped springs and plainer axleboxes (soon altered); single coal rail.

1912 February, second Bowen Cooke tender photographed on *Prince of Wales*, having solid top with double bead and straight-topped springs. Latter used widely as replacements on earlier Whale and Bowen Cooke tenders.

1913 Third Bowen Cooke tender with flared coping and single bead on first production 'Claughtons'.
1914 August, plain black livery for all engines as wartime economy measure, with 'Claughton' No. 260 *W. E. Dorrington* being the first so treated.
1915 Brass numberplates replaced by cast-iron at heavy repairs as wartime economy (drawing dated April).
1916 Final type of Bowen Cooke tender, with square-ended frames having 'square oval' cut-outs and slightly modified axleboxes.
1917 March, naming discontinued after 'Claughton' No. 155 *I. T. Williams*. Motor fitting with vacuum control tried on '4ft. 6in. 2-4-2 Tank' No. 839.
c 1919 Pyrometers and superheater dampers removed, although some lasted into LMS period.
1921 Beardmore 'Princes' built with lamp irons instead of sockets. October, directors resolved that the 'pre-war practice of lining and varnishing engines and naming of passenger engines be resumed'.
1922 Oil boxes on handrails of many classes, as a result of modified lubrication designed by Beames.
1923 Range of boilers with Belpaire fireboxes designed by Beames for many classes. Ross pop safety valves widely used instead of enclosed Ramsbottom type.
LMS Period Standard LNWR lamp sockets replaced by lamp irons, LNWR buffers by parallel-sided standard LMS type, sides of the cab roofs of larger engines cut back to suit Midland loading gauge and, later on, LNWR 5-spoke smokebox door wheel replaced by two handles.

Bibliography

The following books are recommended as further sources of information on LNWR engines.

Ahrons, E. L. *The British Steam Railway Locomotive 1825-1925* Reprinted by Ian Allan, London, 1967
Baxter, Bertram & Baxter, David *British Locomotive Catalogue 1825-1923 Vols 2A and 2B. London & North Western Railway and its constituent companies* Moorland, Ashbourne, 1978 and 1979
Bennett, Alfred Rosling *The Chronicles of Boulton Siding* Reprinted by David & Charles, Newton Abbot, 1971
Cotterell, S. & Wilkinson, G. H. *The London & North Western Locomotives* Holland, Birmingham, 1899
Hambleton, F. C. *John Ramsbottom, The Father of the Modern Locomotive* Stephenson Locomotive Society, 1937
Hambleton, F. C. *Locomotives Worth Modelling* Model & Allied Publications, Hemel Hempstead, 1977
Hawkins, Chris & Reeve, George *LMS Engine Sheds Vol 1: The LNWR* Wild Swan Publications, Upper Bucklebury, Berks, 1981
Head, Sir Francis Bond *Stokers and Pokers* Reprinted by Frank Cass, London, 1968
Livesey, H. F. F. *The Locomotives of the L.N.W.R.* Railway Publishing Co., London 1948
Maskelyne, J. N. *Locomotives I Have Known* Model & Allied Publications, Hemel Hempstead, 1980
Nelson, Jack *LNWR Portrayed* Peco Publications, Seaton, Devon, 1975
Nock, O. S. *LNWR Locomotives of C. J. Bowen Cooke* Bradford Barton, Truro, 1977
Nock, O. S. *The LNWR Precursor Family* David & Charles, Newton Abbot, 1966
Nock, O. S. *Premier Line, The Story of London & North Western Locomotives* Ian Allan, London, 1952
Reed, Brian *Crewe Locomotive Works and Its Men* David & Charles, Newton Abbot, 1982
Reed, Brian *Loco Profile No. 15, The Crewe Type* Profile Publications, Windsor, 1971
Roberts, John Easter *Hazards of the Footplate* Author, 1980
Roberts, John Easter *North Western Engineman* Dalesman, Nelson, Lancs., 1977
Tuplin, W. A. *North Western Steam* Allen & Unwin, London, 1963

In addition, innumerable articles have appeared in the following technical and enthusiast periodicals: *Engineering*, *Railways*, *Railway World*, *Stephenson Locomotive Society Journal*, *The Engineer*, *The Locomotive*, *The Railway Gazette*, *The Railway Magazine* and *Trains Illustrated*. And last, but by no means least, the publications of the London & North Western Railway Society, *Premier News* and *Premier Portfolios*, invariably contain information on locomotives.